THE BEST OF
THOROUGHBRED
HANDICAPPING

JAMES QUINN

THE BEST OF
THOROUGHBRED
HANDICAPPING

LEADING IDEAS
AND METHODS

Revised • Updated • Expanded

Published by
Daily Racing Form Press
100 Broadway, 7th Floor
New York, NY 10005

ISBN: 0-9700147-7-5
Library of Congress Control Number: 2002114414

Cover and jacket designed by Chris Donofry

Text design by Neuwirth and Associates

Printed in the United States of America

All entries, results, charts and related information provided by

EQUIBASE
C O M P A N Y

821 Corporate Drive • Lexington, KY 40503-2794 Toll Free (800) 333-2211 or
(859) 224-2860; Fax (859) 224-2811 • Internet: www.equibase.com

The Thoroughbred Industry's Official Database for Racing Information

Dedicated to Louis Eilken

Former director of racing at Canterbury Park and racing secretary at Santa Anita Park

And a dear friend
who loved anthologies

And told me
he liked this one best of all.

ACKNOWLEDGMENTS

I AM INDEBTED to the authors whose work has been represented in these 50 essays. Collectively, their contributions have transformed the study and practice of the great game of Thoroughbred handicapping. That which formerly had been considered dubious to scandalous today enjoys a basis in scholarship and even science. It has been no small feat.

Whether racegoers will become loyal participants in the parimutuel wagering games offered by racetracks depends ultimately on their ability to handicap intelligently and wager effectively. The sources of instruction represented here are offered to racing's customers and handicappers everywhere as the best of the past 40 years. For dedicated practitioners of the art, these writings also deserve notice for making these the most provocative and promising of times.

Alphabetically, I wish to acknowledge Tom Ainslie, Andrew Beyer, Tom Brohamer, Gibson Carothers, Charles Carroll, Mark Cramer, Steve Davidowitz, Fred Davis, Burton Fabricand, Steve Fierro, Cary Fotias, Milt Gaines, Bonnie Ledbetter, Dave Litfin, Huey Mahl, Barry Meadow, Dick Mitchell, James Quinn, Bill Quirin, Steve Roman, Howard Sartin, William L. Scott, Alan Shuback, Mike Watchmaker, and William Ziemba.

Also, from an earlier time, Robert Saunders Dowst.

Moreover, many excellent handicappers and students of the game provide local products and services that can be fairly characterized as reflecting the state of the art in information and expertise. Three that have influenced my thinking and in that way have contributed to this recollection are Paul Braseth, of Seattle, Ron Cox, of San Francisco, and M. Scott McMannis, of Chicago. Also, for their regular and excellent articles on handicapping and wagering in *Daily Racing Form,* Dave Litfin, of New York, Brad Free, of Los Angeles, and Steve Klein, of Lexington.

To them, and to their colleagues at North American racetracks large and small, my firm salute.

James Quinn
Los Angeles, California

CONTENTS

PERSPECTIVES

WHEN THE ORIGINAL edition of this anthology was published in 1987, I observed that a review of the literature of Thoroughbred handicapping could not have been written as recently as 20 years before. The field by 1965 had continued virtually barren of the kind of literary product that invites a serious recollection and critique. The published voices of intellectually substantial authors Robert Saunders Dowst, Ray Taulbot, Robert Rowe, and few others represented from 1935 through 1964 only occasional and largely lost reverberations in a vast and untamed wilderness. Of handicapping instruction and its market, to the extent either was recognized to exist at all, the instruction was cast as dubious to scandalous, and the market was thought to consist of dreamers, drifters, and hard-core gamblers.

Those days had ended. An explosion of good work followed, and in the period between 1965 and 1985, the field luxuriated in an outpouring of books that not only became standards, but also altered the general practice for the better and for all time.

Now I am pleased to observe how well the good work has continued. This second edition of *The Best of Thoroughbred Handicapping* presents 49 essays its author considers to represent the field at its best and brightest, and although 13 of the original essays have been eliminated, a new and fresh 13 essays have taken their rightful place. The new essays represent seven new authors, as well as additional contributions from the original roster, such that this updated and expanded anthology represents no fewer than 21 authors and 27 books and articles, all of them characterized by the kinds of scholarly contributions that were unprecedented just a generation ago.

Even the scientific method has wedged its way into the study of handicapping, lending its rigor, and demanding that future claims of success unsupported by facts cannot be held as tenable. Owing to the best probability studies yet conducted in this misunderstood field, the art of handicapping enjoys a scientific basis at last. It has been no small feat.

As with any of its kind, this collection has been necessarily selective. Although the second edition should be considered even more comprehensive and diverse, no doubt some meritorious books have been left out. In most cases, disregard for meaningful work is more apparent than real. Where substance has overlapped among authors, priority was afforded those books that either have been more recently distributed or have gained national recognition and impact, such that points of departure and frames of reference might be more commonly recognized and shared.

Priority was awarded too to information attending to fundamental kinds of questions and problems. The wider the scope of a text or the broader the problem area, the more likely the contribution has been included here. Well-defined practices, techniques, and methods, such that the majority of practitioners at most tracks might actually use the tools, these were especially emphasized.

Alternatively, there is wonderful merit to the argument that nothing is so practical as a pertinent idea properly applied. Important ideas about Thoroughbred handicapping and parimutuel wagering find their full expression in these pages. Where ideas dominate, a concentrated attempt to translate the guidance into appropriate practices has been made, either by citing the author's application, if available, or by inventing a tenable alternative.

The condensed history of the subject can be captured in remarkably few pages.

Prior to 1965, the ideas and practices promoted by serious writers such as Dowst, Taulbot, Rowe, and few others were welded into hard and fast systems for beating the game. The rules were fixed. They allowed for little discretion and judgment. The presuppositions courted the existence of some unique, mystical secret for beating the races, and once the cat was out of the bag, the fortunate few would prosper. The legacy of those times persisted into the 1960's among fast-buck artists and systems merchants who peddled their insubstantial, ill-tested, overpriced wares on the pages of *Daily Racing Form,* local newspapers, and numerous periodicals.

In the middle to late 1960's, Tom Ainslie captured the imaginations of thousands of horseplayers and handicappers when he showed that the art of successful handicapping consisted of understanding the interrelationships and priorities among numerous factors, each of which played a part in the outcomes of races. Ainslie referred to his method as comprehensive handicapping. He set down specific guidelines for interpreting the past-performance data and encouraged handicappers to proceed by (a) reducing a field to its logical contenders, (b) separating the contenders on pace and various "plus" factors, and (c) making selections or passing races altogether, passing when races proved either too contentious or unpredictable.

Ainslie's method depended exclusively on information available in the past performances, plus a final inspection of the horses at the paddock. While he provided an excellent treatment of the arithmetic and economics of playing the game, Ainslie did not distinguish between underlays and overlays, but rather between selections and eliminations. At the moment of its publication, comprehensive handicapping was without doubt the most important contribution ever. It remains historic, a break with a notorious past that legitimized handicapping intellectually, not only to horseplayers and handicappers, but also to book publishers, who suddenly recognized a hungry market they previously did not know even to exist.

In the 1970's and 1980's a new and influential wave of writers, several with advanced academic credentials, concentrated on one or a combination of handicapping factors in greater depth. They promoted their ideas and practices as "methodologies" that combined systematic techniques and an ultimate reliance on interpretation and judgment. The new-wave writers had in common a reliance on information not contained in the past-performance lines.

In 1975, Andrew Beyer popularized advanced methods of speed handicapping. He later promoted the fusion of speed handicapping and trip handicapping. Beyer's influence proved enormous, and suddenly the esoteric art of handicapping had its second leading figure. Almost two decades later, Beyer's speed figures having impacted the general practice in ways that could no longer be ignored or denied, even by executives and industry officials not well connected to the gaming aspects of the racetrack, the Beyer Speed Figures became an official part of the past performances. Information had begun to replace data, and Beyer had earned a deserved niche in the history of the sport.

Among a wealth of contributions to handicappers of various persuasions, William L. Quirin documented the advantages of early speed at all racetracks, the significance of pedigrees in turf racing, and the importance of pace pars in speed handicapping. Quirin also developed a numerical method of analysis called race shapes that utilized pace figures and speed figures in combination, an approach to figure handicapping that has been gaining greater influence among practitioners even today. In 1979, Quirin delivered the best scientific probability studies of handicapping factors ever conducted. The practice of handicapping had a scientific basis at last.

The present author developed an analytical means of class evaluation that concentrated on the class demands of eligibility conditions, and related the performance profiles of horses to the conditions of races. The approach struck a chord among handicappers that previously had experienced problems identifying the authentic contenders in nonclaiming races. Years later I developed an innovative approach to figure handicapping on the turf from track to track that depended upon the final fractions of route races and horses' late speed.

William L. Scott concentrated on form analysis and methods of evaluating the class and form dynamics. A valuable nugget was Scott's discovery of the "fabulous five-furlong workout," a critical indicator of peaking form, notably at midlevel and minor tracks.

Steve Davidowitz popularized the importance of track bias—a term he coined—trainer patterns, and an analytical approach utilizing results charts he called the key-race method. In a remarkable revision of his signature text, *Betting Thoroughbreds,* in 1995 Davidowitz expanded his explorations of those topics, developed a means of connecting the Beyer Speed Figures to fractional times, and explored virtually every important factor of handicapping and betting as only a dedicated professional is equipped to do.

Bonnie Ledbetter persuaded all of us as to the importance of equine body language, and she identified six classic profiles of the Thoroughbred's on-track appearance and behavior. Her spade-work has been carried forward impressively by Joe Takach and others.

Mark Cramer focused on the development and testing of spot-play methods that not only toss profits for a time and under specific conditions, but also represent subtle variations of the classical ideas and methods. Cramer's "contrarian" thinking and "kinky" handicapping have continued to the present, as revealed by a succession of books that have made him one of the most prolific of all the handicapping authors.

In the mid-1980's, Dick Mitchell elaborated the first computerized model of the handicapping process. The output converted handicapping ratings of any kind to accurate probabilities and betting lines, which in turn could be converted to optimal bet sizes. A mathematician having more than 100 graduate hours on that elusive subject, Mitchell's writings on the mathematical principles and calculations that control parimutuel wagering and effective money management are the best on the topics, and have filled a tremendous void in the literature.

William T. Ziemba proved mathematically a fail-safe method of place and show wagering that depended upon inefficiency of markets principles and the public's well-established accurate handicapping when betting to win. The wagering model proved sufficiently powerful that it could be endorsed by the renowned Dr. Edward Thorp, who wrote the foreword to Ziemba's text.

Steve Roman invented the remarkable Dosage Index, altering for all time the matings of Thoroughbreds on farms and the purchasing of yearlings at auctions, not to mention the handicapping of the Kentucky Derby, the Belmont Stakes, and the graded stakes among leading horses at the classic distances. Roman's continual research on the industry's roster of *chefs-de-race* and his writings on the relations between pedigree and performance mark him indisputably as the nation's leading authority on bloodlines.

Howard Sartin developed a computerized method of pace analysis that depended upon velocity, a measure of speed divided by time, instead of time. The methodology and pace ratings that evolved iteratively among Sartin and his followers for a decade introduced to the wider audience the concepts and procedures of pace analysis that by now dominate the common practice.

THE NEW METHODS tended to be technical and heavily analytical, and they depended for their success upon information resources not contained in the past performances. The selections and overlays they yield are not accessible from strictly recreational handicapping. A higher level of expertise is required.

Since the original edition of this anthology, a number of influential books have continued to broaden the knowledge base.

In 1991, the most important of these texts came indelibly to life when Tom Brohamer delivered *Modern Pace Handicapping*. Brohamer communicated the ideas and procedures of the Sartin methodology as never before, and he formulated the telltale concepts and principles of contemporary pace analysis—energy distribution, turn time, track profiles, decision models, the importance of the second fraction, the identification of running styles—that have altered forever the practice of pace handicapping, even as Beyer had altered forever the practice of speed handicapping. In a recent amplification of the earlier text, Brohamer in 2000 delivered an extended chapter that relates the concepts of pace analysis to the use of the Quirin-style speed and pace figures. Pace analysts and speed handicappers alike cannot afford to neglect this book.

In a life change that would prove beneficial to all Thoroughbred handicappers, Barry Meadow in the late 1980's vacated his position as a leading expert on harness racing and began the pursuit of success in the Thoroughbred arena. No sooner had he arrived than Meadow wrote the definitive text on money management and betting strategy at the races, a highly practical guide, filled with tactics and charts for every straight and exotic wager on the menus. Meadow's unequivocal allegiance to setting 100 percent betting lines for every race they analyze, and restricting the action to overlays in every race they play, has put handicappers without a previously decent regard for these basic principles forever in his debt.

A New Mexico archaeologist, Charles Carroll, in 1991 presented the results of an extended scientific inquiry into the nature of "real speed." Confining his methods to the handicapping of sprints, Carroll delivered an alternative and innovative approach to speed handicapping that utilized speed-per-length as a baseline standard, and compared the "real speed" of horses to the fastest horses ever at the various sprint distances.

New York professional Dave Litfin in the mid-1990's delivered the best treatment yet on pattern recognition, along with expert illustrations of several relatively obscure patterns that pay especially well. Another New York professional, Cary Fotias, published as recently as 2001 a provocative softcover that relates speed-figure patterns to pace ratings, and in turn those critical relationships to form cycles, an empirically documented methodology that can predict when horses should be expected to demonstrate peaking form. Fotias has referred to his ratings, rather enigmatically, as The Xtras.

Linking his fortunes to Meadow's earlier work, Nevada professional Steve Fierro in 2001 published a softcover that not only demanded of serious handicappers that they apply no-nonsense business principles to their handicapping ventures, but also supplied them with ready-made "templates" of betting lines that contained the fair-value odds of three- and four-horse contender scenarios, once the handicappers had attached their personal fair-value odds to their number one choices.

And in a magazine article the author has judged the best ever on a topic that has grown tremendously in popularity and importance to the average horseplayer since the first edition of this collection in 1987, Minneapolis and southern California handicapper Gibson Carothers has revealed to the smaller and moderate bettors who formerly have competed at the mercy of the high rollers and the syndicates when betting the pick six, how they might tackle the most exotic wager of all, not only on a level footing, but also effectively.

All of it, and much more, has been rediscovered in detail in these pages. The years since the first edition have been characterized too by a pair of overarching developments that cannot go unremarked: (1) the increasingly useful and divergent online information resources, and (2) the rejuvenation under new ownership and management of the *Daily Racing Form*. The latter development has been so innovative and helpful to handicappers everywhere, this second edition begins with a discussion of the new and improved *Daily Racing Form* as prologue to the larger text.

Taken in its entirety, if the literature of handicapping well and betting intelligently suggests anything approaching certitude about playing the races, it might be this: Where knowledge and skill have risen to that certain threshold that begs success, the application of money-management principles and procedures that maximize profits at that level of proficiency will certify financial gain. If the ideas and methods to be found here do not work well enough for handicappers, the explanation is almost surely a shortage of know-how. The burden rests, as always, with improving one's knowledge and skill in handicapping.

These fine pearls from the literature are intended to help horseplayers everywhere accomplish precisely that.

Prologue

THE NEW AND IMPROVED
DAILY RACING FORM

A BANNER DAY FOR horseplayers went unheralded during August of 1998, when Steven Crist of New York expropriated an investment of more than $40 million from Wall Street and purchased *Daily Racing Form,* the newspaper of Thoroughbred racing, which contains the past performances of the horses, the lifeblood of the sport and industry. Crist is one of us, a horseplayer.

Crist had been a journalist—he covered Thoroughbred racing for *The New York Times* for a decade—a writer, a racetrack executive, and even a newspaper executive, roles that no doubt enhanced his credibility as editor and publisher to the industry he would now survey and serve, but it would be his background as a handicapper and bettor that would matter most to his paper's audience, the consumers who are also horseplayers, handicappers, and bettors. The new publisher's background as a handicapper and bettor would serve another and greater purpose not well appreciated by the sport and industry. It has saved the newspaper, if not from extinction, then from a gradual decline that had already begun and could have accelerated into a disastrous plunge.

In the age of information, by the late 1990's, data-based companies that had failed to adapt to the new technologies, to computerized production systems and the centralizing role of databases, not to mention to the most critical adaptation of all, the overarching importance of supplying customers with information instead of data, had fallen haplessly behind the times. *Daily Racing Form (DRF)* had stumbled enough to suggest it would be much more a part of the problem than a part of the future. Competition, in the form of national databases that contained the data items capable of producing alternative versions of the past performances, had materialized as never before, and two companies had developed products and markets that would rival both the exclusivity and superiority of *DRF*'s past performances. These were challenging times, and other and harsher competition for the handicapping market could be expected to rear its ugly head.

In his inaugural editorial, the new publisher advised *DRF*'s audience they could expect changes for the better in the past performances, but he cautioned the market the changes would be incremental and carefully timed, a lesson Crist attributed to his exciting but frustrating one-year experience in 1991 as editor of *The Racing Times.* People who are betting their money on the outcomes of the races want change for the better, all right, but they do not want to be overwhelmed by a landslide of changes all at once. Crist promised as well gradual improvements in the editorial content, in the various simulcast editions of the paper, and in the paper's notorious circulation and distribution systems, the latter an eternally bothersome problem to the game's best customers that never seemed to trouble top management.

And so it has happened, and continues to happen, just as Crist announced it would in the summer of 1998, except that the incremental changes in all directions have been more numerous and wonderful than anyone could have anticipated. The past performances during Crist's tenure have been characterized by more and better information, such that the ideal, that handicappers might have access to the complete array of information they need to make effective handicapping and wagering decisions, without the historical burdens of extensive data processing, may be within reach.

Before examining how the past performances have been expanded and improved, it's important to appreciate the distinction between data and information. Data consists of elements of facts or items of calculation. Examples would include final times, fractional times, running positions, and beaten lengths. Data are useful as a basis for discussion, calculation, or summarization. Data are not useful for decision making and problem solving.

Information is processed data. Information has meaning. It tells users something they did not previously know. When related to a goal or problem, information represents a basis for making a decision or solving a problem. Data that have not been processed lack meaning, and do not represent information, which had been characteristic of the data items of the past performances until a decade ago. Executives in the organization want information, not data, and so do handicappers. Final times remain raw data, for example, unrefined, unprocessed, and not adequately related to making effective handicapping decisions.

Final times become information, or speed figures, by calculations that involve other data items, including par times, projected times, daily track variants, and beaten lengths. Final times are converted to speed figures; data are converted to information. Speed figures appear in the past performances now—eliminating the onerous data-processing tasks—and so does information that facilitates class evaluation, form analysis, trainer-pattern recognition, identifying distance and surface preferences, trip handicapping, and a better understanding of foreign imports.

When the author began to play the races, the past performances looked like the record shown for the 1973 four-year-old claiming horse Son Diver.

Son Diver **122** **Ch. h (1969), by Swoon's Son—Deep Blue Sea, by Nasrullah.**
Breeder, T. Gentry (Ky.). 1973 19 4 2 1 $24,870
Owner, H. V. Howley. Trainer, J. A. Licausi. 1972 3 1 0 2 $3,712

Dec28-73^{9}Aqu	1 1-8	1:53⅕ft	2¼	▲120	$1^{3\frac{1}{2}}$	$1^{2\frac{1}{2}}$	1^2	1^2	C'roAJr^{10}	c5000	69	SonDiver120	NavyNo	MightlyBully	10
Dec 4-73^{7}Aqu	1 1-8	1:50⅕ft	6-5	▲114	1^h	1^h	4^1	5^7	Vel'q'zJ^2	11000	78	Bold Wit 113	Spread the Word	Sig	7
Nov22-73^{7}Aqu	1 1-8	1:51⅕ft	8-5	▲118	2^h	$1^{1\frac{1}{2}}$	1^3	$1^{3\frac{1}{2}}$	Vel'q'zJ^2	c8500	80	SonDiver118	DoubleyRoyal	Privado	9
Nov19-73^{9}Aqu	1 1-8	1:50⅗ft	14	113	1^h	$1^{\frac{1}{2}}$	$1^{2\frac{1}{2}}$	1^6	Vel'q'zJ^5	10500	83	Son Diver 113	Never Or Now	Chili II.	12
Nov13-73^{2}Aqu	6 f	1:11⅕ft	5½	116	$7^{4\frac{1}{4}}$	$5^{3\frac{3}{4}}$	$3^{3\frac{1}{2}}$	$2^{4\frac{1}{4}}$	G'tinesH^7	c6500	83	HolmesSmarty116	SonDiver	BeR'stl'ss	12
Oct31-73^{1}Aqu	6 f	1:11⅕sy	23f	112	$10^{7\frac{3}{4}}$	8^8	$7^{7\frac{1}{2}}$	$7^{6\frac{1}{4}}$	Gusti'sH^{10}	9000	81	Steal aDance116	StansStory	Chili II.	13
Oct22-73^{9}Aqu	6 f	1:10⅘ft	19	116	$12^{9\frac{3}{4}}$	10^7	$8^{9\frac{1}{4}}$	$8^{6\frac{1}{2}}$	GustinesH^4	9000	82	HeadTable116	Messmate	IrishMate	12
Oct11-73^{1}Bel	6 f	1:10⅗ft	35	114	$5^{1\frac{3}{4}}$	1^h	1^h	2^{nk}	GustniesH^9	7500	90	SatansStory112	SonDiver	NavyNo	11
Sep28-73^{5}Atl	1 1/16	1:45⅗ft	5½	115	2^h	1^1	$5^{6\frac{1}{2}}$	6^{17}	Arist'neM^6	8000	62	Fal!Rush110	Enoc-A-Nee	PlumGood	8

Handicappers were not provided even the fractional times of races, such that a pace analysis was impossible without access to the results charts. The making of speed figures was strictly an individual task, and the data-processing burden was severe, such that few individuals bothered. No information was provided about trips, trainers, jockeys, pedigrees, or workouts, not to mention indices of distance and surface preferences. No wonder practically everyone believed you couldn't beat the races. For everyone except dedicated professionals, the requisite information was missing.

By 1978, the fractional times had arrived in the past performances (see Baederwood, next page). Fast forward to the successive iterations of the past performances of 1989 (King of Bazaar), 1992 (Private Access), and 1995 (Apendix Joe). The occasional alterations proved useful to a degree, especially when professional speed figures were published in 1992, after *Daily Racing Form* had purchased the assets of the defunct *Racing Times*, but the iterations of the past can scarcely match the comprehensive information resources and utility value of the present past performances.

Baederwood B. c. 3, by Tentam—Royal Statue, by Northern Dancer
Br.—Taylor E P (Md)
Tr.—Bardaro Anthony J
114
Own.—Bright View Farm

	St.	1st	2nd	3rd	Amt.
1978	3	1	1	1	$6,515
1977	0	M	0	0	

2Aug78- 2Mth sly 6f :22⅖ :46 1:11⅗ 3↑Md Sp Wt 6 1 2hd 1hd 1½ 16 Nied D 117 *1.70 83-22 Baederwood 1176 Revivalist 1226 Silent Bid 1102 Easily 8
18Jly78- 5Mth fst 6f :22⅕ :46 1:12⅗ 3↑Md Sp Wt 7 4 3nk 1½ 1½ 2½ Nied D 116 3.80e 77-27 Ray A Day 1221¼ Baederwood 1165ColumbusBound1162½ 2nd best 8
1Jly78- 9Mth fst 6f :21⅘ :45⅕ 1:11 3↑Md Sp Wt 12 4 57½ 58 48 310 Nied D 116 6.00 75-20 Really And Truly 1165 RayADay1225Baederwood116nk No mishap 12
LATEST WORKOUTS Aug 10 Mth 5f fst 1:04⅖ b Jly 31 Mth 4f sly :49 b Jly 26 Mth 5f fst 1:03⅖ b Jly 17 Mth 3f my :37⅘ b (d)

King Of Bazaar Ch. g. 5, by Air Forbes Won—Blue Period, by Arts and Letters
DELAHOUSSAYE E 116 Br.—Crutcher Dr R R (Ky) Tr.—Hess R B Jr $16,000
Own.—Five Friends Stable Lifetime 22 4 1 3 $37,210

1989	15	2	1	2	$17,735
1988	1	0	0	0	
Turf	1	0	0	1	$990

12Oct89-5SA 6½f :221 :45 1:171ft 15 116 85½ 84½ 62¾ 62 DelahoussayeE 7 16000 82-16 Prime Concord, Art'sAngel,Valdad 11
12Oct89—Crowded last 1/16
28Aug89-1Dmr 6f :22 :444 1:09 ft 24 116 96¾ 87½ 86½ 56½ Davis R G 3 20000 87-14 MuchFineGold,Lrk'sLegcy,Romxe 11
13Aug89-3Dmr 7f :222 :45 1:23 ft *2½ 118 73½ 83¾ 54 45½ Black C A 3 c16000 82-14 Kamikaze, Contravene, Shirkee 9
13Aug89—Lugged in early
6Aug89-2Dmr 6½f :22 :45 1:164ft 5½ 118 44 43½ 33 21½ Olivares F 11 12500 82-14 Mr. Spade,KingOfBazaar,Barnhart 12
6Aug89—Wide into stretch
16Jly89-4Cby 7½f ①:23 :4641:31 fm 3½ 117 77 84¾ 65 32½ Lozoya D A 8 22500 86-09 WnglssFlght,AmcsCror,KngOfBzr 10
29Jun89-7Cby 6½f :221 :45 1:161ft 3½ 118 63½ 62 51½ 11½ Lozoya D A 7 20000 89-16 KingOfBazr,TexsTrio,WildRedBerry 7
29Jun89—Lacked room.
18Jun89-8Cby 6½f :221 :45 1:162ft 7½ 118 65¾ 54¾ 33½ 33 Lozoya D A 1 Aw12000 85-13 AlbmSlmmer,Sugr'sBest,KingOfBzr 6
19May89-6Cby 6f :222 :452 1:102m 5½ 116 62¾ 31½ 2hd 1nk Lozoya D A 8 12500 94-14 KingOfBzr,Lngoldyon,Dle'sDoublD. 8
19May89—Five wide
7May89-11TuP 6½f :213 :432 1:143ft 27 115 106½ 77½ 77¾ 65 EstradJJr8 Stll Slw H 93-13 ToghOpposton,Hndsomls,PsAKttn 13
26Apr89-11TuP 6½f :23 :451 1:16 ft *9-5 114 2½ 42½ 68 43 Salvino D M 1 Aw4700 88-19 Lord Felon, Sky Ballet, Mojo Man 7
Speed Index: Last Race: -2.0 3-Race Avg.: -1.6 9-Race Avg.: +1.6 Overall Avg.: +1.0
Oct 5 SA 6f ft 1:143 H Sep 28 SA 5f ft 1:034 H Sep 22 SA 5f ft 1:032 H Aug 25 Dmr 3f ft :394 H

Private Access B. g. 4, by Private Account—Empress of Canada, by Accomplish
$16,000 Br.—Indian Creek & Tenney E W (Ky)
Own.—Burnside Charles F Tr.—Ritchey Tim F (37 6 6 3 .16)
119
Lifetime 14 3 4 0 $26,775

1992	7	2	2	0	$18,592
1991	5	1	1	0	$6,383
Turf	10	1	3	0	$10,415
Wet	2	2	0	0	$12,960

9Oct92- 8Pha sly 1⅛ :464 1:112 1:523 3↑Alw 16616 78 1 3 23 23 31½ 1nk Salvaggio M V Lb 116 3.50 75-27 PrtAccss116nkPlcnPss119½BttlnBlds112 Altrd crs; drvg 7
9Oct92-Originally scheduled on turf
20Sep92- 6Pha fst 7f :221 :451 1:24 3↑Clm c-13000 63 4 8 88 89 712 69¼ Taylor K T b 118 6.40 78-18 RoughRogue122nkStoneBluff116½FrnchDt116 No factor 9
20Sep92-Claimed from Augustin Stables, Sheppard Jonathan E Trainer
11Sep92- 2Med fst 1116 :484 1:122 1:434 3↑Alw 17000 76 1 2 2hd 2hd 23 21½ Taylor K T b 116 .90 87-07 ToYou1121½PrivteAccess11613Impressions116 Good try 3
11Sep92-Originally scheduled on turf
25Aug92- 7Atl fm *1 ①:471 1:122 1:381 3↑Clm 20000 78 4 4 48 55 41 22½ Carberry M O b 119 7.20 101-07 DncngJsn1122½PrvtAccss119½BD'Argnt117 Gained place 10
23Jly92- 9Atl sly 1116 :464 1:121 1:45 3↑Clm 12500 71 3 3 33½ 42 2hd 1no Taylor K T b 117 2.20 85-22 PrvtAccss117noPoppoln1223¾RrWthKlss117 Long drive 7
18Jun92-10Atl fm *1116 ①:49 1:133 1:472 3↑Clm 20000 62 3 5 33½ 53¾ 63¾ 42½ Taylor K T 117 *.90 79-17 TngoBet117hdSunriseWillie1172½ScrtBy119 Belated bid 9
15May92- 7GS fm 1 ①:463 1:113 1:373 3↑Clm 20000 78 8 9 99 96¾ 46½ 43¾ Castaneda K 115 5.10 100-03 StrppdCpn1173StrlngSnshn113½Wddm115 Finished well 10
8Jun91♦5Epsom(Eng) gd 1116 1:431 ① Croydex Hcp 1016¾ O'Gorman S b 107 25.00 — — DominionGold133nk Bellefan1102½ Frar130 Prom, wknd 14
21May91♦1Beverley(Eng) fm*1116 1:464 ① Windmill Inn Stks(Mdn) 11 Swinburn W R b 121 *.65 — — PrivateAccess1211 Baresi1237 Carnwth133 Led thruout 7
LATEST WORKOUTS ●Oct 4 Del 5f fst 1:004 B Sep 4 Del 4f my :493 B

Apendix Joe Dk. b or br g. 6
Own: Akin & Akin & Winning Ways Stable
Sire: Jett Sett Joe (Bold Joey)
Dam: Easter Ballad (Skin Head)
Br: Hank Feenstra (BC-C)
DESORMEAUX K J (145 26 25 22 .18) $40,000 Tr: Shulman Sanford (72 13 14 9 .18)
L 121
Lifetime Record: 31 13 4 4 $167,392

1995	7	4	2	1	$100,550	Turf	0	0	0	0
1994	9	3	0	0	$18,540	Wet	6	2	1	0
Hol	3	3	0	0	$61,600	Dist	8	3	1	1

1Jun95- 7Hol fst 6½f :22 :443 1:084 1:152 Clm 50000 94 2 4 1hd 1hd 1hd 1hd Desormeaux K J LB 118 fb *2.60 92-13 Apendix Joe118hd Total Tempo116½ Heavenly Crusade1162 Very
14May95- 4Hol fst 6½f :214 :434 1:083 1:15 Clm c-40000 99 7 2 2½ 1hd 11½ 1hd Desormeaux K J LB 118 fb *.90 94-09 Apendix Joe118hd Utmost1172¾ Sky Kid116½ Lugg
Claimed from Mevorach Samuel, Lewis Craig A Trainer
29Apr95- 8Hol fst 6f :213 :443 :57 1:10 Clm 50000 94 6 1 3nk 2hd 1½ 12 Desormeaux K J LB 116 fb *.90 90-13 Apendix Joe1162 Seattletoo118¾ Resting Motel116½ 4w
6Apr95- 3SA fst 6½f :214 :443 1:084 1:15 Clm 50000 99 2 4 11 1½ 2hd 2hd Desormeaux K J LB 116 fb 2.00 97-11 Cantua Creek116hd Apendix Joe1161½ Resting Motel1161¾ Dueled, 2
18Mar95- 3SA fst 6½f :212 :433 1:083 1:152 Clm c-40000 92 4 1 2½ 21 21½ 31½ Black C A LB 116 fb 4.70 93-10 Mr Peter P.116½ Sugar Ray Dancer1161 Apendix Joe1163 W
Claimed from Feenstra & Veitch & Whyte, Olivares Frank Trainer
18Feb95- 5SA fst 6f :211 :434 :561 1:084 Clm 40000 85 7 5 2hd 2hd 2hd 23½ Black C A LB 117 fb *2.90 89-08 Moscow M D1173½ Apendix Joe1174 Belle Grande1171 Dueled, 2
29Jan95- 7SA fst 6½f :212 :434 1:083 1:153 Clm 32000 93 5 1 13 16 18 11½ Valenzuela P A LB 117 b 38.70 94-09 ApendixJoe1171½ Mr.C1Prospctor116½ Outlwd117½ Popped gate,
17Dec94- 8YM my 1 :23 :47 1:131 1:41 3↑Alw 7200NC 50 4 2 21½ 33½ 57 619½ Winnett B G Jr LB 116 fb *1.10 40-50 Aly's Act1192 I Sea Alertly1172 Computer Chip1186 Brok
27Nov94- 7YM sl 6f :231 :473 1:01 1:151 3↑CtyOfYakimaH15k 89 1 2 1½ 15 15 17½ Winnett B G Jr LB 119 fb *.90 60-31 Apendix Joe1197½ Computer Chip1174 Shady Move11610 As rider p
16Nov94- 8YM my 5½f :232 :481 1:014 1:09 3↑Alw 8000NC 78 3 2 1½ 12 12 11½ Winnett B G Jr LB 117 fb 8.80 70-35 Apendix Joe1171½ Shady Move1171½ Computer Chip1171½ Held adv.
WORKOUTS: Jun 10 Hol 4f fst :472 H 5/51 Apr 23 SA 4f fst :471 H 6/34 Apr 18 SA 4f gd :491 H 7/46 Mar 27 SA 4f fst :47 H 3/43

Examine the records of World Trade and Ultimate Warrior, two of the horses entered in an allowance/optional claiming race at Churchill Downs, on June 12, 2002.

8 Churchill Downs

OClm 62500

5½ Furlongs (1:022) **ALLOWANCE OPTIONAL CLAIMING. Purse $52,700 (includes $11,700 KTDF – KY TB Devt Fund) FOR THREE YEAR OLDS AND UPWARD WHICH HAVE NOT WON $7,670 THREE TIMES OTHER THAN MAIDEN, CLAIMING, OR STARTER OR CLAIMING PRICE OF $62,500. Three Year Olds 116 lbs.; Older 122 lbs. Non-winners of $18,800 twice since March 1 allowed, 3 lbs. $14,600 twice since February 1, 5 lbs. $12,400 twice in 2001–2002, 7 lbs. CLAIMING PRICE $62,500 (Races for $50,000 or less not considered).**

START 5½ FURLONGS FINISH

3 World Trade
Own:Diamond A Racing Corporation
Green, Gold Chevrons, Gold Hoop On Green
DAY P (152 49 23 21 .32) 2002:(542 123 .23)

B. c. 3 (Feb) KEESEP00 $150,000
Sire: Storm Cat (Storm Bird) $500,000
Dam: Daring Bidder(Bold Bidder)
Br: Allen E Paulson (Ky)
Tr: Howard Neil J(19 5 2 2 .26) 2002:(66 12 .18)

L 113

Life	9	3	1	2	$85,685	92	D.Fst	9	3	1	2	$85,685 92
2002	6	3	0	1	$75,175	92	Wet(340)	0	0	0	0	$0 –
2001	3	M	1	1	$10,510	82	Turf(325)	0	0	0	0	$0 –
CD	2	1	0	0	$28,525	92	Dst(340)	2	0	0	1	$4,510 59

30Apr02-9CD	fst 6f	:211 :441 :562 1:094	Alw 45500N2X	92 3 4	32½ 31½ 22 1hd	Day P	L 118	5.10	89–16	World Trade118hd Guernica1182½ Thunder Boot1181½	Bmp start,forced in 6
13Apr02-4Kee	fst 6f	:212 :45 :572 1:101	Alw 57000N2X	70 3 4	32½ 32½ 45½ 49¾	Albarado R J	L 120	3.40	78–10	Still Be Smokin'1161¾ Guernica1204 Twin Talk1164	Flattened out 7
23Mar02-7TP	fst 6f	:214 :443 :571 1:104	Hansel58k	72 3 4	41½ 32 34½ 32½	Day P	L 113	*1.40	85–11	StormCommndr113nk WorldChmpn1132¼ WrldTrd1131½	3 wide, lacked bid 6
16Feb02-7FG	fst 6f	:214 :452 :573 1:102	Alw 30000N1X	88 4 2	32½ 22½ 1½ 1½	Albarado R J	L 119	1.60	89–11	World Trade119½ *Lott*1191 Wadsworth1194½	Surged clear, held on 6
28Jan02-10FG	fst 6f	:213 :45 :572 1:102	Md Sp Wt 30k	90 3 5	1½ 12½ 14 110	Perret C	L 120	*1.80	89–17	*WorldTrde*12010 CowboyCt120½ Connor'sGlory1201½	Opened up, drew off 12
7Jan02-6FG	fst 6f	:222 :463 :583 1:113	Md Sp Wt 30k	65 10 1	62¼ 3nk 33 46½	Albarado R J	L 119	*1.40	76–16	*Guernica*1192¼ Texan Storm1192 Checota1192	Three wide bid, faded 10
21Dec01-10FG	fst 6f	:22 :46 :582 1:103	Md Sp Wt 30k	82 5 3	1hd 11½ 2½ 22	Albarado R J	L 119	3.80	89–15	*Clergy*1192 WorldTrade1193 SqureExpecttion1191	No match for winner 9
25Jly01-6Sar	fst 5½f	:222 :451 :571 1:033	Md Sp Wt 41k	59 9 1	2½ 2hd 26 38¾	Gryder A T	118	9.00	90–05	Trumn'sRidr1187¾ BullisticFlght1181 WorldTrd118¾	Between rivals, tired 9
23Jun01-2CD	fst 5½f	:222 :454 :573 1:034	Md Sp Wt 40k	59 5 1	2hd 1hd 33½ 610	Melancon L	118	5.90	89–13	*JumpStart*1182¼ CsChic1132¼ *RequestForProle*1184½	Dueled,led,weakened 12

WORKS: ●Jun7 CD 4f fst :471 B *1/31* Jun1 CD 5f fst 1:00 B *3/32* May26 CD 4f fst :484 B *14/32* May19 CD 5f fst 1:021 B *20/35* May9 CD 3f fst :362 B *8/25* Apr23 CD 4f fst :492 B *22/53*
TRAINER: 31-60Days(61 .16 $0.95) Dirt(177 .19 $1.42) Sprint(74 .14 $1.20) Alw(103 .23 $1.52)

4 Ultimate Warrior
Own:L T B Inc & Ryan James
Gold, Gold/blue Stars On White
$62,500
BOREL C H (229 31 40 32 .14) 2002:(581 69 .12)

Gr/ro h. 5
Sire: Iroquois Park (Chief's Crown) $1,500
Dam: Jodi Z.(Hard Work)
Br: Bernard Flint & James Ryan (Ky)
Tr: Flint Bernard S(56 2 14 8 .04) 2002:(231 38 .16)

L 115

Life	29	7	6	4	$411,407	108	D.Fst	22	5	6	3	$305,996 108
2002	2	1	0	1	$33,429	97	Wet(350)	4	2	0	1	$105,190 105
2001	5	0	1	0	$11,921	99	Turf(261)	3	0	0	0	$221 77
CD	8	0	2	1	$36,860	104	Dst(325)	5	0	1	1	$21,349 99

4May02-8Mnr	fst 5f	:213 :453 :58	3↑ Panhandle H78k	82 2 2	2hd 2hd 1½ 35	Murphy C K	LB 118	3.30	85–18	JeaniesRob1192½ MoMon1182½ UltimateWrrior1181	Battled to lane, short 8
12Apr02-9Kee	fst 6f	:22 :451 :573 1:10	4↑ Clm 50000	97 4 2	12 13½ 13 15	Martin E M Jr	L 116	5.20	89–16	Ultimate Warrior1165 District1163 Canfield1166¾	Controlled pace,drivg 9
2Aug01-9EIP	fm 5½f	Ⓣ :212 :444 1:02	3↑ Alw 24095N2Y	75 5 2	1hd 1hd 21½ 68¼	Dasilva A5	L 111	3.20	87–05	Fantastic Finish1231½ Final Row1233 Coup1161½	Dueled,tired 6
14Jly01-8Crc	fst 2f	:204	Rocket Man H50k	— 4 9	63½ 84	Chavez J F	L 122	*.60	96–09	Puma122¾ Roy's Ruckus1221 Texas Code122½	Off a step slow 9
16Jun01-7CD	gd 5f	Ⓣ :22 :45 :572	3↑ Alw 47960C	68 9 10	53¾ 63¾ 109¾ 106¼	Day P	L 117 fr	*1.30	87–07	Nice N' Salty117nk Morrow115hd Traversteed115½	Hopped start, tired 10
24May01-9CD	fst 5f	⊗ :22 :451 :572	3↑ Alw 58500C	99 3 2	1hd 11 2hd 22	Day P	L 119 r	*.60	99–12	*RobinDeNest*1192 UltimateWrrior1192¼ GmbleLes1172	Exch bumps start 7
5May01-2CD	fst 6f	:204 :433 :553 1:081	3↑ Alw 55125N$Y	91 6 1	1½ 1hd 2hd 64½	Chavez J F	L 119 r	3.70	92 —	LkPontchrtrn119½ *BtOnSunshn*117¾ *BrghtVlour*117nk	Face pace,faltered 9
15Dec00-4Crc	fst 6f	:213 :443 :571 1:102	3↑ Rexon'sHopeH27k	108 4 3	11 11½ 11½ 12¼	Chavez J F	L 118	*.50	98–18	UltimtWrrior1182¼ *Alc'sNotbook*116½ StormyDo1162½	Inside, proved best 6
24Nov00-10CD	fst 6f	:213 :451 :57 1:092	3↑ Alw 49820N$Y	104 3 7	31½ 21 21 2¾	Day P	L 119	2.70	97–12	StrightMn118¾ *UltimteWrrior*119¾ CllieAndJke114no	Stalked,4w,2ndbest 7
7Oct00-3Med	fst 6f	:22 :444 :564 1:094	BergenCounty100k	89 3 2	12 11½ 3nk 43¼	Alvarado R Jr	L 124	2.50	87–15	Max's Pal124no *Trounce*113¾ Stormin Oedy1192½	Rated,dueled,weakened 5
16Sep00-9Pha	fst 6f	:214 :443 :563 1:092	GallantBobH150k	107 1 2	11½ 11½ 12 1nk	Alvarado R Jr	L 119	*1.70	93–19	Ultimate Warrior119nk Trounce1123 Stormin Oedy1165¾	Drifted out, drvg 6
19Aug00-10AP	fst 6f	:222 :452 :572 1:093	Bet Twice67k	96 5 1	11 1½ 1hd 31¼	Desormeaux K J	L 122	*1.50	97–08	KingsCommnd1181¼ *ClssicAppel*122no *UltimteWrrior*1221½	Lost place late 7

WORKS: Jun1 CD 4f fst :472 B *3/44* ●May25 CD 4f fst :462 H *1/38* May17 CD 4f fst :48 B *2/34* Apr25 CD 4f fst :474 B *3/38* Apr4 CD 4f fst :482 B *9/34* ●Mar28 CD 4f fst :473 H *1/24*
TRAINER: 31-60Days(149 .19 $1.29) Dirt(784 .21 $1.68) Sprint(556 .20 $1.60) Claim(264 .17 $1.48)

All of the following has been bright and new.

Above the eligibility conditions, to the far right of the 8th, at Churchill Downs, the class level of the race is summarized succinctly, in this case as "Oclm 62500," signifying an optional claiming race, although handicappers are required to read the conditions of eligibility to identify the allowance classes that remain eligible.

To the far right, above the running lines, the lifetime records of the horses are summarized, including their records for this year and last, at this track, on today's surface, and at today's distance. For each category, a lifetime top speed figure, called a Beyer Speed Figure (named for speed handicapper and author Andrew Beyer), is provided, and these can be compared to the speed figures of recent races.

In parentheses, to the right of the categories of wet tracks (Wet), turf, and distance, appears a numeral called a Tomlinson Rating, which denotes a horse's potential to run well on the surface or at the distance. Guidelines for interpreting the Tomlinson Ratings appear at the end of this prologue.

The jockey of World Trade is Pat Day, and the trainer is Neil Howard, and for each in parentheses are provided their numbers of races, winners, and win percentages for the current meeting (Churchill Downs) and for the current calendar year (2002). Casual handicappers realize at a glance that Day and Howard represent outstanding connections. The same information for Calvin Borel and Bernard Flint (for Ultimate Warrior) is not as powerful, perhaps, but the jockey and trainer are acceptable journeymen, as 11 percent winners represents a useful standard—it corresponds to 11 percent of the starters in a race, or one horse in a nine-horse field, which can be accepted as a typical field size—and the jockey and trainer satisfy the standard, although trainer Flint has been "cold" at Churchill Downs (2 winners for 56 starters, or 4 percent).

Next, handicappers encounter up to 12 recent running lines (20 for Grade 1 stakes horses). From left to right, the information includes the date of the horse's last race, the race number, the abbreviated racetrack name, the track condition, the distance of the race, fractional times and final times, and the names of stakes or specific class levels, including the comparative purse values for all but the graded stakes; the Beyer Speed Figures, which tell how fast the horses have run in the past, essential information; the post positions and points of call, which provide the running positions and beaten lengths at various stages of the races, and now include the two-furlong call in route races; the jockey, medication-equipment-weight, and the odds to $1.00; another speed rating and track variant, now based upon three-year track records; the company lines, trip information, and field size.

At the far left, the running lines have been separated by thin horizontal lines, which indicate layoffs of 30 days or longer.

Below the running lines, as many as 12 recent workouts are provided and each has been ranked as to how fast the time was in relation to the times of the other horses working out that day at that distance. A "bullet" to the left of the workout date indicates the workout was the fastest at the distance on that morning, as with World Trade on June 7 (best of 31) and Ultimate Warrior on May 25 (best of 38). Below the workout line is a valuable innovation, Trainer Form, the record for the trainer in six or fewer categories of performance relevant to today's race. As many as 29 trainer-pattern categories can be reported, and for each category handicappers see the number of starts, win percentage, and rate of return on a series of $2 bets. The information covers the current season and the preceding calendar year, an excellent baseline. The 29 categories of Trainer Form appear at the end of this prologue.

The header information provides information about pedigrees and auction prices that can be helpful at times. World Trade is a son of the leading sire Storm Cat, and handicappers can see that Storm Cat's present stud fee is no less than $500,000. World Trade was sold at the Keeneland September sale for $150,000, although it's important to realize the correlation between the price of a yearling at auction and its performance on the track is virtually zero. Ultimate Warrior is far more common. He was bred in Kentucky, but not sold at auction, and his sire, Iroquois Park, stands for a humble $1,500.

DRF provides for many tracks a handicapping service, "A Closer Look," a capsule analysis of each horse's credentials, which appears in the far-right column, beside the past performances. The capsule analysis is provided by a professional handicapper, who will likely supply additional information, and the service can be especially useful in the races for maidens, which appear on every program. Casual and experienced handicappers are urged to develop the habit of consulting "A Closer Look."

Extremely valuable information is provided now about the numerous imports from the several countries that lately have infiltrated allowance and stakes races in the United States. Where formerly handicappers found virtually nothing of interest, now they get everything they need to know. As this was written, the best Thoroughbred in the world on dirt was the four-year-old Street Cry. Examine the colt's past performances.

On March 23, 2002, Street Cry won the Dubai World Cup (Grade 1), the world's richest race ($6 million), going away by more than four lengths. Trip notes are provided under the company lines, often indicating the import's running style. Street Cry is a stalker, or a colt that prefers to track the pace, before pouncing. Most important is the Timeform rating for the performance, which appears to the far left, under the racetrack name, and is recorded as a numeral, often accompanied by a symbol. Street Cry was assigned a Timeform rating of 127 + for his Dubai World Cup. The rating of 127 means Street Cry can be considered a Group 1

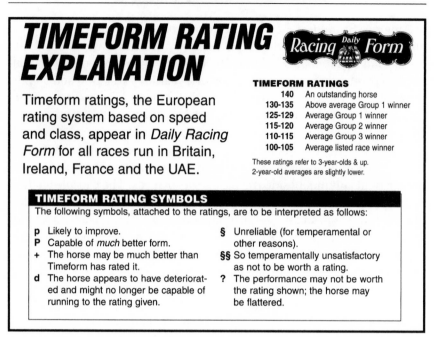

TIMEFORM RATING EXPLANATION

Timeform ratings, the European rating system based on speed and class, appear in *Daily Racing Form* for all races run in Britain, Ireland, France and the UAE.

TIMEFORM RATINGS

140	An outstanding horse
130-135	Above average Group 1 winner
125-129	Average Group 1 winner
115-120	Average Group 2 winner
110-115	Average Group 3 winner
100-105	Average listed race winner

These ratings refer to 3-year-olds & up.
2-year-old averages are slightly lower.

TIMEFORM RATING SYMBOLS

The following symbols, attached to the ratings, are to be interpreted as follows:

p Likely to improve.
P Capable of *much* better form.
+ The horse may be much better than Timeform has rated it.
d The horse appears to have deteriorated and might no longer be capable of running to the rating given.

§ Unreliable (for temperamental or other reasons).
§§ So temperamentally unsatisfactory as not to be worth a rating.
? The performance may not be worth the rating shown; the horse may be flattered.

horse, and the plus sign means "the horse may be much better than Timeform has rated it." Handicappers that want a better understanding of the relative class of European imports should pause now to review the Timeform ratings and symbols presented above.

Handicappers might have noticed that until the Dubai World Cup, Street Cry had never been assigned a Group 1 rating. The colt had improved, and seriously, as a new four-year-old. (The Timeform ratings of European horses should be evaluated analytically, not numerically, and bear no arithmetical relationship to *DRF*'s Beyer Speed Figures.)

Online, *Daily Racing Form*'s past performances can be downloaded two days in advance, at approximately 7:00 p.m. EDT on Thursday, for example, for the Saturday program. The past performances can be purchased online in daily, monthly, quarterly, and annual packages. Handicappers can download for free a software program, *Formulator 3.1* currently, that allows the user to customize the past performances, such that the internal fractions might be viewed or printed out—crucial for analyzing turf routes—or the lifetime records of horses can be accessed—helpful for pattern recognition—with a couple of clicks. *Formulator 3.1* has embedded each horse's morning-line odds in the past performances, a convenient service for simulcast bettors and off-track account wagering.

As a valuable service to simulcast players, *Daily Racing Form* now publishes *DRF Simulcast Weekly*, a weekly compilation of the results charts for all operating racetracks. *Simulcast Weekly* also provides an array of Beyer Pars for selected class levels at all operating tracks, and it supplies in one convenient repository the Beyer Speed Figures for all recent winners of all races at all tracks.

The editorial content of the paper is so much better than before, most dedicated handicappers will actually enjoy reading it. Features and columns by leading handicappers are served up daily, including the popular *Washington Post* columns by Andrew Beyer. National correspondent Jay Privman and executive columnists Jay Hovdey and the venerable Joe Hirsch are excellent fixtures, and business reporter Matt Hegarty has added elements of news reporting and in-depth investigative journalism that have been unprecedented. On the business of racing, Hegarty is just terrific. On Sundays, also unprecedented, handicappers are exposed to the critical thinking of editorials, one of them typically a hard-hitting, on-the-nail piece by Crist himself, and to the constructive sounding off by readers, in a full page of Letters to the Editor.

Not to be forgotten are the expert handicappers hired by the new management team to analyze the races everywhere. Where previously the *DRF* handicappers might be thought second-rate, they now are unmistakably first-rate. Dave Litfin in New York, Steve Klein in Kentucky, and Brad Free in southern California warrant special recognition, and Klein is a master of the overlay. National handicapper Mike Watchmaker performs an onerous and thankless role exceptionally well, and Michael Hammersley qualifies as an expert analyst, wherever he chooses to play. On event days, throughout the Triple Crown, during the week of the World Thoroughbred Championship races (aka the Breeders' Cup), and at other special times, the paper and its handicappers shine ever more brightly, in special sections and expanded coverage that continues a trend Crist began so impressively at *The Racing Times*.

All said and done, the *DRF* is a remarkably energized daily that handicappers can be proud to call their own.

TOMLINSON RATINGS

MUDDERS

Mud Rating of **320+**

Merits further consideration as a horse who could run particularly well over a wet track.

DISTANCE

Ratings from 0-480, with a rating of **320** considered average.

Ratings are keyed to the distance of the race in which the horse is entered in today, and helps determine which horses are bred for speed and which may be bred for distance.

TURFERS

Turf Rating of **280+**

Merits further consideration as a horse who could run particularly well over the grass.

If properly utilized these ratings will prove to be extremely useful especially in the following races:

a) Most maiden races.

b) Most 2-year-old-races.

c) Races switched to a main track listed as "sloppy" or "muddy."

d) With horses trying mud, slop, or turf for the first, second or third time.

e) Handicapping younger horses with a limited number of starts at the distance in question.

TRAINER FORM

Comprehensive Trainer Statistics: There are 29 trainer statistics that DRF is tracking, covering every trainer's record over this year and last year in a variety of situations. Up to 6 of these categories will show up under the bottom PP, depending on the number of applicable statistics. Each trainer stat will list:

· the number of Starts for the trainer in this category,
· the win percentage for the trainer in this category
· and the $2.00 Return On Investment for the trainer in this category.

TRAINER FORM CATEGORIES

1. First North American Start
2. 1st Race After Claim
3. 1st Race With Trainer
4. 180 Days Since Last Race
5. 60-180 Days Since Last Race
6. 1-7 Days Since Last Race
7. 1st Time Starter
8. 2nd Start of Career
9. 1st Time Turf
10. 1st Time Blinkers

11. 1st Time Lasix
12. 2 Year Olds
13. Dirt to Turf
14. Turf to Dirt
15. Blinkers On
16. Blinkers Off
17. Sprint to Route
18. Route to Sprint
19. 31-60 Days Since Last Race.
20. Dirt

21. Turf
22. Sprints
23. Routes
24. Maiden Claiming
25. Maiden Special Weight
26. Claiming
27. Allowance
28. Stakes
29. Graded Stakes

CHAPTER 1

SPEED POINTS

DEVELOPED INGENIOUSLY AND tested successfully by William Quirin, professor of mathematics at Adelphi University in New York, and major contemporary figure in handicapping instruction, the technique explained and illustrated below, of assigning speed points to horses, is the best-known predictor of which horses are likely to control or contest the early pace.

How important is early speed? Consider the facts:

1. Horses that run first, second, or third at the first-call positions in the past performances win five of every nine races at all major tracks.
2. Horses that run first, second, or third at the first-call positions win far more than their fair share of all races (179 percent) and as a group throw a profit of approximately 28 percent on the invested dollar when bet to win.
3. Though early-speed horses perform best in sprints, the above statistics hold relatively stable at all distances.
4. Horses able to get a clear early lead at the first call (one length or better) are among the best bets at racetracks when sent off at odds of 10-1 or lower. These win almost three times their rightful share of races and return an astonishing 80 percent on the dollar. As a group, these front-runners represent perhaps the most consistent

overlays in racing. Taking pains to predict which horses might earn the early lead seems well worth the effort.

The practice of assigning speed points relies on the first-call positions of horses in *Daily Racing Form's* past performances.

For sprints, or races around one turn, the first-call position occurs after the horses have raced for a quarter mile.

Speed points are assigned and totaled for three recent qualifying races, but never referring back to more than the latest five races. Three races are used because a series of performances represents a far better predictor of what should happen today than does any single race.

Here are the rules and some illustrations:

For horses in sprints, award speed points as follows:

1 point   for any sprint in which the horse ran 1-2-3 at the first call

and

1 point   for any sprint in which the horse ran within two lengths at the first call

0 points   for any other sprint performance

0 points   for any route performance, *unless* the horse ran within one length of the lead at the first call, in which case the race is passed (receives a bye)

Exception: at seven furlongs, a horse is eligible for 2 points only if it led at the first call; if the horse was merely second or third, or within two lengths, it gets just 1 point

Each horse starts with "1" speed point, and the total for its three "rated" races is added to "1." At that point, horses will be assigned between 1 and 7 speed points.

To get a bonus point, for a total of 8, the horse must have led or raced within a neck of the leader in each rated race.

Crimson Sister (next page) in her most recent race earns a point for position (3rd), but none for beaten lengths (2½). Two back she earned no speed points. Three back she raced on the lead and gets two speed points. Total: 3 + 1, or 4 speed points.

1 Crimson Sister
Own:**Banks Ann & Lazenby Virginia**
Green/white Quarters, White $32,500
JOHNSTON J A (—) 2002:(290 39 .13)

B. m. 6
Sire: **Discover (Cox's Ridge) $2,000**
Dam: **Crimson Carrie(Crimson Battle)**
Br: **Parrish Alma M (Ky)**
Tr: **Banks David P** (—) 2002:(43 7 .16)

L

30 Jun01– 7AP fst 6f	:221 :452 :574 1:11 3↑ ⒻAlw 32000N2x	45 3 1	32½ 86½ 99¼ 913¾	Meche L J	L 120 f
8 Jun01– 8CD fst 6f	:212 :452 :58 1:111 3↑ ⒻAlw 37625N2x	74 7 2	62½ 44 43¼ 44	Peck B D	L 115 f
23May01– 1CD fst 6½f	:23 :46 1:104 1:172 4↑ ⒻClm 40000 (40–30)	80 5 1	1hd 21 32 23½	Borel C.H	L 116 f
27Apr01– 5Kee fst 7f	:222 :454 1:112 1:243 4↑ ⒻAlw 54000N1x	75 3 2	2hd 1hd 12 11¾	Guidry M	L 116 f
17Mar01– 7Mnr my 1	:241 :482 1:144 1:413 3↑ ⒻAlw 21600N1x	48 4 31	43¼ 43½ 610 414¾	Leeds D L	LB 117
19Feb01– 8Mnr fst 6f	:221 :453 :584 1:122 3↑ ⒻClm c-(10–9)	56 6 5	64¾ 54½ 54 31¾	Andrews M E	LB 118
Claimed from Baird John W & Harbison Velma for $10,000, Baird John W Trainer 2001(as of 02/19): (408 92 61 63 0.23)					
22Jan01– 7Mnr gd 1	:241 :48 1:123 1:391 3↑ ⒻClm c-(10–9)	63 5 11 11 11½ 11½ 1hd		Leeds D L	LB 118

For horses in routes, award speed points as follows:

1 point	for any route in which the horse ran 1-2-3 at the first call

and

1 point	for any route in which the horse ran within three lengths of the leader at the first call
0 points	for any other route performance
1 point	for any sprint in which the horse ran 1-2-3 or within three lengths at the first call

and/or

1 point	for any sprint in which the horse ran within six lengths of the leader at the first call
Note:	Any sprint in which the horse was neither 1-2-3 nor within six lengths of the lead at the first call is passed (given a bye), and the handicapper refers back to the next most recent race, never going back more than five races.

As with sprints, each horse is awarded "1" point to start, and at this point has earned from 1 to 7 speed points. For routes, the bonus point goes to any horse earning a 7 that was on the lead or within one length in each of its rated races.

Apply the rules for routes to the Hawthorne Handicap (Grade 3), run at Hollywood Park on April 28, 2002. Each runner's speed points are shown as a numeral to the right of the horse's name.

Try to obtain the same speed-points totals.

8 Hollywood Park

ⒻHawthorne H-G3

1 1/16 MILES (FINISH ▲ ASTART)

1 1/16 MILES. **(1:40) 29th Running of THE HAWTHORNE HANDICAP. Grade III. Purse $100,000 added. Fillies and mares, 3-year-olds and upward. By subscription of $100 each on or before Wednesday, April 17, or by supplementary nomination of $5,000 each by Saturday, April 20. $1,000 additional to start, with $100,000 added. The added money and all fees to be divided 60% to the winner, 20% to second, 12% to third, 6% to fourth and 2% to fifth. Closed Wednesday, April 17 with 11 nominations.**

Ask Me No Secrets 8

Own: Shultz Earl H
Yellow Yellow Seahorse In Green Ball
MCCARRON C J (2 0 1 0 .00) 2002:(218 43 .20)

B. f. 4
Sire: Seattle Slew (Bold Reasoning) $300,000
Dam: In On the Secret(Secretariat)
Br: Earl H Shultz (Ky)
Tr: Hofmans David (—) 2002:(59 8 .14)

L 119

Life	5	3	1	1	$207,600	104	D.Fst	4	2	1	1	$184,800	104
2002	3	2	0	1	$176,400	104	Wet(320)	0	0	0	0	$0	–
2001	2	1	1	0	$31,200	91	Turf(280)	1	1	0	0	$22,800	90
Hol	1	0	1	0	$8,400	91	Dist	3	2	1	0	$160,800	100

16Mar02-10OP fst 1 1/16 :232 :473 1:122 1:442 3↑ ⒻOP BC-G3 100 2 11 11½ 1½ 11½ 14½ Smith M E L 116 1.80 86–20 AskMeNoSecrets1164½ RdN'gold116hd Dscpt1182¼ Comfortable pace,clear 5
9Feb02-8SA fst 1⅛ :481 1:123 1:37 1:491 4 ⒻLa Canada-G2 104 2 21 21 2½ 1hd 32 McCarron C J LB 115 14.50 88–11 Summer Colony1191 *Azeri*1151 *Ask Me No Secrets*1151½ Bid,led,held 3rd 6
13Jan02-2SA fst 1 1/16 :223 :454 1:102 1:432 4↑ ⒻAlw 54000N1X 95 6 2hd 21 21 1½ 12 Delahoussaye E LB 117 *.60 87–19 AskMNoScrts1172 *StrshpSrtog*1173 Whoopddoo1174 Re-bid,led,driving 7
25Nov01-2Hol fst 1 1/16 :231 :464 1:113 1:434 3↑ ⒻAlw 49560N1X 91 2 2½ 2½ 2hd 1hd 21 Delahoussaye E LB 118 *1.40 83–18 ContinentlLu1201 *AskMNoScrts*1185½ PotrGirl1213½ Vied,led,outfinished 6
20Oct01-5SA fm *6½f Ⓣ :222 :44 1:071 1:13 3↑ ⒻMd Sp Wt 39k 90 1 12 74¾ 78 42½ 12½ Delahoussaye E LB 120 8.00 95–07 AskMNoScrts1202½ Stormscp1201½ *Apollo'sMusic*1221 Off bit slow,rallied 12

WORKS: Apr24 Hol 4f fst :50 H *25/32* Apr18 Hol 7f fst 1:291 H *2/3* Apr9 Hol 6f fst 1:141 H *3/6* Apr3 Hol 6f fst 1:152 H *3/3* Mar27 Hol 6f fst 1:161 H *4/6* Mar12 Hol 5f fst 1:022 H *12/20*
TRAINER: 31-60Days(58 .17 $1.49) Dirt(133 .16 $1.74) Routes(117 .18 $1.77) GrdStk(24 .29 $1.95)

Alexine (Arg) 3

Own: Hubbard &Masterson &Rio Claro Tbrds
White White Lion On Red Ball On Back
STEVENS G L (2 0 0 0 .00) 2002:(148 21 .14)

Gr/ro m. 6
Sire: Runaway Groom (Blushing Groom*Fr) $20,000
Dam: Sentimental Gift(Green Dancer)
Br: Paula Machado & Linneo Eduardo De (Arg)
Tr: Mandella Richard (—) 2002:(101 18 .18)

L 119

Life	19	8	1	4	$404,911	98	D.Fst	2	1	0	0	$67,635	97
2002	4	1	0	1	$85,635	98	Wet(365)	0	0	0	0	$0	–
2001	3	2	0	1	$122,500	96	Turf(290)	17	7	1	4	$337,276	98
Hol	0	0	0	0	$0	–	Dist	1	1	0	0	$49,635	96

31Mar02-8SA fst 1 1/16 :231 :461 1:101 1:422 4↑ ⒻⓇSantaLucia H82k 96 7 57½ 58 44 22 1½ Stevens G L LB 117 *1.40 92–08 Alexine117½ Cashmina1163½ **De Goddaughter**1152½ Reeled in leader late 7
10Mar02-8SA fst 1⅛ :471 1:111 1:361 1:49 4↑ ⒻSMargaritaH-G1 97 7 62½ 52½ 53½ 43½ 48 Blanc B LB 115 17.60 83–16 *Azeri*1153 Spain1181 Printemps1164 Chased 3wd,no rally 7
2Feb02-3GG gd 1 1/16 Ⓣ :24 :483 1:131 1:44 + 4↑ ⒻBrownBessH-G3 96 2 42 43 42½ 33 32 Alvarado F T LB 117 3.90 87–16 Janet1231¾ *Impeachable*115nk Alexine1172 Saved ground,missed 2d 5
13Jan02-8SA fm 1⅛ Ⓣ :472 1:11 1:351 1:471 4↑ ⒻSanGorgnioH-G2 98 6 53½ 65½ 63 52½ 53½ Blanc B LB 117 9.10 90–14 Tout Charmant1202 *Janet*1191 Vencera115nk 3wd move,outkicked 8
1Dec01-8TuP fm 1 Ⓣ :234 :474 1:104 1:363 3↑ ⒻQueenOGreenH75k 96 8 86¼ 74½ 64½ 65 1no Blanc B L 122 *1.00 99–01 Alexine122no Miss Pixie114nk Deliciosa116no 7w, just up mid track 10
12May01-3BM fm 1⅜ Ⓣ :491 1:132 1:381 2:17 3↑ ⒻYerbaBuenaH-G3 95 1 11½ 13 2hd 33 31 Blanc B LB 119 1.50 103–04 Janet115¾ *Keemoon*121nk *Alexine*1195 Set pace, game try 4
8Apr01-8BM fm 1 Ⓣ :232 :47 1:104 1:36 3↑ ⒻMissAmericaH100k 96 10 78 65¾ 42½ 32 1¾ Blanc B LB 117 2.90 97–03 Alexine117¾ Matiere Grise1161 Vapor Trail115no 4w 2nd turn,steady bid 10
5Nov00-8SA fm 1⅛ Ⓣ :47 1:103 1:35 1:464 3↑ ⒻLasPalmas H-G2 85 4 79½ 810 913 84½ 65½ Stevens G L LB 116 7.50 90–12 SmoothPlyer117hd BeutifulNois115nk Hppynunoit1211½ Pulled early,inside 10
7Oct00-9SA fm 1¼ Ⓣ :511 1:163 1:401 2:024 3↑ ⒻYellwRibbon-G1 89 6 21 21 21 54 65 Flores D R LB 123 4.20 73–22 TranquilityLke1231 SpnishFern123¾ Polire123nk Stalked pace, weakened 6
9Sep00-8Dmr fm 1⅛ Ⓣ :471 1:111 1:352 1:47 3↑ ⒻRamona H-G1 98 2 42½ 43 33 31½ 32 Solis A LB 115 2.10 100–03 CaffeLatte1171¼ *ToutCharmnt*120¾ Alexine1152½ Came out,bid,outkicked 7
17Aug00-7Dmr fm 1 Ⓣ :223 :46 1:094 1:342 3↑ ⒻAlw 70000N$mY 97 7 32½ 32 31½ 2½ 1½ Solis A LB 123 3.70 93–09 Alexine123½ Beautiful Noise1211 Coracle1171½ 3wd bid,held gamely 8
Previously trained by Alfredo Gaitan Dassie
26Feb00♦ San Isidro(Arg) fm *1⅜ Ⓣ LH 2:124 3↑ ⒻClasico Juan Shaw-G2 Stk 42600 12½ Robles P 132 *1.70 Alexine1322½ Crazy Ensign1195 Eterna Girl119nk 11
Well placed in 3rd,led 2f out,drew clear.Batty Dualidad 4th

WORKS: ●Apr19 SA 6f fst 1:114 H *1/9* Mar28 SA 3f fst :364 H *7/15* Mar23 SA 4f fst :53 B *40/40* Mar6 SA 4f fst :491 H *22/42* Feb28 SA 6f fst 1:13 H *5/19* Feb21 SA 5f fst 1:01 H *16/35*
TRAINER: Dirt(214 .17 $1.91) Routes(239 .22 $2.10) GrdStk(59 .17 $1.93)

De Goddaughter 6

Own: Bonde & Golden State Racing LLC
Gold, Black Golden State Stable
ESPINOZA V (6 1 2 0 .17) 2002:(346 56 .16)

B. f. 4
Sire: De Niro (Gulch) $2,000
Dam: Say Forever(Little Current)
Br: Parrish Hill Farm (Ky)
Tr: Bonde Jeff(1 0 1 0 .00) 2002:(96 23 .24)

L 113

Life	17	4	2	3	$143,552	89	D.Fst	12	3	1	2	$105,852	89
2002	3	1	1	1	$42,927	89	Wet(290*)	3	1	1	1	$33,850	85
2001	13	2	1	2	$85,025	85	Turf(260)	2	0	0	0	$3,850	80
Hol	0	0	0	0	$0	–	Dist	5	1	0	2	$42,927	89

31Mar02-8SA fst 1 1/16 :231 :461 1:101 1:422 4↑ ⒻⓇSantaLucia H82k 89 5 32½ 31½ 31½ 32 34 Espinoza V LB 115 b 10.90 88–08 **Alexine**117½ Cashmina1163½ De Goddaughter1152½ Loomed 1/4, weakened 7
2Mar02-8GG fst 1 :22 :453 1:102 1:36 3↑ ⒻSacramento H55k 88 3 34½ 43½ 21 21 22 Gonzalez R M LB 117 b 7.50 88–14 SecretLiison1162 DeGoddughtr1172 PrincssVy115½ Bid 4w 2nd trn, hung 11
24Jan02-4GG fst 1 1/16 :23 :462 1:103 1:43 4↑ ⒻAlw 40000NC 88 4 12 12½ 11½ 11 11½ Gonzalez R M LB 115 b 3.70 88–20 DeGoddaughter1151½ MyFirstLdy114½ LindsyJen117½ Fine rating, driving 7
31Dec01-4GG my 1 :22 :452 1:10 1:36 3↑ ⒻAlw 40000NC 85 5 45½ 33½ 2hd 2½ 22 Gonzalez R M LB 115 b 1.80e 90–16 FullScrmAhd1152 *DGoddghtr*1154½ LndsyJn120¾ Drifted out,bumped 1/8 7
2Dec01-3GG wf 1 1/16 ⊗ :224 :454 1:092 1:413 ⒻMomentToBuyH59k 85 8 21½ 21 21 22½ 32½ Gonzalez R M LB 115 b 11.70 92–09 LindsyJen1162 *SuperTuesdy*117½ DGoddughtr1151½ Pressed, outfinished 9
17Nov01-3GG fst 6f :214 :44 :554 1:074 3↑ ⒻCamillaUrsoH55k 71 4 3 73½ 65½ 48 410 Lopez A D LB 116 b 3.10e 89–07 HllOfGold1193½ Cresinhrjns1203 TimForRomnc1163½ Checked after start 7
20Oct01-9BM fst 6f :22 :442 :563 1:091 3↑ ⒻCHRussell H50k 80 7 1 41½ 42½ 33½ 36 Warren R J Jr LB 115 b 10.10e 89–08 *HallOfGold*1164½ Creaseinherjens1221½ DeGoddughter1154 4w turn, wknd 7
1Sep01-9BM fst 6f :214 :441 :563 1:093 3↑ ⒻMaeDeVolSprH53k 81 1 6 65½ 64½ 54½ 46 Warren R J Jr LB 115 b 3.10e 87–12 Slewsbox1213½ Carson Jen1161½ Phaenna1181 Svd grnd, no rally 7
11Aug01-10Bmf fm 1 Ⓣ :231 :47 1:112 1:371 ⒻFloralFiesta44k 64 4 45 32 31 64 68¼ Alvarado F T LB 119 b 6.40 85–07 Plnncmtbbpn1191 ClrMSpcl1152 SngOfThMmnt1152 3w 2nd turn, empty 7
4Jly01-8Mth fst 170 :223 :461 1:112 1:42 ⒻSerena'sSong50k 60 7 78½ 66¾ 55 511 617 Alvarado R Jr L 116 b 42.30 72–18 Astrid1124¾ Latour1181½ Strike It Up1217¾ Middle move,empty 8
9Jun01-5Del fst 1 1/16 :243 :491 1:134 1:46 ⒻSusan's Girl75k 34 5 55½ 53½ 54½ 510 532 Tohill K S L 117 7.30 45–34 Strike It Up1195 Lady Andromeda1152 Emery Board1226¾ Trailed 5

L'Emeraude (Fr) 2

Own: Amerman Racing LLC
Navy Blue, White Bars On Sleeves, Navy
VALDIVIA J JR (2 0 0 0 .00) 2002:(237 27 .11)

Gr. f. 4
Sire: Vert Amande*Fr (Kenmare*Fr)
Dam: Abigaila*Fr(River River*Fr)
Br: Lellouche Elie & Lellouche Sylvain (Fr)
Tr: Frankel Robert(2 0 2 0 .00) 2002:(136 31 .23)

L 112

Life	10	3	0	0	$53,542	86	D.Fst	0	0	0	0	$0	–
2002	1	0	0	0	$380	84	Wet(—)	0	0	0	0	$0	–
2001	6	2	0	0	$42,027	86	Turf(278*)	10	3	0	0	$53,542	86
Hol	0	0	0	0	$0	–	Dist	0	0	0	0	$0	–

Previously trained by Hennig Mark
26Jan02-6GP fm 1⅛ Ⓣ :502 1:151 1:382 1:50 + 4↑ ⒻAlw 38000N3X 84 7 42 42 42½ 42¼ 83¾ Coa E M L 117 n 18.40 80–14 SltyYou1172¼ SmmrSolstc117nk TopFloorSt119nk Saved ground, gave way 11
15Nov01-8Aqu fm 1 Ⓣ :231 :463 1:111 1:361 3↑ ⒻAlw 48000N3X 86 7 612 611 63 41½ 63½ Gryder A T L 115 9.10 93–14 Nouvelle121½ Unbridled Vice121nk Slipping1171½ Inside, no response 10
19Oct01-9Med fm 1 1/16 Ⓣ :232 :473 1:114 1:43 ⒻMissLiberty100k 77 5 125¾ 126½ 104 102 73½ Bailey J D L 115 *1.10 81–09 MdAccss112nk DHThGddssAtrd116 DHAtrlFlttr1141¾ Mild bid when clear 12
Previously trained by Elie Lellouche
9May01♦ Saint-Cloud(Fr) sf *1 5/16 Ⓣ LH 2:223 ⒻPrix Cleopatre-G3 Stk 56600 42½ Bonilla D 121 16.00 Spring Oak1211½ Epistole1211 Zghorta121hd 8
Timeform rating: 103
·Towards rear,lacked room 3-1/2f out,finished fast,just missed 3rd
11Apr01♦ Saint-Cloud(Fr) hy *1 5/16 Ⓣ LH 2:411 ⒻPrix Penelope-G3 Stk 56800 56¼ Peslier O 126 2.00 Baldwina1264 Nadia126¾ Bellona1261½ 5
Timeform rating: 102

```
Queen of Wilshire                              Ch. m. 6                                          Life 16 5 6 2 $239,442 99   D.Fst      9 4 3 1  $131,175 97
Own: E A Ranches                               Sire: Major Impact (Roberto) $5,000               2002  4 0 3 0  $67,947 99   Wet(315)   0 0 0 0       $0  -
Red Red Ea On Yellow Ball On Back              Dam:  Rampart Street(Dixieland Band)        L 115 2001  2 1 0 0  $35,400 94   Turf(305)  7 1 3 1  $108,267 99
VALENZUELA P A (6 2 1 1 .33) 2002:(340 45 .13) Br:   Jacques D Wimpfheimer & Edgar Cullman (Ky)  Hol   3 1 0 1  $22,800 94   Dist       0 0 0 0       $0  -
                                               Tr:   Vienna Darrell(2 0 0 1 .00) 2002:(120 23 .19)
  Entered 26Apr00- 3 HOL
 7Apr02-5BM  fm 1     (T):241 :474 1:112 1:343 3+(F)MsAmericaH100k    99 3 12 12 12 2hd 22       Baze R A     LB 117 b *1.50 100-06 CrzyEnsign1162 QunOfWilshr1172½ DsprsdRwrd1151½  Easy lead, gave way 6
 7Mar02-7SA  fm *6½f  (T):213 :434 1:07 1:131 4+(F)WntrSolstceH82k    95 9 1 1hd 1hd 11 3¾       Flores D R   LB 118 b  3.70  90-09 PennyMrie118no TwinSet116¾ [D]QueenOfWilshire1181½  Drifted in bit late 9
  Disqualified and placed 4th
18Feb02-9SA  fm 1     (T):232 :473 1:112 1:352 4+(F)BuenaVistaH-G2    97 3 1½ 11 11 11½ 2nk      Flores D R   LB 116 b  6.00  85-15 Blue Moon113nk Queen OfWilshire1161 OldMoney118nk  Inside,caught late 7
16Jan02-7SA  fm 1     (T):221 :451 1:094 1:35 4+(F)Alw 65000N$mY     95 4 12 12½ 12 11 21½      Pincay L Jr  LB 117 b  5.80  85-18 OldMoney1171½ QueenOfWilshire1172½ Kalatiar1231  Fought back rail lane 6
15Dec01-3Hol fm 1 1/16 (T):241 :483 1:121 1:431 3+(F)Dahlia H-G2      92 7 42 31½ 21½ 21½ 53¼   Pincay L Jr  LB 117 b  5.30  74-25 Verruma115½ Vencera1151½ Heads Will Roll1171  Pulled,stdied 6-1/2 8
 4Oct01-7SA  fm 1     (T):23  :462 1:101 1:342 3+(F)OClm 100000N      94 4 11 11 11½ 11½ 1¾     Pincay L Jr  LB 118 b 13.00  95-06 Queen Of Wilshire118¾ Nashoba120nk Vencera1181  Strong hand ride 9
 2Dec00-3Hol fst 6f        :221 :45  :57  1:10 3+(F)Corona H82k      89 5 2 53½ 43 44 45        Nakatani C S LB 117 b  4.60  82-19 Theres'sTizzy1201½ Hookedonthefelin122no SqullCity1163½ Off rail, no rally 5
 1Nov00-2SA  fst 6½f       :214 :44 1:084 1:153 3+(F)OClm 80000N      96 5 1 2hd 21 22 21¼       Pincay L Jr  LB 118 b  *.90  89-18 SqullCity1111¼ QunOfWilshir1183 LdingLight1181½  Dueled,stalked,2d best 5
19Oct00-7SA  fst 6½f       :212 :441 1:092 1:161 3+(F)(R)Cascapedia60k 97 5 2 31 21 21½ 2½        Espinoza V   LB 116 b  9.70  86-19 Hookedonthflin122½ QunOfWilshir1161¼ Nny'sSwp1161½  Willingly to wire 7
 2Sep00-1Dmr fst 6½f       :22  :451 1:102 1:17 3+(F)OClm 80000N      89 4 1 4½ 31 1hd 1¾        Espinoza V   LB 117 b  *.90  88-13 QueenOfWilshire117¾ Gilly'sGhazi1171½ AnnieLil114½  4wd to turn,gamely 8
18Dec99-7Hol fst 6f        :22  :45  :571 1:093 3+(F)Corona H90k      94 2 5 2½ 2hd 22 34        Espinoza V   LB 111 b 16.20  85-14 Theres'sTizzy1173½ Funllover115½ QunOfWilshir111hd  Inside duel,held 3rd 8
14Nov99-2Hol fm 1 1/16 (T):241 :474 1:114 1:422 3+(F)Alw 43050N2X     86 4 11 11 1½ 2½ 32¼      Espinoza V   LB 117 b *1.10  79-19 RnbwAmthyst117¾ DstyHthr1151½ QnOfWlshr1171  Angled in,outfinished 5
WORKS: Apr22 SA 6f fst 1:174 B 9/9  Apr15 SA 4f fst :481 B 9/45  Apr3 SA 4f fst :512 H 35/39  Mar28 SA 5f fst 1:021 H 29/32  Mar20 SA 4f fst :493 H 33/46  Feb26 SA 3f fst :361 B 5/10
TRAINER: Turf/Dirt(19 .16 $1.47) Dirt(111 .21 $1.36) Routes(211 .17 $2.07) GrdStk(54 .11 $1.32)
```

```
Stormy Society                                      B. f. 4 OBSAUG99 $60,000                         Life 19 7 3 1 $216,894 100  D.Fst      16 5 3 1  $157,014 100
Own: Cono & Eastern Sky Unlimited Trust             Sire: Storm Creek (Storm Cat) $15,000            2002  3 2 0 0  $54,600 100  Wet(335*)   2 2 0 0   $59,880  71
Red, Black Horse On Purple Panel On Back            Dam:  Social Desire(Raised Socially)       L 112 2001 13 3 3 1 $121,434  79  Turf(275)   1 0 0 0        $0  51
SOLIS A (5 1 0 1 .20) 2002:(391 71 .18)             Br:   Mockingbird Farm Inc (Fla)                 Hol   0 0 0 0       $0   -  Dist        8 3 3 0  $115,486  79
                                                    Tr:   Paasch Christopher S(1 0 1 0 .00) 2002:(68 11 .16)
31Mar02-8SA  fst 1 1/16    :231 :461 1:101 1:422 4+(F)(R)SantaLucia H82k 66 2 21 21 21½ 46 717      Valenzuela P A LB 115 b 4.20 75-08 Alexine117½ Cashmina1163½ De Goddaughter1152½  Forced pace, tired 7
10Mar02-3SA  fst 1         :231 :464 1:111 1:363 4+(F)OClm 80000N       100 1 11 11½ 13½ 14 11½    Valenzuela P A LB 118 b 9.80 88-16 StormySociety1181½ Eline'sAngl1186½ StrshipSrtog120½  Inside,clear,held 5
  Previously trained by Depaulo Michael P
 4Jan02-10GP fst 1⅛ (X):502 1:161 1:414 1:541 4+(F)Alw 34000N1X          81 6 11½ 1½ 1½ 11½ 15      Guidry M      L 117 b  2.30 66-32 Stormy Society1175 Ready11718 Festive Madam1171  Inside, drew away 7
 2Dec01-10WO fst 1 1/16    :23  :472 1:123 1:453 3+(F)Alw 58100N1X      68 10 1hd 1hd 1hd 3½ 45½   Husbands P    L 117 b *2.30 72-13 BandLady118½ MKitty1172¾ ChrmingMelody1092¼  Faltered upper stretch 10
21Oct01-7WO  fst 1 1/16    :241 :483 1:131 1:453   (F)Clm 45000 (50-45) 79 3 1hd 2hd 11 15 13½    Husbands P    L 116 b  3.30 78-20 Stormy Society1163½ Dime Across1162¾ Fafnir1191½  Much the best 7
27Sep01-6WO  fst 1 1/16    :231 :473 1:131 1:472   (F)Clm 50000 (50-45) 71 2 11 11 1½ 12½ 2½      Husbands P    L 119 b  2.55 68-30 HaggledKiss116½ StormySociety1192¼ Stephanie'sWager1142¼  Just failed 8
 1Sep01-7WO  fst 7f        :221 :452 1:123 1:261 3+(F)Alw 52800N1X      31 2 1 2hd 1hd 72½ 821¼   Husbands S P  L 115 b  7.00 52-22 RoylDllince1181¾ ExplosiveAmy1181 RivrZupprdo118½  Eased late stretch 8
19Aug01-1WO  sly 1 1/16    :233 :48  1:131 1:462   (F)Clm 50000 (50-45) 71 2 11½ 12 12½ 13 1½     Husbands P    L 119 b  *.95 74-21 StormyScty119½ RdngThWvs1162¾ DmAcrss116nk  Led throughout,driving 5
 3Aug01-7WO  fm 1      (T):221 :443 1:092 1:343 3+(F)Alw 58100N1X      51 10 49 812 84½ 107½ 1113 Husbands P    L 116 b 30.20 79-09 Soundtrck115nk MrjorieDw112nk SkippingSton116½  Lacked late response 12
 6Jly01-4WO  fst 1 1/16    :23  :463 1:12 1:474    (F)Clm 50000 (50-45) 67 5 2hd 11 1½ 2hd 22¼    Husbands P    L 119 b  3.95 65-33 CosaRar1162¼ StormySociety1193¾ AwesomeDeed1169  Good effort inside 7
24Jun01-7WO  fst 7f        :222 :45  1:102 1:234 3+(F)Alw 52800N1X      63 5 1 3nk 1hd 2½ 67       Husbands P    L 115 b  6.05 78-10 Petal118nk Royal Dalliance1184 Falwyn1151¼  Tired late stretch 7
21Apr01-6WO  fst 7f        :224 :462 1:124 1:262   (F)Alw 52800N1X      58 10 1 1hd 1hd 4¾ 46     Ramsammy E    L 117 b  2.60 66-22 FleurDeSel1172¼ SnowyWger1173¾ MinesInGr117no  Weakened late stretch 10
WORKS: Apr21 Hol 5f fst 1:02 H 29/37  Apr14 Hol 4f fst :484 H 14/34  Mar24 SA 5f fst 1:022 H 45/56  Feb25 GP 6f fst 1:143 Hg 2/2  Jan30 GP 4f fst :493 B 18/37
TRAINER: Dirt(176 .14 $2.12) Routes(104 .12 $1.32) GrdStk(22 .14 $1.33)
```

```
Verruma (Brz)                                  B. f. 6                                           Life 18 9 2 0 $412,643 103  D.Fst       7 3 1 0   $83,618 103
Own: Clifton & Lester                          Sire: Emmson*Ire (Ela-Mana-Mou)                   2002  2 0 1 0  $60,000 103  Wet(295)    0 0 0 0        $0   -
White, Dark Green Star, White Cap              Dam:  Call Box*GB(Caerleon)                 L 116 2001  9 4 1 0 $270,228  99  Turf(284*) 11 6 1 0  $329,025  99
GOMEZ G K (—) 2002:(174 18 .10)                Br:   Haras J B Barros (Brz)                      Hol   0 0 0 0       $0   -  Dist        2 0 1 0   $60,000 103
                                               Tr:   Chapman James K (—) 2002:(25 2 .08)
 6Apr02-11OP fst 1 1/16     :232 :472 1:12 1:423 4+(F)ApplBlssomH-G1     98 2 32½ 31½ 42 52½ 57       Gomez G K      L 114  13.20 88-15 Azeri1171¾ Affluent118¾ Miss Linda1182  Forward, little left 5
17Feb02-8SA  fst 1 1/16     :234 :48  1:121 1:44 4+(F)SantaMariaH-G1     103 2 54½ 53¾ 52½ 21 2hd     Gomez G K     LB 114  25.80 84-18 Favorite Funtime116hd Verruma1141 Printemps1164  Tight,steadied 7/8 7
31Dec01-8SA  fm *6½f   (T):214 :441 1:083 1:15 3+(F)Monrovia H-G3       90 9 8 1111 1213 119¾ 42¾    Nakatani C S  LB 117   5.90 82-15 Paga1171¼ Twin Set115½ Impeachable1151  Swung out, late bid 13
15Dec01-3Hol fm 1 1/16 (T):241 :483 1:121 1:431 3+(F)Dahlia H-G2         99 1 64 74½ 74¼ 43 1½       Gomez G K     LB 115   4.20 77-25 Verruma115½ Vencera1151½ Heads Will Roll1171  Split foes,rail rally 8
25Nov01-5Hol yl 1⅛     (T):503 1:142 1:38 1:50 + 3+(F)Matriarch-G1       74 3 66 911 1010 1011 912¼   Baze T C      LB 123  38.20 67-19 Starine1232½ Lethals Lady120nk GoldenApples1203  Steadied 3/8,weakened 12
  Previously trained by Penna Angel Jr
26Oct01-5Bel fm 1 1/16 (T):251 :484 1:13 1:42 3+(F)Athenia-G3           96 5 32 32 3nk 2hd 1no       Velazquez J R  L 114   3.70 86-15 Verruma114no Siringas1121 Freefourracing113hd  3 wide move, prevailed 8
 8Oct01-9Bel gd 1      (T):222 :454 1:104 1:344 4+(F)Alw 56000N$Y        98 3 810 88 84¾ 31½ 1no      Velazquez J R  L 120   2.80 84-24 Verrum120no [D]MySweetWstly116hd SilvrRil1206¾  Inside move, swung out 10
22Sep01-9Bel fst 1     (X):223 :453 1:092 1:35 3+(F)NoblDamselH-G3       79 2 56½ 65½ 65½ 511 510     Santos J A     L 114   8.90 82-11 Tugger1191 Shine Again123hd Tippity Witch1133¾  Inside, no response 6
 5Aug01-6Mth fm 1⅛     (T):483 1:122 1:36 1:472 3+(F)Eatontown H-G3      84 5 53 66¼ 54 55 46        Coa E M        L 115   2.50 90-04 Cousin Gigi1152½ Quidnaskra1161 Crystal Sea1132½  5wd far turn,no rally 8
27Jun01-7Bel fm 1⅛     [T]:471 1:113 1:353 1:472 4+(F)Alw 54000N$YmT     92 6 55 54½ 54 2hd 1no      Prado E S      L 116   3.50 92-11 Verruma116no Babae120½ Zeiting1201½  3 wide move, driving 7
 4Jun01-8Del gd 1 1/16 (T):221 :461 1:111 1:441 3+(F)Rosenna75k          89 3 511 510 62¾ 42 21      McCarthy M J   L 115   4.30 85-17 Quidnaskra1151 Verruma115no Pretty Dutch115nk  Gamely, up for 2nd 8
  Previously trained by F Monteiro
22Aug99♦ Cdad Jardim(Brz) fm *1 (T)LH 1:341  (F)GP Barao de Piracicaba-G1   64½ Queiroz A  123  -  Hail Glory123 Buque de Noiva123 Breeder's Song123  18
                                              Stk 41200
WORKS: Apr20 Hol 4f fst :481 B 7/43  Mar30 Hol 6f fst 1:142 H 8/16  Mar23 Hol 5f fst 1:012 H 21/44  Mar16 Hol 4f fst :503 H 37/42  Mar4 Hol 4f fst :474 H 4/21  ●Feb9 Hol 6f fst 1:121 H 1/11
TRAINER: Dirt(139 .15 $1.54) Routes(34 .12 $1.10) GrdStk(20 .15 $1.25)
```

Regarding interpretation and use, handicappers should honor these guidelines:

1. A horse with 4 speed points or more is said to have early-speed dependability. That is, such a horse is most likely to be among the early leaders.
2. Horses that have at least 4 speed points and stand alone as the highest-speed-point horse in the field win frequently enough to

return about a 4 percent profit on the dollar. In three of four races one horse stands alone as having the highest speed-point total.

3. Horses with at least 5 speed points and at least 2 points' advantage over their nearest rivals do better. That kind wins almost twice its rightful share of races and returns a 10 percent profit.

4. A horse having 8 speed points is most likely to battle the early pace or to set the pace alone. If no other horse has a high speed-point figure, its chances of winning increase terrifically. But if the race contains a 7 or 6 or both, an early speed duel is likely, and this will decrease the high-figure horse's chances.

5. The best way to estimate the high-speed-point horse's relative chances is to calculate its speed-point percentage. Simply add each horse's speed points and divide the sum into each of the three top-figure horses. Suppose the speed points in an eight-horse field are 4-2-7-4-1-4-5-2. The sum of speed points is 29. The top three-figure horses have a speed-point percentage equal to $\frac{7}{29}$, $\frac{5}{29}$, and $\frac{4}{29}$, or 24 percent, 17 percent, and 13 percent, respectively. Studies indicate horses having speed-point percentages of 30 percent or greater are most likely to dominate the early pace.

Early Speed and Early Pace

EXPERIENCE WITH SPEED POINTS is tantamount to a deeper understanding of early pace. As Tom Brohamer has observed, pace analysis begins, and often ends, with a careful analysis of the early pace. As is true of any rating method, the procedure is terrifically less important than the meaning of the ratings.

Keep these definitions in mind:

    8-7   speed points means high early speed
    6-5   speed points means good early speed
      4   speed points means acceptable early speed
  3-2-1-0   speed points means poor early speed

If two or more horses have high early speed, the pace will likely be normal to fast. That means horses running behind the early pace will have a better chance. In the Hawthorne Handicap, three of the seven runners, Ask Me No Secrets, Queen of Wilshire, and Stormy Society, showed high early speed. It's true too that two-horse duels do not necessarily ruin the horses engaged in them, but three-horse duels usually do. The high-quotient-of-speed lineup for the Hawthorne Handicap meant that closers Alexine and Verruma might be advantaged by the early pace.

Remember this crucial distinction among front-runners having high early speed (8-7 points). Many of them will be need-to-lead types. Unless they can secure the front, they do not win. Moreover, if they cannot get the lead, not only do they not win, they do not run second and third, completing exactas and trifectas. Instead, they normally will finish up the course. Handicappers can throw them aside, and confidently. Brohamer has asserted that need-to-lead front-runners that cannot get the lead are among the worst bets in handicapping.

Of Ask Me No Secrets, Queen of Wilshire, and Stormy Society, which are need-to-lead front-runners?

Ask Me No Secrets and Queen of Wilshire have won from slightly behind the pace, but Stormy Society (seven wins) has not. Stormy Society is a need-to-lead front-runner that cannot secure the lead today; out. Handicappers easily recognize the pattern of wire-to-wire wins interspersed with finishes out of the money. Occasionally, a need-to-lead front-runner that does not win will hold second, as did Stormy Society at Woodbine on September 27, when it has been clear inside the eighth pole and is passed late. But when challenged early, they routinely finish up the course, and handicappers should anticipate that.

At the opposite pole of the speed-points scale, horses having poor early speed (3-2-1-0 points), the key consideration is these horses' customary position at the second call, or pace call, which occurs after four furlongs in sprints and after six furlongs in routes. The horses should be "up close," at least twice in the past seven or eight races. "Up close" means within 2¾ lengths in sprints and within 3½ in routes, which represent flexible, even liberal, guideposts. Horses that are "up close" have striking position. If horses have poor early speed and no striking position at the second call (six-furlong call in routes), they represent poor bets to win. But they do run second and third regularly, completing exactas and trifectas, and handicappers had best expect that.

The two horses on page 8 competed in the Kings Point Handicap for New York-breds at Aqueduct on April 28, 2002. Assign the speed points. One of the two is routinely "up close" after six furlongs, and can be backed to win. The other is almost never "up close" at the pace call, and can be backed to place and to show, but not to win. Review the records closely.

```
5 Gander                              Gr/ro g. 6                                              Life 41 10 7 6 $1,317,688 110   D.Fst     34 8 4 6
  Own:Gatsas Thoroughbreds            Sire: Cormorant (His Majesty) $6,500                    2002  1  0 0 0         $0  89   Wet(355)   3 2 0 0
  White Royal Blue Ball               Dam:  Lovely Nurse(Sawbones)                    L 124   2001 10  2 1 2   $557,060 110   Turf(270)  4 0 3 0
VELAZQUEZ J R (124 30 24 17 .24) 2002:(457 94 .21)   Br: Rugnetta Angela (NY)                 Aqu   5  0 1 1    $16,410  95   Dist      14 3 1 3
                                      Tr:   Terranova John P II(17 3 3 1 .18) 2002:(42 7 .17)
3Feb02-6SA fst 1⅛ :473 1:113 1:361 1:483 4↑ SanAntonioH-G2 89 6 64 52¼ 52½ 65¾ 711½ Stevens G L LB 116 b 9.40 81-17 Redattore116½ Euchre1191½ Irisheyesareflying1171 3w
23Nov01-11CD fst 1⅛ :471 1:11 1:353 1:481 3↑ Clark H-G2 103 8 108¾ 107 44 44 52 Chavez J F L 115 b 3.80 93-09 Ubiquity113nk Include1201 Mr Ross114hd 8w
27Oct01-10Bel fst 1¼ :47 1:111 1:354 2:003 3↑ BC Classic-G1 102 8 128¾ 116½ 53½ 107¾ 910 Espinoza V L 126 b 80.75 81-12 Tiznow126no Sakhee1261¾ Albert The Great1262¾ Check
28Sep01-8Med fst 1⅛ :483 1:114 1:352 1:47 3↑ Med Cup H-G2 104 1 11½ 1½ 11 2hd 1hd Velazquez J R L 114 b 4.10 92-09 Gander114hd Broken Vow120nk Include12115 Pace,
19Aug01-9Sar fst 1¼ :481 1:12 1:363 2:012 3↑ Sar BCH-G2 107 2 1½ 11½ 2½ 42 46¼ Bridgmohan S X L 115 5.30 92-08 Aptitude1224¼ Perfect Cat1151 A Fleets Dancer1151 Set
28Jly01-6Sar fst 1⅛ :463 1:101 1:344 1:474 3↑ Whitney H-G1 110 6 22 22 32 42 32¼ Bridgmohan S X L 113 35.50 100 — Lido Palace1152 Albert The Great124nk Gander113nk Goo
23Jun01-9Rkm fm *1⅛ Ⓣ 1:461 3↑ NHSweepstkH-G3 88 6 31 31½ 3½ 23 27 Gryder A T LB 117 2.50 87-08 Hap1237 Gander1171¾ Flash Of Joy1131¼ 3w, le
10Jun01-7Bel fst 1⅛ :462 1:10 1:342 1:472 3↑ Brooklyn H-G2 103 3 42 41 42½ 45½ 46¾ Velazquez J R L 115 6.40 86-12 AlbertTheGreat1223¼ PerfectCt1153 TopOfficil113½ Cha
10May01-5Bel fst 1 1/16 :224 :452 1:092 1:41 4↑ Alw 50000N4X 109 4 2½ 2½ 1½ 13 15¼ Velazquez J R L 116 *.65 92-08 Gander1165¼ Jarf1205¾ Open Sesame1161 Too'
3Mar01-10GP fst 1¼ :461 1:104 1:363 2:024 3↑ Gulf Park H-G1 85 5 2hd 3½ 68½ 59½ 517 Velazquez J R L 115 b 5.20 66-24 Sir Bear116½ Pleasant Breeze1151½ Broken Vow1146 B
3Feb01-11GP fst 1⅛ :464 1:11 1:36 1:484 3↑ Donn H-G1 97 2 31½ 31½ 31½ 35 311¾ Velazquez J R L 115 b 13.90 81-13 Captain Steve1201¼ AlbertTheGreat11910 Gander1151½ Cha
4Nov00-10CD fst 1¼ :472 1:12 1:36 2:003 3↑ BC Classic-G1 97 11 104 61¾ 74¾ 97¼ 913 Velazquez J R L 126 b 64.60 94 — Tiznow122nk Giant'sCusewy1223¼ CptinSteve122hd 5-6 wic
WORKS: ●Apr24 Bel 5f fst :59 B 1/30 Apr16 Bel 6f fst 1:141 B 1/3 Apr10 Bel 5f fst 1:004 B 2/10 ●Apr4 Bel 5f fst :594 B 1/10 Mar29 Bel tr.t 4f fst :483 B 19/73 Mar23 Bel tr.t 4f fst :491 B 37/102
TRAINER: 61-180Days(22 .27 $3.19) Dirt(147 .16 $1.64) Routes(73 .11 $0.77) Stakes(13 .00 $0.00)
```

```
6 Galactic                            Gr/ro g. 6                                              Life 43  4 4 14   $229,463  95   D.Fst      26 1 4
  Own:DeFalco B & Mermini P A & R J   Sire: Tank's Number (Tank's Prospect) $2,000            2002  4  0 1 2    $17,505  91   Wet(350*)   7 3 0
  Black, Light Blue Diamond Frame And 'k',  Dam: Princess Nova(Morning Bob)           L 114   2001 13  2 1 4    $92,028  95   Turf(160*) 10 0 0
DAVIS R G (87 19 12 16 .22) 2002:(173 37 .21)   Br: Team Martin & Zacarias Aragon (NY)        Aqu  12  2 1 4    $81,994  94   Dist       19 4 3
                                      Tr:   Carlesimo Charles Jr(7 1 1 2 .14) 2002:(15 1 .07)
3Apr02-7Aqu fst 1⅛ :49 1:144 1:41 1:54 4↑ Clm 50000(60-50) 83 5 511 58 44½ 44½ 35½ Davis R G L 114 4.20 60-35 Willimthenchnted1191 ReefChief1214½ Glctic1141½
14Mar02-3Aqu fst 1⅛ :481 1:13 1:38 1:504 4↑ Clm 40000(40-35) 86 3 58½ 56¾ 54 42½ 3¾ Davis R G L 117 3.05 81-22 Badger Gold120½ Borntoberegal115nk Galactic117½
3Feb02-9Aqu fst 1 1/16 ⊡ :242 :483 1:132 1:454 4↑ Clm c-(30-25) 83 3 89½ 84½ 105¼ 84½ 73 Bridgmohan S X L 118 *1.85 74-19 K.O.'sCrypto123¾ AloneAtHome116hd Zachrov1231
   Claimed from Castle William J & Friedman Stuart for $30,000, Laboccetta Frank Jr Trainer 2002(as of 02/03): ( 65 17 12 6 0.26 )
13Jan02-8Aqu fst 1⅛ ⊡ :48 1:121 1:372 1:501 4↑ Alw 46000N2X 91 5 55 42½ 42½ 21½ 2hd Bridgmohan S X L 115 3.90 86-19 YankeeDoodleBoy120hd Galactic1151 PaynesBy1185¾
29Dec01-5Aqu fst 1 1/16 ⊡ :24 :473 1:122 1:434 3↑ Alw 46000N2X 82 2 813 89¾ 85½ 58½ 58¾ Bridgmohan S X L 116 8.50 78-16 John Little1211 Quiet One1196¼ Ghost Story119no
24Nov01-1Aqu fst 1⅛ :49 1:14 1:39 1:513 3↑ Clm c-(30-25) 80 8 69½ 68¼ 63¾ 54½ 32¼ Santos J A L 115 3.55 76-16 Drawing Away1141¼ K. O.'s Crypto1131 Galactic115nk
   Claimed from Aragon Zacarias for $30,000, Martin Carlos F Trainer 2001(as of 11/24): ( 182 22 29 23 0.12 )
21Oct01-9Bel fst 1⅛ :474 1:111 1:362 1:49 3↑ Ⓢ EmpireClsscH250k 82 3 76 710 811 710 710¾ Santos J A L 114 29.50 74-22 ScottishHlo1201¾ Duplicitous1152¾ SrtogSunrise1182
28Jun01-8Bel fm 1¼ Ⓣ :494 1:132 1:364 2:001 3↑ Alw 46000N2X 82 4 95¼ 95¾ 85¼ 86¼ 65¾ Pitty C D L 121 16.50 84-14 MelNDve1212¼ NorthernFntsy1211½ Zfonic'sSong1231
17Jun01-6Bel sly 1 ⊗ :231 :46 1:103 1:353 4↑ Alw 46560N3X 88 3 311 311 45½ 33½ 34¾ Pitty C D L 116 2.85 84-19 Top Bunk1163 Polish Miner1161¾ Galactic1162¾
28May01-8Bel my 1⅛ :47 1:13 1:384 1:514 3↑ Alw 44000N1X 95 6 710 711 51½ 1½ 13¾ Pitty C D L 121 5.60 71-26 Galactic1213¾ Peak Dancer1212¾ Tampa1164
20May01-8Bel fm 1⅛ Ⓣ :473 1:111 1:353 1:481 3↑ Ⓢ Kingston H86k 94 4 1213 117½ 118¼ 93½ 31¾ Pitty C D L 113 75.50 86-15 Pebo's Guy1191½ John Paul Too114nk Galactic1131½
29Apr01-6Aqu fst 1⅛ :501 1:141 1:383 1:511 3↑ Alw 44000N1X 90 3 42½ 41 42 23 22 Pitty C D L 121 14.50 78-15 Call It Off1212 Galactic1213½ Cypress1211¾
WORKS: Mar30 Bel tr.t 3f fst :37 B 7/47 Mar8 Bel tr.t 4f fst :52 B 35/36 Mar2 Bel tr.t 3f fst :373 B 19/44
TRAINER: Dirt(70 .06 $1.50) Routes(27 .04 $0.78) Stakes(4 .00 $0.00)
```

Handicappers must allow three exceptions to the instinctive elimination to win of horses having poor early speed and no striking position at the second call:

1. Turf races
2. The track profile favors deep closers
3. The horse enjoys a significant class edge, which usually occurs in stakes races or on the turf.

For horses whose past performances do not yet contain five races, Quirin has projected speed-point totals from points already earned. Consult this table:

POINTS

Career Starts	0	1	2	3	4	
one start	0	3	5	x	x	Projected Points
two starts	0	1	3	4	5	

The zeros are included because, in Quirin's original technique, horses that earned no speed points beyond the one given, and did not beat at least half the field to the first call in any of the three rated races, were penalized by having the original point taken away.

Interestingly, in the 2002 Hawthorne Handicap at Hollywood Park, the front-runners Ask Me No Secrets and Stormy Society were late scratches. Now Queen of Wilshire had a two-point advantage over the other early speed, and a serious pace advantage over favorite Alexine and second choice Verruma.

In a five-horse field, Queen of Wilshire went wire to wire and paid $6.80.

EIGHTH RACE
Hollywood
APRIL 27, 2002

1 1/16 MILES. (1.40) 29th Running of THE HAWTHORNE HANDICAP. Grade III. Purse $100,000 added. Fillies and mares, 3-year-olds and upward. By subscription of $100 each on or before Wednesday, April 17, or by supplementary nomination of $5,000 each by Saturday, April 20. $1,000 additional to start, with $100,000 added. The added money and all fees to be divided 60% to the winner, 20% to second, 12% to third, 6% to fourth and 2% to fifth. Closed Wednesday, April 17 with 11 nominations.

Value of Race: $106,100 Winner $63,660; second $21,220; third $12,732; fourth $6,366; fifth $2,122.   Mutuel Pool $342,597.00 Exacta Pool $187,552.00   Quinella Pool $23,904.00 Trifecta Pool $170,679.00

Last Raced	Horse	M/Eqt. A.Wt	PP	St	1/4	1/2	3/4	Str	Fin	Jockey	Odds $1
7Apr02 5B M2	Queen of Wilshire	LBb 6 115	1	1	1 1½	1 3	1 2½	1 1½	1 no	Valenzuela P A	2.40
31Mar02 8SA1	Alexine-ARG	LB 6 119	3	5	5	3 hd	3 2½	2 2½	2 4½	Stevens G L	1.40
6Apr02 11OP5	Verruma-BR	LB 6 116	5	3	4½	5	4 1	3 1	3½	Gomez G K	2.20
31Mar02 8SA3	De Goddaughter	LBb 4 113	2	2	2 2	2 2	2 hd	4 4	4 6	Espinoza V	11.00
26Jan02 6GP8	L'Emeraude-FR	LB 4 114	4	4	3 1	4 2	5	5	5	Valdivia J Jr	10.20

OFF AT 4:55 Start Good. Won driving. Track fast.
TIME :24, :471, 1:103, 1:362, 1:43 (:24.05, :47.31, 1:10.70, 1:36.42, 1:43.16)

$2 Mutuel Prices:

2-QUEEN OF WILSHIRE	6.80	3.00	2.20
4-ALEXINE-ARG		2.60	2.10
6-VERRUMA-BR			2.20

$1 EXACTA 2-4 PAID $7.40 $2 QUINELLA 2-4 PAID $6.60 $1 TRIFECTA 2-4-6 PAID $16.40

Ch. m, by Major Impact-Rampart Street, by Dixieland Band. Trainer Vienna Darrell. Bred by Jacques D Wimpfheimer & Edgar Cullman (Ky).

QUEEN OF WILSHIRE sped to the early lead, set the pace under a long hold a bit off the rail, came out some into the stretch and held on gamely under urging. ALEXINE (ARG) pinched back a bit at the start then steadied off heels in the opening strides, settled inside, moved up on the second turn, came a bit off the rail into the stretch, bid inside through the drive and continued gamely to the wire to just miss. VERRUMA (BRZ) settled three deep early then off the rail on the backstretch, angled in and inched forward on the second turn, came off the rail in midstretch, was no match for the top pair but held third. DE GODDAUGHTER broke out a bit, raced outside the winner early then stalked that one off the rail on the backstretch and outside the runner-up on the second turn and was edged for the show. L'EMERAUDE (FR) chased between horses early then outside a rival, continued off the inside on the second turn, angled in some and weakened.

Owners— 1, E A Ranches; 2, Hubbard R D Masterson Robert Rio Cl; 3, Clifton or Lester; 4, Golden State Racing & Bonde Jeff; 5, Amerman Racing Stables

Trainers— 1, Vienna Darrell; 2, Mandella Richard; 3, Chapman James K; 4, Bonde Jeff; 5, Frankel Robert

Scratched— Ask Me No Secrets (16Mar02 10OP1), Stormy Society (31Mar02 8SA7)

$2 Daily Double (7-2) Paid $34.20; Daily Double Pool $27,216.
$1 Pick Three (3-7-2) Paid $49.50; Pick Three Pool $63,102.

CHAPTER 2

OPTIMAL BETTING

IN A BEAUTIFULLY concise and possibly perfect technical paper on money management delivered in 1979, the redoubtable Huey Mahl took bettors of games by the hand, escorted them to the mountaintop, and there explained the facts of life in language so clear and persuasive that anyone who listened and learned the truth need never be troubled again. Handicappers sufficiently skilled in their art that they are capable of making seasonal profits by betting on horses can take it as gospel that the source of their greatest possible prosperity is Mahl. The method of the man is called optimal betting, and it is exactly that.

Handicappers in consultation with Mahl will at least find answers to all the eternal questions. They can consider themselves for now and evermore enlightened on the following.

1. What exactly is the nature of a gamble?
2. Whether to bet at all, or how to determine whether they can expect positive results?
3. How to bet, or how to maximize the utilization of capital?
4. How much to bet, or how to relate the size of the bet to their advantage in the game?
5. How not to bet, or how to run advantage into disadvantage, and certain profits into certain losses?

6. How to use a simple mathematical formula to determine the optimal size of the bet?

As Mahl tells, a gamble consists of three elements: the event, the proposition, and the bet. The handicapper's event is the horse race. Nobody bets on that. Handicappers bet on the propositions offered by other handicappers, not so dissimilar from neighborhood bar bets, specifically on the odds spreads that reflect all the players' opinions regarding the winning chances of each horse. Because the proposition is framed by the public—fallible and possibly badly informed people—bettors sometimes encounter propositions that offer a positive expectancy. That is, bets on certain kinds of propositions have been known historically by the bettor to achieve positive results. Winning bettors bet on propositions whose outcomes they know to be ultimately and necessarily positive. To this incredibly important point we shall return immediately.

First, Mahl considers the actual bet. It is the single aspect of the gamble over which the bettor exercises complete control, or relative lack of the same. The prime considerations are method and size. The flat bet (same amount each bet) turns out to serve a critical function. It determines whether the bettor has a positive expectancy. Handicappers need to know first of all whether a season's selections win or lose money. They also need to know the average mutuel on winning bets. Flat bets, of a season's duration, tell handicappers whether they are playing a losing game. Those that are best retreat to a study of handicapping and postpone the wrestling with money-management methods. None that counts will matter anyhow, unless flat bets first determine a positive expectancy.

Handicappers discovering a positive expectancy with flat bets have a satisfactory basis for assuming profits over time, the critical point previously remarked, but should consider whether that method gets the most from their money. Mahl says no. He hastens to comment on the variation of flat betting referred to as unit betting, whereby handicappers bet more on some bets than others, either when pressing good luck or having high confidence in the expected outcome. This works well enough when winning streaks occur, but as Mahl explains, unit betting has a great capacity for converting a positive expectancy into loss. If handicappers lose the big ones and win the little ones, to use Mahl's metaphor, they are deep in mashed potatoes again.

Flat betting is also held to be ultraconservative. It takes quite a season to make any real money with that method. And the question and answer remain. Are flat bets the best way to appreciate a bankroll? No. At some point beyond the expectancy that signals positive results, handicappers are urged to entertain money management capable of maximizing results.

There is really only one: optimal betting. Optimal betting holds that the bettor gets maximum appreciation on investment only by sizing the bet as a percentage of bankroll equal to the bettor's advantage over the game. Mahl provides the formula that determines the bettor's advantage and therefore the percentage of capital to the bet. Handicappers will arrive at that great divide momentarily.

First, the rationale for the method and Mahl's explanation of the occasional reverent references among punters to the Kelly Criterion. It came to pass that J. L. Kelly Jr., a mathematician with Bell Telephone in the 1950's, solved a greatly technical communications problem by using complex calculus formulae he published in a treatise entitled "A New Interpretation of Information Rates." How Mahl came to prosper by the article is strictly coincidental: Kelly used gambling as the analogy for his problem solving.

Kelly told of baseball results passing along a ticker wire into an illegal bookie parlor. A telephone man, he said, could interrupt the wire flow, intercept the transmission, and make a bet with the bookie before reconnecting the wire and transmitting the results. Kelly asked how much the telephone man should bet on the game. Since the outcome was 100 percent certain, the telephone man should bet every penny he owned, and make a 100 percent profit. The operating principle was maximum utilization of capital, or optimal betting, the putting of money to work in the most effective manner.

Next Kelly assumed the possibility of a transmission error. If the telephone man intercepted the wire once a week, how much should be bet each time? To frame the next question differently, since the outcome was now something less than 100 percent certain, how to determine the size of the bet or percentage of bankroll the telephone man could afford each week and still achieve optimal results in terms of bankroll appreciation?

Mahl perceived that in each case Kelly was betting on a sure thing. The single difference was the difference between 100 percent profit maximization (based on certainty) and something less than 100 percent profit maximization (based on some advantage less than certainty). What Kelly and his calculus went on to prove, Huey Mahl translated into the first axiom of betting. For optimum results, the size of the bet, taken as a percentage of the bettor's bankroll, should be equivalent to the bettor's advantage over the game.

In any game having a one-to-one (even) proposition, Kelly showed that a bettor's advantage was equal to P-Q. Mahl translated the symbols to Win Percentage – Loss Percentage, a remarkably simple way to calculate your advantage over a game, as illustrated in the blackjack sample below. Blackjack counters who determined the remaining cards in a deck presented propositions that were 52 percent favorable to the player, 48 percent unfavorable, knew they enjoyed a 4 percent advantage. Thus, they bet 4 percent of their bankroll. If the bankroll was $1,000, the bet each time was $40.

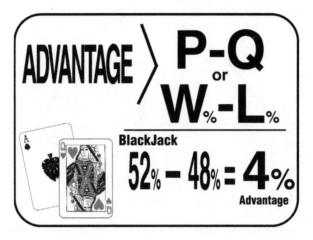

The graph illustrates a feature of the method almost universally ignored or misunderstood. To wit, a bankroll grows positively and reaches a peak when the percentage bets are equal to the advantage. If the bettor bets in amounts larger than the advantage, however, the bankroll will begin to decrease, eventually converting positive results (+) into losses (−). Even though the bettor holds an advantage over a game, if the bettor bets too much, the bettor will lose.

Mahl supposes a guy has a 10 percent advantage over his pals in a nightly bar bet. Thus he wins 55 percent of the time, loses 45 percent. If the guy's playing with $1,000 to start, then his first bet is $100 (10 percent advantage), and changes thereafter only as the bankroll changes. Suppose the guy gets greedy, says Mahl. And starts to bet 20 percent of his bankroll. By betting twice his advantage (2A on the graph), the guy ends as a loser for sure. That indeed the greedy bettor will lose is a mathematical certainty. A crucial principle of optimal betting techniques is this: The bettor will win less if he bets more at a certain point, that point being any percentage of capital beyond the bettor's advantage over the game.

Now to handicapping, where the one-to-one relationship is replaced by parimutuel betting odds. The adjustment to the optimal-betting formula is simple. It divides the loss percentage by the average payoff to $1. Thus,

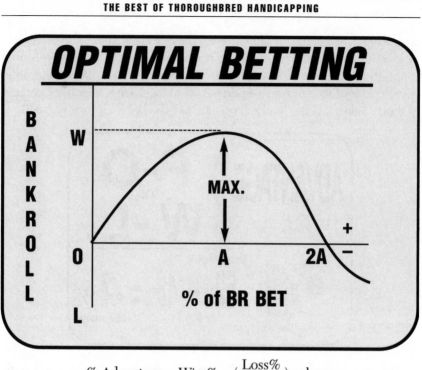

$$\% \text{ Advantage} = \text{Win } \% - \left(\frac{\text{Loss}\%}{\$ \text{ Odds}}\right), \text{ where}$$

$ means average payoff to $1. If handicappers can pick 40 percent winners at an average mutuel of $5 (odds 3 to 2, payoff to $1 is $1.50), they have no advantage over the game, as

$$40\% - \left(\frac{60\%}{\$1.50}\right) = 40 - 40 = 0\% \text{ Advantage}$$

Such handicappers have no advantage betting the races until they either raise their proficiency level (percentage of winners) or average mutuel, or both. In like manner, handicappers can calculate their advantage over the races and set the size of their bets equivalent to their advantage. In practice, this requires nothing more than records indicating the seasonal win percentage and average mutuel.

Handicappers who wish to make optimal profits but do not have the performance data to plug into Mahl's formula can start today to establish their advantage. Whatever other practices are engaged, take $100 and make a series of 200 bets ($2) to win on prime selections. Calculate the win percentage and average win mutuel. Plug the data into the formula. That is the best available estimate of your personal advantage. Establish a betting bankroll and begin. The size of each bet across a season equals your advantage over the game. The advantage changes when (a) handicapping knowledge improves; or (b) methods of selection are systematically altered; or (c) personal judgment is impaired; or (d) the conditions of racing are fundamentally changed, e.g., bad weather, new track. A new baseline is needed.

Fixed-percentage wagering principles and methods have long been touted by handicappers as avenues to maximizing profits when winning and minimizing losses when losing, but the conventional percentages to be bet have been concerned with avoiding bankruptcy and not with maximizing utilization of capital, and therefore not with maximizing profits. The traditional 5 percent guideline is the classic example. This serves to avoid calamity, but winning players wish instead to maximize gains. Optimal betting permits the bettor's true advantage to work toward the best possible financial return.

Estimates of advantage can be continually calculated, after perhaps each series of 200 bets. In the beginning, if estimated advantages are not thought precise, an underestimate represents a more favorable type of error than an overestimate. The overestimate leads to betting more than the true advantage allows, which leads to ruin, as Mahl has shown. The underestimate merely assures that the bettor will be winning at something less than an optimal rate of profit, a sorry but not desperate state of affairs.

The beauty of Mahl's optimal betting is that it guarantees the best of handicappers the greatest rewards. Experts capable of 40 percent winners at average odds of 5-2 enjoy a 16 percent advantage over the game. Each of their bets can be 16 percent of capital, yielding a return far greater than the flat-bet 40 cents on the dollar. If 40 percent winners average 2-1 on win bets, they can invest 10 percent of capital at each risk.

Handicappers that win 30 percent at 3-1 on average hold a 7 percent advantage. They can risk just 7 percent of capital each bet. If they bet 10 percent, they will lose.

As all know, the crowd wins 33 percent of its bets, loses 9 percent on the dollar. Its advantage is negative, a -9 percent, because its winners average 8-5 odds, or $1.60 to $1.

Optimal betting also reveals the handicapping pretenders for the varmints they are. Prophets of 50 percent winners at average odds of just 5-2 hold an insurmountable 30 percent advantage. They have the game by the throat. All they need to do is wager 30 percent of a fat bankroll each bet and it's a guaranteed gold mine. If such claims were true, these hucksters would be wasting their time hawking leaflets.

In determining advantage, handicappers benefit if they refine first estimates successively as more data accumulate. The tendency to define advantage in terms of best results or results recently achieved leads inevitably to overestimation and therefore to the betting of more capital than true performance warrants. Once upon a time, not repeated since, the writer hit 42 percent winners at Hollywood Park, average mutuel $8.40 ($3.20 to $1). The advantage was approximately 24 percent. To press a 24 percent betting advantage at Del Mar (next stop) that season, where win percentage was 29 and average mutuel $6.20, would have meant tapping out. Stable estimates, conservatively interpreted, are the best estimates for Mahl's formula.

To fly close to reality, when betting to win, the attainable results obtained by competent handicappers can be summarized by holding the average odds on winners constant at 5-2 at four levels of proficiency.

30% at 5-2	advantage, 2%
33% at 5-2	advantage, 6%
35% at 5-2	advantage, 9%
40% at 5-2	advantage, 16%

Most handicappers do not keep records that can inform them of their proficiency in handicapping and of the corresponding betting advantage, and will not bother to complete the task. If handicappers are willing instead to assume an advantage over the game consistent with the above estimates, they can begin betting at the optimal percentage.

Money-management experts Dick Mitchell and Barry Meadow have cautioned that handicappers suffer a tendency to overestimate their true advantage. The correction is betting a half-Kelly, or half the estimated percentage advantage. At 33% win-proficiency, average odds of 5-2 on winners, handicappers best bet 3% of the bankroll instead of 6%. The bankroll may grow at less than the optimal rate, but no one should be tapping out.

Profits will depend upon (a) the amount of the original bankroll, (b) the number of bets, and (c) the order of winning and losing wagers. All competent handicappers can know for sure is they will be winning in accord with their handicapping proficiency. That is, they will win as much precisely as they are capable of winning.

CHAPTER 3

THE KEYS TO
OLDER MAIDENS

DRF PRESS MANAGER Dean Keppler wondered whether the probability data collected by Fred Davis in 1974 remained valid. Davis had used a 300-race sample to demonstrate how older maidens (three-year-olds, three and up, four and up) that had finished second last out were a significantly better bet to win than first-time starters. In the Davis sample, second-place finishers had represented 9 percent of the starters but 24.6 percent of the winners, while first-timers had represented 6.8 percent of the starters, but only 3 percent of the winners, a 274 percent advantage to the experienced runners. Sadly, first starters were winning less than 50 percent of their rightful share of the races.

In all probability, the advantage belongs still to the second-place finishers last out, but it's true too that the handicapping of maiden races has been altered in other and far more significant ways. Nowhere else in handicapping has the impact of the information age been greater than with older maidens. Races where handicappers formerly had been groping in the dark have now been illuminated by a variety of information resources not previously available.

The transformation has proved so dramatic that enlightened handicappers that stick to the facts can expect to collect on approximately 40 percent of their bets to win with older maidens, average odds near 5-2, which throws a tantalizing 40 percent profit. The new keys to older maidens restrict support to three types:

1. horses that have recently have matched or exceeded par,
2. first starters that satisfy minimally acceptable standards associated with the sire, trainer, and workout pattern, and
3. second starters

No one should doubt the importance of a par figure among experienced maidens.

Maidens, the lightly raced kind in particular, that have equaled par will be extremely difficult for first starters to beat, even when the first starters possess greater talent and are training like blazes. Inexperience defeats them. Handicappers should expect that. In a six-week handicapping program I conducted with partner Tom Brohamer for several summers at Del Mar, once we encountered a dozen maidens that had matched par. All twelve won.

In the absence of local pars, or of pars published in *Daily Racing Form,* handicappers can trust the following estimates of Beyer Speed Figure pars for major, mid-level, and minor tracks. Major tracks means New York and southern California. Mid-level tracks include the flagships of Florida, Kentucky, Illinois, Maryland, New Jersey, and Louisiana, as well as northern California. Minor tracks encompass the others.

	Colts	Fillies
Major	88	83
Mid-level	79	74
Minor	69	64

The bad news is the older maidens that have matched par will be highly visible to all the bettors. They often will be notoriously overbet. No play. In one enticing situation, however, older maidens that have matched par will still be overbet, but no bargains whatsoever, and irresistible favorites to play against. We will return to that point momentarily.

First starters should satisfy three standards. The sires have won with 11 percent of their first starters. The trainers have won with 11 percent of their first starters. Two or more of the workouts have been "sharp." The standards are flexible, even liberal, and should not be violated. The 11 percent is a probability statistic that is not plucked from midair but rather corresponds to one starter in a nine-horse field. The sire-and-trainer win percentages should correspond to their percentages of starters. Handicappers can award extra credit for win percentages that exceed 20 percent. Sires tend to be more important with two-year-olds (because they are easier to train) and trainers tend to be more important with three-year-olds, because they can be difficult to train.

Sharp workouts means faster than 12 seconds per furlong at four and five furlongs (if urged, all maidens can train quickly at three furlongs), or faster than 48 seconds at four furlongs and faster than 1:00 at five furlongs; faster than 1:13 at six furlongs; faster than 1:27 at seven furlongs. At deeper, slower tracks, add a second to each time barrier. No extra credit is awarded for breezing vis-a-vis handily or for workouts out of the gate. Two sharp workouts are more meaningful than one, because most maidens will train swiftly if asked, and eventually they will be asked, but two or more fast workouts should indicate the horses have been doing it on their own. They possess authentic speed.

A caution on workout patterns is in order. Numerous trainers routinely work their maidens quickly. Bob Baffert leaps to mind. His workouts look fast, faster, and fastest. Now the importance of sharp workouts has been reduced to zero. Unless his maidens have been working out slowly, in which case they can be dismissed, Baffert's scintillating workout patterns amount to standard operating procedure. Handicappers should not be fooled. This is local knowledge. Handicappers have numerous incentives for understanding the habits of local trainers.

All three criteria of sire-trainer-workouts should be acceptable. Trainer statistics are now published in *Daily Racing Form,* of course, but sire statistics are not, and often will remain out of reach for recreational handicappers. A convenient resource of *Daily Racing Form,* however, frequently will be "A Closer Look," the capsule commentaries provided by *DRF* handicappers in the columns to the right of the past performances. When maidens are the menu, the *DRF* handicappers routinely will provide the sires' win percentages with first starters, or they may allude to the statistics, reporting that the sires are "average," "okay," "acceptable," or "below average," and the information can be taken at face value.

A common scenario finds two of the sire-trainer-workout factors acceptable, but the third unacceptable. No play on favorites, or on low-priced contenders, although overlays might be backed, notably in below-par fields. If two of the sire-trainer-workout factors are unacceptable, pass. Occasional winners will not redeem the long-term losses.

The new and best bets in races for older maidens are the second starters. These good things not only win significantly more than their rightful share, but also they pay better than they should. The public tends to overestimate the high-figure horses among experienced maidens, as well as the lickety-split workouts of first starters from top barns, but they often will underbet the second starters, and these can be expected to improve by three to five lengths. Using the Beyer Speed Figures, normal improvement can be projected by adding three to five lengths, or eight to 13 points, to the speed figure of the debut.

In two common situations, second starters will represent an especially ripe advantage. One, the high-figure maidens remain slightly below par, and the second starters show speed figures within three to four lengths: e.g., a more experienced New York maiden shows a Beyer 85, and a second starter shows a Beyer 79. Prefer the second starter. In other similar situations, the high-figure maidens will be at par, or slightly above perhaps, but the horses have since lost a couple of times, failing repeatedly when they were expected to win. This is a variation of the Davis data on horses that have finished second last out, but have finished second and third repeatedly without winning. These are unreliable maidens, and must be avoided at low odds.

A trickier situation involves second starters who have one dull line, but otherwise may look attractive. Maybe the workouts have impressed, or the odds in the debut were short, or the trainer wins with second starters at a high percentage, or the horse suffered a troubled trip and should benefit from a jockey change or blinkers-on today. Second starters do improve dramatically, and handicappers must remain on alert. Second starters having one dull line may be difficult to evaluate, but if the surrounding dope is positive, the field is suspect, and the odds are attractive, the bet makes sense.

EXAMINE THE RECORDS of the six three-and-up maidens below. The fillies lined up for a six-furlong sprint at Hollywood Park, on May 4, 2002, and the race illustrates several keys and complications inherent in numerous races for older maidens. The Beyer par is 83.

---

4 **Hollywood Park**　　　　　　　　　　　　Ⓕ**Md Sp Wt 43k**　　START ▼ ⟨ 6 FURLONGS ⟩

6 Furlongs (1:07²) MAIDEN SPECIAL WEIGHT. Purse $43,000 (plus $12,900 CBOIF – CA Bred Owner Fund) FOR MAIDENS, FILLIES AND MARES THREE YEARS OLD AND UPWARD. Three Year Olds 117 lbs.; Older 123 lbs. (Horses which have started for $40,000 or less in their last 3 starts least preferred).

Magnetic	Dk. b or br f. 3 (Apr)			Life	0 M 0 0	$0	–	D.Fst	0 0 0 0	$0
Own: Tailwind Racing Inc	Sire: Royal Academy (Nijinsky II) $20,000			1994	0 M 0 0	$0	–	Wet(350*)	0 0 0 0	$0
White, Black Yoke, Red Chevrons	Dam: Grandmother(Gulch)			1993	0 M 0 0	$0	–	Turf(360)	0 0 0 0	$0
	Br: Tailwind Racing Inc (Cal)		117							
ALMEIDA G F (6 1 2 0 .17) 2002:(134 10 .07)	Tr: McAnally Ronald(6 0 2 1 .00) 2002:(111 12 .11)			Hol	0 0 0 0	$0	–	Dist	0 0 0 0	$0

WORKS: May1 Hol 5f fst 1:01⁴ H 14/37　Apr25 Hol 5f fst 1:00 Hg5/25　Apr24 Hol 5f fst 1:00 Hg4/31　Apr19 Hol 5f fst 1:01² Hg 15/41　Apr12 Hol 5f fst 1:01⁴ H 18/37　Apr5 Hol 5f fst 1:02² H 15/23
Mar22 Hol 4f fst :49 H 14/27　Feb23 SLR 5f fst 1:01¹ H 2/7　Feb16 SLR 5f fst 1:01⁴ H 2/9　Feb9 SLR 5f fst 1:03⁴ H 12/14　Jan26 SLR 4f fst :49³ H 17/24
TRAINER: 1stStart(34 .12 $1.63) Dirt(185 .13 $1.75) Sprint(185 .11 $1.50) MdnSpWt(110 .11 $1.48)

Ask Dorothy
Own: Frankfurt Stable
Red, Black 'fs' In White Circle On Back,
JAUREGUI L H (6 1 1 0 .17) 2002:(83 9 .11)
Ch. f. 3 (May)
Sire: Smart Strike (Mr. Prospector) $30,000
Dam: Psychic Spirit(Deputy Minister)
Br: Curt Mikkelsen & Trish Mikkelsen (Ky)
Tr: Drysdale Neil(3 1 0 0 .33) 2002:(68 12 .18)
L 117
Life 1 M 0 0 $0 70 | D.Fst 1 0 0 0 $0 70
2002 1 M 0 0 $0 70 | Wet(435*) 0 0 0 0 $0 –
2001 0 M 0 0 $0 – | Turf(290*) 0 0 0 0 $0 –
Hol 0 0 0 0 $0 – | Dist 1 0 0 0 $0 70

6Apr02-11SA fst 6f :212 :44 :57 1:101 ⒻMd Sp Wt 48k 70 9 10 1114 1010 913 77¾ Nakatani C S B 120 41.20 79–10 MinisterThatcher120nk MissTropics1203 Nzreen1201 Passed tiring rivals 11
WORKS: Apr30 Hol 5f fst 1:011 H 15/26 Apr24 Hol 5f fst 1:042 H 30/31 ●Apr18 Hol 6f fst 1:124 H 1/12 Apr12 Hol 3f fst :361 H 6/20 Mar31 Hol 6f fst 1:17 H 11/11 Mar25 Hol 5f fst 1:003 H 11/33
TRAINER: 2ndStart(18 .17 $1.14) 1stLasix(66 .15 $1.10) Dirt(57 .19 $1.29) Sprint(52 .12 $0.55) MdnSpWt(63 .14 $1.24)

Favorite Fashion
Own: Golden Eagle Farm
Burgundy, Gold Eagle On Back, Gold
TRUJILLO E (15 1 1 4 .07) 2002:(160 22 .14)
B. f. 4 KEENOV98 $90,000
Sire: Seattle Slew (Bold Reasoning) $300,000
Dam: Chelsea Favourite(Diesis*GB)
Br: John D Gunther (Ky)
Tr: Spawr Bill(5 1 0 0 .20) 2002:(172 32 .19)
L 118⁵
Life 1 M 0 0 $960 69 | D.Fst 1 0 0 0 $960 69
2002 1 M 0 0 $960 69 | Wet(300) 0 0 0 0 $0 –
2001 0 M 0 0 $0 – | Turf(315) 0 0 0 0 $0 –
Hol 0 0 0 0 $0 – | Dist 0 0 0 0 $0 –

7Apr02-2SA fst 6½f :213 :444 1:093 1:161 3↑ ⒻMd Sp Wt 48k 69 4 5 2½ 45 46½ 59½ Pincay L Jr LB 124 f .90e 82–11 *AffrsOfStt*1171½ PcfulPlc1171 Sophstctdblff1176 Angled in turn,wkened 7

Jade Vixen
Own: Lewis Beverly J & Robert B
Green, Yellow Hoops/sleeves, Yellow
PEDROZA M A (20 1 6 4 .05) 2002:(223 24 .11)
B. f. 3 (Apr) KEESEP00 $220,000
Sire: Jade Hunter (Mr. Prospector)
Dam: Wixon*Fr(Fioravanti)
Br: Allen E Paulson (Ky)
Tr: Baffert Bob(14 3 3 1 .21) 2002:(224 48 .21)
L 117
Life 0 M 0 0 $0 – | D.Fst 0 0 0 0 $0 –
2002 0 M 0 0 $0 – | Wet(330) 0 0 0 0 $0 –
2001 0 M 0 0 $0 – | Turf(280) 0 0 0 0 $0 –
Hol 0 0 0 0 $0 – | Dist 0 0 0 0 $0 –

WORKS: May1 Hol 5f fst 1:013 H 13/37 Apr24 Hol 5f fst 1:01 Hg8/31 Apr17 Hol 5f fst :594 Hg2/19 Apr11 Hol 6f fst 1:151 H 4/6 Apr3 Hol 5f fst 1:012 H 13/26 Mar28 Hol 6f fst 1:151 H 10/22
Mar21 Hol 5f fst 1:004 H 9/20 Mar15 Hol 5f fst 1:013 H 15/33 Mar3 Hol 4f fst :483 H 4/15 Feb19 Hol 3f fst :374 B 12/21 Jan25 Hol 3f fst :364 H 3/11 Jan19 Hol 3f fst :38 B 10/16
TRAINER: 1stStart(113 .20 $2.06) Dirt(749 .22 $1.68) Sprint(570 .21 $1.54) MdnSpWt(230 .20 $1.92)

Stormscape
Own: Gann Edmund A
Red White Eg On Back Blue Sleeves
BAZE T C (23 3 3 4 .13) 2002:(282 25 .09)
Dk. b or br f. 4
Sire: You and I (Kris S.) $12,500
Dam: Bright Storm(Storm Bird)
Br: Edmund A Gann (Ky)
Tr: Frankel Robert(6 0 4 0 .00) 2002:(142 31 .22)
L 123
Life 5 M 2 2 $28,500 86 | D.Fst 3 0 1 1 $15,380 86
2002 1 M 0 1 $5,520 81 | Wet(270*) 0 0 0 0 $0 –
2001 4 M 2 1 $22,980 86 | Turf(220) 2 0 1 1 $13,120 84
Hol 1 0 0 1 $5,040 86 | Dist 1 0 0 0 $940 76

10Mar02-4SA fm *6½f Ⓣ :214 :441 1:072 1:133 3↑ ⒻMd Sp Wt 46k 81 7 3 32 33 22½ 33 Desormeaux K J LB 124 *1.80 86–11 FanAppeal1171 SultrySound1172 Stormscape124nk 3wd into lane,held 3rd 9
20Oct01-5SA fm *6½f Ⓣ :222 :44 1:071 1:13 3↑ ⒻMd Sp Wt 39k 84 8 1 41½ 44½ 31 22½ Desormeaux K J LB 120 *3.00 92–07 AskMNoScrts1202½ Stormscp1201½ *Apll'sMsc*1221 Bid btwn late,2nd best 12
2Sep01-10Dmr fst 6f :214 :443 :571 1:101 3↑ ⒻMd Sp Wt 47k 76 6 4 52½ 46 44½ 58 Gomez G K LB 118 *1.80 81–11 Nicky's Intuition1183 Forever Holy1182½ Maud1182 Angled in,no late bid 10
4Aug01-6Dmr fst 6½f :221 :45 1:102 1:17 3↑ ⒻMd Sp Wt 47k 75 11 2 51¾ 42½ 22 22½ Gomez G K LB 118 *2.20 85–09 *SmrtStrt*1182½ Stormscpe1182½ *MyNmeIsSue*1233 Chased outside,2nd bst 12
11Jly01-2Hol fst 6½f :221 :45 1:09 1:151 3↑ ⒻMd Sp Wt 42k 86 2 2 1hd 2hd 32 34½ Gomez G K LB 117 10.00 90–12 *TamaraPrincess*1171 *DoubleCt*1173½ Stormscpe1172 Inside duel, held 3rd 6
WORKS: Apr28 Hol 5f fst 1:014 H 27/40 Apr22 Hol 5f fst 1:002 H 11/32 Apr15 Hol 5f fst 1:004 H 7/28 Apr8 Hol 6f fst 1:141 H 5/12 Apr1 Hol 5f fst 1:022 H 20/24 Mar25 Hol 4f fst :484 H 11/29
TRAINER: Turf/Dirt(33 .12 $0.93) 31-60Days(162 .25 $1.92) Dirt(142 .29 $2.06) Sprint(120 .24 $2.22) MdnSpWt(54 .28 $2.56)

Summerwood
Own: Jones Aaron U & Marie D
White, Red Cross Sashes, Red Diamonds
VALENZUELA P A (36 8 6 7 .22) 2002:(370 51 .14)
Dk. b or br f. 3 (Feb) KEEJAN00 $350,000
Sire: Boston Harbor (Capote) $23,000
Dam: Rutledge Place(Caro*Ire)
Br: Rutledge Farm (Ky)
Tr: Inda Eduardo(3 0 0 1 .00) 2002:(39 5 .13)
L 117
Life 1 M 0 0 $0 33 | D.Fst 1 0 0 0 $0 33
2001 1 M 0 0 $0 33 | Wet(335) 0 0 0 0 $0 –
2000 0 M 0 0 $0 – | Turf(272) 0 0 0 0 $0 –
Hol 1 0 0 0 $0 33 | Dist 0 0 0 0 $0 –

23Jun01-7Hol fst 5½f :214 :451 :581 1:05 ⒻMd Sp Wt 42k 33 8 5 43½ 46 812 813½ McCarron C J LB 118 5.10 74–11 RorngBlz1181½ *RchMusq*1183 BlondAmbton1183 Lugged out wide,wkend 8
WORKS: May2 Hol 3f fst :351 Hg5/26 Apr27 Hol 5f fst 1:011 H 28/64 ●Apr21 SA 6f fst 1:12 H 1/24 Apr14 SA 5f fst 1:001 H 5/32 Apr8 SA 5f fst 1:024 H 34/40 Apr1 SA 6f fst 1:15 H 9/11
TRAINER: +180Days(8 .13 $0.53) 2ndStart(14 .21 $3.20) Dirt(79 .24 $1.85) Sprint(66 .24 $1.90) MdnSpWt(47 .17 $1.17)

A reliable point of departure in examining maiden races for older horses is to look first for the horses that have matched par. Stormscape jumps out. The four-year-old exceeded par in her debut at Hollywood Park on July 11, 2001, but failed to follow up by winning as the favorite in each of her next two. She since has exceeded par once more, on the turf at Santa Anita, and last out on the same course she ran within a length of par. Stormscape has finished second twice and third twice, and she is the prototype of the high-figure maiden, above par, that handicappers should aim to defeat. Out of the Bobby Frankel barn, Stormscape is a virtual cinch to be the overbet favorite here, and she is a far cry from a trustworthy winner. Handicappers must recognize Stormscape for the vulnerable favorite she will be, or the game already has been lost.

Next we examine the first starters. As indicated by *DRF* handicapper Brian Pochman in his "Closer Look" comments, Magnetic has an "above average" sire with first-timers in Royal Academy. Trainer Ron McAnally wins with 12 percent of his first starters, and that is acceptable. Magnetic shows no sharp workouts. No play as the favorite, or if the odds fall below 5-1, but Magnetic might be backed at 6-1 or greater, as handicappers prefer.

Jade Vixen is a Baffert first starter. Baffert wins with 20 percent of his first starters and, according to Pochman, the sire Jade Hunter gets "average results" with firsters. So far, so good, but the workout pattern is plainly unacceptable. Only the 59⅗hg three back on April 17 fits the definition of a sharp workout. One is not enough. More importantly, for a trainer that works his maidens fast, faster, and fastest, the workout pattern of Jade Vixen is depressingly slow. When trainers that work maidens fast are working them slowly, it's almost always because the horses themselves are slow. No play on the Baffert maiden at any price.

Given an above-par-figure horse that should be overbet and unreliable, and no first starters that satisfy the three criteria of sire-trainer-workouts, the trio of second starters represents the crux of the handicapping. Ask Dorothy and Favorite Fashion show dull lines, but the Beyer Speed Figures of 70 and 69 can be projected by the normal improvement pattern of three to five lengths, or by eight to 13 points. In projecting Beyer figures for second starters, handicappers prefer that the projections reach par. A five-length improvement for Ask Dorothy would result in a Beyer 83, which touches par, and for Favorite Fashion in a Beyer 82, a half-length shy of par. At 6-1 or higher, either filly should be preferable to Stormscape. For one reason, the improvement in the second start may surpass five lengths. It may be seven, eight, 10, or 12 lengths, which would topple Stormscape absolutely.

Summerwood shows the kind of dull line that cannot be projected using speed figures. The surrounding information presents a mixed message, which is not unusual. Summerwood has not run for 11 months, but that lengthy a layoff is not an elimination factor with maidens. The second finisher in her debut returned to win. Jockey leader Chris McCarron is gone, but Pat Valenzuela jumps aboard, and he has been the hottest jockey on the grounds. Summerwood was backed to 5-1 in her debut, which is healthy support. The three-year-old filly has recorded one sharp workout, the 1:12h, best of 24, three back, on April 21. Trainer Eduardo Inda deserves extra credit with second starters, where he scores with 21 percent and shows a dollar profit of 60 percent.

As with Ask Dorothy and Favorite Fashion, Summerwood is preferable to Stormscape at 6-1 or greater, and the three second-starters might be covered in a pick three moving forward. The results flattered the analysis, but although Stormscape disappointed as expected and at 6-5, and

Summerwood won, the winner's odds at 7-2 off one dull race proved too short to support for long-term profits.

FOURTH RACE	6 FURLONGS. (1.07²) MAIDEN SPECIAL WEIGHT. Purse $43,000 (plus $12,900 CBOIF – CA Bred Owner Fund) FOR MAIDENS, FILLIES AND MARES THREE YEARS OLD AND UPWARD. Three Year Olds 117 lbs.; Older 123 lbs. (Horses which have started for $40,000 or less in their last 3 starts least preferred).										

Hollywood
MAY 4, 2002

Value of Race: $43,000 Winner $25,800; second $8,600; third $5,160; fourth $2,580; fifth $860.   Mutuel Pool $613,151.00 Exacta Pool $381,580.00   Quinella Pool $39,205.00 Trifecta Pool $374,226.00

Last Raced	Horse	M/Eqt. A.Wt	PP	St	¼	½	Str	Fin	Jockey	Odds $1
23Jun01 7Hol8	Summerwood	LB 3 117	3	3	2²	1hd	12½	11½	Valenzuela P A	3.60
5Aug01 3Emd4	Infernal Mcgoon	LB 3 117	5	6	7	6½	31½	2no	Valdivia J Jr	25.40
10Mar02 4SA3	Stormscape	LB 4 123	2	5	3½	3½	21	34	Baze T C	1.20
6Apr02 11SA7	Ask Dorothy	LB 3 117	4	4	5hd	7	7	4½	Jauregui L H	9.20
7Apr02 2SA5	Favorite Fashion	LBf 4 118	7	2	6³	5hd	61	51	Trujillo E5	4.10
	Magnetic	B 3 117	1	7	4hd	41½	4hd	62½	Almeida G F	20.00
	Jade Vixen	LBb 3 117	6	1	1hd	21	5hd	7	Pedroza M A	5.50

OFF AT 3:39 Start Good For All But INFERNAL MCGOON. Won driving. Track fast.
TIME :22², :454, :583, 1:114 (:22.45, :45.94, :58.68, 1:11.98)

$2 Mutuel Prices:

5–SUMMERWOOD	9.20	5.60	3.00
7–INFERNAL MCGOON		14.20	4.60
4–STORMSCAPE			2.40

$1 EXACTA 5–7 PAID $85.90 $2 QUINELLA 5–7 PAID $102.80 $1 TRIFECTA
5–7–4 PAID $264.30

Dk. b. or br. f, (Feb), by Boston Harbor–Rutledge Place, by Caro*Ire. Trainer Inda Eduardo. Bred by Rutledge Farm (Ky).

SUMMERWOOD broke in a bit, went up inside to duel for command, inched clear into the stretch and held sway under urging. INFERNAL MCGOON stumbled at the start, settled off the rail, moved up a bit off the fence leaving the turn, swung four wide into the stretch and just got the place. STORMSCAPE chased between horses on the backstretch and outside a rival on the turn, came three deep into the stretch and just lost second. ASK DOROTHY stalked the leaders three deep between horses then off the rail on the turn, steadied in tight off heels into the stretch and lacked a further response. FAVORITE FASHION chased outside on the backstretch and four wide on the turn, came five wide into the stretch and did not rally. MAGNETIC broke a bit inward and bobbled slightly, saved ground stalking the pace, waited a bit in close off heels leaving the turn and weakened. JADE VIXEN broke sharply, angled in and dueled outside the winner, dropped back between foes into the stretch and had little left.

Owners— 1, Jones Aaron U & Marie D; 2, One Horse Will Do Corporation; 3, Gann Edmund A; 4, Frankfurt Stable; 5, Golden Eagle Farm; 6, Tailwind Racing Inc; 7, Lewis Robert B & Beverly J

Trainers—1, Inda Eduardo; 2, Sahadi Jenine; 3, Frankel Robert; 4, Drysdale Neil; 5, Spawr Bill; 6, McAnally Ronald; 7, Baffert Bob

Scratched— Hide The Chianti, Sevens Wild (25Aug01 5DMR2)

Although second starters in races for older maidens will be handicappers' best pals, it's important to remember the rationale. The second starters improve dramatically because they possess considerable talent they did not reveal in their debut, due to inexperience. Do not confuse second starters in maiden races with the same horses in maiden-claiming races. Second starters in maiden-claiming races have little or no talent. They should never be expected to improve. Drop-downs from maiden special weights, however, usually possess enough talent to handle many maiden-claiming fields.

CHAPTER 4

STANDARDS OF
ACCEPTABLE FORM

SOMEWHERE BETWEEN THE mid-1960's and the mid-1980's, and increasingly so since then, the standards of recent action that handicappers depend upon when evaluating horses' current form have evolved from a gradual shift to a monumental change. Where before the standards were conservative, today they are liberal. Where once the guidelines demanded strict compliance, now they allow for lenient acceptance.

Once upon a time, for example, handicappers were warned not to accept horses in sprints unless they had raced within the past 30 days. In routes, the horses were required to show a race plus two workouts within the past 30 days. Horses that had run within the past two weeks must still have shown a workout. And sprinters that had not run in 45 days could be backed only if (a) they had been working out every four to five days, and (b) they had won following similar layoffs. Those days are gone, the guidelines passé.

Recent Action. Of horses that have run within the past 30 days, good races can be defined still as a finish in the money, or within two lengths in sprints, within three lengths in routes. The good recent races always should be rated, using whatever methods handicappers prefer.

Good races apart, what about the concept of "acceptable form" among horses having recent action (have run within the past 30 days)? Handicappers can expect the horses will win their rightful share if the records conform to these guidelines:

1. Horses are acceptable on form if they were "up close" at the stretch call of their most recent race. If the most recent race looks poor due to a legitimate excuse, use the second race back, provided that race occurred within 30 days of the most recent race. The "up close" standard varies with the distance, as follows:
   a. up to 6.5f, up close means within 2¾ lengths
   b. at 7f and 1m, up close means within 3¾ lengths
   c. at 8.5f and farther, up close means within 4¾ lengths

2. Horses that are dropping in class are acceptable on form if they were up close at any call. So a claiming horse exiting a $25,000 race where he was beaten 12 lengths at the finish and 8½ lengths at the stretch call and 6½ lengths at the pre-stretch call and 2½ lengths at the first call, is entered today for $16,000. Is that horse acceptable on form? Yes, he was "up close" at the first call in a higher-class race. The horse showed something against better and may improve dramatically today. Most handicappers would toss those horses on form, but the evidence indicates they win their fair share. Probe deeper.

3. In a shorter race—route to sprint, seven furlongs to six furlongs, nine furlongs to a mile—horses are acceptable on form if they were up close at the pre-stretch call. In the route-to-sprint situation, however, the horses that win their fair share will have run on the front, or within one length of the leader, at the four-furlong and six-furlong calls of the route.

The "up close" standard for recent action is best applied early in the handicapping process, when handicappers are identifying contenders. Later, when separating contenders, the notion of acceptable form might be discounted in favor of improving form, or peaking form, or declining form, or questionable form. But it's a careless mistake to eliminate the eventual winners prematurely, by applying standards of form analysis that have been shown to be too strict, too conservative.

Short Layoffs. Horses are acceptable off layoffs of 31-60 days, provided they show a four-furlong workout or longer within the past seven days. The time of the workout is unimportant. A variation of the guideline accepts horses off short layoffs if they show two or more workouts at any time during the interval, although when the workout within the past week is missing, these horses will win somewhat less than their rightful share. Rate the good races in the previous form cycle, and be strict about the horses that have not trained in the past seven days.

Long Layoffs. Horses are acceptable off layoffs of 61-365 days and longer, provided they show a five-furlong workout within the past 14 days. Is that a liberal form standard? It works. Again, the time of the workout is unimportant. The five-furlong workout can be embedded in a regular pattern too, where the most recent workouts are shorter but the longer workout appears more than two weeks ago.

Many handicappers discard horses that have been away for 90 days or longer, unless they have run well fresh, or enjoy a significant class edge, or are trained by a horseman that wins with a high percentage off long layoffs, but probability data reveal this to be a mistake. Long-layoff returnees showing the five-furlong workout win their fair share. They cannot be ignored.

The five-furlong workout standard will be met by a large majority of horses in New York and especially in southern California, where sunny weather year-round permits the horses to train regularly, but the situation changes dramatically at mid-level and minor tracks. Now the horses will be cheaper and more arthritic, and they train less frequently and at shorter distances. As simulcast handicappers will attest, the five-furlong workout in the past 14 days will frequently be missing at mid-level and minor tracks. Those horses can be discarded as noncontenders on form. Even at the flagship ovals of Florida, Kentucky, New Jersey, Maryland, Illinois, and Louisiana-Texas, whenever the five-furlong workout is missing, horses returning from long layoffs are best eliminated.

In New York and in southern California, the horses most likely to win off lengthy layoffs will combine a longer workout, at least one, and preferably more than one, with an edge in class. In all cases following long layoffs, handicappers should rate horses acceptable on current form by using the good races in the form cycle just prior to the layoff, and not just the last running line.

Positive Patterns. Acceptable form can be distinguished from positive form, or improving form. Later in the handicapping process, handicappers will evaluate contenders more closely on current form, not to mention hurry to relate the form factor to matters of speed, class, and pace. Award credit for positive form when any or a combination of the following patterns can be observed.

1. The horse has been "up close" at every point of call.
2. The last running line shows a "big win," defined as a win by three lengths or greater.

3. Front-runners and pressers flash obviously improved early speed, perhaps for a couple of races following a layoff and a dull effort or two.

4. Deep closers show much-improved form, defined as a mid-race move that passes other horses, before a flattened run through the stretch, or even a bid-and-hung maneuver approaching the wire.

5. In claiming races, an impressive win, followed by a multiple rise in class, provided the speed figure of the last-out victory matches par for today's higher level.

6. A pair of improving sprints, usually following a layoff, followed by a stretchout to a more comfortable route. A positive variation of the two-sprint stretchout is a sprint and a route, followed by another route.

7. Following a claim by an established claiming trainer, a much-improved performance, especially accompanied by a class rise, provided the horse has back class at today's level.

8. Following a much-improved performance, notably a big win, a quick return to competition, of five days, seven days, or 10 days.

9. Any improvement, followed by a drop in class and a switch to a leading rider.

10. A short series of increasingly dull efforts, preceded by strong performances, first Lasix today.

Peaking Form. A few trusty form patterns typically indicate a peak performance is looming.

1. The third start following a long layoff, whenever the second start following the layoff has been a definite improvement over the first start following the layoff. The pattern is especially positive among sprinters. The third start is usually best, and the fourth start should be positive too.

2. Any improved performance resulting in a win, followed by a return to action in seven days or fewer.

3. Among three-year-olds, a positive form reversal, or a much-improved race, followed by much-improved workouts, followed by a return to competition within three weeks.

4. The ability to set or attend a seriously faster early pace, without falling apart in the stretch (a finish within six lengths), followed by a quick reentry at the same class level or lower, provided the horse has one of the two highest pace figures in the race.

Negative Patterns. Several seemingly positive form patterns are more likely to result in negative consequences. Handicappers should not be fooled. Beware of the following patterns.

1. The last running line shows a win, but the horse has failed to return to action for more than six weeks. A form problem should be assumed. The exception will be graded stakes horses shopping for the next logical opportunity. The pattern is deadly among claiming horses. Throw them out.

2. Horses four and up have delivered a lifetime best effort last out, as indicated by a lifetime top speed figure. The best-ever performance should not be repeated, and often results in a setback.

3. Horses returning from lengthy layoffs have experienced an overexertion first race back, as indicated by a win or close finish in excellent time. Referred to colloquially as the "bounce" pattern, two of three of these horses regress if returned to action within six weeks. An exception will be off-pace turf horses at the route. Of horses that bounce, handicappers can anticipate a bounce-back performance next time, typically resulting in a speed figure that exceeds the comeback effort.

4. Following a long layoff, one sprint, followed by a stretchout to the route. The one-sprint stretchout is bad news. In New York and southern California, exceptions can be horses having a class edge.

5. Need-to-lead front-runners that have won their last race, perhaps the last two races, but cannot secure the lead today. Not only do these front-runners fail to win, but also they routinely finish out of the money, not completing exactas and trifectas.

6. Following a claim of a horse in positive form, an absence of 30 days or longer, followed by a drop in class below the claiming price. The only exceptions are trainers that win on the drop first start following claims.

7. Multiple Grade 1/Grade 2 winners that return from lengthy layoffs and are entered in ungraded stakes or under classified allowance conditions. Form is usually short, or the horses are not well intended, and the odds are invariably low.

Early eliminations include horses having poor early speed and unacceptable form; unacceptable form in combination with an inferior trainer (5 percent winners or lower); unacceptable form in combination with unsuitable or inferior class.

Finally, when identifying contenders, early in the handicapping process, and current form appears murky and inconclusive, give the horses the benefit of the doubt. Accept them. Rate the good races. Suspend final decisions on form until later.

CHAPTER 5

DROP-DOWNS IN
CLAIMING RACES

WHICH IS THE better bet, a claiming horse moving up in class or its counterpart, a claiming horse moving down? It's the horse moving down, by a landslide!

In fact, claiming horses dropping in class by 30 percent or more after a recent decent race represent the most powerful probability statistic yet discovered in handicapping. These horses represent approximately 2.8 percent of the starters in claiming races, but they win almost 11 percent of the races.

That is, horses dropping 30 percent or more in claiming price win 378 percent their rightful share of these races!

In general, drop-downs in claiming races represent 15 percent of the starters, but 30 percent of the winners. Drop-downs win twice their fair share of the claiming races. Moreover, the greater the drop in claiming price, the more likely the horses will win.

Remember to require that the drop-downs show a decent recent race. A finish first, second, or third, or within three lengths of the winner, is a good race. Acceptable, too, is a race that shows high early speed until the pre-stretch or stretch calls. So is a race that shows a pre-stretch or stretch gain of two or more lengths while beating at least half the field.

By combining the key findings of recent probability studies and the traditional emphasis on current form, handicappers have practically arrived at knowledge as to what kind of horse represents the ideal play in claiming races.

The ideal claiming-race contender combines:

1. Early speed
2. Improving or peaking form
3. A drop in class

CHAPTER 6

THE KEY-RACE
METHOD WITH CHARTS
(REVISITED)

HANDICAPPERS WITH RESULTS CHARTS hold a razor's edge. The charts contain the keys to unlocking class within a class. Whether it's purse comparisons for open but ungraded stakes, restrictions, or specifications limiting eligibility to allowance races, or restrictions in claiming races having the same purse values, results charts tell the tale regarding numerous class changes of one kind or another. Handicapping author Steve Davidowitz years ago revealed a simple procedural method with charts that absolutely pinpoints the best races within a class.

The idea is to use a collection of charts to identify "key" races. Key races are those that are so competitive that several horses in the field win next out. As Davidowitz says, key races bring together either the best fields or fields of horses unusually fit and ready, and in either case several of them are likely to win next time when, presumably, matched against a more ordinary lot. Once key races have been identified, handicappers can fairly expect big efforts from horses that raced well in them.

The procedural steps are simple. First, for the most recent race in the charts, check the date and race number of the winner's previous start. Fanmore, for example, last raced on January 1, 1994, in the eighth, at Santa Anita.

THIRD RACE
Santa Anita
JANUARY 15, 1994

1⅛ MILES. (Turf)(1.43⁴) ALLOWANCE. Purse $60,000. 4-year-olds and upward which are non-winners of $22,500 other than closed or claiming at one mile or over since October 1. Weights: 4-year-olds, 120 lbs. Older, 121 lbs. Non-winners of such a race since August 1, allowed 2 lbs. Of such a race since June 1, allowed 4 lb. Of such a race since April 1, 6 lbs.

Value of Race: $60,000 Winner $33,000; second $12,000; third $9,000; fourth $4,500; fifth $1,500. Mutuel Pool $439,640.00 Exacta Pool $349,708.00 Quinella Pool $43,740.00 Minus Show Pool $22,254.20

Last Raced	Horse	M/Eqt.	A.Wt	PP	St	¼	½	¾	Str	Fin	Jockey	Odds $1
1Jan94 8SA2	Fanmore	B	6 116	1	2	1¹	1¹	1½	1½	1¹	Desormeaux K J	0.40
30Dec93 8SA2	Myrakalu-Fr	LB	6 115	4	3	3½	3hd	2¹½	2⁷	2⁶	Stevens G L	3.40
5Dec93 7Hol5	Dick Tracy-Fr	LB	5 115	3	1	2²	2²	3¹	3²	33½	Black C A	13.30
5Dec93 7Hol6	Peter Davies	L	6 115	5	4	4¹⁰	4¹⁰	4⁸	43½	4½	Solis A	10.00
7Sep93 Lch4	Navire-Fr	LB	5 117	2	5	5	5	5	5	5	McCarron C J	8.30

OFF AT 1:31 Start Good For All But NAVIRE. Won handily. Time, :24⁴, :48², 1:12, 1:35⁴, 1:48² Course firm.

$2 Mutuel Prices:

1–FANMORE	2.80	2.20	2.10
4–MYRAKALU–FR		2.40	2.10
3–DICK TRACY–FR			2.10

$2 EXACTA 1–4 PAID $5.60 $2 QUINELLA 1–4 PAID $4.00

B. g, by Lear Fan–Lady Blackfoot, by Prince Tenderfoot. Trainer Frankel Robert. Bred by Johnson Don & Trimble Ann M (Ky).

FANMORE quickly sprinted to a short lead inside DICK TRACY, responded gamely when challenged by MYRAKALU leaving the backstretch, repulsed that rival's bid in midstretch while in hand and continued in hand to the wire. MYRAKALU outside PETER DAVIES early, moved up alongside the winner approaching the second turn but could not get by. DICK TRACY prompted the early pace outside the winner while appearing rank, then was not a factor after six furlongs. PETER DAVIES saved ground to no avail. NAVIRE dwelt at the start to be off far behind and was not a factor.

Owners— 1, Juddmonte Farms; 2, Recachina Dion A; 3, Taub Stephen M; 4, Lucayan Stud Ltd; 5, Cohen & Red Baron's Barn
Trainers— 1, Frankel Robert; 2, Lukas D Wayne; 3, Hendricks Dan L; 4, McAnally Ronald; 5, Vienna Darrell
Scratched— Alzarina (25Jlv93 DLB3)

Second, find the chart for the indicated race, and however the winner had performed, circle its name. As seen on the next page, Fanmore had finished second of eight on January 1 at Santa Anita. The circle means Fanmore has won his next race.

Third, repeat the procedure for the winners of the previous 10 days of racing, encompassing as many as 90 to 100 races. Trace the winners to their previous performances and circle their names in those back charts. Valuable information will emerge, in particular the identity of highly competitive races, as indicated by several circles on the same chart. Handicappers would look eagerly for the other horses in the key races in their next starts. The best performers in these races can be followed indefinitely, as they win successively after shining in the key races.

Handicappers occasionally will encounter a key race such as the second example on the next page.

Handicappers at Aqueduct would look longingly for the next appearances of Finney Finster and Just Like Pa.

IN HIS CONTINUOUS research of the method, Davidowitz found the key-race method particularly potent among maiden races. Since maidens lack class in any categorical sense, the key-race procedure with charts

EIGHTH RACE
Santa Anita
JANUARY 1, 1994

1⅛ MILES. (Turf)(1.434) 47th Running of THE SAN GABRIEL HANDICAP. $100,000 Added. Grade III. 4-year-olds and upward. By subscrition of $100 each to accompany the nomination, $1,000 additional to start, with $100,000 added, of which $20,000 to second, $15,000 to third, $7,500 to fourth and $2,500 to fifth. Weights Tuesday, December 28. High weights preferred. Starters to be named through the entry box by the closing time of entries. A trophy will be presented to the owner of the winner. Closed Wednesday, December 22, 1993 with 23 nominations.

Value of Race: $110,300 Winner $65,300; second $20,000; third $15,000; fourth $7,500; fifth $2,500. Mutuel Pool $569,996.00 Exacta Pool $527,625.00 Quinella Pool $71,183.00

Last Raced	Horse	M/Eqt.	A.	Wt	PP	St	¼	½	¾	Str	Fin	Jockey	Odds $1
20Nov93 6Hol3	Earl Of Barking-Ir	LB	4	118	8	8	7½	6hd	4hd	21	1no	McCarron C J	3.70
28Nov93 5Hol4	Fanmore	B	6	116	3	4	61½	4hd	32	1hd	25	Desormeaux K J	2.50
5Dec93 7Hol2	Navarone	LB	6	119	6	7	8	8	74	52	3½	Stevens G L	1.90
20Nov93 4Hol4	D'arros-Ir	LBb	5	114	7	6	2½	23	22	3½	42	Nakatani C S	14.10
20Nov93 6Hol13	Eastern Memories-Ir	LB	4	116	2	1	11	11	1hd	44	51¼	Delahoussaye E	12.20
19Dec93 7Hol2	Bossanova	LBb	5	114	1	3	3hd	31	51½	62	62¾	Solis A	9.50
12Dec93 4BM1	Ranger-Fr	LB	4	115	5	2	41½	52	62	712	718	Boulanger G	11.10
12Dec93 8Hol6	Square Cut	LB	5	115	4	5	5½	73½	8	8	8	Antley C W	33.40

OFF AT 4:13 Start Good. Won driving. Time, :24, :472, 1:11, 1:36, 1:483 Course firm.

$2 Mutuel Prices:

9-EARL OF BARKING-IR	9.40	4.40	2.80
3-FANMORE		3.80	2.60
7-NAVARONE			2.60

$2 EXACTA 9–3 PAID $40.80 $2 QUINELLA 3–9 PAID $17.60

B. c, by Common Grounds–The Saltings, by Morston. Trainer Cross Richard J. Bred by O'Callaghan Gay (Ire).

EARL OF BARKING settled off the early pace slightly off the rail after angling inward into the first turn, moved up inside into the second turn, swung four wide into the lane and just bested FANMORE under urging in a long drive. FANMORE saved ground down the backstretch, moved up inside on the second turn, swung out for the drive to gain the lead in midstretch and battled gamely inside the winner to just miss. NAVARONE unhurried to the second turn, moved up outside on that bend and into the stretch but could not make up the needed ground. D'ARROS prompted the pace outside EASTERN MEMORIES to midstretch and weakened. EASTERN MEMORIES sped to the early lead inside, held the advantage to midstretch and weakened. BOSSANOVA was not far back a bit off the rail down the backstretch, then weakened. RANGER, outside FANMORE early, angled in for the second turn and did not rally. SQUARE CUT, a bit wide on the first turn, raced outside the winner early on the backstretch, gave way readily and was not persevered with in the stretch.

Owners— 1, Pabst Henry; 2, Juddmonte Farms; 3, Hibbert R E; 4, Wall Peter; 5, Team Valor & Amerman & Stibor; 6, Kenis & 3 Plus U Stable; 7, Lonergan Frank; 8, E W Racing Stable

Trainers—1, Cross Richard J; 2, Frankel Robert; 3, Rash Rodney; 4, Frankel Robert; 5, Hennig Mark; 6, Van Berg Jack C; 7, Bonde Jeff; 8 Devereux Joseph A

FIRST RACE
Aqu
July 15, 1976

1⅛ MILES. (1:47). CLAIMING. Purse $7,500. For 3-year-olds and upward. 3-year-olds, 116 lbs.; older, 122 lbs. Non-winners of a race at a mile and a furlong or over since July 1 allowed 3 lbs.; of such a race since June 15, 5 lbs. Claiming price $8,500; if for less, 2 lbs. allowed for each $250 to $8,000. (Races when entered to be claimed for $7,000 or less not considered.)

Value to winner, $4,500; second, $1,650; third, $900; fourth, $450. Track Mutuel Pool, $106,946. OTB Pool, $87,971.

Last Raced	Horses	Eqt	A	Wt	PP	St	¼	½	¾	Str	Fin	Jockeys	Owners	Odds to $1
25Jun76 6Bel3	Charms Hope	b	5	113	1	2	44	43	47	3½	1nk	MVenezia	J J Stippel	2.50
7Jly 76 1Aqu1	Finney Finster	b	4	117	3	7	68	52	31½	2h	21¼	ASantiago	Camijo Stable	5.60
9Jly 76 1Aqu1	Good and Bold		5	110	4	1	14	16	16	13	31¾	BDiNicola5	Emmarr Stable	3.00
9Jly 76 1Aqu6	Just Like Pa	b	3	109	2	4	3½	31½	2h	48	49	DMontoya†	Audley Farm Stable	8.50
8Jly 76 1Aqu1	Wave the Flag		6	115	5	6	7	7	7	56	54½	RHernandez	O S Barrera	3.40
1Jly 76 2Aqu1	Jolly Mister	b	4	113	6	5	51	67	6½	612	622	PDay	Stan-Mar Stable	7.30
9Jly 76 3Aqu5	Acosado II.		4	117	7	3	25	23	51	7	7	JVasquez	Bellrose Farm	11.90

†Five pounds apprentice allowance waived.

OFF AT 10:30 PDT. START GOOD. WON DRIVING. Time, :24; :47⅕, 1:12⅗, 1:39⅗, 1:53⅖. Track fast.

$2 Mutuel Prices

1-CHARMS HOPE	7.00	4.00	2.60
3-FINNEY FINSTER		6.20	3.60
4-GOOD AND BOLD			2.80

B. h, by Abe's Hope—Cold Dead, by Dead Ahead. Trainer, F. J. Horan. Bred by Criterion Farms (Fla.).

CHARMS HOPE, unhurried early, rallied approaching the stretch and outfinished FINNEY FINSTER. The latter, off slowly, advanced steadily to loom a threat near midstretch and continued on with good courage. GOOD AND BOLD tired from his early efforts. JUST LIKE PA rallied leaving the far turn but lacked the needed late response. WAVE THE FLAG was never close. JOLLY MISTER was always outrun. ACOSADO II tired badly.

Charms Hope claimed by M. Garren, trainer G. Puentes; Good and Bold claimed by S. Sommer, trainer F. Martin.

Claiming Prices (in order of finish)—$8000, 8500, 8250, 8250, 8250, 8000, 8500.

regularly spots the most competitive of races for maidens. Other statistical evidence supports Davidowitz on the point, as it shows that a good previous performance represents a strong predictor of success among maidens.

For the same reason, Davidowitz recommends the approach for isolating competitive races among younger horses on turf, where few if any of the horses have much of a track record.

Handicappers can fairly extend the same logic to allowance races for nonwinners of one or two allowance races, and here a twist on the Davidowitz procedure is in order. The horses competing under preliminary nonwinners allowance conditions remain relatively unclassified. If the charts for these races reveal no circles, or a single circle for only the winner, mark the quality of the races down. The races reveal the horses do not boast much class at all.

Under any conditions, a pattern appreciated by many handicappers reveals a circle for the winner and for the fourth or fifth finisher. Handicappers would watch like detectives for the next appearances of the second, third, and fourth horses. If they look solid, they very probably are.

After his key-race method had appeared in print in the original *Betting Thoroughbreds*, in 1977, Davidowitz began to receive tips from other professionals on ways to improve the power of the method. He listened, and credits among others Ron Cox of San Francisco, and Mark Cramer, now in Paris, with contributions to the chart notations. Examine the notations in the sample chart on the next page, along with the legend that defines the notations.

Circles always indicate the horses that have won their next start, but a new symbol, an underline, indicates the horses that finished second in their next start. In the sample chart, three horses have been underlined: Perfect Start, Three Dreams, and Dancing Chas. Five of the seven horses in The Meadowlands route finished first and second in their next starts, a leg up on the exotic wagering in those races.

Davidowitz encourages handicappers to respect the power of the method by including his favorite key race of all. Naturally, it was run on the grass. It was August 5, 1972, at storied Saratoga. Examine the result chart on page 36.

Handicappers see no circles. As Davidowitz explains with delight, every horse in the field won its next race. A week later Scrimshaw won the first division of Saratoga's Bernard Baruch Handicap, and a half hour later Chrisaway won the second division, and paid 50-1. Days later Chartered Course won a daily-double race, and paid $25. Toward the end of Saratoga, Mongo's Image won an allowance race at 8-1.

SIXTH RACE

Meadowlands

SEPTEMBER 5, 1994

1 MILE 70 YARDS. (1.391) CLAIMING. Purse $15,000. 3-year-olds and upward. Weights: 3-year-olds, 116 lbs. Older, 122 lbs. Non-winners of three races at a mile or over since July 25, allowed 3 lbs. Two such races, 5 lbs. One such race, 7 lbs. Claiming price $20,000; for each $1,000 to $16,000, allowed 1 lb. (Races where entered for $15,000 or less not considered).

Value of Race: $15,000 Winner $9,000; second $3,000; third $1,800; fourth $750; fifth $150; sixth $150; seventh $150. Mutuel Pool $143,167.00 Exacta Pool $196,246.00

Last Raced	Horse	M/Eqt.	A.Wt	PP	St	¼	½	¾	Str	Fin	Jockey	Cl'g Pr	Odds $1
24Aug94 5Mth1	Perfect Star	Lbf	7 115	6	6	5³	4²	2½	2⁵	1³	Lopez C C	20000	1.40
26Aug94 7Mth1	Three Dreams	Lb	5 115	2	3	1½	11½	1³	1¹	2³	Santagata N	20000	6.90
28Aug94 4Mth4	Nauset Flash	Lf	7 114	1	2	6²	6hd	7	4hd	33½	Chavez J F	19000	6.00
26Aug94 7Mth2	Smart Time	Lf	6 115	5	1	4³	5²½	4hd	3hd	43½	Marquez C H Jr	20000	4.40
19Aug94 10Mth1	Sabinal	Lb	4 117	7	7	7	7	5¹	6¹⁰	5½	Torres C A	18000	4.70
23Aug94 6Mth7	Dancing Chas	Lb	5 115	3	5	3½	3³	3²	5½	6	Castillo R E	20000	30.80
21Aug94 1Mth5	Funinthesun	Lbf	8 115	4	4	2⁵	23½	6hd	7	—	McCauley W H	20000	6.40

Funinthesun:Eased

OFF AT 3:06 Start Good. Won driving. Time, :21⁴, :45, 1:10, 1:35², 1:39¹ Track fast.

(Equals Track Record)

$2 Mutuel Prices:

7-PERFECT STAR	4.80	3.20	2.60
2-THREE DREAMS		6.60	5.00
1-NAUSET FLASH			4.20

$2 EXACTA 7-2 PAID $32.80

Dk. b. or br. g, by Morning Bob-Faneuil Lady, by Diplomat Way. Trainer Lotti Gene A Jr. Bred by Farnsworth Farm (Fla).

PERFECT STAR began moving to contention three wide through the far turn, moved to equal terms with THREE DREAMS a sixteenth out, then was going away to the finish. THREE DREAMS made all the pace, then was no match for the winner late while clear for the place. NAUSET FLASH rallied mildly to gain a share. SMART TIME went fairly evenly. SABINAL failed to reach serious contention. DANCING CHAS tired from his early efforts. FUNINTHESUN was used early and was being eased in the stretch.

Owners— 1, Team Stable Inc; 2, Jones Anderson Farm; 3, Pierce Sheila; 4, Conover Stable; 5, Golden Key Racing Stable; 6, Mamone Raymond; 7, Picciolo Frank J

Trainers— 1, Lotti Gene A Jr; 2, Cash Russell J; 3, Pierce Joseph H Jr; 4, Tammaro John J III; 5, Brown Steven R; 6, Vincitore Michael J; 7, Durso Robert J

Three Dreams was claimed by Angelo Frank; trainer, Iwinski Allen.

Scratched— Will To Reign (23Aug94 6MTH5)

KEY RACE SYMBOLS

↑ indicates a jump up in class

↓ indicates a drop in class

~ indicates no class change

Ⓣ indicates a turf race

⊗ indicates a wet track race

Sp indicates a switch to a sprint

Rt indicates a switch to a route

"KR" indicates a *very fast race* for the class and distance, a potential Key Race. As a rule of thumb, I insist on clockings ⅗ of a second faster than normal to qualify

Head Table alone did not race again at Saratoga. Davidowitz hunted for him meticulously day after day in the *Daily Racing Form* entries. "I was prepared to fly anywhere," said Davidowitz, "but he never showed up."

EIGHTH RACE
Saratoga
AUGUST 5, 1972

$1\frac{1}{16}$ MILES.(turf). (1.39 2/5) ALLOWANCES. Purse $15,000. 3-year-olds and upward which have not won three races other than maiden, claiming or starter. Weights, 3-year-olds, 117 lbs. Older, 122 lbs. Non-winners of $7,200 at a mile or over since July 1, allowed 2 lbs. $6,600 at a mile or over since June 17, 4 lbs. $6,000 at a mile or over since May 15, 6 lbs. (Maidens, claiming and starter races not considered inallowances.)

Value of race $15,000, value to winner $9,000, second $3,300, third $1,800, fourth $900. Mutuel pool $128,695, OTB pool $70,388.

Last Raced	Horse	Eqt.	A.	Wt	PP	St	1/4	1/2	3/4	Str	Fin	Jockey	Odds $1
23Jly72 ^{8}Del^{2}	Scrimshaw		4	116	2	2	7^{1}	$7\frac{1}{2}$	4^{1}	1^{3}	1^{4}	Marquez C H	2.40
20Jly72 ^{6}Aqu^{4}	Gay Gambler		3	108	8	8	$9^{1\frac{1}{2}}$	9^{5}	9^{8}	$8^{1\frac{1}{2}}$	$2^{1\frac{1}{2}}$	Patterson G	5.60
22Jly72 ^{6}Aqu^{3}	Fast Judge	b	3	111	7	7	6^{2}	6^{1}	$6\frac{1}{2}$	4^{hd}	3no	Velasquez J	10.00
28Jly72 ^{6}Aqu^{1}	Straight To Paris		3	115	9	3	$2\frac{1}{2}$	$2^{1\frac{1}{2}}$	$2\frac{1}{2}$	$2\frac{1}{2}$	4no	Vasquez J	2.70
25Jly72 ^{9}Aqu^{1}	Search the Farm	b	4	116	3	9	$8^{1\frac{1}{2}}$	$8^{1\frac{1}{2}}$	8^{1}	6^{hd}	5no	Guadalupe J	11.20
23Jly72 ^{8}Del^{3}	Chrisaway		4	116	4	6	$5^{1\frac{1}{2}}$	4^{hd}	$7\frac{1}{2}$	$7\frac{1}{2}$	6^{2}	Howard R	25.30
25Jly72 ^{9}Aqu^{5}	Navy Lieutenant	b	4	116	1	1	$3\frac{1}{2}$	5^{1}	$3\frac{1}{2}$	$5\frac{1}{2}$	7^{4}	Belmonte E	10.90
25Jly72 ^{7}Aqu^{4}	Head Table	b	3	113	10	5	4^{1}	3^{1}	$5\frac{1}{2}$	9^{10}	8^{2}	Baeza B	7.50
17Jly72 ^{8}Del^{3}	Mongo's Image		3	111	5	4	$1^{1\frac{1}{2}}$	$1\frac{1}{2}$	1^{1}	3^{hd}	9^{10}	Nelson E	28.70
21Jly72 ^{7}Aqu^{5}	Chartered Course	b	4	116	6	10	10	10	10	10	10	Arellano J	16.70

Time, $:23\frac{1}{5}$, $:46\frac{2}{5}$, $1:09\frac{4}{5}$, $1:34\frac{3}{5}$, $1:40\frac{4}{5}$ (Against Wind in Backstretch). Course firm.

$2 Mutuel Prices:

2-(B)- SCRIMSHAW	6.80	3.60	3.20
8-(H)- GAY GAMBLER		7.00	4.80
7-(G)- FAST JUDGE			5.60

B. g, by Jaipur—Ivory Tower, by Hill Prince. Trainer Lake R P. Bred by Vanderbilt A G (Md).
IN GATE AT 5.23; OFF AT 5.23 EASTERN DAYLIGHT TIME. Start Good Won Handily

SCRIMSHAW, taken back after breaking alertly, swung out to go after the leaders on the far turn, quickly drew off and was never seriously threatened. GAY GAMBLER, void of early foot, was unable to split horses entering the stretch, altered course to the extreme outside and finished strongly. FAST JUDGE, reserved behind the leaders, split horses leaving the far turn but was not match for the top pair. STRAIGHT TO PARIS prompted the pace much of the way and weakened during the drive. SEARCH THE FARM failed to menace. CHRISAWAY raced within easy striking distance while outside horses much of the way but lacked a late response. NAVY LIEUTENANT, a factor to the stretch while saving ground, gave way. HEAD TABLE was finished leaving the far turn. MONGO'S IMAGE stopped badly after showing to midstretch.

Owners— 1, Vanderbilt A G; 2, Whitney C V; 3, Wygod M J; 4, Rokeby Stable; 5, Nadler Evelyn; 6, Steinman Beverly R; 7, Sommer S; 8, Happy Hill Farm; 9, Reynolds J A; 10, Camijo Stable.

Trainers— 1, Lake R P; 2, Poole G T; 3, Nickerson V J; 4, Burch Elliott; 5, Nadler H; 6, Fout P R; 7, Martin F; 8, Wright F I; 9, Reynolds J A; 10, King W P.

Head Table returned to the races on April 21, 1973, fully nine months following the key race. He won by six. Commented Davidowitz, "That's weird."

CHAPTER 7

THE PRINCIPLE OF
MAXIMUM CONFUSION

A MELANCHOLY THOUGHT FOR many handicappers regards the collective wisdom of the betting public. No matter the genius of the individual handicapper, the crowd as a whole does it better. Imagine a select group of notable handicappers, to include perhaps Robert Dowst, Colonel Bradley, Howard Rowe, Ray Taulbot, Tom Ainslie, Andrew Beyer, Steve Davidowitz, William Quirin, Tom Brohamer, Barry Meadow, Mark Cramer, Steven Crist, and the top two or three professionals on every local circuit. Could these experts not excel the crowd?

They could not.

Assuming they play every race, performing at their best, the small group of experts could be expected to lose approximately 15 percent on investment. Public choices lose only 9 percent. Actually, the experts' 15 percent loss would mean they estimated the real winning probabilities of horses exceedingly well, losing merely the house take. Yet the public, a crowd that includes those little old ladies from Pasadena, their intuition and hatpins and all the rest, estimates horses' actual chances so mysteriously well it loses less than 10 percent and has outperformed every public selector in the history of the sport.

Thus, and not very surprisingly, it has come to pass that perhaps the surest mechanical betting approach ever devised departs from the scientifically established performance of the betting public, yet the system gathers dust on bookshelves and is scarcely remarked in the literature.

That is because the approach has been promoted in the strictest mathematical terms, together with theory, symbols, and formulae that might have guaranteed profits, but also discouraged mastery.

Regardless, the principle underpinning the system can be readily understood by anyone, however averse to mathematics. There is, too, a convenient alternative to grappling with the math. It substitutes intuition, of a practiced kind, and a normative measure of success.

In his eloquent and rigorous book *Horse Sense*, in which probability theory and mathematical methods are applied to betting propositions at the track, professor of ocean sciences Burton Fabricand befriends handicappers with a concise and lucid explanation of the Principle of Maximum Confusion. The principle derives from the proposition that the betting public achieves its time-honored 9 percent loss on favorites by overbetting some and underbetting others. Fabricand postulates the existence of races where the crowd underestimates the favorite's true probability of winning by more than 9 percent, that is, enough to turn loss into gain. The underestimated favorite presents handicappers with the only kind of favorable bet—a true overlay. Opposed to the underestimated kind is the overbet favorite, the kind that counterbalances the books into the 9 percent loss. The handicapper's task is to distinguish profitable favorites from the others.

Enter the Principle of Maximum Confusion. This holds that the public is most likely to underestimate the true winning probabilities of favorites in races where the past-performance record of the favorites is highly similar to one or more other horses. The intuitive rationale for the principle is the crowd's superior handicapping; that is, there must be some reason or reasons not immediately obvious for the public to make one horse its choice, notwithstanding its similarity to other horses. Yet the public is sufficiently confused that it bets too much money on the similar horses. Thus, its favorite is underbet. The public's confusion is held to be maximal if enough other horses look enough like the favorite to make the favorite a good bet.

As to the converse of this circumstance, where one horse looks superior in every fundamental respect, it is certain the outstanding record will not be lost on the betting public. This kind is regularly favored by form players, public selectors, and experts, such that few would argue the horse does not deserve to be favored. But, as Fabricand notes, the question is not whether the horse should be favored, but whether it should be bet. His answer to that rhetorical question is a resounding no. Why? Because the horse looks so obvious to all, it will almost certainly be overbet, or at least properly bet. No chance for profits long-haul. Fat chance for losses of at least 9 percent.

How might handicappers apply the Principle of Maximum Confusion, thus assuring themselves of continuous profits at upward of 10 percent? The trick is to recognize those races where the favorite is so similar to other contenders that the public gets very confused. Fabricand supplies handicappers with seven rules comprising the definition of similarity, as well as the probability formulae for applying the betting methods. Here we present a simplified version of the definition rules, and an alternative to the math.

To wit, the favorite is similar to another horse if:

1. Both show a race within the past 29 days, and
2. Both have raced at today's track, or neither has, and
3. The favorite's last race was at a class level equal to or lower than the similar horse's, and
4. There is less than a nine-pound weight shift between the two horses off their latest races, and
5. Both are male, or the favorite is female, and
6. Both last-race finishes were the same, greatly similar, or the favorite's last-out finish was slightly inferior to the other horse's, and
7. For sprints, the favorite is a sprinter (does not show a route in its PP's); for routes the favorite is a router (last three races occurred in routes) or a sprinter that won its last race.

All seven rules of similarity must be satisfied, according to Fabricand.

All kinds of races are susceptible to the principle, from the cheapest maidens to the highest class stakes. This is understandable, since the public is known to estimate the winning probabilities of favorites equally well regardless of the class of the race.

Handicappers that have isolated betting favorites that are similar to other horses in the field can fairly assume the public has been maximally confused. They can therefore presume the favorite will be underbet, and proceed to bet on it. To check the validity of the assumption, handicappers can employ a precious normative measure—their personal past performance with the principle. Allow a distribution of 30 bets. The criterion of success is upward of 10 percent profit.

Of money management, the betting method should not be one sensitive to large mutuels. Favorites, even underestimated ones, do not yield these. Flat bets, of small amounts during the testing period, are appropriate. Bets might be enlarged in some proportion to the public's under-estimation of its favorite's true chances, as handicappers intuit them, and this is surely preferable as the method becomes successfully familiar and habitual.

Reliance on norms (subjective standards) as substitutes for rigorous mathematical formulae is perfectly acceptable with complicated methods of handicapping and betting at racetracks, as the most meaningful index of performance at the track is one's personal performance. Once goals and criteria of success have been established, and notwithstanding the rigor or lack of the same of one's applications, whatever the idea or method under experiment, satisfactory results can be readily determined, repeated, or even improved. Unsatisfactory results can be eliminated, merely by eliminating the activity contributing to the inadequate performance. If the Principle of Maximum Confusion does not work well enough as applied by individual handicappers, the normative approach will reveal that at small cost. These handicappers can abandon the principle and return to the normal routine.

Even in the worst of scenarios, practice with the principle might prove beneficial. Its application will reverse a greatly unfortunate tendency. Handicappers long have relished the overbet favorite. They anticipate the overlay elsewhere, if not so successfully. Much less enthusiasm is held toward underbet favorites. Many handicappers would benefit on both accounts by changing tactics. Rather than buck overwhelming favorites by plunging on reasonable horses at reasonable prices, as is far too often done, stimulating action but not profits, handicappers can concentrate on underestimated favorites. When favorites are highly similar to non-favorites, as Fabricand tells, the crowd will be uncharacteristically confused, and handicappers benefit by backing the nervous public choices. The Principle of Maximum Confusion will be on their side. It assures they will be betting a series of true overlays, and this without the customary demand for full-dress handicapping.

What could be less complicating than that?

CHAPTER 8

THE RACE WAS
WRITTEN FOR HIM

A THIRST AMONG HANDICAPPERS for knowledge about eligibility conditions accounted for the instant success of the most comprehensive treatment of that topic yet published. In this author's *The Handicapper's Condition Book,* horses well suited to race conditions were elaborately described, and contrasted to horses not so well suited to conditions. Where more than one kind of horse fit the conditions nicely, these were profiled in descending order of preference, though handicappers were cautioned to consider the suitable profiles as interchangeable, depending on factors other than class. The book defined the role of race conditions as essentially prescribing or limiting the class of the horses eligible to compete. Many handicappers regarded the work as an advanced treatment of the class factor. They were largely correct.

From time to time at every major track the racing secretary writes a race specifically for one horse, almost invariably a star of the division, if not the local, regional, or national champ. The star's trainer may complain that he needs an overnight race to prepare for the upcoming stakes. Or a preliminary stakes may be wiped out by rain, hindering the big shot's conditioning and necessitating an overnight substitute race before the next big stakes on the agenda.

Once upon a Saturday, long ago, the fourth race at Santa Anita early in January was carded specifically for the Eastern stakes invader Five Star Flight, there to contest that track's Strub series, three closely matched graded stakes uniquely limited to new four-year-olds. The first leg of the Strub series had been covered with mud a week before, and Five Star Flight had scratched out. Thus an overnight race was written for him, to ensure his continued conditioning. The conditions of eligibility for the special race looked like this:

4 **Santa Anita**

7 Furlongs (1.20) Classified Allowance. Purse $40,000. 4–year–olds and upward. Non–winners of $19,500 since December 25, which are non–winners of two such races since July 20. Weights, 4–year–olds, 121 lbs. Non–winners of two such races since April 20 allowed 3lbs; of such a race since September 29 or a race of $22,500 in 1991,5lbs; of a race of $19,500 since July 20, 8lbs. (Claiming races not considered). Value of race $40,000, value to winner $22,000, second $8,000, third $6,000, fourth $3,000, fifth $1,000. Mutuel pool $281, 671. Exacta Pool$407,330.

By barring winners of first money since only December 25, the racing secretary kept the Eastern horse clear of extra-sharp stakes winners at the young meeting, notably the winner of the Malibu Stakes, the previously referenced first leg.

On the rare occasions when this occurs, handicappers gaze upon the miserly odds on the big shot under overnight conditions and scream that the race was written for him. True enough, but upsets are common enough under these circumstances. Five Star Flight finished fourth of five on his special day. After all, the stars come into the race short on a fundamental factor of handicapping, current form. So they sometimes lose.

In contemporary racing, characterized by a proliferation of stakes, and the classified races at some major tracks virtually extinct, division leaders more frequently return to action in stakes. The comeback stakes will typically be preliminary to bigger objectives. The division leaders that are authentic Grade 1 winners will be warming up. Few will be well intended to win a preliminary stakes with an all-out effort.

During winter of 2002, Kentucky Derby winner Monarchos returned at odds-on in a preliminary stakes at Gulfstream Park and at 1-10, no less. Siphonic returned in a preliminary stakes at Santa Anita. Both horses lost. Handicappers in the know should have anticipated the flops.

LATER IN THAT Santa Anita season, juvenile-filly division leader Bella Bellucci returned at odds-on in a minor stakes at six furlongs and got up to win in the last jump. Handicappers who cashed tickets might have noticed trainer Neil Drysdale's post-race observation, that his division leader was not well intended. She won regardless, in part because the front flight fell apart, in part because division leaders have the talent to win, even when unintended.

Handicappers having a grasp of eligibility conditions and stepping-stone stakes need not be fooled. Avoid the multiple Grade 1 and Grade 2 division leaders whenever they return to competition under the less than optimal conditions.

The screaming handicappers can benefit in this regard from recognition of a much greater truth about eligibility conditions. If not for a particular horse, in fact every race on the card is written with a particular kind of horse in mind. That's the racing secretary's main purpose, to provide winning opportunities for every horse in the barns. Handicappers who learn to recognize in the past performances the kinds of horses most likely to win each kind of race have leaped ahead of the crowd by miles.

From the *Handicapper's Condition Book,* here are the conditions of eligibility in major racing and the kind of horses best suited to each. If it sets up as the only horse of its kind in the field, the race was written for him.

Maidens, three and up, or four and up, any distance
The horse that finished second or third last time out, provided the Beyer Speed Figure matches par.

Maiden claiming, all ages, any distance
The horse moving from a maiden or maiden special weight race, provided form is intact, it has a front-running or pace-pressing running style, and its pace figures for either of its previous two races are among the top two in the field.

Allowance, nonwinners of two races, or nonwinners of a race other than maiden or claiming
Lightly raced younger maiden winners that have raced close once or twice with above-average clockings under similar conditions.

Allowance, nonwinners two times other than maiden or claiming
Lightly raced impressive younger horses, especially nicely bred improving three-year-olds, that recently have won an allowance race easily or impressively in better-than-average (par) time.

Allowance, nonwinners three times other than maiden or claiming
Impressive winners of two recent allowance races that have performed evenly or better in a graded stakes.

Allowance, nonwinners four times other than maiden or claiming
Previous stakes winners, preferably of open or graded stakes.

Conditioned stakes, bars previous stakes winners or winners of a specified amount since a specified date
Horses that recently have finished in the money or have run close in an open or graded stakes of relatively high purse value, provided form remains intact or continues in the improvement cycle.

Stakes, Grade 1
Previous Grade 1 and Grade 2 stakes winners, preferably of two or more such races.

Stakes, Grade 2
Previous Grade 1 or Grade 2 stakes winners, preferably a well-meant Grade 1 horse.

Stakes, Grade 3, listed, or ungraded but open
In the absence of well-meant Grade 1 or Grade 2 winners, a recent persuasive winner of a listed stakes, preferably of a purse comparable to or greater than today's.

Classified allowances, relatively unrestricted
Any horse whose basic class, as indicated by purse values won, restrictions of prior classified conditions, or the quality of horses engaged in its recent best efforts, is superior to today's conditions, especially open stakes winners, provided form is acceptable and the distance, footing, and probable pace are comfortable.

Classified allowances, relatively restricted
Currently sharp horses that have been competing for purses of comparable or better value and are particularly well suited to today's distance, footing, and probable pace.

Claiming races, three and up, four and up, all prices
Any horse dropping in claiming price by 30 percent or more, provided form is acceptable, improving, or peaking, and the horse has high-to-satisfactory early speed or the top speed figure.

Claiming races, three-year-olds, January-October

Horses that are dropping from an allowance race, as long as the horse exhibited some ability in the allowance race, e.g. early speed, a mid-race move, an even effort, a finish within six lengths.

Starter races, all ages, all prices

Horses that have won or run close previously at the highest open claiming price, especially a horse that has won a prior race in the starter series, or one that became eligible by a drop in claiming class last time out.

Regarding classified allowance conditions, relatively unrestricted conditions are not very restricted at all. They are open to all but the classiest horses on the grounds. Thus, class rules. Relatively restricted conditions bar all horses that have accomplished anything of late, and therefore provide ordinary and inferior horses a better chance to win. Thus, class bows to form.

Of claiming conditions, the ideal bet in any claiming race is the horse that combines (a) high early speed; (b) peaking form; and (c) a drop in class. The 30 percent or greater drop in claiming class is handicapping's most powerful probability statistic. It wins 378 percent of its rightful share of claiming races.

CHAPTER 9

BEYER SPEED

IN THE MID-1970's speed handicapper Andrew Beyer provoked a renaissance of his specialty and numerous successive investigations into same by describing an original and persuasive method of estimating the true speed of horses. Beyer's method concentrated on specifying final times that reflected the relative abilities of horses, and not just time differences due to differences in track surfaces. He flatly claimed his advanced technique for calculating daily variants as providing the best estimates available anywhere. He further assailed the concept of parallel time, replacing that with a concept of proportional time and controversial techniques for calculating the proportions.

Now that the smoke has cleared, Beyer has been sustained. Not only that, he, along with selected others, can be justly credited for stimulating several scientific advances in speed handicapping that are genuinely useful and effective. So effective that all serious handicappers, regardless of religion, are fairly recommended to include among their weapons adjusted final times, calculated in the manner promoted by Beyer.

The advances in speed handicapping, theory and method, have proved so conclusively effective that they have rendered obsolete for all times traditional practices associated with unadjusted final times (raw times), "speed ratings" as calculated by *Daily Racing Form,* or variants not sensitive to the influence of class. Before reviewing Beyer's method, it's instructive to consider those steps now fundamental to the effectiveness of any method of speed handicapping. To wit:

1. The construction of par-time tables for class-distance categories at the local track
2. The calculation of daily variants that reflect differences in class and the influences of track surfaces
3. The conversion of raw final times into adjusted final times
4. The conversion of adjusted final times into speed figures
5. The modification of the basic figures
6. The interpretation of the figures, in a context of full-dress handicapping that considers the fundamentals

Practiced speed handicappers complete the steps listed, but proceed variously at each step. At step one, some handicappers construct local par-times tables, and many more purchase the pars constructed by others. When it comes to calculating daily variants, procedures, and the resulting variants, differ practically in exact proportion to the number of handicappers calculating them. Thus adjusted final times differ variously, and so, too, the ultimate speed figures, even before these have been variously adjusted for beaten lengths, distance changes, or track class.

Beyer Speed Figures reach to the farthest frontier yet explored in speed handicapping. Beyer discounts par times, arguing the averages obscure class within a class, bringing together as they do time differences above and below average by several lengths. He replaces par times with projected times, estimates of how fast a small number of well-known horses should run. Thus, projected times are expected standards against which actual running times can be more reliably compared.

The concept of projected times poses difficulties in practice, and Beyer's personal illustrations dramatize these. Beyer describes Horse A, with an adjusted time of 1:11, coming off a 30-day layoff to beat by one length Horse B, with an adjusted time of 1:12. Beyer projects that A should beat B in 1:11⅘, finishing four ticks slower than normally—a concession to form analysis. The alternative finds A winning in the customary 1:11, but meaning that B, only a length in arrears, would have improved four lengths. That projection is held not tenable. Convenient, but loose, and open to considerable if irreconcilable argument. Beyer's projections depend on (a) form; (b) trainer intentions; (c) early pace; and by extension, (d) any fundamentals of handicapping that might reasonably explain time differences.

If speed handicappers would rely on projected times of individual horses to calculate daily variants and determine speed figures, they might most advantageously depend on that small category of horses alluded to by Beyer—those horses with highly reliable speed figures. Those final times are most stable and therefore most reliably projected. Where a half dozen of these can be spotted on a single card, the projected times represent best estimates of true speed. Variations from these times can lead handicappers to daily variants and speed figures well beyond the ken of the crowd, and of handicappers without figures. But handicappers need to be cautious about their everyday projections. Assumptions about the influences on final time of form, or trainer intentions, or early pace, are tricky at best. Handicappers best choose to be accurate rather than clever.

Of variants, Beyer cites a pair of classic problems. As illustrated in *Picking Winners*:

Race	Projected Time	Actual Time	Difference
1	1:13	1:13⅗	slow by ⅗
2	1:12⅕	1:13	slow by ⅘
3	1:12⅘	1:13⅘	slow by 5/5
4	1:12	1:10⅖	fast by 8/5
5	1:12	1:12⅘	slow by ⅘

Beyer notes that the fourth race looks perplexing. He suggests that the track appears dull, but that this race is completed eight ticks faster than expected. Beyer first focuses on his projected time, in this case trying to find basis for a projection of 1:09⅘, which would mesh with the others. Failing this, he concedes the point, asserts that the race defies explanation—in terms of speed handicapping—and recommends the race be excluded from the variant's calculation. By extension, all extreme times, whether fast or slow, are best subjected to elision, if not to explanation. This is fair practice, by all means. In all statistical compilations, averages are oversensitive to extremes, a distortion wisely eliminated.

Here is another kind of problem:

Race	Projected Time	Actual Time	Difference
1	1:12	1:11⅖	fast by ⅗
2	1:13	1:12⅕	fast by ⅘
3	1:12⅕	1:11⅕	fast by 5/5
4	1:11	1:10⅕	fast by ⅘
5	1:11⅗	1:12⅕	slow by ⅗

Beyer Speed			
6	1:12	1:12⅕	slow by ⅕
7	1:10⅘	1:11⅗	slow by ⅘
8	1:11	1:11⅖	slow by ⅖
9	1:13	1:13⅕	slow by ⅕

The track condition has changed abruptly during the card, perhaps for no apparent reason. Beyer's solution? Construct two variants. For races 1 through 4, fast by ⅘; for races 5 through 9, slow by ⅖.

The critical problem of comparing times earned by horses competing at different distances leads speed handicappers to the conversion of adjusted final times into speed figures and introduces the notorious concept of parallel time. This logic suggests that horses that run such-and-such at six furlongs can be expected to run so-and-so at 1⅛ miles. Beyer cites Laurel, where his arbitrary speed figure of 80 equals six furlongs in 1:13 equals seven furlongs in 1:26⅕ equals 1⅛ miles in 1:54. In other words, an 80 is an 80 is an 80 is an 80, distance notwithstanding.

Is there basis in fact for the logic? Actually, studies of sprint final times indicate that time differences as between distances are equivalent at most tracks. But when sprint times are compared with route times at various tracks, the equivalence disappears. And the headaches begin.

Conceding that fast horses might be expected to change distances in time different from the time needed by slow horses, Beyer escorts handicappers closer to reality by promoting the concept of proportional time. Because one length or one-fifth second has greater value in faster races or at shorter distances, speed handicappers are urged to determine the percentage of a race one length (one-fifth second) represents. Again using Laurel's pars, Beyer shows that in running 1:13 at six furlongs, a horse has covered the distance in 365/5, such that one-fifth represents .28 percent of the entire race. At seven furlongs in 1:26⅕, one-fifth is 1/431 or .23 percent of the race.

In that way one-fifth second is weighted for all distances at the local track. By moving the decimal point an integer to the right for convenience, handicappers can construct a speed figure table that reflects proportional time. If 1:13 is set at 80, 1:12⅘ is really .28 percent better, such that 1:12⅘ is set at 82.8. Yet a change from 1:26⅕ to 1:26 corresponds to a change from 80 to 82.3, reflecting the .23 percent one-fifth represents at seven furlongs.

By this method, a portion of the Laurel speed chart at six and seven furlongs would look like this:

Six Furlongs		Seven Furlongs	
1:12	94.0	1:25⅕	91.5
1:12⅕	91.2	1:25⅖	89.2
1:12⅖	88.4	1:25⅗	86.9
1:12⅗	85.6	1:25⅘	84.6
1:12⅘	82.8	1:26	82.3
1:13	80	1:26⅕	80.0
1:13⅕	77.2	1:26⅖	77.7
1:13⅖	74.4	1:26⅗	75.4

By removing the decimal points and rounding the numbers, handicappers can construct a speed-figure table for every time at every distance at the local track. All that is needed are the basic equivalent times at each distance. Par times for a common class of horse at the regularly run distances will do.

Beyer's chart does not pretend that every horse should cover an additional furlong in equivalent time, such as the 13⅕ seconds difference between six furlongs at Laurel in 1:13 and seven furlongs there in 1:26⅕. If a Laurel sprinter covers six furlongs in 1:10, the concept of proportional time would require its seven-furlong time be something faster than 1:23⅕. If a plodder goes six in 1:14⅘, its seven-furlong time must be something slower than 1:28. The faster horse would run the extra furlong proportionately slower than 13⅕.

Referring to Aqueduct's basic time equivalents, Beyer's speed chart shows that a horse than runs six furlongs in 1:09⅘ (a raw figure of 124) should cover seven furlongs in 1:22⅖ (also a figure of 124), covering the extra furlong in 12⅗ seconds. But a horse running six in 1:14⅕ (a figure of 64) should go seven in 1:27⅗ (also a 64), covering the last eighth in 13⅖ seconds. In this way, proportional time replaces parallel time. Speed handicappers fly closer to reality by simulating Beyer. Figures in hand, they have a basis for comparing times at different distances, assuming the horse will be comfortable enough at the distance to approach their proportional times.

Beyer emphasizes the convenience of speed figures, once handicappers become familiar with them. Class-distance par times, for instance, can be converted to figures. When actual race times are converted to figures from simple reference to the speed chart, the actual figures can be compared to the par figures, in this way producing race variants, and ultimately the daily variant. Beyer supplies the following illustration from Aqueduct:

Class	Distance	Par	Time	Actual Figure	Difference
$10,000	1 mile	97	1:37⅖	100	fast by 3
F-Maiden	6F	90	1:11⅘	97	fast by 7
$15,000 Alw	7F	113	1:23⅖	112	slow by 1
Stakes	1⅛M	119	1:49⅗	122	fast by 3
$17,000	6½F	102	1:17⅗	105	fast by 3

Averaging the differences, Aqueduct's daily variant this day equaled –3. When a horse that competed this day runs again, speed handicappers will have subtracted three points from its figure. Beyer also provides handicappers with a standardized chart for beaten-lengths adjustments. The numbers, which are reprinted at the end of this piece, are likewise subtracted from the winner's figure, after the variant has been added or subtracted.

Even as Beyer's method of speed handicapping was gaining recognition as something new and worthwhile, other forces were gathering throughout racing that would enhance the fundamental importance of speed. Racing days were increasing terrifically, lowering the quality of the general competition, thus assuring that more races than ever would go to the cheaper speed. State-bred breeding programs were materializing to fill racing cards, and these depended on speed as the trump. Probability studies began to demonstrate the importance of early speed, such that horses first, second, or third at first calls throughout the land were winning almost 60 percent of the races. Racetrack surfaces were changing, favoring the speed. Suddenly the game had turned toward the speed horses. Beyer speed was fairly perceived as the surest route to the winner's circle.

Notwithstanding all the attention to speed and early speed, a significant point is that speed handicapping certified handicappers as consistent winners only after it had encompassed the relative influence of class. Par times and projected times are sensitive to class levels and real abilities. In a separate chapter of *Picking Winners* on class, Beyer asserts his belief that class is relatively unimportant. Speed is the way and the truth. But Beyer's own method, paradoxically, belies his beliefs about class and reassures handicappers using figures that speed and class are interlocking and had better not be conceptualized or treated separately.

Nowhere is evidence for the point more convincing than Beyer's final chapter of his book's trilogy on speed handicapping, "Speed Handicapping: III." In this chapter Beyer offers interpretative guidelines and illustration of speed figures at work. He introduces the material by recall-ing the beatings he endured when in his earlier days he accepted the fig-ures on faith, and with blind ambition attempted to beat the races with them and them alone. It didn't work for Beyer, and it won't work for handicappers who repeat the blind ambition. Beyer's method improved once he began winnowing out horses that did not measure up on other handicapping fundamentals. These include class, form, distance, pace, trainer, and footing criteria. Of speed figures, Beyer provides the follow-ing lessons:

- Discount figures a horse has earned with the assistance of strong track bias.
- Discount figures a horse has earned on a wet track, especially if the track is fast today.
- Discount figures a horse has earned by opening a big lead and main-taining it wire to wire.
- Distrust an outstanding figure resulting from a single exceptional performance.
- The latest figure is the most important, but consistently higher fig-ures than those earned by the competition today represent the most unshakable bets of speed handicapping.

Beyer's Beaten-Lengths Adjustment Chart

(To use, look down the left column for the beaten lengths. Move right across the row to the column for today's distance. Subtract the number from the winner's figure.)

Margin	5 Fur.	6 Fur.	7 Fur.	Mile	1⅟₁₆	1⅛	1½
Neck	1	1	1	1	0	0	0
½	1	1	1	1	1	1	1
¾	2	2	2	1	1	1	1
1	3	2	2	2	2	2	1
1¼	4	3	3	2	2	2	1
1½	4	4	3	3	3	2	2
1¾	5	4	4	3	3	3	2
2	6	5	4	4	3	3	2
2¼	7	6	5	4	3	3	2
2½	7	6	5	4	4	4	3
2¾	8	7	6	5	5	5	3
3	9	7	6	5	5	5	3
3¼	10	9	7	6	5	5	4

			Beyer Speed				
3½	10	9	7	6	6	6	4
3¾	11	9	8	7	6	6	4
4	12	10	8	7	7	6	5
4¼	12	10	9	8	7	7	5
4½	13	11	9	8	7	7	5
4¾	14	11	10	9	8	8	5
5	15	12	10	9	8	8	6
5½	16	13	11	10	9	9	6
6	18	15	12	11	10	9	7
6½	19	16	13	12	11	10	8
7	20	17	14	13	12	11	8
7½	22	18	15	13	13	12	9
8	23	20	17	14	13	13	10
8½	25	21	18	15	14	13	10
9	26	21	18	15	14	13	10
9½	28	23	19	16	15	14	11
10	29	24	20	18	17	17	12
11	32	27	23	20	18	18	13
12	35	29	25	21	20	20	14
13	38	32	27	23	22	22	15
14	41	34	29	25	23	23	16
15	44	37	31	27	25	25	17

To be sure, if the winner's figure for a one-mile race is 108, what figure is assigned to a horse beaten six lengths?

The answer is 97.

Speed figures can be trusted to explain whether horses moving up or down in claiming price can be expected to win.

Professional speed handicappers have taken Beyer's concept of projected times to heart, applying the idea to horses whose times they understand particularly well. Speed figures of that kind represent the most advanced stage of the art.

CHAPTER 10

PARS

AMONG THE MOST significant of all the scientific discoveries yet produced by probability studies of handicapping is the absolute correlation of speed and class. Not only do final times improve as class levels rise, the time differences tend to be standard from track to track. The practical consequences of this phenomenon have benefited handicappers throughout the nation. They have been forever relieved of the research drudgery formerly required to construct accurate class-distance tables. As accurate pars (average final times recorded by a class of horses at a specified distance) precede the making of accurately adjusted final times and speed figures, handicappers without pars can receive little nourishment from their numbers.

Following Bill Quirin, par-time tables for all classes and distances can be constructed for claiming races once the local pars for a particular class at the regularly run distances have been determined. Quirin recommends $10,000 claiming horses represent the baseline. Of a single quiet afternoon, local handicappers need to consult their tracks' latest results charts and record the final times for $10,000 older claiming horses at each distance. Only fast surfaces qualify. A sample of 15 races yields stable estimates. Throw out extreme times. Average the other final times.

The baseline erect, consult the table of standard claiming-price adjustments abstracted here (next page) from Quirin's studies and plug in the final times for each class at each distance.

To construct par-time tables for nonclaiming horses, handicappers need baseline data for nonclaiming maidens at the various distances. The maiden baseline data in hand, standard adjustments for class, sex, age, and time of season fall neatly into place. The standard adjustments follow:

Nonclaiming Class Adjustments

	Sprints	Routes
Maidens	0	0
NW 1	−2	−3
NW 2	−4	−5
NW 3	−5	−7
Classified Alw	−7	−10
Stakes	−9	−12

Par Times for Claiming Races

	3½F	4F	4½F	5F	5½F 6F 6½F	7F 7½F	1M 1 40M	170M 1¹⁄₁₆M	1⅛M
$50,000	−3	−4	−5	−5	−6	−7	−9	−9	−10
$40,000	−3	−4	−5	−5	−6	−6	−8	−8	−9
$35,000	−3	−4	−5	−5	−6	−6	−8	−8	−8
$30,000	−3	−4	−5	−5	−5	−5	−6	−6	−7
$25,000	−2	−3	−4	−4	−4	−4	−5	−5	−6
$20,000	−2	−2	−3	−3	−3	−3	−4	−4	−4
$18,000	−2	−2	−2	−2	−2	−2	−3	−3	−3
$15,000	−1	−1	−2	−2	−2	−2	−2	−2	−2
$13,000	−1	−1	−1	−1	−1	−1	−1	−1	−1
$10,000	0	0	0	0	0	0	0	0	0
$8,500	+1	+1	+1	+1	+1	+1	+1	+1	+1
$7,500	+1	+1	+1	+2	+2	+2	+2	+2	+2
$6,500	+1	+1	+1	+2	+3	+3	+3	+3	+3
$5,000	+2	+2	+2	+3	+4	+4	+4	+4	+4
$4,000	+3	+3	+3	+4	+5	+5	+5	+5	+5
$3,500	+3	+3	+3	+4	+5	+5	+5	+6	+6
$3,200	+4	+4	+4	+5	+6	+6	+6	+7	+7
$3,000	+4	+4	+4	+5	+6	+6	+7	+8	+8
$2,500	+5	+5	+5	+6	+7	+7	+8	+9	+9
$2,000	+5	+5	+6	+7	+8	+8	+9	+10	+11
$1,750	+6	+6	+7	+8	+9	+9	+10	+11	+12
$1,500	+6	+6	+7	+8	+9	+10	+11	+12	+13
$1,250	+6	+7	+8	+9	+10	+11	+12	+13	+14
$1,000	+6	+7	+8	+9	+10	+11	+13	+14	+15

So $5,000 claimers normally run six furlongs four-fifths of a second slower than $10,000 claimers do, at any track. And $20,000 claimers normally cover 1⅛ miles four-fifths of a second faster than $10,000 claimers do. Anywhere.

Standard par-time adjustments, various:

Fillies and Mares (all classes). Sprints +2, Routes +3.
Maiden claimers (same age, sex, and class). Sprints +5, Routes +7.
Seasonal adjustments for nonclaiming maidens and nonwinners allowances.

Jan.-Feb.	−2
Mar.-Apr.-May	−1
June-July-Aug.	0
Sept.-Oct.	+1
Nov.-Dec.	+2

For races restricted to three-year-olds in claiming races, classified allowance races, and stakes races at various times of year.

	6F	6½F	7F	1M-1 40M	1 70M-1¹⁄₁₆M	1⅛M	
+9						Jan. 1	+9
+8						Feb. 1	+8
+7					Jan.1	Mar. 15	+7
+6					Feb. 1	May 1	+6
+5				Jan.1	Apr. 15	June 1	+5
+4		Jan. 1	Jan.1	Apr. 15	June 1	July 1	+4
+3	Jan. 1	Feb. 1	Mar. 15	June 1	July 1	Aug. 1	+3
+2	Apr. 15	June 1	June 15	July 15	Aug. 15	Sept. 15	+2
+1	July 1	Aug. 1	Aug. 15	Sept. 15	Oct. 15	Dec. 1	+1
0	Nov. 1	Dec. 1	Dec. 15	—	—	—	0

For example, in comparison to races open to older horses, claiming races for three-year-olds at six furlongs are completed three-fifths slower on January 1, one-fifth slower on July 1, with no difference by November 1.

If handicappers determine the local par for $10,000 older claiming males at six furlongs is 1:11, they can readily answer the following by consulting the adjustment charts:

1. What is the par for older $4,000 males at six furlongs?
2. What is the six-furlong par for $20,000 older mares?
3. What is the six-furlong par for $12,500 older males?
4. What is the six-furlong par for $8,000 three-year-olds during May?

In like manner, handicappers can determine the following pars, if they know older nonclaiming maidens at the mile average a final time of 1:38, at 1 1/16 miles average 1:44⅗, and at 1⅛ miles 1:51⅖.

What is par for NW 3 males traveling 1 1/16 miles on July 4?

What is par for NW 1 older fillies and mares at 1⅛ miles February 15?

What is par for stakes fillies, three-year-olds, going one mile on October 20?

What is par for classified three-year-old fillies traveling 1⅛ miles August 15?

The first three pars would be 1:43⅕, 1:51⅖, and 1:36⅖, respectively.

The fourth question's par requires these adjustments:

Classified	–10
Fillies	+3
Three-year-olds, August 15, at 1⅛ M	+3

Par is 1:51⅖, minus 4, or 1:50⅗.

The most constructive use of pars for handicappers, regardless of persuasion, is the calculation of daily track variants sensitive to class differences. Handicappers who compare actual times to par times and average the differences for a nine-race card have calculated a variant sensitive to both class levels and track surfaces. When the variant is added to or subtracted from the raw final times, the resulting times are adjusted final times that represent better estimates of true speed.

Properly adjusted final times help handicappers understand class within a class, and they have reliable application to the calendar's largest category of races, claiming races open to older horses. Adjusted final times also reflect the relative quality of maiden races, providing indicators as to which of these winners might proceed successfully to preliminary nonwinners allowance competition. Variants calculated by reference to par-time tables can be obtained within minutes. Many professionals recommend calculation of both a sprint and a route variant, by averaging the day's time differences (par plus or minus raw times) in each category.

Handicappers can honor the dramatically improved role of speed in handicapping by spending the time and effort to obtain pars and daily variants. Those who do will prosper with a set of adjusted final times that shed light on numerous handicapping mysteries.

CHAPTER 11

THE SECOND COMING
OF ANDREW BEYER

Late in 1983, handicappers were served a second helping from the storied horseplaying individualist Andrew Beyer—a book on the art of "trip" handicapping, with chapters on modern betting strategy and the indispensable attitudes and work habits of racetrack winners.

Eight years after his *Picking Winners* revealed an original and effective method of adjusting the raw final times of Thoroughbreds, enabling American horseplayers to estimate the true speed of racehorses more reliably and popularizing speed handicapping to an extent hardly imagined by the author, Beyer returned with new perspectives on beating the game.

Profits on speed horses had slowed to trickles, Beyer complained, with so many mathematical types, computer whizzes, and numbers merchants spewing forth speed figures and thereby lowering track odds on top-figure horses everywhere, sending hundreds of them postward as underlays. The customers beating the game in the 1980's, asserts Beyer, were the trip handicappers, and in *The Winning Horseplayer* he proceeded to provide handicappers with the first comprehensive, experimental treatment of that fashionable topic.

Trip handicapping should not impact as widely on the general practice of handicapping as did Beyer's speed methodology, but Beyer accomplishes something crucially important in this book that he failed to do sufficiently in *Picking Winners*. He integrates trip handicapping with the handicapping process as a whole. He combines that which is essentially a technique—evaluating horses' trips—with a basic, fully developed, and demonstrably effective handicapping orthodoxy, his own speed handicapping methodology. Thus what is promoted in *The Winning Horseplayer* is not merely the technique, which, if so promoted, thousands of handicappers might wrongly substitute for the art of handicapping, but fully formed methodology that embraces both the incidental (trips) and the fundamental (speed and pace).

In his first contribution to the handicapping literature, Beyer refused to relate adjusted final times to other important factors of handicapping. Class was ardently eschewed, pace ignored. Speed figures, standing alone, represented the truth and the way. To handicappers not particularly persuaded of numerical differences of one, two, or a few points as the means to distinguish horses competing in a complicated game characterized by a sizable error factor, Beyer's speed handicapping, though itself laborious and rigorous, could not fairly substitute for the full-dress handicapping routine. Without interpretation guidelines, applying the numbers might become something of a parlor game, and the interpretive guidance seemed too often to be missing.

Beyer speed survived and prospered nonetheless, as the methodology was sound and, more importantly, because its speed quotient is an intrinsic characteristic of the racehorse. But if its speed ability supplies evidence about a horse that is intrinsic and fundamental, its trips do not. Trip handicapping is situational and circumstantial, and its importance to the correct analysis of any race may be incidental, not fundamental. The handicapper's capitulation to trip handicapping as a first and last resort can therefore be terribly misleading, unless trip analysis can be carefully entwined in a broader context of fundamental handicapping.

Beyer handles these issues impressively. Not only are trip analyses related to other crucial situational variables, notable track biases and pace, but in the book's most influential chapter Beyer cleverly interweaves trip information and speed figures. The lesson for handicappers of all persuasions should not be lost—trip information must be integrated with a handicapping orthodoxy that is far more fundamental, much more encompassing. Beyer makes that case well. This point of view might become *The Winning Horseplayer*'s most valuable legacy.

As Beyer says, trip handicapping involves a scheduled observation of horses in competition. The schedule of observations does not include watching the horses one has bet from flagfall to finish, a deeply ingrained tendency handicappers will have a devilish time changing. Beyer provides handicappers with tested procedures for watching races effectively, along with surprisingly simple notations for recording what has been systematically observed. The notation should not be underestimated. It is crucial to effective trip handicapping, which relies not only on observation skills but also on the efficient recording of all the combustion. Beyer's notations can be found at the conclusion of this piece. Surprising, too, and happily so, is the lack of emphasis on the kinds of racing trouble that regularly beset horses and jockeys—stumbling at the start, taking up, checking, shuffling back, altering course, getting blocked, etc. Beyer instead concentrates more on running position, especially on the turns and entering the stretch.

When position is related to the presence or absence of a track bias, and in turn to considerations of pace, handicappers can readily appreciate the advantages trip handicapping promises. In a typical illustration, the notation 3B, 4T, 5E of a horse racing in outside paths down the backside, around the far turn, and into the stretch can denote either a positive or a negative trip, depending on the bias, or perhaps on the pace set by front-runners.

Beyer does something else in *The Winning Horseplayer* perhaps unexpected by his legions of speed fanciers—he achieves a point of view about trips vis-à-vis speed that handicappers everywhere might usefully ponder. In contrasting the two methods he now employs in combination, Beyer notes that whereas speed handicapping is mainly objective, trip handicapping is highly subjective; whereas speed handicapping is analytical, trip handicapping is visual; whereas speed handicapping is quantitative, trip handicapping is qualitative. Beyer avoids the temptation to translate into numbers information that is inherently descriptive. Beyer does not modify his speed figures with trip adjustments. He illustrates how those who do so might go badly astray and implores handicappers not to descend into those well-concealed traps.

Instead, Beyer recommends handicappers ask a series of logical questions about the trip information at hand. He lists the questions. Drawing on his extensive experience with trip information, Beyer then profiles the kinds of horses he most prefers and those he most strongly resists when trips have been juxtaposed to biases, pace, and speed figures. All of it adds up to a powerful methodology that combines vital information from the past performances and vital information obtainable during the actual races.

Moreover, the practical problems many might expect to limit the successful practice of trip handicapping—notably getting to the racetrack daily—have been vastly overdrawn in Beyer's view. Indeed, handicappers hesitant to embrace trip handicapping because they cannot attend the races every day should not be so put off. Beyer shows that by attending the track twice a week, handicappers are able to see 80 percent of a week's trips. They just have to arrive in time to see the previous day's replays. In this way, two days' attendance equals four days' trips.

With respect to modern betting strategy, Beyer promotes the advantages of exotic wagering, whereby handicappers can scramble key selections and the other contention of decipherable races. By this approach big money may more often result at small risk. Underlays in the win pools might become overlays in exotic combinations. Even prime selections bet seriously to win might be protected in the exotics, with smaller wagers on marginal horses that Beyer refers to as savers, meaning of one's capital.

What Beyer espouses most is flexibility in betting strategy, counseling handicappers to free themselves of practices that demand comparable amounts be bet on each selection; that is, fixed-percentage wagering. Beyer contends that handicapping selections reflect an array of opinions having numerous gradations of strength, such that the size of the wagers should be proportionate to the differences of one's opinions.

When betting seriously to win, Beyer advises handicappers to ask what would be the largest amount they could comfortably risk in the best of situations; that is, when the prime selection and all the attending circumstances of the race appear to be ideal. From that threshold handicappers are urged to downscale win bets in accord with the rigor of their opinions. Beyer's personal ceiling is $3,000, an amount he invests a few times a season. Thus for him, $100 spent on exotics represents one-thirtieth, or 3 percent, of his maximum, a comfortable risk.

Beyer does not expect others to implement his betting strategy as he does, but he cautions that risk capital should be relatively sizable to begin. In recounting how an acquaintance who had a $2,000 bankroll to start soon lost confidence and was forced to quit the game, Beyer concludes that the man's bankroll was too thin to begin with.

To be sure, $100 equals 5 percent of a $2,000 stake, a relatively bold investment strategy, as computer simulations have shown. Studies also having revealed that handicappers are mostly spinning wheels with bets to win on horses at 3-1 odds or lower, Beyer's more aggressive strategy offers handicappers an alternative for backing all those properly bet horses that do figure.

Beyer concludes his discourse by noting that winning attitudes belong to those who can deal effectively with (a) anger and (b) self-pity. He maintains that winning horseplayers are most likely to be those who collect the most meaningful information and work the hardest to interpret it smartly.

Those of us who have enjoyed opportunities to play the races for a time with Andy Beyer usually have chronicled the experiences to friends and others by adding to the man's legend as a big bettor and aggressive gambler. So be it. But few make the effort to point out, as Beyer gently does in *The Winning Horseplayer,* that his big bets are carefully structured and are based not only on considerable and fundamental information, but also on comprehensive skill in interpreting it.

And almost no one stops to mention that Andy Beyer collects more information and works harder with it than just about anybody else playing this difficult, challenging parimutuel game. If anyone doubts this or cares to dispute the point, let them read in this book how deliberately and painstakingly Beyer prepared for his 1983 attack on Santa Anita, beginning a year earlier in Washington, D.C. Beyer is a serious, studious, rigorous professional. When handicapping for profit, he's hard at work for long, long hours, to be sure. His books prove the point unmistakably.

A Notation System for Trip Handicapping

STAGES OF THE RACE

G	The gate; anything that happens at the start of a race
FT	First turn
B	Backstretch
T	Turn
E	Entering the stretch
S	Stretch

THE PACE

Duel	A horse fighting for the lead.
Stalk	A horse sitting behind a duel for the lead.
Move	A horse accelerates strongly in a way that almost makes his rivals look as if they are standing still.
MIHP	Move into hot pace. A horse makes a strong move, but does it at a time when the leaders are accelerating, too.
Inherit	A horse gets the lead by taking over from rivals who have collapsed.

TYPES OF TROUBLE

Slo	A horse breaks from the gate behind the field.
Rush	A horse rushes into contention suddenly after breaking slowly.
Steady	Mild trouble, caused by a lack of running room.
Alter	A horse is forced to alter his course sharply.
NP	No push; the jockey is not asking his horse to run at some stage of a race.
Stiff	A jockey has not asked his horse to run at any stage of the race.

(Continued)

TYPES OF TROUBLE (Continued)

V   Vise; a horse is in heavy traffic without encountering actual interference.

GP   Good position; a horse is in the clear with no rivals inside or outside him.

POSITIONS ON THE TRACK

Rail   A horse on the innermost part of the track. Each successive horse width from the rail is described as the 2-path, the 3-path, and so on. A notation of 3T would indicate a horse in the 3-path of the far turn.

TRACK BIASES

GR   Good rail

GR+   Very strong good rail

BR   Bad rail

BR+   Very strong bad rail

S   Speed-favoring track

S+   Very strong speed-favoring track

C   Track that favors closers

CHAPTER 12

TRACK BIASES

IF THERE IS one pervasive influence on the handicapping experience, wrote Steve Davidowitz in *Betting Thoroughbreds,* track bias comes very close to filling the bill. Davidowitz went on to argue that handicappers who did not weigh the significance of the track surface could not expect to make profits. However much they catered to track bias before Davidowitz anointed the factor to cardinal status, handicappers everywhere paid even more devotion to their ovals afterward. Davidowitz, whose writings more than those of others reflect a studied synthesis of widely diverse experiences, excepted no racetracks. He insisted biases operate everywhere, only more or less so.

Some specific examples are worth repeating. At Pimlico in Maryland the tendency for inside posts at 1 1/16 miles to dominate when the first turn is a short way from the gate is sharply exaggerated, biased toward posts 1, 2, and 3, and away from posts 9, 10, 11, and 12. Many racetracks share that bias to various degrees. Davidowitz names Fair Grounds and Churchill Downs, where conventional wisdom unwisely believes stretch runs of 1,300-plus feet eliminate post-position biases. But the two turns are acutely sharp and favor speed horses that can accelerate around them.

At Delaware Park, Philadelphia Park, and other tracks where winter racing endures, Davidowitz says the extra topsoil mixed with antifreeze agents affects track surfaces notably. The effectiveness of the antifreezing varies significantly. In consequence, the rail may be a paved highway or it may be a swampy trap.

Racetracks also change surfaces. Storied Saratoga changed in 1974 from a graveyard for front-runners to a freeway where they might threaten time records. Speed on the rail can be a tremendous positive bias.

When horses switch courses on the same circuit, handicappers aware of the biases at each track can make the quickest adaptations, as horses cannot. Calder-to-Gulfstream is cited as from endurance to lickety-split speed. Yet speed horses at Calder today cannot be tossed aside as formerly, when that track was new.

Of weather, a sudden rainstorm on an otherwise normal surface usually places a premium on early speed. But if the rain continues for a few days, handicappers experience the bane of all abnormalities, unpredictable results. The same sorry situation results from a sudden frost or extreme heat.

Davidowitz reassures handicappers they can readily spot significant track biases when at the track. Observation skills make the difference. Here are the guidelines:

1. Watch the turns. Are horses gobbling up ground on the outside, or is the rail the only place to be?
2. Watch the break from the gate. Are particular post positions sluggish during the early going, even when occupied by early-speed horses?
3. In route races around two turns, watch the run to the clubhouse turn. Do horses exiting the outside posts settle into position comfortably, or are they laboring noticeably?
4. Watch the top jockeys. Do the best riders continually direct their mounts to one part of the track? Handicappers are advised that most jockeys remain insensitive to biases themselves, but that every track's colony contains one or two who know where to be after two or three turns of the course.

   For infrequent track visitors or handicappers arriving from out of town, Davidowitz urges consultation with recent results charts. Look for running patterns that reflect biases. Underline phrases and clauses that betray strong biases.

Track Profiles In 1991, along came Tom Brohamer with his observations on modern pace handicapping, one of which was the importance—and simplicity—of constructing "track profiles." While concerned with the position and beaten lengths of recent winners at the first and second calls, track profiles can complement the discovery of biases due to track surfaces with the discovery of biases reflected by running styles.

As did Davidowitz, Brohamer urged handicappers that cannot attend the races regularly to spend five minutes a day with the local results charts. Now the task requires the recording of positions and beaten lengths of each winner at a specific distance at the first and second calls.

The data for a few days only allows handicappers to identify running styles that have been favored at the distance. Brohamer relates a trip to Las Vegas in the summer of 1989, and his interest in playing the races at the new Arlington Park. Brohamer consulted the results charts at Arlington Park for the three days of August 19-21. Examine Brohamer's five-race track profile for Arlington's one-turn mile on August 20-21, and the conclusions he reached.

	Dist	Ent	1Call	2Call	%E	ESP
20Aug89	8	7	3/10+	3/6½	N/A	P/S
"	8	8	4/2	1/½	"	P
"	8	6	5/4½	4/2	"	S/P
"	8	8	5/6½	5/6	"	S
21Aug89	8	8	3/1	2/½	"	P

Now consider Brohamer's three-part conclusion from the limited data:

First, handicappers should not consider any front-runner that might attempt a wire-to-wire theft. The track profile is clear. Wire-to-wire types will be at a severe disadvantage.

Second, strongly prefer pressers and sustained runners.

Third, avoid deep closers unable to stay in touch with the leaders by the second call. Deep closers are poor bets most times, at most tracks, unless the track profile at a specific distance convinces you otherwise.

In using results charts, Brohamer reminds recreational handicappers who rarely consult the charts that the exponents indicating beaten lengths refer to a horse's lengths in front of the horse directly behind it. If the winner of a one-turn mile at Arlington Park at the first call was running fourth, handicappers must examine the three horses in front of the winner at the first call, and sum the lengths by which they led the winner at that call.

Simulcast handicappers should appreciate the utter simplicity of constructing track profiles once they review the results charts. The recommended resource is *DRF Simulcast Weekly* (published by *Daily Racing Form*), which provides the weekly charts for all operating tracks.

Devotees of track profiles advise recreational handicappers who want to convert exacta and trifecta tickets to profits to compile track profiles, not only for the winners, but also for the horses that have finished second. Often, the two profiles will be dissimilar and can reveal that distinct running styles have been finishing first and second. That is nice to know.

CHAPTER 13

COMPREHENSIVE HANDICAPPING

Promoted by Tom Ainslie variously in his seven books and private method, "comprehensive handicapping" as method recognizes that all the factors of handicapping play a part in the outcome of races. Arguing that all the factors of handicapping are intertwined, Ainslie makes systematic the player's handling of each, underscoring their interrelations, and establishing their priorities under various conditions of racing. Because the method features the interactions among several factors, it is essentially analytical and evaluative in approach, asking handicappers to break down races into component parts, put those pieces together again into a new coherent whole, and make final decisions with a judgment formed by extensive knowledge and experience. Not easily susceptible to quantification, the method relies on qualitative analyses. Because the method derives only from fundamental and comprehensive knowledge about the sport of racing and skill of handicapping, it not only achieved a breakthrough of its own, equipping thousands of racegoers with considerable knowledge and systematic procedure encompassing the entire range of the handicapping art, but also advanced the frontiers of knowledge about the sport itself.

And because it depends on fundamental knowledge, the method begs revision whenever the knowledge base of handicapping gets extended through research or changes in the sport itself. First set forth in *The Compleat Horseplayer* (1966), and following successive revisions from

1968 through 1986, the latest version incorporates well the new evidence regarding the importance of early speed and the need to liberalize standards of form.

Taking distance and form as the starting points, and proceeding to jockeys, weight, class, age, sex, and consistency, Ainslie first presents elimination guidelines, standards of performance against which horses' records must pass muster, or the horses themselves are eliminated from further consideration. The survivors are the contenders. These are next differentiated on pace. The separation process continues by comparing the horses' records on a list of plus factors, these designed to reflect the subtleties of handicapping. Next come the paddock and post-parade inspections, where horses that figure best on paper must look acceptable in the flesh. If selections survive all of this, handicappers can finally check the odds and decide whether they have found a good bet.

In systematic but not mechanical manner, handicappers proceed to apply a series of negative guidelines that identify contenders to the application of a series of positive guidelines that separate the contenders. Noting that handicappers might start with any factor that suits their personal tastes, as comprehensive handicapping eventually must touch all the factors, Ainslie recommends distance and form considerations to begin, as these two factors reliably eliminate the largest number of noncontenders.

Of class, Ainslie reminds us that the handicapping process sometimes ends abruptly here, if one horse outclasses its rivals notably. Handicappers already know that the horse is suited to the distance and in acceptable form. If a final check indicates that the horse's class edge should not be nullified or seriously blunted by today's probable pace, it figures, and the handicapping for all practical purposes has been completed.

To separate contenders, Ainslie emphasizes that pace analysis supersedes pace ratings, and in the latest edition of the method he stresses that pace analysis should begin by estimating the influences and probable effects of the early speed. Where early speed looks inconclusive, pace analysis concerns the relationship between fractional times and final times. Ainslie sets out to find the horse that either will set and maintain the fastest fractions or will track and overcome the early fractions. The Plus Factors cover the full range of the handicapping process but many of them reflect the critical interplay as between class and form.

If no horse qualifies, or too many do, comprehensive handicapping has found the race unplayable, and therefore unbeatable. The method is designed to determine whether one horse has an unusually good chance to win, and not to provide action on unreliable horses or overly competitive races.

Full-dress comprehensive handicapping is more intricate than the above capsulization suggests. Once unfit, outclassed, and horses ill suited to the distance are eliminated by applying the negative guidelines, what counts is how handicappers relate performance on each factor to all others. Weight and post-position performance normally have incidental effects on race outcomes, for example, but those influences will have more or less effect depending on the horses' comfort with the distance, degrees of class, or relative fitness. To attempt a condensation of comprehensive handicapping as method almost necessarily violates the basic tenet of the method, which, after all, honors comprehensiveness. For now, it will be instructive to review some of the basic elimination guidelines for the fundamental factors of distance, form, and class. These eliminate systematic errors of the grossest sort. Handicappers who continually support horses whose records violate one or more of the following precepts are prone to mistaken judgments of the most fundamental character.

The following guidelines apply to horses aged three or older.

Of distance, a horse qualifies at today's distance if (a) it has won a race of this exact distance; or (b) it has finished close (within three lengths) to the winner at today's distance in respectable time and the race occurred this season; or (c) it finished fourth and within two lengths of the winner at the distance this season.

The concept of "respectable time" has been defined in terms of *Daily Racing Form*'s speed ratings, not to be confused with Beyer Speed Figures. The cutoffs are:

90—Sprints of handicap and stakes quality
88—High-grade allowance sprints
85—Handicaps and stakes run around two turns
80—High-grade allowance routes, lesser allowance sprints, and sprints for claiming horses valued above $7,500
78—Cheap claiming sprints
73—Route races for better claimers
69—Route races for claimers valued at $4,000 or less

Excepting the occasional sprinter that might take the early lead and control the pace, horses four and older competing at new distances are best eliminated.

Of form, when analyzing claiming races:

(a) Horses at seven furlongs or less must have raced within the past calendar month at today's track, a sister track, or a track of superior class.

(b)   A horse at longer than seven furlongs must show a race within the past month plus two workouts in the meantime. If it has raced within two weeks and shows one workout, it is acceptable. If it has raced within the past week, no workouts are necessary.

(c)   A horse entered at seven furlongs or less can be regarded as a potential contender even if it has been unraced for 45 days, providing it has been working out at intervals of four or five days and has previously won after absences of such lengths.

When considering allowance, handicap, and stakes horses, these need not have raced so often to maintain sharpness, but they are seldom acceptable unless they have worked out frequently, recently, and with respectable times (12 seconds a furlong).

Regarding basic fitness and soundness standards:

(a)   Throw out any horse that bled, ran sore, or finished lame in its last race.

(b)   Throw out any horse that lugged in or bore out in its last race.

(c)   Throw out any horse that is stepping up in class after a race it won while losing ground in a driving stretch run.

(d)   Throw out any cheaper four-year-old or older horse that engaged in driving finishes in each of its last two races.

(e)   Throw out any horse aged five or older whose best effort at today's distance occurred in its last race, unless the horse is a male that demonstrated reserve speed in that race.

(f)   Throw out any claimer whose last race was a "big win" more than two weeks ago.

Of class, eliminations remain consistent with these guidelines:

(a)   No horse aged four or older is acceptable in a handicap or stakes unless it usually runs in such company and either has won or finished in the money when so entered.

(b)   No three-year-old is a good candidate in a handicap or stakes race against older horses unless it has already beaten such a field, or has been running with exceptional power against its own age, suggesting a clear edge in intrinsic class and condition.

(c)   To be acceptable as a contender in an allowance race, a horse whose last start was in a claimer should have won an allowance race on this circuit or one of equal class, or should be facing other nonwinners of such allowance races, and should not be asked to defeat another contender that has run in the money in a handicap or stakes within the last three months.

(d) In claiming races no horse can step up as much as 50 percent when comparing the top price today with the claiming price at which the horse was entered last time.

(e) In maiden races and races for nonwinners of two races, three-year-olds are almost invariably better prospects than the older, chronic losers they meet in such fields.

(f) No horse can be conceded an advantage in class because it has raced against higher-class horses than it will meet today unless the horse beat at least half the field or showed high early speed in the higher-class race.

Because the method is at once basic and intricate, comprehensive handicapping is simultaneously appropriate for beginners and intermediate-to-advanced handicappers. Because it is comprehensive, the method has something for practically everyone, regardless of persuasion.

The elimination guidelines can be considered ultraconservative in the modern game. They should not be helpful in identifying overlays having a decent chance to win, but they can be useful in evaluating favorites and low-priced contenders rather strictly on the form, class, and distance factors.

CHAPTER 14

UNIT WAGERS
AT THE ODDS

THE RECORDS OF professional handicappers have taught them how to make seasonal profits. These result from betting to win, but not so often at odds below 3-1. To be sure, horses at 8-5 might represent outstanding overlays (true chances better than public odds), and these can be bet confidently. An overlay at any price is part of a mathematical pattern that must end in success. Yet the record shows that handicappers earn their profits from bets on better-priced horses. The dividing line is reported at 2-1. Above that, handicappers' win percentages may drop, but not enough to alter the profit picture. Students of win-loss ratios above and below odds of approximately 3-1 report that handicappers win frequently enough at the higher odds to concentrate the higher bets there.

The implications of this for unit wagering ($2 or $5 or $20 or $200 or whatever) are clear, if difficult to apply. The size of the bets should increase as the odds increase.

Various experts have recommended the following escalation:

At 3-1 or below, one unit
At 7-2 or 4-1, two units
At 9-2 or 5-1, three units
At 6-1, four units
At 7-1 or above, five units

All studies agree that handicappers win enough at the higher odds to justify the higher wagers. At the same time, unit wagering at 3-1 or below amounts to little more than spinning wheels. Neither the profits nor the losses become significant. If unit bets correlate with size of the odds, a $20 bettor will bet $100 when his selection goes at 7-1 or greater. If he is the kind of handicapper that wins 40 percent on the dollar, raising the bets as odds grow will improve the rate of return.

Tom Ainslie, who long has advocated fixed percentage wagering, advises that unit wagering in ratio to the odds should not be tried with 5 percent of capital as the basic unit. Otherwise, handicappers bet 25 percent of capital when the 10-1 horses arrive. Theoretically, this works, but few of us have the temperament for the bets. Ainslie recommends 1 percent as the base, thus 5 percent on the longshots.

To sustain profits that are not seasonal, perhaps weekly or monthly, unit wagering in this manner can include place bets. The pros tolerate place bets when (a) horses stand out at 7-2 or greater; and (b) the favorite figures to lose. If both conditions prevail, handicappers can bet one unit to win and two units to place when their selection is (a) 7-2 or better in a field of seven starters or more; (b) 3-1 in a six-horse field; and (c) 5-2 in a field fewer than six.

To repeat, the race favorite must smell like a loser.

Perhaps the most simplified of all the acceptable long-term wagering methods, the main problem experienced with unit bets that increase as odds increase is the psychology of the approach. Having been conditioned forever to bet more on shorter-priced horses, handicappers have difficulty extinguishing that baseless approach and learning to bet more when the risk goes up. Regardless, as the books assert, there can be little doubt many handicappers can tolerate the new approach and profit extensively from it.

CHAPTER 15

PADDOCK INSPECTIONS REVISITED

Until Bonnie Ledbetter broke into print with descriptions of equine body language, handicappers assigned most if not all horses with copious kidney sweat to the no-bet category. None could be fairly regarded as a betting stickout. All worlds change. Sweating horses are sometimes the sharpest horses in the field. The sweat is part of a keyed-up profile of the sharp, impatient horse clamoring for competition. Handicappers can now not only recognize the sharp horse that might be sweating, they can distinguish it unmistakably from the frightened horse that is sweating as well. Ledbetter has spelled out the differences.

Ledbetter has also revealed that the most critical object of the handicapper's paddock and post-parade inspections is a part of the horse barely touched by previous literature—the ears. More on that momentarily.

In a collaboration altogether helpful and rewarding to handicappers everywhere, when Tom Ainslie combined the body language of horses, as supplied by Ledbetter, to formal principles of handicapping, the resulting inspections guidelines served to extend the knowledge base in the esoteric area tremendously and to alter several preexisting notions that no longer apply.

Even the foundations of the paddock visit have been shaken. The purpose heretofore was to look for negative signs. If horses that figured on paper failed the paddock inspection, races were passed, or at times second choices were upgraded. Handicappers now are advised that horses inseparable on paper can sometimes be distinguished in the paddock and post parade. This represents a fundamental departure in procedure. If contenders are separated at the paddock, previous unplayable action increases, and handicappers had better understand what they are about.

Ainslie reminds us that 90 percent of all races are won by horses described as sharp, ready, or dull. The remaining 10 percent are taken by frightened, angry, and hurting horses, which handicappers presumably avoid. Sweat and kidney lather can be characteristic of both sharp and frightened horses, which represent by far the most interesting dichotomy of body language. Handicappers can support sharp horses on those grounds alone, avoid frightened horses for like reasons. They should set out to become expert about the two profiles. Ledbetter and Ainslie are greatly reassuring on the point, asserting that the body language of each kind is unmistakable.

Of the sharp horses, these may not only sweat but also dance and wheel almost fractiously, affecting apprehension or nervousness, but otherwise are the embodiment of health and vigor. The coat luxuriates with a shine or dapple. Mane and tail gleam. Neither fat nor bony, its rear muscles haunch and perhaps ripple. The animal prances on its toes, a picture of eagerness, often with neck arched, head tucked downward toward the chest, the ears pricked forward, tail up to signal readiness. The horse is alert to the crowd and surrounding commotion. It is not quiet in the saddling stall, but rather full of itself, almost showing off, head in the air, dancing confidently, and this language intensifies during the parade to the post. The lead rider may have to take a short hold of it in the parade, lifting its nose in the air, lest the sharp horse throttle the lead pony. When warm-ups begin, the sharp horse strides out strongly off the haunches in the first couple of strides, tail up, muscles tensing. Sometimes the horse's head will almost touch its chest, neck arched, ears pricked fully forward. The horse almost lunges into the gate and once inside stands firm, back feet planted, fronts at times shuffling and restless. It springs out of there like jet propulsion. There might not be many of these sharpsters, but they are well worth the hunt. They are, in the banker's lexicon, bettable.

The sharp horse's opposite number, the frightened horse, begs the player's automatic elimination. Its sweat and fractiousness are not symbols of excitement but of fear. Reluctant and resistant en route to the paddock ceremonies, there, and in the walking ring, its head is held high and in continuous motion, eyes rolling so that the whites become visible, ears flicking rapidly in all directions, unsynchronized. Leg action in front is high and uncoordinated, tail swishes from side to side or up and down.

The handler might control the horse with a stud chain over the nose, under the lip, or across the mouth. The horse fights the chain, perhaps moving in a semicircle in front of the lead horse, pulling and yanking to get away from it all.

During saddling, walking, and mounting, the horse washes out and moves about kicking and stomping in unorganized maneuvers. Eyes roll, ears flick, nostrils flare. It resists its handlers, who in turn fight back. In the walking ring the frightened horse may wheel and circle away as the jockey attempts to mount. During the post parade the jockey has a tight hold, even as the horse clings to the lead pony as much as possible, perhaps extending its head and neck across the pony. If the lead rider prevents that with the chain, the horse's head is high, eyes and ears moving wildly, the front legs stepping high and sideways. The lead horse proceeds straight down the course, but the frightened horse moves in short, spastic jumps at an angle to the pony.

Before the starting gate arrives, all energy and hope have been lost. This kind also throws tantrums in the gate, casting itself or hanging over the partitions. Coincidence determines what happens when the gate opens. Often, frightened horses burst out first, as if fleeing, but they exhaust themselves in a panicky run long before the homestretch. If they break tardily, they typically show keen bursts of speed that catch the others but deplete the horses of late speed, such that they are absolutely exhausted just as the stretch run begins.

Handicappers already may be familiar with the ready, dull, and hurting horses, but not so with the angry horses, characterized by Ledbetter as the sour kind easily provoked during the prerace ceremonies. Ill-tempered, angry horses range from mildly irritated to wildly furious, and all but the mildly irritated should be expected to lose. Angry body language differs from the language of fright, but the result is the same. Angry horses rarely sweat. The telltale sign of its annoyance is flattened ears or, in furious moments, ears pinned directly onto the head. Handicappers should not fail to consult Ledbetter for the angry profile and are well advised to renew acquaintances with the ready, dull, and hurting kind.

Handicappers are also alerted that sharp horses can turn angry during any phase of the prerace ceremonies, if distracted or upset by handlers or circumstances. If horses behave fractiously when parading before the stands, dancing sideways, rearing, or bucking, heads tossing up and down, and tails swishing, handicappers who have not visited the paddock and many who have will have difficulty recognizing whether the horses remain sharp or are seriously fractious. What differentiates the two conditions at this crucial point is the position of the ears. The ears of the sharp horse remain alert and in the forward position, or perhaps turned backward to the chirping rider, but straight. But if the ears flatten or become pinned or assume the airplane position, even as the tail swishes and pops irritably, the horse is now out of sorts. Handicappers should continue to watch the horse, paying attention to the ears. If they remain flattened or pinned, avoid the horse.

Ainslie relates the body language of horses to the fundamental factors of handicapping in numerous important ways. A few:

Closely matched contenders can sometimes be separated at the paddock. If one looks particularly sharp, and the odds beckon, the bet makes sense. These horses not only are overlays and figure well enough on fundamentals, they look like winners in the flesh. In this special context, handicappers prosper by inspecting horses for positive signs of fitness and readiness.

Dramatically improved form together with dramatically improved appearance equals a potentially sweet bet.

Of horses that appear dull or hurting, only those that have won previously when in comparable condition can be considered a potential play.

The most debilitating and negative experience for a young horse is the stumble or actual fall. As Ledbetter tells, for a horse, loss of balance is perceived as a threat to survival.

If a horse's behavior deteriorates as soon as the jockey climbs aboard, and the jockey has lost with the horse while others have won, handicappers can fairly assume incompatibility between horse and rider. They should not expect a triumphal return.

More than ever before, handicappers can prepare themselves to benefit from the body language of horses. The language is not learned quickly. Familiarity and practice make the difference. The study of horses' body language moves from Ledbetter and Ainslie to the paddock, walking ring, and post parade, and back again, numerous times a season.

CHAPTER 16

BRED FOR GRASS

PEDIGREE STUDIES HAVING largely revealed that breeding for performance represents the sport's richest crap shoot, breeding as a factor in handicapping has merited only limited application. William Quirin's probability studies changed that forevermore. They demonstrated irrefutably that talent on turf is strongly related to pedigree. Moreover, horses whose breeding promises good performance on turf regularly win at boxcar prices when first tried over grass. If the dirt performances have been ranged from ordinary to awful, the public will shy from the horses, but handicappers in the know can back them enthusiastically when they switch to the grass.

Quirin identified a prepotent sire line as well as the contemporary sires and broodmare sires whose descendants ran best on the lawn. The sire line of Prince Rose was the prepotent family. Handicappers can still appreciate the important influence of Princequillo, whose grandson Stage Door Johnny was one of the most influential turf sires of recent generations. Two sons of Princequillo, Prince John and Round Table, exerted tremendous influence on successful grass racing. Another son, Prince Chevalier, engendered a less well known but important line.

Probability studies have identified the sires and broodmare sires that afford handicappers not only a significantly better than expected chance of winning, but also of netting profits on a series of $2 wagers. Refer to the *Daily Racing Form* chart later in the chapter.

Even today, the entire Princequillo line wins approximately 160 percent their expected share of turf races and returns handicappers a $2 net profit while doing so.

As broodmare sires, the entire lines of Prince Rose and Princequillo win much more than expected with $2 profits ranging from $3.49 to $3.61, powerful performance statistics.

Quirin combined the data on these sires along with selected others in numerous ways to discover the most propitious ways handicappers might proceed toward profits in turf racing. These findings can be accepted as maxims:

1. Horses with potent turf breeding should be bet when attempting their first or second starts on grass. The horses are generally underbet, in opposition to horses that have raced on turf without winning, and therefore represent overlays that yield seasonal profits.
2. Most profits await handicappers who play turf breeding on horses that go postward at odds of 10-1 or greater. This might represent the richest source of longshots handicappers have ever discovered scientifically!
3. If both sire and broodmare sire are influential turf parents, results can be expected to be all the better.
4. The first start on grass of appropriately bred horses can be either a sprint or a route.
5. Good form on dirt is not a prerequisite for backing horses with turf breeding when they switch to grass. Dirt form helps, but is not necessary. Poor dirt form horses win less frequently, but return larger profits.
6. The most rewarding second start on turf is one that immediately follows the first start. If the horse returns to dirt before a second start on grass, its attraction diminishes greatly—no play.
7. Horses that win the first turf start do very well when bet right back, but horses that lost their first start "with honor," finishing within a length of the winner, do even better. These win 313 percent their appropriate share of their next races, and return a 30 percent dollar profit.
8. Appropriately bred horses do best when their first turf start occurs in maiden races or in nonwinners allowance races.

Quirin's updates of his original tabulations appeared annually for a time, but no longer. The researcher found that horses carrying the blood of stallions on the original list do especially well themselves. Handicappers can expect the descendants of these sires to carry the cause:

Secretariat	Majestic Light
Tentam	King Pellinore
Big Spruce	Fifth Marine
Shredder	Little Current

Daily Racing Form routinely publishes a table of leading contemporary turf sires. Here is the list of leaders for 2003 and beyond:

A.P. Indy	Kingmambo
Abstract	Kris S
Alphabet Soup	Lite the Fuse
Avenue of Flags	Local Talent
Benton Creek	Lord At War ((ARG)
Bold Laddie	Mister Jolie
Danzig	Mr. Prospector
Delineator	Northern Trend
Dixie Brass	Nureyev
Exclusive Era	Once Wild
Fabulous Champ	Pick Up The Phone
Falstaff	Quiet Enjoyment
Forest Wildcat	Rhodes
Free at Last	Royal Academy
Frency Deputy	Smokester
Frosty The Snowman	Storm Cat
Game Plan	Strodes Creek
Glitterman	Tale of The Cat
Gold Ruler	Tejano Run
Grand Slam	Valid Appeal
In Excess	Valid Expectations
Is It True	Valid Wager

The Tomlinson Ratings

NEW YORK INVESTMENT BANKER and horse owner Lee Tomlinson took up the handicapper's cause after the Quirin sires lists were discontinued. Using proprietary formulae, Tomlinson created his Tomlinson Ratings for evaluating horses making their first and second starts on the turf.

Tomlinson studied the sons and daughters of sires and of the broodmare sires. The research provided a rating for sires and broodmare sires ranging from zero to 300. Manuals that listed as many as 11,000 sires were published and handicappers were advised to add the rating for a horse's sire to one-half the rating for the same horse's broodmare sire.

Tomlinson supplied a cut-off value of 280 and horses rated there or above 280 were held to have high potential for turf racing. Soon the long-shots with strong Tomlinson Ratings began to win, and users not only were impressed, but also licked their chops over the exciting new edge.

Daily Racing Form eventually purchased the Tomlinson Ratings and they have printed them in the lifetime-statistics tables of the past performances for all users to see. The ratings appear in parentheses to the right of the word "Turf."

When maidens on the grass are the menu, the Tomlinson Ratings are indispensable, and they take precedence over trainer, jockey, and workouts. The higher the rating, the better. In practice, ratings above a threshold level of 360 can throw seasonal profits when used to back horses at 10-1 or greater. Handicappers must remember that in concert with high Tomlinson Ratings, the inexperienced grass starters should be accompanied by high odds. Tomlinson Ratings are not recommended to support first and second starters on the turf as favorites or low-priced contenders. The ratings best support overlays and longshots, an especially agreeable circumstance.

The Tomlinson Ratings will be helpful whenever younger, lightly raced horses are switching to the turf for their first or second try. Winners can be uncovered in the allowances, the stakes, and even in the claiming races. A particularly useful application supports inexperienced grass runners on the second attempt, when the first attempt has been good and occurred within the past 30 days.

A less apparent application, urged by Tomlinson himself, supports European imports having *low* Tomlinson Ratings for the turf, when the horses are being switched from the grass to the main tracks in the United States.

CHAPTER 17

AN APPROACH
TO NONCLAIMING
THREE-YEAR-OLDS

I N *THE HANDICAPPER'S CONDITION BOOK* this writer argued that nonclaiming three-year-olds present handicapping problems peculiar to them. In contrast to older, well-established horses, their class levels remain uncertain, form cycles uneven, and distance-footing-pace preferences elusive. Not much about them is reliably known or understood for a time, not even to their owners and trainers. This regularly contributes to upsets of one kind or another, as either horses do not repeat big wins or others in apparently dull form snap suddenly to life and win waltzing.

What to do?

The proper solution treats nonclaiming three-year-olds as the developing horses they are. It requires of handicappers that they analyze three-year-olds' past-performance lines using methods particularly suited to younger, still developing horses. Such methods must diverge from absolute commitment to class-consistency handicapping, or speed handicapping, or even comprehensive handicapping, as these rely one and all on recent races and best efforts to provide telltale indicators of what should happen today. For older horses, recent races and best efforts normally supply accurate and stable indicators of true performance. But the past performances of nonclaiming three-year-olds may provide neither.

An alternative to common practice was termed total-performance handicapping and demanded study of the entire three-year-old record. Only in this way, handicappers were advised, could they appreciate a young racer's pattern of development. All three-year-olds were held to proceed to true levels of performance by one or an admixture of four patterns of development that were characterized as stereotypical. Further, by recognizing the attributes of class young horses demonstrate in today's race, handicappers best understand whether horses fit conditions. The stereotypical patterns of development are reproduced here. The class demands of races progress from the moderate speed and basic competitiveness of maiden races to the increasingly necessary combinations of speed, endurance, and competitiveness required to win allowance, classified, and stakes races. Handicappers equipped to identify performance patterns and to match attributes of class to the class demands of races not only eliminate errors of the grossest kind, but also zero in on nonclaiming three-year-olds that outclass eligibility conditions or fit those conditions especially well.

In practice, total-performance handicapping systematically examines three component parts of a three-year-old's record. Present performance refers to the last out or two and indicates whether the current form can be regarded as weak or strong under today's conditions. The power component begins the critical assessment of class and potential class. Handicappers find the horse's best performance under the most difficult conditions it has faced. What qualities of class and potential does the race provide? Next, handicappers examine the race following the power performance, to determine whether the expected improvement or performance actually occurred. Are the power performance and its aftermath consistent or contradictory? If consistent, contradictory, or inexplicable, how to reconcile?

Finally, handicappers supplement indices of current form and class potential with information about the entire pattern of development. They go back to the first three-year-old race and proceed upward through the past performances to the present. This procedure illuminates overall achievement and potential, yields best indications of distance-footing-pace preferences, often explains apparent inconsistencies and contradictions in the recent record, and determines whether the horses fit today's condition well, outclass them altogether, or merely figure to lose.

Here's an instructive example of how total-performance handicapping can expose attractive nonclaiming three-year-olds that really do not fit the race as potential winners should. It's October 1980 at Santa Anita. Read the conditions, and apply the proposed method to Back'n Time's entire three-year-old record.

7th Santa Anita

1 MILE

1 MILE. (1.33⅗) ALLOWANCE. Purse $40,000. 3-year-olds and upward, which have not won two races of $13,750 at one mile or over since April 7. Weights, 3-year-olds, 116 lbs.; older, 120 lbs. Non-winners of $13,750 since July 21 allowed 2 lbs.; since June 1, 4 lbs.; since April 7, 6 lbs. (Races when entered for $40,000 or less not considered.)

Back'n Time

110

Dk. b. or br. c. 3, by First Back—Exigency, by Prize Host
Br.—Post Time Stables (Cal)
Tr.—McAnally Ronald

Own.—Post Time Stables

1980 5 3 0 1 $24,825
1979 0 M 0 0

21Sep80–100MF	6f	.21²	.43⁴	1.07⁴ft	*1-2	113	1hd	1⁴	1⁷	1⁶	Valenzuela P A¹	Alw 98 Bck'nTime,VoomVoom,AmnBrothr 9
6Sep80–7Dmr	6f	.21²	.44	1.08²ft	*1-2	118	1½	1³½	1⁴	1⁴½	Pincay L Jr⁴	Alw 95 Back'nTime,StatelyNtive,BronzeStr 7
22Aug80–6Dmr	6f	.22	.44¹	1.08¹ft	*3-5	117	1¹½	1⁵	1⁹	1¹⁰	Pincay L Jr³	5 Mdn 97 Back'n Time,Trammell uck,Donald 11
13May80–2Hol	6f	.21⁴	.44¹	1.10¹ft	5½	118	42½	31½	32½	32½	McHargueDG⁵	M50000 84 Olympd'sSon,WurfrdBlly,Bck'nTm 11
5Jan80–3SA	6f	.21³	.45	1.10³ft	13	118	52½	63½	83½	59½	McHargueDG⁹	5 Mdn 76 WoodlndLd,SgcosStory,FortClgry 12

Oct 28 SA 1 ft 1:43² h ● Oct 15 SA 7f ft 1:25¹ h Oct 8 SA 6f ft 1:14² b Oct 1 SA 4f ft :50⁴ b

As *The Handicapper's Condition Book* explained:

This classified mile admitting three-year-olds during Oak Tree at Santa Anita 1980 provides an instructive note on which to end this discussion.

To recall, classified conditions of fall can often favor late-developing three-year-olds, which have projected a higher class under nonwinners conditions. The colt Back'n Time certainly fits that description. Moreover, six months of the core season have elapsed since April 7, the specified date of the classified restrictions. Any horse that has won two or more routes of classified or stakes quality has effectively been barred from the competition, the usual layups excepted. The conditions are thus relatively restrictive. So much more in favor of developing three-year-olds.

Does Back'n Time figure to win in a breeze? Not according to total-performance handicapping procedures, which are enlightening in this instance, as is so often the case.

Having won a maiden race and two allowance races, Back'n Time can be credited with having proceeded to advanced nonwinners allowances. Its power performance Sept. 21 at Del Mar surely indicates Back'n Time will be a monster sprinting under NW3 conditions if not pressed hard on the front. What the victory says about the future races under classified or stakes conditions at longer distances or on turf is far more speculative, much more risky.

The total record is similarly of concern. After a hapless performance Jan. 5, the colt was not favored in a maiden claiming sprint four months later, which it lost. No one wanted the claim. Next came the rejuvenating workouts and the devastating maiden and preliminary nonwinners races at Del Mar. Back'n Time might have an exceptional future, after all.

But the time to bet on it was not the Oak Tree classified mile. Not only was the fast colt attempting a distance of two turns for the first time, but also it was jumping greatly in class. Do the Del Mar races support the combined moves? They do not. Anyone who watched the Del Mar romps saw a fast but free-running colt, and ability to get middle distances had to be of concern. With classier horses running at it, that concern should have mounted. At low odds, handicappers prefer to pass, rather than risk good money.

Back'n Time weakened in the final sixteenth of the Oak Tree mile and lost the decision to a middling classified miler of no previous distinction. Had better horses been eligible, Back'n Time would have lost more persuasively, notwithstanding its strong betting favoritism. As events proceeded, a nondescript animal proved good enough to handle this developing three-year-old. But the race was written for just that kind of nondescript classified maverick. I hope handicappers who begin paying stricter attention to racing conditions will stop betting on young colts that are not favored by the conditions, and therefore do not figure to win.

Three-year-olds' patterns of development:

The races entered by nonclaiming three-year-olds often reveal them as horses of a kind. Developing horses proceed to the core of competition in one of four stereotypical patterns, depending on abilities exhibited in their earliest races. They can be referred to as Class A, B, C, or D. Here are the four patterns handicappers can identify.

Class A
Maiden, nonclaiming
Allowance, nonwinners other than maiden or claiming
Allowance, nonwinners twice other than maiden or claiming
Allowance, nonwinners three times other than maiden or claiming, or conditioned and open stakes
Allowance, nonwinners four times other than maiden or claiming, or open stakes, listed or lower grade
Grade 2 stakes
Grade 1 stakes

Class B
Maiden, nonclaiming
Allowance, nonwinners other than maiden or claiming
Allowance, nonwinners twice other than maiden or claiming
Allowance, nonwinners three times other than maiden or claiming, or conditioned and open stakes

Claiming races, at relatively high price brackets, or allowance, non-winners three times other than maiden or claiming

Claiming races, at high-to-moderate price brackets, or classified allowances, or minor stakes or conditioned stakes

Class C

Maiden, nonclaiming

Allowance, nonwinners other than maiden or claiming

Allowance, nonwinners twice other than maiden or claiming, or claiming, at relatively high price brackets

Claiming races, at high-to-moderate price brackets, or allowance, non-winners once or twice (if eligible)

Claiming races, at moderate-to-low price brackets

Class D

Maiden claiming

Claiming races, at moderate-to-high price brackets, or allowance, non-winners other than maiden or claiming

Claiming races, at moderate-to-low price brackets

Claiming races, at relatively low price brackets

The classifications overlap, the sequences vary. Class A three-year-olds of April, competing then in nonwinners three times allowances or conditioned stakes, may be struggling against Class C claiming horses by September.

Handicappers often get a direct line on three-year-olds by examining the sequence of good performances, however embedded in the total record.

CHAPTER 18

ABILITY TIMES

SOCIAL-SCIENCE RESEARCHERS refer to operationally defined variables that exist solely in testable hypotheses as constructs. These are usually single measures of two or more factors whose true relationships are otherwise difficult to define. The measures are admittedly artificial and sometimes arbitrary, obtaining validity only to the extent that they can be shown to work admirably well for given purposes in the real world.

Who would have believed it? The study of the great game of handicapping had by 1982 become so scientific a pursuit that handicappers have now had delivered to them the game's first demonstrably effective construct. It has been called ability times. In *Investing at the Racetrack*, author William L. Scott carefully defines ability time as "an artificially constructed time element out of a portion of a race, designed to represent both speed and class."

Having determined through extensive preliminary research of his own that speed and class were two of the three factors that distinguished Thoroughbreds the best, Scott next set out to represent horses' abilities in terms of their combined speed and class. He succeeded, notably, with the discovery of ability times, an invention Scott ultimately converts to standard figures, to be modified in turn by considerations of form and early speed.

It is all curiously compelling, particularly the logic that not only sustains Scott's fundamental ideas but also supports his numerous adjustments to the basic times and figures, as well as his rules for constructing "ability" figures and for applying them. What makes Scott's logic still more compelling is his repeated assertion, so true, that however much other handicappers beg to differ with it, this is precisely what works. That is to say, Scott's arguments have been handed down after the fact. They evolve only after months of laborious empirical research have finally revealed the winning formulae.

Although Scott's pursuit of a speed-class figure that reflects horses' basic abilities was only part of a more ambitious campaign to prove a fail-safe system of handicapping for profit, the ability-time construct will undoubtedly be lifted out of that grand context. On the thought that speed handicappers and class handicappers everywhere might wish to incorporate into their methods an adjusted time that represents both factors satisfactorily, Scott's methods for constructing ability times can be usefully generalized here.

Scott's measure of racing ability in sprints is the final-quarter time of the race, called lead time, modified by two adjustments: for lengths gained and for energy expended. The calculation is quite easy.

Consider the latest race of the New York claiming sprinter Self Pressured:

Here are the procedures that apply:

1. The lead time from the quarter pole to the finish, or second call to final call, is 25 seconds.
2. Between the two calls, Self Pressured is credited with gaining only one length.

The horse actually gained five lengths, as indicated in the past-performance line, but Scott found that the lengths-gained calculation should not be made from a second-call-beaten-lengths number greater than eight lengths. Thus Self Pressured advanced from "eight" lengths behind at the second call to seven lengths at the final call, a gain of one length.

In Scott's formula for lengths gained (shown at the end of the article), which translates lengths gained to fifths of seconds, and is based on the finding that five lengths gained equates to four-fifths of a second, a gain of one length equals one-fifth second gained.

The lengths-gained time equivalent is subtracted from the lead time for the race. Thus Self Pressured's ability time, adjusted for lengths gained (1), is 24⅘.

3. The energy adjustment concerns the expenditure of early speed and depends on a horse's ability to reach the second call in less than 47 seconds (46 seconds in California). If the horse does, no adjustment is made. If a horse runs to the second call in 47 seconds or slower, an adjustment is required according to the following formula:

47 to 47⅘	add ⅕
48 to 48⅘	add ⅖
49 to 49⅘	add ⅗
50 to 50⅘	add ⅘

Twelve lengths behind a 45⅗ lead time at the second call, Self Pressured is estimated to have run to the quarter pole in a tardy 48 seconds, a ⅖ penalty.

By adding ⅖ to 24⅘, handicappers arrive at Self Pressured's ability time. It is 25⅕.

REGARDING THESE CALCULATION rules, and numerous others in the original work, the researcher's chant applies. To wit, these are the rules that work best. In technical language, they are empirically valid.

Scott recommends handicappers calculate several ability times in a horse's past performances and use the two best. At sprint distances other than six furlongs, as with Self Pressured on March 17, final times must first be equated to six-furlong final times, and Scott provides a formula for the conversion.

Interestingly, Scott's use in sprints of final-quarter times as indicators of speed-class dynamics traces to his discovery that differences in final-quarter times for horses racing over fast and slow track surfaces respectively, that is, California strips and Eastern strips, were smaller than comparable differences in final times. Where final-time differences were of a full second or greater, final-quarter times often differed by as little as two-fifths or one-fifth. Scott replicated that finding when studying fast and slow surfaces in Florida. Thus he reasoned the final-quarter times represent a truer index of basic ability across horse populations than final times, track speed notwithstanding.

In route racing the distances from the second call to the finish varied so that they rendered those time comparisons impractical. Scott found that for those regularly run routes where the first and second calls represent four and six furlongs, the most accurate estimates of basic ability relied on the time differences between the four-furlong and six-furlong calls. Lead times are calculated, and the lengths gained and energy adjustments are applied, as for sprints. Where the two calls do not represent four and six furlongs, Scott has treated each distance independently. Handicappers wanting to calculate ability times for horses in the various route races should consult Scott in his provocative book.

There handicappers will find, too, the means for converting ability time to speed-class figures, based on fundamental considerations of form and early speed. They will discover much else besides, all of it adding up to a veritable model of empirical research at the racetrack. Few handicappers might choose to apply Scott full-scale. On the other hand, few can afford to ignore this large, meticulous field study and the significant contributions it contains. For example, the formula just below:

Scott on Lengths Gained:

Therefore, we now adopt a 5-for-4 formula for lengths gained as converted to fifths of seconds. We shall equate five lengths with four-fifths of a second. We can also deal with fractional lengths with more flexibility, and these fractional lengths will embrace slight shadings of error and leave us with a more realistic rating all around. Here is a simple chart showing how we will treat lengths behind in terms of fifths of a second where a gain is involved.

This is one of the most important tools to be applied in rating horses. You must learn this formula, accept it, apply it. It is relatively easy to learn, even though it may look difficult. As soon as you use it a few times, it will become much easier. Surrounding five for four, it flows up and down in proper sequence.

Gain in Lengths	Gain in Fifths of Seconds
Less than One	None
1 to 1¾	One
2 to 2¾	Two
3 to 3¾	Three
4 to 4¾	Three
5 to 5¾	Four
6 to 6¼	Four
6½ to 7¼	Five
7½ to 8	Six
8 and More	Six

Handicappers might fairly substitute Scott for their own beaten-lengths calculations, and anticipate better results.

CHAPTER 19

HORSE AND JOCKEY SWITCHES

PROBABILITY STUDIES DEMONSTRATE generally that changes of jockey, weight, and post position have incidental effects on race outcomes, except when combined with changes that are more fundamental. Handicapper-writer-lecturer Mark Cramer has combined the fundamental and the incidental to elaborate a demonstrably effective system of play at major tracks that over successive monthly time frames has provided handicappers with unusually complementary rewards, high action, and high profits. The profits regularly soar. A May 1981 workout at Hollywood Park returned 98 percent on investment. A December workout returned 91 percent, after Cramer lopped off two longshot winners as not representative. Cramer's data indicate that handicappers can expect approximately 33 percent winners on 60 to 65 plays a month, with average winning mutuels near $11. The longest losing skein has been seven.

The system is pleasing to the handicapping taste as well, and readily digested. If two events occur simultaneously, Cramer hypothesized, (a) a class drop and (b) a favorable jockey change, the trainer has a live horse and is taking out insurance. The rationale for the system emphasizes trainer intentions. As all know, when the horse is primed to win, its chances improve against easier competition and with superior jockeys. Regardless of whether the race is actually easier or the jockey better, trainers perceive these differences and believe the switches favor their horses.

Systematizing the rationale involves two simple rules:

1. The horse must be taking a drop in class.
2. The trainer must be switching jockeys from either a lower to a higher category of winner, or from within the same winning category, unless the jockey switch is to a rider that handled the horse in its latest victory, or to a rider that is perceived as a specialist under today's conditions.

The class drops are defined as (a) stakes to allowance, (b) allowance to claiming, and (c) higher claiming to lower claiming. Magnitude of the drop is irrelevant.

Jockeys are categorized by win percentages. Jockey standings for the past season and the current meet produce a normal curve that identifies "leading," "excellent," and "good" categories. To illustrate, Cramer notes the final 1980 standings in southern California showed that Laffit Pincay Jr. and Chris McCarron won at above 20 percent, with the next best jockeys clustered near 15 percent. Pincay and McCarron were defined as "leading." The next cluster, "excellent," included Eddie Delahoussaye, Sandy Hawley, Bill Shoemaker, and Darrel McHargue. At "good" were jockeys Patrick Valenzuela, Fernando Toro, and Terry Lipham. The curve is regenerated after each meeting. Jockeys are systematically added, dropped, or reclassified.

In categorizing jockeys, handicappers are best guided by two indices: current win percent, and trainer perceptions. Is the jockey winning consistently? Is the jockey "hot," and perceived to be "hot"? Remember, the jockey changes can be from any lower to higher category, or from within a given category that is favorable.

To break ties (more than a single horse qualifies), a horse must have any one of the following attractions:

1. Switching to a rider who has won before with the horse.
2. Switching to a "leading" jockey.
3. Dropping from allowance to $40,000 claiming or less.
4. Switching to a rider with a well-known talent for the type of race; for example, in southern California, jockey Pat Valenzuela is widely perceived as a talented rider on front-runners, amazingly adept at breaking first and fast out of the gate.

If ties are unbroken and two horses qualify, play both.
If three or more horses qualify as an unbroken tie, discard the race.

Successive workouts with the system indicate a normal distribution of winners, similar to results achieved by fundamental handicapping selections, with profits unbiased by unrepresentative longshots. Implementing the system requires neither results charts nor arithmetic, just the past performances. All qualifying horses must be played, irrespective of odds.

The results of two monthly workouts six months apart are highly similar, as indeed are the workout distributions themselves:

Results of System Workouts

	May 1981	December 1981
Playable races	65	62
Amount invested ($2 base)	$130	$124
Profit	$127.60	$104
Percentage of winners	35	33
Return on investment (dollar)	.98	.91
Average mutuel	$11.20	$11
Most successive losses	5	5

The continuity and internal consistency of Cramer's system at southern California tracks suggest that when drop-downs are mounted by more favorable jockeys, handicappers have come within an arm's length of systematic profits. To the extent the findings generalize to other major tracks, handicappers everywhere can enjoy the same sweet fruits of Cramer's research.

CHAPTER 20

TREND ANALYSIS

WHETHER TOTALIZATOR ACTION signifies inside money or not is less important to handicappers than whether the action represents a betting trend that wins frequently enough to matter. A field study of parimutuel price fluctuations lasting an amazing 18 years has identified only two winning betting trends. At the same time it reveals a losing trend that often fools handicappers into expressing false confidence with real money. In presenting his research, engineer Milt Gaines muddied the issues with extravagant claims of financial success traceable solely to biased samples of exotic wagering, and weakened his case with sloppy illustration, yet some of the substantial evidence not only survives, it may be persuasively useful to handicappers who prefer their key selections get inside support on the board. Gaines is not a handicapper, rather a tote watcher and trend taker. Thus his method is trend analysis. When Gaines spots a winning betting trend, he bets. As he carefully points out, the best of all worlds unites a winning betting trend with solid handicapping selections.

The two betting trends that frequently signify inside action ("insiders" are held to have more information or knowledge than the average customers), and win, are characterized by odds lines moving in opposite directions. In one the odds first fall below the morning line, shift quickly upward, and finally fall again. In the second, the odds first change to a line higher than the morning line, eventually but not immediately fall significantly lower, and may rise again near the end of the betting. Gaines presents two variations of each pattern, detailing each trend in terms of the kinds of odds changes handicappers should expect as the minutes before post time trickle there. Here we illustrate the two positive trends, and describe the variations. Of much concern, too, is a variation of the most frequently successful trend that is an abject loser. That trend, too, is illustrated below.

The most frequently successful betting trend Gaines refers to as an H1 trend. (H honors the late Lou Holloway, who studied price fluctuations and trend analysis and delivered, in 1957, the most important work on the topic, *The Talking Tote*.) It looks like this:

Morn Line	Open Line	10 Min Line	5 Min Line	2 Min Line	Bet Line	Close Line
4-1	8-5 9-5	2-1 5-2	3-1 3-1 3-1	5-2 8-5	8-5	8-5

or like this:

10-1	2-1 5-2	3-1 4-1	6-1 8-1 8-1	6-1 5-1	9-2	9-2

An H1 trend satisfies these rules:

1. The first odds change (Open Line) shows a line lower than the morning line by at least half.
2. The odds move upward until post time nears (2 Min Line).
3. The odds drop once or twice near the end of betting.

Gaines refers to Step 2 as absorption, meaning that the public interprets the early inside betting as dropping the horse below its true odds, and therefore not worth a bet, thus the odds steadily rise. Step 3 Gaines calls confirmation, whereby the inside money that did not bet early now reacts to the public's misinformed generosity. Late betting is essential to an H1 trend. If it does not occur, no play.

In a positive variation of H1 (H6), the initial change is lower than the morning-line odds, but not by half. The subsequent trends remain firm.

In a more important variation of H1 called H2, the well-backed horse can be fully expected to lose. In the opening flash, the odds indeed fall below the morning line by at least half. But they stay low. In fact, they never again exceed the first flash (Open Line). Gaines provides this example of H2:

Morn Line	Open Line	10 Min Line	5 Min Line	2 Min Line	Bet Line	Close Line
2-1	1-1 1-2	1-2 1-2	4-5 3-5	4-5 4-5	3-5	1-2

H2 horses are getting strictly public money. These likely look solid in the past performances and were probably selected by several public experts. The inside money steers clear of this kind, and Gaines advises handicappers to do the same. The horses are underlays. As such, a series of bets on them guarantees loss. Gaines's data support the point. If handicappers believe the horses won't lose, Gaines urges they pass the races.

More common than the H1 trend, but not as successful, is H8. It goes like so:

Morn Line	Open Line	10 Min Line	5 Min Line	2 Min Line	Bet Line	Close Line
5-1	12-1 16-1	14-1	12-1 8-1 6-1	7-1 8-1	9-1	10-1

To qualify as an H8 trend:

1. Open odds (Open Line) must be at least twice the morning line.
2. Several successive drops must occur prior to the 2 Min Line. Importantly, the drops must each be more than a single point.
3. Near the end of betting, the odds rise again.

In this trend the inside money bets between the end points of the public action. The horses figure better than the public realizes, and the insiders know it. Since inside money tends to be big money, odds can be expected to drop by more than a single point. At lower odds, the drop simply might skip the next logical level, that is, the 4-1 horse drops to 3-1, skipping the conventional 7-2 level.

H8 horses being common, these often find their way into races that also contain H1 horses. If the two trends conflict, and just one H1 trend has begun, handicappers should back the H1 horses relentlessly. Gaines's data show that the H1 horses win 70 percent of the races where this type of conflict arises. But if two or more H1 horses have been entered against a single H8 horse, the H8 horse figures to upset. Handicappers' money belongs on H8.

Trend analysis is held applicable at both major and minor tracks. Here are selected guidelines supports by Gaines's data.

1. Do not consider trends until a meeting has been active for at least two weeks. Insiders are less likely to bet until form over the track begins to emerge.
2. Do not bet trends where one or more horses in the race are first-time starters. Maiden and juvenile races are susceptible to trend analysis, but not until all starters have started previously.
3. Do not bet on a trend until the final two minutes. The later the better, especially when considering the H1 trend.
4. Be skeptical of early action on the strongest of public selectors' horses. Winning trends on horses not selected by public selectors represent much better bets.
5. Demand that the bettable horses be outstanding illustrations of the winning trends. If trends look vague or ambiguous, pass. Best bets equal outstanding trends combined with outstanding handicapping selections.
6. Beware of races having two H1 trends, especially at smaller tracks. The insiders are playing games.

CHAPTER 21

PACE ANALYSIS
BEATS PACE RATINGS

PACE AS A fundamental factor in handicapping can be mishandled as readily as any other, perhaps more so. Among the most serious malfunctions has been the tendency to treat a horse's performance during a single race segment, or combinations of segments, as the critical index of its pace ability. It's a variation on the strictly rhetorical question: Which is the most important factor in handicapping? Pace fanciers seek to know: Which is the most important segment of the race? The answer to both questions is the same: None.

The early Ray Taulbot, for example, promoted pace to the half-mile in sprints, and to the three-quarters in routes, as the critical indicators. His contemporary Hugh Matheson argued the opposite, that the third quarter-mile of sprints, the third- and fourth-quarter times of routes, were most important. Huey Mahl proposed a hybrid approach, whereby the first quarter combined with the final quarter told the tale. Colonel E. R. Bradley remains celebrated for his lasting remark that any horse that last time out had completed the final quarter-mile of a race in 24 seconds or less was worth a bet next out.

None of these assertions squares with the classic definition of pace, which is that pace refers to the relationships between running styles, fractional times, and final times. Thus it should not be surprising that the most comprehensive study of pace yet conducted has revealed that segments of the race are not as important as the race taken in its entirety.

Even as no single factor is most important in handicapping, no single segment of a race's pace should be considered most important, at least not in the absolute sense many handicappers set sail to discover.

John Meyer, publisher of the *National Railbird Review,* selected thousands of races nationwide to study the relative importance of eight pace segments. Defining pace as a rate of speed, measured by dividing distance by time (feet divided by seconds equals feet per second), Meyer asked what percentage of winners in four types of races also had run at the fastest pace during each of the segments.

Here is a summary of the findings:

Percentages of Winners by Pace Segments During Which They Ran at the Fastest Rate of Speed

Type of Races	Start to 1st Call	1st Call to 2nd Call	2nd Call to Finish	Average Pace, 1st 3 Calls
Dirt sprints	.25	.19	.09	.31
Dirt miles	.21	.16	.26	.16
Dirt routes	.43	.09	.09	.27
Grass routes	.20	.17	.23	.27

	Start to 2nd Call	Start to Finish	1st and Last Call Combined	3rd and 4th Calls Combined
Dirt sprints	.22	.41	.19	.03
Dirt miles	.16	.32	.26	.26
Dirt routes	.43	.39	.17	.09
Grass routes	.12	.30	.17	.27

The relatively high percentages in the "Start to Finish" column indicate that generally the greatest number of winners can be found by determining which horses can maintain the highest rate of speed throughout the race, and not just for particular segments of races.

As 43 percent of Meyer's winners in dirt routes (1¹⁄₁₆ miles to 1½ miles) also had shown the highest rate of speed to the first call, and to the second call, a much higher winning percentage than that of the sprints, Meyer suggests handicappers pay greater attention than traditionally supposed to early pace leaders in routes.

In both dirt sprints and dirt routes, speed to the first call is associated with many more winners than speed demonstrated between first and second calls, or between the second call and the finish. In the same kinds of races, however, speed from the start to the first call and speed from the start to the second call are associated with comparable percentages of winners. Apparently handicappers can fairly interchange first- or second-fraction times in their calculations of pace ratings.

Handicappers who concentrate their pace calculations on the combined final segments (third and fourth calls) of races are working with less than 5 percent of the winners in sprints and less than 10 percent of the winners in routes. Such handicappers will be making many dismal forecasts. Only slightly more advantaged are handicappers who combine the first and last calls in their pace ratings, as Mahl has recommended.

Meyer concluded handicappers will be keeping company with the greatest number of winners if they base pace calculations on entire race segments. Thus his findings support the definition of pace as the relationships between fractional times and final times.

The Meyer study supports, too, a conclusion about pace far more fundamental. Pace analysis supersedes pace ratings. Instead of rushing to ratings, by focusing on the rate of speed dished out during one favored race segment or another, handicappers benefit if first they consider how races might be run today, which horses might contest or press the lead at the various points of call, and what might be the likely effects of the pace confrontations at each point. This kind of pace analysis will be most effectively completed in a broader context that simultaneously considers class and form. To put it simply, pace analysis extends a fundamental kind of race analysis.

And so it goes, if a horse that figures to contest the early pace also figures to be outclassed by early rivals, it does not figure to win, its previously high ratings notwithstanding. Likewise, the prospects of horses suited to the class demands of early pace duels, but short of form, or dulling in form today, are dim prospects. Such horses might lose even if they carry the race to the second or third calls, and even if they wield the highest pace ratings. The high ratings presumably were earned when the horses raced in tip-top shape.

After analyzing which horses should do what, in relation to the probable pace to each point of call, and deciding what the likely effects at each call will be, handicappers have identified those horses that figure to survive a comprehensive pace analysis.

Now handicappers can rate the identified horses, relying on key races within recent times and applying methods whose resulting numbers reflect horses' abilities at both fractional points and final points.

As Meyer's study reminds us, when handicappers set out to discover with arithmetic whether one horse is likely to set and maintain the fastest pace or to track and overcome that pace, they best limit the calculations to horses that have already distinguished themselves as genuine contenders on pace, as revealed by pace analysis.

When, at last, pace ratings are employed to separate contenders, Meyer recommends that handicappers calculate horses' rates of speed in feet per second. The method describes a ratio between distance traveled and time recorded and eliminates the common practice whereby one length is equated to one-fifth of a second. The one-to-one equation is not sufficiently accurate.

By Meyer's method, a horse that ran a furlong (660 feet) in 12 seconds would be credited with a rate of speed at 55 feet per second. The horse that does a furlong in 11⅗ seconds goes 56.9 feet per second. When a final time is considered, the beaten-lengths adjustment used by Meyer is 11 feet per length. The small differences in feet per second that normally result from these pace calculations need not be so upsetting to handicappers. As Meyer shows, even tiny differences in feet per second translate to significant differences in ground covered during the race. To illustrate the point, Meyer shows how a .05 feet-per-second difference represents approximately a yard of ground in a six-furlong sprint completed in 1:11 seconds.

Or enough to explain the difference between victory and defeat.

CHAPTER 22

RACE SHAPES

In *THOROUGHBRED HANDICAPPING: State of the Art,* Bill Quirin lays down a speed-pace methodology that simultaneously accomplishes the following:

1. Adjusts fractional times to tenths of seconds indirectly, simply by noting the pace pars associated with speed pars (final times).
2. Makes speed figures that are compatible with the sum of the old-style speed ratings and track variants of *Daily Racing Form.* The compatibility renders the comparisons of all horses facile, regardless of distance or racetrack.
3. Introduces the concept of par variants (the average differences from track records across the same sample of races on which par times for the various class-distance categories were established) and ingenious procedures by which all shippers can be reliably evaluated.
4. Shows how to predict speed figures (final times) today, based upon the pace figures contending horses will be forced to exhibit.
5. Uses pace and speed figures to illustrate nine configurations of pace, or race shapes, and tells the kinds of horses that should benefit from each.

The concept of race shapes emphasizes an interpretive function of speed handicapping, which methods that focused on final times alone did not permit. The nine shapes prove to be extraordinarily useful to all of us.

In this essay I suggest a truncated variation of Quirin's method for recreational handicappers who eschew figures but are willing to adjust raw times utilizing pars and daily variants.

First, some additional discussion of Quirin's speed-pace technique is important.

In recommending that pace pars be stated in tenths of seconds, Quirin notes that studies of thousands of races show that class-distance speed pars (final times) differ by just one-fifth of a second. These differences are one-half as great at the pace call. Quirin refers to the phenomenon as a telescoping effect. One-half of one-fifth is one-tenth. The second call is used in both sprints and routes. Since the telescoping effect has been statistically verified at 50 percent, once final times are known, the associated pace adjustments are readily inferred.

The truly ingenious part emerges, too, from statistics. Quirin has discovered that a $10,000 claiming horse is a $10,000 horse is a $10,000 horse anywhere, from New York to Maryland to Florida to Oaklawn to southern California, as reflected by the times these horses normally run. By assigning a figure of 100 to the regularly run $10,000 distance pars, an amazing assortment of comparisons become tenable. Speed handicappers who have ignored pace pars are urged to consult with Quirin. A practical imperative for doing so is the reduced odds now offered regularly on final-figure horses. A caution is that Quirin's method is technical, laborious, and complicated. Yet it's a greatly intelligent extension of modern speed methodology.

The present purpose, however, is more concerned with the interpretations plausible once the pace-speed figures have been elaborated and juxtaposed.

Quirin recounts the hilarious symposium exchange with Andrew Beyer on the subject:

Beyer: "What do you do with your pace and speed figures once you have them?"

Quirin: "I look at them."

THE REACTION, of course, was laughter. But Quirin was serious, pressed the point, and won it.

He reminds handicappers that state-of-the-art figures have not only a predictive value but also an interpretive function. To interpret past performances, it's best to examine speed-pace figures analytically. The pace figure help explain the speed figure. Quirin discusses nine possible explanations, or nine configurations of pace. He refers to the nine as race shapes.

Using figures for sprints and speed pars (final times) of 105, Quirin interprets the nine race shapes in terms of the running style each favors:

Average-Average (105-105): A completely typical race for the class. Favors no particular running style.

Average-Fast (105-108): An average pace leading to an above-average speed figure. Usually the result of a strong front-running performance.

Average-Slow (105-102): An average pace that fell apart, with nothing able to rally in the stretch and sustain the figure. A rallying performance here can be deceptive, warns Quirin, not as good as it might appear.

Fast-Fast (108-107): The most impressive shape of all. Anything close at the wire has raced exceptionally well.

Fast-Average (108-105): An above-average performance if by a front-runner. If won from behind, the winner was taking advantage of an exceptionally quick pace.

Fast-Slow (108-102): An above-average pace that had a telling effect. Not a bad performance if won in front, but exceptionally weak if the winner ran late.

Slow-Fast (102-108): An exceptionally strong performance by a horse that got away with leisurely fractions. Especially impressive if won from behind.

Slow-Average (102-105): The winner was able to finish strongly and record an average figure despite a slow pace. Usually won by a front-runner, but most powerful when won by a stretch-runner.

Slow-Slow (102-102): A complete washout. Nothing in the field was able to run early or late. Most unimpressive are front-runners unable to capitalize on an advantageous slow pace.

HANDICAPPERS WITHOUT FIGURES can incorporate pace into their procedures by resorting to adjusted times. They will need speed and pace pars, of course, plus daily variants.

In Quirin's applications, when the adjusted speed-pace times of sprints are two lengths faster than par, respectively, the race is Fast-Fast.

In routes, three lengths faster at the fractional and final calls equals Fast-Fast.

Two lengths slower at each call is Slow-Slow in sprints, three lengths is Slow-Slow in routes.

A sprint having adjusted times two lengths fast at the pace call and a length slow at the final call is Fast-Average.

A route having adjusted times two lengths fast at the pace call and four lengths slow at the final call is Average-Slow. And so forth.

Once the daily variant has been tabulated, identifying a day's race shapes consumes roughly 20 minutes. First adjusted times are calculated. Then adjusted times are compared with the pace-speed pars. The race shapes can be quickly recorded. Handicappers benefit if they immediately consider which horses in the field benefited from the shape of the race.

A two-year application of the method at Santa Anita Park has persuaded me the Fast-Fast shape is tremendously advantaged in claiming races. It beats the other shapes repeatedly, often at double-digit prices. The same finding may generalize well to other major tracks.

The interpretive value of numerical handicapping ratings has long been a debatable item. The numbers can sometimes obscure the relationships they're intended to clarify. Speed figures have disappointed many users repeatedly on precisely this point. The numbers too often have been more impressive than their interpretations. Quirin's speed-pace methodology and the race shapes they represent narrows several of the interpretation gaps.

If two horses brandishing the same speed figures exit a Slow-Average race, the first front-runner, the second a closer, which is more impressive? It's the closer.

Two closers earn the same speed figures. One exits a Fast-Average race. The other exits a Slow-Fast race. Which most likely warrants the bet next time? It's the Slow-Fast pattern.

Which is the more impressive winner of two Fast-Average races having similar final figures, the speed horse or the closer?

Modern speed handicappers are fully expected to know.

CHAPTER 23

FORM DEFECTS,
FORM ADVANTAGES

THE CONTINUOUS EMPIRICAL research on Thoroughbred form indicates that horses can be absent from the races for six months or more, but if they have worked five furlongs or longer within 14 days of today's race, they are acceptable. In 1968, Tom Ainslie's classic chapter on form advised handicappers that horses that did not show a race and a workout within the past 17 days, or if unraced, had not worked out within the past 12 days, should be eliminated.

The divergent views reflect the most significant trend in form analysis across the past decades, a dramatic shift from conservative to liberal interpretations of form patterns. If the publication in 1984 of William L. Scott's *How Will Your Horse Run Today?* means anything, it is this: Handicappers will get more from their wagering dollars as soon as they begin to liberalize their standards of acceptable form. Remaining rigid or even strict with traditional form guidelines means eliminating too many winners, many of them at juicier prices than "good form" horses have normally returned.

Scott's intention with his form research was to identify more specific handicapping guidelines than had previously been clarified, a purpose at which he succeeded impressively, but the specifics speak volumes about the more general trends that all smart handicappers must abide.

Besides the warning to loosen the grips on firmer form standards, handicappers need to be cautioned more specifically that recency has been greatly overrated. Handicappers have known for years now, since the first national probability studies hit the market in the mid-1970's, that powerful stretch performers won no more than the expected share of their next starts. Often they were overbet. Scott's descriptive data support the probabilities. The book awards pluses to four of the five form factors its author studies, but no matter what, horses cannot be considered at advantage next time due to outstanding performance in the stretch.

Before summarizing Scott's specific findings, it is important to understand the evolutionary context. Historically, the American horseplayer has confronted two persistent, fundamental problems with form analysis. First, operational definitions of good and bad form were practically nonexistent prior to 1968. Because the horse populations and racing calendars were so different, Robert Saunders Dowst, the leading handicapping author of the 1930's and 1940's, virtually ignored the form factor.

No one else much bothered with the matter until Ainslie set forth his numerous elimination and selection guideposts. Since then, more rigorous examinations of specific "good" and "bad" form standards have crystallized the second historical problem—horses having "good" form regularly collapse on the profit criterion. Positive-form horses win more races than probability estimates would expect, but they also toss considerable losses while winning. The probability studies of form proved mainly that the public bets too much money on good-form prospects. These go postward as underlays and are often favored to win.

In the 1990's several handicapping authors attacked the form factor with empirical studies–based upon their extensive personal experience— intended to identify patterns that might project to improved form, or peaked form, next time. Good form that would underpay was eschewed. Hidden form that would overpay was relished.

The publication of professional speed figures by *Daily Racing Form*, and other sources, led to the fascinating trend whereby figure patterns were recognized as contributing to positive or negative form next out. One of the best, most comprehensive treatments of figure patterns as harbingers of improving and declining form on record was published by *DRF*'s New York handicapper Dave Litfin in 1995, and that work is summarized elsewhere in this anthology.

In *Kinky Handicapping* (TBS Publishing 1993), the peripatetic Mark Cramer examined virtually every generally accepted principle of form analysis, in all cases looking for logical opposites that also win. Cramer's discoveries shed light on hidden-form patterns that not only win enough, but also pay well.

One of the most recent examinations of form, by Cary Fotias, has uncovered a dynamic relationship between early pace and peaking condition, a contribution not to be missed by the thousands of modern handicappers that now use pace figures.

The latest contribution to form analysis comes from Joe Cardello, whose *Speed to Spare: Beyer Speed Figures Uncovered* (DRF Press, 2003), gives readers an entirely new perspective on pattern recognition, probably the most important skill in using the Beyer figures correctly.

What has been needed by casual users of the *Daily Racing Form* are carefully observed empirical studies of highly specific form indices that operate within the well-established parameters of recent action and acceptable performance. Author Scott has contributed exactly that kind of research, precisely those kinds of results, concentrating first in 1981 on a 433-race sample encompassing Belmont Park, The Meadowlands, Keystone, and Bowie racetracks, next testing initial discoveries variously at selected tracks around the nation, and culminating with a 500-race national replication during 1982.

A key result has been designated the "form defect," or a disadvantage on form that predicts reliably which horses will probably lose. As form defects are often characteristic of favorites and low-priced underlays, those eliminations open the handicapping decisions to solid prospects at better prices, the overlays found to enjoy form advantages, and these can be incorporated into the rating processes of whatever methods handicappers of varying persuasions might prefer. A third rating category has been called neutral. Neutral ratings are acceptable, but inconclusive.

Scott explored five topics of interest, after his original investigations identified these as the directions of most promise. The five include recency, the last usable running line, stretch performance, last-race winners, and declining-improving cycles of performance. There are four rating symbols:

0   Form defect: Eliminate

N   No significant impact, or neutral: Accept

+   A plus factor: Give extra credit

U   Unknown: Do not rate

It's instructive to list Scott's crucial results in regard to recent action. The first plus factor will be familiar to handicappers, but the second will not, and the remaining four findings suggest that in the future more horses than ever will be acceptable on recency.

+   Has run within seven days or fewer of today's race
+   Has run within 21 days of today and has either:
     a. a 5f bullet workout within 14 days
     b. a 5f workout that is exceptionally fast, such as 59⅗ in the East or Midwest, or 58⅗ or less in the West
N   Has run within 21 days of today's race
N   Has run within 28 days of today's race and has worked 4f within the past week
N   Regardless of layoff time, has worked 5f or longer within 14 days
O   Has not run in 21 days, without a qualifying workout

Scott has labeled his plus factor for exercise in the morning "the fabulous five-furlong workout," explaining the move is both unusual and tremendously impactful at all tracks below the rank of New York and southern California. Scott makes clear that sharp recent action is more of an advantage to racehorses than dull recent form is a disadvantage.

Scott shows handicappers how best to evaluate what he calls "the last usable running line," which is normally the last race, provided it was run within the past 28 days and was not unrepresentative due to class or footing differences or to notable trouble lines. The rating depends on the presence or absence of "up close" position, usually at the stretch call. Being "up close" is defined variously, in relation to distance, as follows:

a.	Sprints up to 6½ furlongs	2¾ lengths
b.	Races at 7f and 1M	3¾ lengths
c.	Races at 1¹⁄₁₆ miles or farther	4¾ lengths

Horses are generally acceptable on performance if they were "up close" at the stretch call, but horses shortening distance by a furlong or more can be up close at the pre-stretch call. Claiming horses dropping in class can be "up close" at any call. A well-defined fall-back/gain-again pattern is also acceptable. A plus is awarded only to horses "up close" at every call of the last race, provided that race is "usable."

All horses that do not qualify for the plus or neutral ratings receive a "0," a form defect, to be eliminated. The exceptions are "U" horses, including first-time starters, first-starters on grass, and foreign horses in their first United States race.

This research recommends handicappers attend more to recent performance patterns than to recent action. That is, performance indices surpass training indices.

Which horses that won last out are likely to repeat today?

In general, and absolutely for horses rising in class, it's the horses grad-uating from a "big win," or victory by at least three lengths, and having another plus factor for form. Maiden graduates must satisfy those twin conditions as well, but horses not moving ahead in class can show two form pluses of any kind, or even a single plus factor if they also reveal high consistency. Scott cautions that as many as nine of ten last-out win-ners do not repeat, and he sets up strict repeat-win conditions to protect handicappers from that downside.

In the book's most complicated and technical sections, Scott presents an arithmetical technique for identifying declining and improving form. The procedure relies on information provided by the *Daily Racing Form*, final times and speed ratings, but three preconditions must coexist before the rat-ings can be calculated. To be eligible, horses must show at least a length gain (closer to the leader) at the stretch calls of their previous two races, and the races must represent the same class and distance. Where those conditions are present, handicappers will apply a handy technique for evaluating declining and improving form numerically. It's a convenient and valid advance.

Scott's kind of research is empirical—descriptive, iterative, laborious, and a function of scheduled observations involving numerous reexami-nations of the same data, until plausible patterns apparent on first obser-vations have been confirmed for the total sample of races. The research method does not examine prearranged hypotheses but instead follows a kind of intuitive search for what works.

Because the research is descriptive, it intends to describe a group or class or predefined populations, or races. These have not been sampled randomly. This reduces the generalizability of the findings, not in any essential way, but in particular variations that may differ from track to track, notably at racetracks with different horse populations and racing programs from the five that comprised this study, including its application for a day at Golden Gate Fields. Minor tracks are not well represented here, and handicappers there and elsewhere are recommended to con-duct local replications.

It's rather easy, to be sure. As one interesting approach, if the per-centage of winners having form defects was divided by the percentage of starters having form defects, say for a group of 250 to 400 races, the resulting quotient would be an impact value (I.V.), or probability index. That value should be 0.5 or lower.

In short replications of two weeks or less, this writer applied the book's findings to Hollywood Park, Keystone, Santa Anita, Golden Gate Fields, and Arlington Park. They worked impressively. They did not work as well for three days at Longacres, a small track near Seattle.

CHAPTER 24

INTERNATIONAL RACING AND THE HANDICAPPER'S NEW EDGE

IT HAS BEEN two decades since the three-year-old English import Tolomeo flew to Chicago, upset the great John Henry in the 1983 Arlington Million, and paid $78.40. The $2 exacta with John Henry on the underside paid $439.20.

As the relevant information was inaccessible in 1983, few Americans realized that Tolomeo was an authentic contender. A month earlier, on July 27, he had finished second of 11, to older handicap horses, no less, in the sixth-richest group event of England, the Sussex Stakes (Group 1). Or that his previous five races had been Group 1 events, and in four he had finished second or third, beaten a head and a neck in two. Or that the bookmakers' odds in England on Tolomeo to win the Arlington Million had ranged from 4-1 to 8-1.

Comes soon a letter from one Winford Mulkey, of Siloam Springs, Arkansas. "Did you know that on the simulcast of the Arlington Million to Louisiana Downs, the winner paid over $200 to win and the exacta ($3) to John Henry paid *six thousand dollars!*" I did not know. Simulcasting remained an infant. Furthermore, had I been in attendance at Louisiana Downs on that memorable August 28, 1983, I could not have seized the moment. I would have not been well-enough informed to use a $30 exacta box between Tolomeo and John Henry, collect nearly $60,000 in a gigantic scoop, and retain bragging rights to the greatest exacta overlay in Thoroughbred racing.

Nonetheless, the 1983 Arlington Million and its provocative result did have a salient effect. It introduced the American horseplayer to the delights of international racing; specifically, to the overlays lying in wait for handicappers willing to come to terms with the records of European imports. During the next six to eight years, the golden years, so to speak, the number of European imports increased terrifically, the odds on most of them remained ridiculously high, and many of them won, and won again. Handicappers aware of the general superiority of European racing, especially in relation to the overnight racing in the United States, prospered handsomely from the international edge.

In his wonderful chapter on European racing in *Bet with the Best* (DRF Press, 2001), *Daily Racing Form* foreign editor Alan Shuback recalls Tolomeo's upset in the 1983 Arlington Million as the start of something new and big for the American horseplayer; namely, the advance of international racing and the opportunities in store for properly armed handicappers. Shuback remembered the race as a personal lesson as well, as he had watched Tolomeo run in Goodwood's Sussex Stakes on his first trip to England during July of 1983. In talking to British observers about the colt, Shuback had learned that Tolomeo should have won the St. James's Palace Stakes (Group 1), where he was beaten a head, following a troubled break, and that his best distance was probably the mile and one-quarter on good-to-firm turf.

As Shuback tells, and handicappers appreciate, so much has changed in regard to the European imports and international racing. The relevant information has improved, and correspondingly the odds have plunged. Still, as the French have admonished, the more things change, the more they remain the same. European turf racing is still superior to the American brand, and European imports still arrive in large numbers, and not only do they infiltrate the daily programs in New York, Florida, Kentucky, and southern California, but also many of them still win as overlays. Not as gigantic overlays, a la Tolomeo, perhaps, but as significant overlays that beg the handicapper's attention.

Shuback's treatment of European racing is the best on record; informative, instructive, and even inspiring in its insistence that the best way for American handicappers to learn about racing on the continent and the horses there that will matter in the months ahead on American programs is to spend two weeks a year in Europe. Shuback even presents the racing itinerary not to be missed.

Before recognizing the essentials of European racing, as revealed by Shuback, handicappers benefit from a terse summary of the sources of their greatest overlays, not only from European imports, but also from the ever-increasing imports from South America, Australia, and to a lesser extent, from New Zealand, South Africa, and lately Dubai. Keeping in mind that European racing is superior to American racing, handicappers should understand that their biggest edge is a function of relative class. Look longingly for situations where imports from Europe should simply outclass the conditions of eligibility and the American horses at those levels.

If the class edge is significant, it does not matter that the imports have not run in six months, or that they will be running on an unfamiliar surface (dirt), or at an unrelated distance (marathoners apart), or that the pace may be faster. The imports will win enough of the races, and several of them will pay much more than they should.

Here are the golden opportunities that repeat themselves weekly:

1. Imports exiting the listed and group (graded) races of England, France, Ireland, Germany, and Italy, where they have exhibited just a trace of ability, and are entered under allowance conditions limited to nonwinners once or twice other than maiden or claiming races.

A relatively new wrinkle in the U.S. nonwinners allowance conditions often supplements the phrase "nonwinners once (or twice) other than maiden or claiming," with "or nonwinners of two (or three) races." As the majority of European imports will have broken their maiden status in non-maiden races, these winners have already won a race (or two) equal to or superior to the American NW1XMC/NW2XMC allowances. If the same imports have shown ability in listed or group stakes as well (early speed, a mid-race move, a finish within six lengths, has beaten half the field), the horses probably possess a significant class advantage. If the imports go as non-favorites, take the money.

2. Imports from South America and Australia that have won the equivalent of a Grade 1 or Grade 2 race there and remain eligible to the nonwinners once or twice allowances here.

When evaluating non-European imports, standards of class evaluation must be tightened, and strictly. International pattern committees evaluate the stakes races of North America and Europe by examining the quality of the past three editions, but local jurisdictions evaluate the stakes races elsewhere. Whereas the former is relatively objective, the latter is highly subjective, rather like Churchill Downs or Santa Anita evaluating its own races. A definite and positive bias creeps into the proceedings.

Unless the imports of South America and Australia already have won a major stakes in the homeland, it's difficult to comprehend their relative class under nonclaiming conditions in the States. Ungraded (or nongroup) and unlisted stakes of Australia and South America can be considered analogous to overnight races in the U.S., but their relative quality remains a mystery. Handicappers best wait to see. The same standards might be applied to the imports of New Zealand, South Africa, and Dubai entered under allowance conditions here, although now the horses should have won or finished close in multiple Group 1/Group 2 stakes in the homeland.

3. European winners and close runners-up of listed and group stakes on the continent entered in minor stakes (unlisted, ungraded, and purses of $100,000 and lower) in the U.S.

Even though the purses of the European listed and group events will be lower than numerous minor stakes in the U.S., the competition is keener. While the U.S. cards thousands of minor stakes races, Europe cards only a couple hundred of the listed and group variety. The class edge of the European imports in minor stakes here can be equally keen. When the imports of South America and Australia are entered in minor stakes here, handicappers find the classier overlays among horses that have won *two or more* Grade 1 or Group 1 stakes in the native land. Unless the records are undeniably strong and the odds are attractive, it's usually best to avoid the imports of New Zealand, South Africa, and Dubai when they appear in U.S. stakes.

The class edge that guides the handicapper so reliably in the above situations recedes when European imports are entered at the listed and graded stakes levels here. Although the comparisons will be complicated, effective handicapping has been bulwarked by new information in the past performances of imports. To appreciate the advances, examine the past performances of the pair of imports on the next page.

In February 1984, Ice Hot was entered at 6½ furlongs on the downhill turf course at Santa Anita under NW4XMC allowance conditions.

On the Preakness undercard at Pimlico, in May 2002, Siringas was entered in the Grade 3 Gallorette Handicap, for fillies and mares, purse of $125,000, at 8½ furlongs on the turf.

Only handicappers in possession of special information not embedded in the past performances could have backed Ice Hot at 5-1 and collected $12.80 when the colt won going away. Not revealed by the past per-

Ice Hot B. c. 4, by Icecapade—Beau Fabuleux, by Le Fabuleux
Br.—On The Rocks Farm (Ky) 1984 11 3 0 4 $52,892
Own.—Paulson A E 113 Tr.—McAnally Ronald 1983 3 1 1 0 $12,279
Lifetime 14 4 1 4 $65,171 Turf 14 4 1 4 $65,171
9Oct83♦3Longchamp(Fra) a7f 1:192fm 5½ 127 ⓘ 1½ DubrecqG Px du Pin IceHot, Lichine, AfricanJoy 10
22Sep83♦5MLaffitte(Fra) a1 1:363gd 23 126 ⓘ 12 AsssnC Hcp de laTamise Ice Hot, Mauve Lilas,WaterMelon 20
4Sep83♦3Longchamp(Fra) a1⅝ 2:053gd 23 122 ⓘ 32½ PiggottL Px del Table H Port Franc, Regal Step, Ice Hot 24
24Aug83♦6Deauville(Fra) a1 1:43 gd 8½ 122 ⓘ 3¾ Gibert A Px de Varavle Dayzaan, Conerton, Ice Hot 7
15Aug83♦3Deauville(Fra) a1 1:392gd 18 118 ⓘ 13 Head F GrdHcp deDevlle BellTempo,FiddlersGreen,Relayeur 17
2Jly83♦5Evry(Fra) a1⅛ 1:592gd 17 128 ⓘ 44½ DbrcqG Px Daphnis(Gr3) Glenstal, Luderic, Redmead 7
Feb 8 SA 5f fr 1:004 h ●Jan 27 SA 5f fr :591 h Jan 20 SA 6f fr 1:122 h Jan 14 SA 6f fr 1:14 h

10 Siringas (Ire) B. f. 4 Blinkers OFF Life 8 3 2 0 $116,879 98 D.Fst 0 0 0 0 $0 –
Own:Skymarc Farm Inc Sire: Barathea*Ire (Sadler's Wells) 2002 2 1 1 0 $32,650 98 Wet(267*) 0 0 0 0 $0 –
Blue, Yellow Triangular Panel, Yellow Dam: In Unison*Ire(Bellypha*Ire) L 112 2001 5 1 1 0 $77,525 96 Turf(340*) 8 3 2 0 $116,879 98
Br: Cyclades Farming Co (Ire)
PRADO E S (—) 2002:(573 113 .20) Tr: Clement Christophe(1 0 0 0 .00) 2002:(108 26 .24) Pim ⓣ 0 0 0 0 $0 Dstⓣ(450) 2 1 1 0 $49,175 98

11Apr02-6Kee fm 1⅛ ⓣ :47 1:112 1:353 1:473 4↑ ⒻAlw 63050N3X 97 6 23½ 23½ 2hd 11½ 21¼ Prado E S L118 b *1.40 98-06 Beefeater Baby1161¼ Siringas1183½ Alida1181 Pressed,led,2ndbest 6
13Mar02-7GP fm 1 1/16 ⓣ :242 :494 1:14 1:444 4↑ ⒻAlw 36000N2X 98 4 11½ 12 11½ 12½ 14 Bailey J D L117 b *.90 72-29 Siringas1174 Cozy Island1212 Herzblatt1175 On rail, widened 7
Previously trained by Bolger James S
26Oct01-5Bel fm 1 1/16 ⓣ :251 :484 1:13 1:42 3↑ ⒻAthenia-G3 96 4 2½ 2hd 1hd 1hd 2no Bridgmohan S X L112 b 16.30 86-15 Verruma114no *Siringas*1121 Freefourracing113hd Vied inside, gamely 8
8Sep01♦Leopardstwn(Ire) gd 1¼ⓣ LH 2:014 3↑ Irish Champion Stakes-G1 620 Manning K J 120 66.00 Fantastic Light130hd Galileo1236 Bach1304 7
Timeform rating: 88 Stk 929000 *Rated in 5th,never a factor*
2Sep01♦Curragh(Ire) yl 1 ⓣ Str 1:391 3↑ ⒻMatron Stakes-G3 107¾ Manning K J 122 6.00 Independence1221 Toroca122hd Danceabout127nk 11
Stk 73300 *2nd after 2f,3rd 3f out,weakened 2f out*
19Aug01♦Curragh(Ire) sf 1 ⓣ Str 1:451 3↑ Desmond Stakes-G3 43 Manning K J 120 *1.75 Hawkeye1231 Pebble Island1231 Maumee1231 6
Timeform rating: 105 Stk 69600 *Tracked in 3rd,4th over 1f out,no late response*
7Jly01♦Leopardstwn(Ire) gd 1 ⓣ LH 1:391 3↑ ⒻBrownstown Stakes (Listed) 1½ Manning K J 112 3.00 Siringas122½ Saying Grace1221 Toroca1221½ 9
Timeform rating: 109+ Stk 43100 *Tracked leaders,dueled 1f out,led 70y out.Katherine Seymour 5th*
31Aug00♦Gowran Park(Ire) yl 1 ⓣ RH 1:393 Bagenalstown EBF Maiden 113 Manning K J 123 6.50 Siringas12313 Elbader128nk Hawkeye1282 16
Timeform rating: 109 Maiden 9700 *Tracked in 4th,rallied to lead 3f out,drew clear final furlong*
WORKS: May12 Bel 3f fst :37 B (d) *2/9* May4 Bel 3f fst :382 B *19/25* Apr3 Pay 4f fst :504 B *6/12* Mar26 Pay 4f fst :501 B *5/18* Mar6 Pay 4f fst :51 B *9/19* Feb20 Pay 4f fst :51 B *9/27*
TRAINER: BlinkOff(5 .60 $4.68) 31-60Days(135 .19 $1.38) Turf(365 .23 $1.69) Routes(401 .22 $1.67) GrdStk(89 .22 $1.81)

formances was the important information that both the Prix du Pin (purse of $22,500) and the Prix de Table (purse of $33,150) were listed stakes and were open to older handicap horses. Ice Hot shaped up as a multiple listed stakes winner lined up against older nonwinners of four allowance races. The class edge was hidden, but real.

If Ice Hot had been entered instead in a stakes race at Santa Anita, the relative class of the import would have been impossible to estimate accurately. No such impediments remain while evaluating Siringas in the Grade 3 Gallorette at Pimlico. The filly fits the level well enough, but enjoys no class edge, and should be considered an underlay as the favorite or a low-priced contender.

The new, improved past performances show that Siringas had won a listed stakes at three at Leopardstown, in Ireland, and had lost by a nose in her first try in the States in the Grade 3 Athenia Stakes at Belmont Park. Following an easy win off the layoff under the NW2XMC conditions she outgunned at Gulfstream Park and another good try under the more advanced NW3XMC conditions at Keeneland, Siringas is returned to Grade 3 stakes competition in her third start following the layoff, often a peak effort. Is she good enough?

Two new sources of information should convince handicappers that Siringas fits the Grade 3 level well. First, as Shuback tells in *Bet with the Best,* the major tracks of Ireland are only two, The Curragh and Leopardstown; nice to know. Siringas had won a listed stakes at a major track. The gradings of European stakes are now provided, along with the equivalent American purse values. Even more telling, *Daily Racing Form* now provides the excellent Timeform ratings for European imports. Consider the Timeform scale of averages for winners at the various stakes levels:

100-105 Listed stakes winners
110-114 Group 3 stakes winners
115-124 Group 2 stakes winners
125-134 Group 1 stakes winners
135 Outstanding horses
140 Exceptional horses

In winning the listed stakes at Leopardstown as a three-year-old running against older fillies and mares, Siringas had earned a Timeform rating of 109 +, the symbol (+) indicating the filly had exhibited the potential to do better. Siringas could be accepted at the Group 3 level at Pimlico, but not at the Group 2 or Group 1 levels. Handicappers should remember the average Timeform guidelines, and apply them dutifully when European shippers enter the listed and graded stakes of the U.S. The habit will eliminate errors of the grossest sort.

ADDITIONAL IMPORTANT INFORMATION now provided by the *Daily Racing Form* past performances includes a second line that typically denotes not only trip information, but also the running styles of the imports. Siringas is best as a presser-stalker. Shuback suggests the most likely winners of U.S. stakes, and the handicapper's most valuable source of overlays, will be imports exiting European races where the winners and close runners-up have proceeded to win a Group 1/Group 2 stakes overseas. These are the handicapper's version of the European key races, and horses to watch. The company lines, supplemented by the alerted handicapper's mental notebook, provide the clues.

In his widely roaming discourse on the topic, Shuback delivers an excellent discussion of the structure of European racing, focused primarily on the stakes competition. For the first time, the allowance races and handicaps of Europe are explained in practical detail. So are the purse structures of England, France, and Ireland, and those in contrast to the important racing in Germany and Italy. Shuback reports the results of a 10-year study of the Group 1 races of those five countries, and provides the rankings of every Group 1 event on the continent.

Which is the higher-rated race of England, the July Cup, or the Cheveley Park Stakes? It's the former. Which of these two Group 1's of France is stronger, the Prix Royal Oak, or the Prix d'Ispahan? It's the latter. Of Italy's eight Group 1 events, which is top rated? It's the Gran Premio di Milano. Name the two increasingly important Group 1 stakes of Germany. They are the Grosser Preis von Baden and the Bayerisches Zuchtrennen, and Shuback cautions that the latter has served its winners as an obscure steppingstone to prestigious U.S. events, citing Timarindas's triumph in the Beverly D. Stakes and Dear Doctor's in the Arlington Million. The information helps enormously.

Shuback has issued another warning handicappers cannot afford to ignore. Be wary of European imports in U.S. stakes if they have already been successful in Group 1 races on the continent. The horses have reached a peak of development and performance under vastly dissimilar conditions. They may dislike, even resent, the change of scene. Little upside is possible and many of the stars will disappoint. Shuback documents the assertion with the names of 17 Group 1 winners of the last 10 years that have failed to fire in U.S. stakes. The exceptions, he notes, Group 1 winners of Europe that have run to their abilities in America, have been far fewer.

On an important, broader point, Shuback classifies the tracks of Europe into four categories, A-B-C-D, from major to unimportant. Here are the A tracks of England, France, Ireland, Germany, and Italy, and handicappers are urged to submit the names to memory.

England	France	Ireland	Germany	Italy
Ascot	Longchamp	The Curragh	Baden-Baden	La Campanelle
Goodwood	Chantilly	Leopardstown	Cologne	San Siro
Newbury	Deauville		Dusseldorf	
Newmarket	Saint-Cloud		Hamburg	
Sandown	Maisons-Laffitte		Munich	
York				
Epsom				
Doncaster				

Although imports exiting stakes at the A tracks of Europe can be accepted at equivalent or higher class levels at all U.S. tracks, Shuback has concluded the Group 1 races of Europe are not equivalent from country to country. The leading races of England, France, and Ireland are superior to the leading races of Germany and Italy. In Shuback's taxonomy, the Group 1's of Germany and Italy should be equated to the Group 2's of

England, France, and Ireland; the Group 2's of Germany and Italy should be equated to the Group 3's of the other three; the Group 3's of Germany and Italy should be equated to the listed stakes of England, France, and Ireland.

As mentioned, Shuback exempts the Grosser Preis von Baden and Bayerisches Zuchtrennen of Germany, as well as the Premio Roma and Grand Premio di Milano of Italy, as Group 1 events eminently worthy of the designations.

Of the inspiring foreign travel that will enhance the handicapping skill of the participants as nothing else might, Shuback recommends a week each in England and France, as follows:

Second and third weeks of June, for the French Derby and French Oaks at Chantilly, near Paris, and the Royal Ascot meet in London;

Fourth week of July, first week of August, for Glorious Goodwood and the first week of Deauville, the resort tracks of England and France, respectively;

Third and fourth weeks of August, for the third week of Deauville and the York August meeting;

Fourth week of September, first week of October, for Ascot's Festival of Racing in London and Arc Weekend at Longchamp in Paris.

No American handicapper could possibly disagree.

Although the generous odds that formerly characterized so many imports that win American races largely have disappeared, the situation can be viewed as analogous to the decline in the payoffs of speed-figure horses. The overlays are fewer and pay less, but they continue to win.

CHAPTER 25

DIALECTICS, OPPOSITE LOGICS, A PRIVATE BETTING PUBLIC, AND THE INFORMED MINORITY

ONE OF THE truly unfettered, acrobatic, inventive, and intellectually distinct minds of Thoroughbred handicapping belongs to Mark Cramer. Original thinking is the man's imprimatur, and in the stimulating *Fast Track to Thoroughbred Profits* he impresses us with it nonstop. This juicy softcover pours unconventional wisdom into our heads from flap to flap. It's must reading for long-suffering handicappers strapped uncomfortably to systematic methods and unshakable ideas.

On Cramer's fast tracks the locomotive is customized handicapping information heavily charged with wager value. The information is neither well understood nor well distributed. Because the information is undervalued, the horses it picks will be underbet. The horses become overlays, the only kind from which talented handicappers can profit.

Moreover, and this is the magnificent part, the information having the greatest wager value is often a dialectic (subtle variation) of conventional handicapping information well understood by all and overused by many. Finish position, final times, and leading jockeys are important pieces of information having scarce wager value. Cramer displaces them with a new hierarchy of information values.

Cramer has been persistently absorbed by the dialectics and opposite logics—in his terms—inherent in the handicapping process. The subtleties and contradictions of routine handicapping puzzles give the game its dynamism for Cramer, and he is not hesitant to scorn the groups he thinks have missed the boat. His main target are the "determinists," handicappers who believe that reality consists of one dimension and that they have discovered it forevermore.

In *Fast Track to Thoroughbred Profits* the author makes plain a wide array of unconventional information brimming with wager value. A delectable, highly identifiable example debunks the class handicapper's customary reliance on average earnings per race as a separation factor.

Cramer recounts an argument with a student who insisted average earnings was an important variable every time.

Cramer held that the information is useful only in certain types of situations. In those situations, furthermore, the public will be aware that average earnings may have handicapping value but will be unaware that the information lacks wager value. When a horse stands out on earnings, it tends to be strongly overbet. No wager value.

Cramer presses on to show that there are two situations where the public disregards the factor of average earnings per race. In both situations—and how many handicappers can guess what they are?—a system of unit wagering on the entry having the highest average earnings per race whenever the horse goes off above 10-1 will show a substantial flat-bet profit. The procedure does not contain much handicapping value and results in few plays, but it contains tremendous wager value.

Average earnings per start acquires maximum wager value when attached to (a) shippers and (b) foreign horses.

In races that pit shippers and foreign horses against the locals, notably on turf, where par times are useless, Cramer points out that average earnings represents the single factor on which the horses can be compared directly. Yet the public will distrust the unfamiliar horses and their earnings. When the unknowns show the highest average earnings and are sent away at 10-1 or greater, a system bet is automatically placed. It works. A salute to dialectical handicapping!

Flexible handicappers will find at least a dozen of these uncut jewels in Cramer's book. To handicappers who insist it's the horses that win races, not their trainers and jockeys, Cramer does not entirely disagree but counters that trainers and jockeys often have greater wager value than horses. To handicappers who insist that horses should be evaluated closely off good races, Cramer counters that bad races generally have greater wager value than good races. And so it goes. The dialectics of handicapping do not turn events upside down exactly, they just change perspectives.

Cramer's coup, however, is his fascinating study of opposite logics, the notion that there are several ways to skin the same race, some of them contradictory but no less valid. Pairs of classic opposites that often represent contenders in the same races are class drops-class rises and early speed-late speed. His chapter "What Other People Think" shows handicappers how to exploit these realities for big profits, and I heartily recommend the methods to everyone. They are especially pertinent in the information age and consistent with the general movement toward information management in handicapping.

Cramer also urges the formation of "private betting publics." These are small circles of three handicappers, each of whom meets these criteria:

1. Has demonstrated proven competence and originality
2. Has averaged between 4-1 and 10-1 on winners, regardless of win percentage
3. Represents a handicapping methodology vastly dissimilar from the other two
4. Has the time for daily in-depth handicapping

Cramer reasons that the consensus betting at the tracks, of the public and of public selectors, reflects intelligent handicapping that fails to be profitable only because the parimutuels pay less as more money is bet. But what, he asks, if the betting public did not show up at the track? Its consensus selections would not be overbet.

The remedy would have handicappers create their own betting public which does not impact the tote board. And what, he asks, if the betting public we created consisted of competent handicappers implementing diverse handicapping methods? This introduces the possibility of an intelligent consensus that differs from the crowd. A greater chance for higher odds and greater handicapping success simultaneously.

Cramer participated in precisely this kind of private betting public for entire meetings in southern California. When the three handicappers agreed, achieved a consensus, bets were placed.

The results are tantalizing. First of all, consensus is reached for slightly less than a play a day. Cramer warns that if more than a play a day is cropping up, the three handicappers are probably beginning to anticipate one another too well, or were not so dissimilar to begin with, and the power of the procedure will erode.

When the three coincided, the win percentage for the summer of 1983 was 60 percent. Cramer felt that statistic unbelievable and replicated the study in the fall. Eureka! Sixty percent winners again. Mysteriously, Cramer begged off reporting profit margins, saying they would differ significantly among threesomes. He did note that horses below 7-5 were bet to place. Interested trios are exhorted to make paper bets first, before springing into action.

Just as fascinating, Cramer hypothesized that when two handicappers (the majority) favored the same horse and the third (the minority) dissented, the majority would outperform the minority.

The results proved otherwise. The dissenter chose the winners exactly as often as the majority. The pattern repeated itself across several samples. The minority voice called the winner just as frequently.

These findings intrigued Cramer. He interpreted the results to indicate a deeper respect for what he has called the informed minority. The trick was to convert the facts into profits. Cramer's fertile mind soon generalized the results to the selections of public selectors.

With public selectors, he asserted, we can assume the minority is just as competent as the majority, "with one added seduction." The majority is overbet and the minority is underbet. Cramer now hypothesized that if we could identify the informed minority among public handicappers, we had an authentic basis for collecting profits.

Cramer concentrated on the nonconsensus selections of public handicappers. Nonconsensus choices would be comparable to the informed minority.

Under the handicapping "consensus" columns of newspapers, Cramer studied the performance of third choices versus first choices. A consensus third choice must have been the first choice of some expert.

In several studies the consensus third choices outperformed the consensus first choices, during both profit and loss cycles. Cramer concluded the consensus top choices were more likely to represent a majority opinion and are overbet, while the consensus third choices represent the informed minority and yield a profit.

These findings sparked a spate of studies of the informed minorities among public handicappers. Results proved consistently positive. In one study, bets supported the top choice of any Los Angeles newspaper selector that went off at 4-1 or better. The high odds suggested that the opinion was a minority opinion held by an expert. The profits were huge.

Next Cramer completed extensive studies of *Daily Racing Form* selectors in 1983, and he contributed these key findings:

"Trackman" functioned in unique ways. He concentrated on the running lines of races, on trip handicapping, if you will, the subtle ways horses run and finish races. When Trackman picked a horse to win, he would often wind up in the position of the informed minority. Cramer isolated two circumstances when Trackman was likely to spot generous overlays:

1. A win selection for a maiden race that was not selected by any other *Form* handicapper
2. A "best bet" for any type of race when no other *Form* handicapper selected the horse on top

During the May-July period in 1983, Cramer reported, the two situations produced a 30 percent profit on 25 percent winners. The informed minority got overlays.

Cramer suggested the *Form*'s "Sweep" offered similar handicapping advantages. Responsible for setting a morning line, Sweep had to attend to each horse's record in detail. When he liked a horse the others did not, Sweep became the informed minority, and handicappers would more likely be gazing at an overlay.

As methodology, to repeat, Cramer's emphasis on the types of information that contain wager value more than handicapping value closely resembles the broader drift in contemporary handicapping toward information management. The directions are promising and will be rewarding to handicappers willing to bear the educational and administrative burdens they entail.

No one delivers the instruction in more imaginative, innovative style than Cramer.

Cramer presently resides in Paris, where he visits a nearby OTB parlor regularly. On a three-week visit to the City of Lights in June 2000, I benefited again from Cramer's idiosyncratic style. He explained I would see two betting lines on my visits to the Parisian tracks. One would show the off-track betting odds only. The second would show a commingling of the off-track betting and on-track betting beginning at 1:15 p.m. Cramer explained that the simulcast money is smart money in the U.S., but off-track money is dumb money in Paris. OTB bettors are chasing the "tierce," an off-track bet only. Most off-track bettors know next to nothing about handicapping the horses.

Cramer advised me to play any horse that had been bet down on-track from its off-track morning odds. On my visit to Maisons-Laffitte, I found two horses in separate maiden races that fit the profile. The first was bet down from 11-1 off-track to 9-2 on-track. The second was bet down from 9-1 off-track to 7-2 on-track. Both won.

Handicappers growing increasingly impatient with the small fields of contemporary racing, and the underlays they present ad nauseam, have every incentive to consult with Cramer on the alternatives to common practice.

That assertion was documented in the extreme in 1993, with Cramer's publication of *Kinky Handicapping*, the ultimate extension of his search for unconventional patterns having substantial wager value.

With 17 chapters loaded with Cramer's opposite logics and dialectics, it's impossible to summarize the book's substance, but a favorite section is entitled, "Can There Be Intense Action Without Love?" which advises handicappers to abandon handicapping in unpredictable races and rely instead on observations of action on the tote. Cramer defines six types of races as typically unpredictable, referred to as Lesser-of-Evils races. They are:

1. Claiming races restricted to nonwinners of two lifetime.
2. An entry-level allowance race in which all the entrants have shown they cannot win at the allowance level.
3. An open claiming race in which none of the horses has ever won at today's level.
4. Any race in which none of the participants can run to par.
5. Any race in which the best horses have running styles contrary to the track profile for the distance but similar to each other.
6. Two-year-old maiden races in which none of the horses has win-early breeding.

Cramer relates his experience with a race at Laurel where all the horses had never won at the claiming level. Handicappers are urged to watch the tote from the opening line. If the morning-line favorite and the second choice on the line drift higher than their morning line, the race is probably a Lesser-of-Evils unpredictable washout. Now handicappers look avidly for nonfavorites that have been dropped below their morning line, the greater the bet-down the better, as long as the odds on these horses show volatility. If the odds on the bet-down nonfavorites do not fluctuate, that's public money only, and a negative pattern. The fluctuation following the opening line indicates that insiders or a well-informed subset of the public prefers the horse.

Those horses qualify as the Lesser-of-Evils candidates. The horses can be backed to win and combined in a variety of exotic wagers, as the odds dictate, and the handicapper's experience allows. Tossing one of four bet-down possibilities because the difference in his morning-line odds and the tote odds was small, Cramer proceeded to combine the other three every which way and walked away with an $875 trifecta.

In case orthodox handicappers have missed the point, other sections of *Kinky Handicapping* have been entitled "Banal Fixations," "The Inaccurate Conception," "Menage A Trois," "Grass Smokers," "Secret Affairs," "X-Rated Factors," "Lecherous Betting," and "Foreplay." The chapters may be X-rated seductive, but the handicapping material is straight-edged and aimed, as always with Cramer, at wager value. It's Cramer at his kinkiest, perhaps, but readers will be in the hands of a savvy, competent, highly experienced handicapper.

CHAPTER 26

ROBERT SAUNDERS DOWST IN THE NEW MILLENNIUM

BEYOND PUBLISHING THE books and magazine articles that established him as the high priest of handicapping in the 1930's and the 1940's, Robert Saunders Dowst went public in 1936 with perhaps the only fundamentally sound system capable of continual seasonal profits. Dowst's system had been born a year earlier in 1935, when a St. Louis betting commissioner, no less, a gentleman sporting the handle of "Liberal Tom" Kearney, burst into print with the unerring observation that the only way to beat the races was to play winners. Other than indicating that the horse Adobe Post in 1934 had won 20 of 50 starts and that a bet on each would have netted profits, the commissioner provided his followers with no directions as to how to select the winners in advance of the races.

But Dowst did.

In *Profits on Horses*, the Dowst Consistency System came to life. In its simplicity and scope it was indeed a system for all times. Dowst postulated two verifiable assumptions, from which he derived one principle of selection and 11 rules of exclusion. Following "Liberal Tom's" magnificent insight, the Dowst system was based on the precept that good horses can beat bad horses. Good horses, said Dowst, were those that beat members of a specific class consistently. Thus, Dowst put forth his two premises: (a) all Thoroughbreds are divisible into fixed classes; and (b) when a horse wins a race or runs close he normally does so by virtue of his own speed, gameness, and quality, and not by the advantage of jockey, post position, or a clever trainer.

The chief difficulty was establishing the operational definition of consistency. After tinkering with diverse formulae, which did not work, Dowst hit on the one that did. To wit, the Dowst principle of selection:

Play to be limited to horses that had won at least a third of their starts while finishing in the money at least half of the time, provided any qualifying horse is the only one of its kind in the race.

A horse with 10 starts this year can be rated on this season's record alone. If starts number fewer than 10, rate the horse on this year's and last year's records cumulatively, regardless of total races.

When the system appeared in book form and in *Esquire*, the national stampede began. As Dowst had predicted, the system rang up munificent profits during the whole of 1936. It repeated the feat in 1937, by which time Dowst had prepared a list of the horses that qualified as a play.

For a time the sweet smell of success permeated the air. The secret of beating the races was out, and it worked. But it came to pass that Dowst was wrong on one important point. Dowst himself had argued the system would remain fail-proof unless so many of the public bet on consistent horses that their prices bottomed out under the weight of the money. Knowing the contrariness of the horseplayer, Dowst dismissed that dismal possibility. On that he erred. The public bet Dowst's consistent horses off the board, and the Dowst Consistency System stopped working.

Five decades later, in the context of contemporary handicapping literature, what is the legacy of Robert Saunders Dowst? Does the Dowst Consistency System deserve a revival?

Dowst on racing and handicapping is not so out of date, as the leading authority of the century's first half left a rich and pungent body of work. He has left to handicappers as a first contribution a theoretical definition of class not yet improved. Good horses still beat bad horses, and a horse's class is arguably best assessed by identifying the specific class of horses it can beat consistently. The Dowst system worked, not because he eventually discovered a working definition of consistency, but because he had precisely comprehended the true nature of Thoroughbred class. Dowst repeatedly contended that class held the key. Indeed the Dowst Consistency System would have been better named the Dowst Class-Consistency System, as the essential ingredient was demonstrated ability against a specific class of horse. Dowst's exclusion rules (reprinted on page 132) honored his high regard for class repeatedly, and Rule 8 prevented play on system horses when "definitely stepped up." Others forbade playing fillies against colts, horses aged seven or older, chronic quitters, and claiming horses valued at $1,500 or less.

When the Dowst system falls flat today is on the center point of consistency. The probability studies of William Quirin concluded that consistency was overrated. Horses that have won three or four of their past 10 starts do win more than their share of races, but (a) the public overbets that kind; and (b) inconsistent horses win enough. Quirin showed that horses that won just one of their 10 previous starts won almost a fair share of their starts. Fred Davis's probability studies supported Quirin on the matter of inconsistency, concluding this was insufficient reason to regard horses as noncontenders, particularly in claiming races.

Yet the Davis data did suggest a modern variation of Dowst. Davis found that recent consistency outperformed consistency. Recent consistency was defined as winning two of the latest six starts. Moreover, recent consistency proved more important among better horses, and in studies of allowance races, recently consistent horses performed significantly better than inconsistent ones (won one or none of their latest six). Davis did not report whether recently consistent horses in allowance races returned profits.

A modified application of the Dowst Consistency System is tenable, at small investment until profit margins are determined. The principle of selection now holds:

Play to be limited to horses in allowance races that have won at least two of their latest six starts, provided any qualifying horse is the only one of its kind in the race.

Before presenting the rules of exclusion, which apply without exception, it's instructive to consider why Dowst's carefully calculated operational definition of consistency no longer applies. To be sure, it's a matter of modern Thoroughbred form—the methods trainers use to regulate form, the demands on form of the modern racing calendars, and the resulting variations in horses' form cycles. Dowst did not take the form factor seriously. Excepting downright unsoundness, his system ignored it. In Dowst's time approximately 8,000 horses were in training to compete on a limited calendar. Relatively sound and able to begin with, when racing began the 8,000 were relatively fit and ready to race. Trainers did not have enough time to race horses into top condition, and fewer horses became severely overworked during the shorter season. On these points times have changed. During 2001, no less than 72,205 horses competed on 7,661 racing days. Untalented, unfit, and overworked horses do not easily become consistent horses. Nowadays handicappers best find the class of the field, not so much by identifying the kinds of horses a horse has whipped consistently, but by closely evaluating form cycles, to determine whether one horse is ready to run at its authentic best today.

Dowst's rules of exclusion:

1. No plays on tracks slow, heavy, muddy, or otherwise off; a track must be fast or good to permit a system wager.
2. No fillies or mares are to be played against colts, horses, or geldings from April 1 to September 1 of each year.
3. No plays on two-year-olds.
4. No plays on aged horses (animals over six).
5. No chronic quitters are to be played.
6. No horse known to have any physical infirmity, to be unsound in any way, is to be played.
7. No horse entered in a claiming race at a valuation under $1,500 is to be played in any event (the modern equivalent of this rule remains unknown, but might hover at $5,000).
8. No horse is to be accepted as a play under this system when definitely stepped up, in comparison with earlier races.
9. No horse otherwise qualifying as a play can be accepted if he is conspicuously overweighted.
10. No sprinters are to be played in route races.
11. No route-type horses are to be played in sprints.

As Dowst insisted, the rules are easy to apply. Only the eighth and ninth, of class and weight, require knowledge and skill in handicapping.

Handicappers interested in pursuing Dowst can consult the following bibliography.

1934 *Playing the Races* (with Jay Craig). New York: Dodd, Mead.
1935 *Winners and How to Select Them*. New York: Cosmic Press.
1937 *Profits on Horses*. New York: William Morrow.
1938 *Horses to Bet*. New York: William Morrow.
1945 *Straight, Place, and Show*. New York: M.S. Mill Company.
1947 *Winners at Prices*. New York: Dodd, Mead.
1954 *In the Stretch*. New York: Dodd, Mead.
1959 *The Odds, the Player, the Horses*. New York: Dodd, Mead.

CHAPTER 27

DR. Z'S SYSTEM

HANDICAPPING AUTHORITIES CANNOT escape the routine question of their fellows, "Do you bet to place? To show?"

Most of them do not, but some do.

Among the minority that do, the reasons are more strongly associated with individual temperament and personality than mathematics. Certain experiences in handicapping have played a highly formative role as well.

Take me. As a rookie handicapper I one day bet three longshots to win and place, fifty-fifty. A longshot won; the favorite ran second. I got $37.80 to win, $9.80 to place. I haven't played a longshot to place since.

When math has been contemplated at all, the typical considerations have involved high-priced horses that figure to be in the money, but not so decisively to win. The basis of the thinking and learning has been knowledge and skill in handicapping, but not betting.

As a result, a sizable amount of nonsense has been circulated on these matters. The conventional strategy has been targeting races where favorites can be discounted. A summary of what experience has taught was presented in Tom Ainslie's *Encyclopedia of Thoroughbred Handicapping*. Show betting was eschewed, but the following prescriptions related wagers to place to the chances of favorites and sizes of fields:

1. In fields of seven or more horses, betting to place is acceptable when the selection is 7-2 or greater and the favorite figures to be out of the money.
2. In a field of six, betting to place is acceptable when the selection is 3-1 or greater and the favorite figures to be out of the money.
3. In a field of five, betting to place is acceptable when the selection is 5-2 or greater and the favorite figures to be out of the money.

Tempting, but wrong. It comes to pass that favorites and short-priced horses represent the best place and show bets of all. Show is frequently juicier than place. In fact, a fail-safe mathematically determined system of place and show wagering pointedly advises handicappers to pass whenever system selections start at odds exceeding 8-1.

The Dr. Z system is predicated on how well the public bets. The public bets fantastically well. It estimates the winning chances of horses very accurately, except for a tendency to underbet its favorite and overbet its longshots. William Ziemba (Dr. Z) calls this phenomenon the favorite-longshot bias. Handicappers tempted to rush out and bet on the most likely 6-5 favorites should understand that those horses enjoy just a 6 percent edge against chance, an advantage easily swallowed up by the track take (circa 17 percent).

The mathematics that prove these points and many more appear in *Beat the Racetrack,* co-authored by Ziemba and Donald Hausch, a book characterized in its foreword by the renowned Dr. Edward Thorp as providing the first system of parimutuel wagering (not handicapping) that actually wins.

The Dr. Z system identifies place and show overlays. It's based on a concept of securities investment called inefficiency of markets. As applied to horse racing, the foundation principle holds that while the public estimates the winning chances of horses exceedingly well (efficiency), it sometimes makes glaring errors when betting to place and show (inefficiency). Ziemba has found that these inefficiencies occur in two to four races a day.

An inefficiency (betting error) occurs when a much lower proportion of the place or show pool is bet on a particular horse than the same horse's proportion of the win pool. When this happens, bettors confront an instance of a pattern that can result in significant long-term profits, between 10 to 20 percent on investment.

An inefficiency is not difficult to spot. Approaching the six-minute mark, bettors examine the tote. They are looking for betting discrepancies in the win-place-show pools. Ziemba supplies the following illustration:

			Horse					
	#1	#2	#3	#4	#5	#6	#7	Totals
Odds	4-5	14-1	6-1	5-2	16-1	11-1	33-7	
Win	8,293	1,009	2,116	4,212	885	1,251	457	18,223
Place	2,560	660	1,386	2,610	696	903	399	9,214
Show	1,570	495	1,860	1,881	543	712	287	6,558

Horse 1 has 44 percent of the win pool, but just 27 percent of the place pool and 23 percent of the show pool. A discrepancy is clear.

An easy way to recognize betting inefficiencies is to examine the total amounts in the win-place-show pools. In the example, the place pool is roughly half the win pool. The show pool is about one-third the win pool. To find a possible place overlay, the bettor would find a horse with significantly less than half its win money bet to place. To find a possible show overlay, the bettor finds a horse with significantly less than one-third its win money bet to show.

When a discrepancy is noted, the bettor must determine if the differences are large enough. As Ziemba puts it, is the bet really good enough?

The answer involves probabilities and the mathematical Expectation of the place and show payoffs. Expectation refers to how much bettors can expect to win for each dollar wagered. At major tracks the Dr. Z system requires an Expectation of 1.14; at other tracks, Expectation must be 1.18.

Ziemba provides the formula for calculating the place bettor's Expectation:

$$\text{EX PL} = 0.319 + 0.559\,\frac{W_i/W}{P_i/P}$$

Where P_i and W_i are the amounts bet to place and win, respectively, on Horse 1, and P and W are the place and win pool totals. I hope that handicappers can agree that the formula is simple.

Expectation for Horse 1 in the example race is 1.20, meaning that bettors can expect to win (net) 20 cents on each dollar wagered, or 20 percent on investment long-range. The advantage amounts to a bet as 1.20 exceeds both 1.14 and 1.18.

While the math constants change, the formula is similar for calculating the show Expectation:

$$\text{EX SH} = 0.543 + 0.369\left(\frac{W_i/W}{S_i/S}\right)$$

The Expectation to show for Horse 1 is 1.24, another good bet.

Studies of Dr. Z's system indicate that the bettable expected values usually range from 1.15 to 1.30, meaning profit rates between 15 and 30 percent. All probabilities considered, a series of 100 bets should begin to yield meaningful profits, which will then accumulate consistently and dramatically.

The optimal-bet sizes are hitched to the Kelly Criterion and the single-race Expectation. Ziemba's chapter on Kelly wagering demonstrates beyond dispute that the method contributes the maximum rate of growth of the bettor's bankroll. No other systematic method rivals Kelly on that standard, especially as time goes by.

A computerized version of the Dr. Z system simplifies everything for the bettor. A hand-held computer at the track is not cumbersome. When four pieces of tote-board data have been entered, the program computes Expectation and identifies the optimal Kelly bet. As technically complicated as the mathematics of the Dr. Z system might be for most handicappers, procedurally the system is stepwise simple, as is true of so many computerized versions of complex methods.

Handicappers should appreciate that serious profits are possible by implementing Dr. Z. They should realize, too, that this is a betting system and must be implemented to the letter of the law. In particular, the size of the optimal bet will be large when Expectation is greatest, such as Spectacular Bid to show in the 1979 Kentucky Derby. The Expectation was 1.85, the optimal wager 38 percent of bankroll. It must be risked.

Dr. Z advocates I have observed have consistently fallen down on the betting requirements. Using a fractional-Kelly betting scheme slows the rate of growth, to be sure, and this amounts to a significant reduction where profits are so slim to begin, as with place and show payoffs on low-priced overlays. Initial capital should be advisedly large.

On the inaugural Breeders' Cup Event Day, November 10, 1984, at Hollywood Park, the famous Dr. Thorp joined Ziemba and three others to try the Z system. In the second race, the Dr. Z horse (Fran's Valentine) finished first but was disqualified and placed 10th for interference. A sizable loss! Five additional overlays were spotted that day. The probabilities were highly favorable, but only Thorp risked the optimal amounts on each. He won $1,851 for the afternoon, thank you. The others did not bet properly. Perhaps I should say "optimally." They therefore won modest amounts instead on a day particularly generous to the system. A system is a system is a system is a system.

Ziemba has posted five cautions when implementing his system. Do not bet:

1. On days when the track is not fast. No exceptions.
2. When minus pools exist or so much will be bet on a single horse that the place and show payoffs on all horses will be $2.10.
3. When the horse in question is greater than 8 to 1. This is due to the longshot bias. These types are so overbet that the payoff you receive will not overcompensate for the attendant risk.
4. When the horse in question is a "Silky Sullivan" type. These horses come from so far back that they typically either win or finish out of the money. Aha! A concession to handicapping!
5. When the expected dollar return is less than 1.14 for the top tracks and 1.18 for other tracks. The tracks where 1.14 represents the expected-value cutoff are:

Arlington Park, Illinois
Aqueduct, New York
Belmont Park, New York
Churchill Downs, Kentucky
Del Mar, California
Emerald Downs, Washington
Golden Gate, California

Gulfstream Park, Florida
Hawthorne, Illinois
Hollywood Park, California
Keeneland, Kentucky
Louisiana Downs, Louisiana
Meadowlands, New Jersey
Monmouth Park, New Jersey

Oaklawn Park, Arkansas
Pimlico, Maryland
Santa Anita Park, California
Saratoga, New York
Sportman's Park, Illinois
Woodbine, Ontario

CHAPTER 28

THE DOSAGE INDEX

WHEN THE COUGAR II colt Gato Del Sol, a longshot, swept from last to first and drew off to win the 1982 Kentucky Derby, the remarkable record of Steve Roman's Dosage Index (DI) as a predictor of classic winners was sustained further still. Damascus excepted, no modern horse having a ratio of speed to stamina—Dosage—in its pedigree above Roman's statistical value of 4.00 had ever won either the Kentucky Derby or the Belmont Stakes. The 1982 pre-Derby favorites loomed as counterpoints to dosage analysts, as each had inherited much more speed than endurance, and each possessed a DI higher than the magic number, but those fast favorites perished badly in the Churchill Downs stretch, true to their pedigree prospects.

When, weeks later, Conquistador Cielo, his DI a soaring 16.0, blitzed the Belmont Stakes field, controversy swirled. Some concluded that Roman's index had been unmasked at last. Indeed, since 1982, three colts having a DI greater than 4.00 have won the Kentucky Derby: Strike the Gold (1991), Real Quiet (1998), and Charismatic (1999).

In his stimulating "Dosage: A Practical Approach" (which appeared exclusively in *Daily Racing Form* during the spring of 1981, and which that paper's former national "Bloodlines" columnist, Leon Rasmussen, promoted frequently and pointedly), author Steven A. Roman explained how to calculate and interpret the Dosage Index, which is a mathematical expression of a Thoroughbred's inherent speed and endurance characteristics, and thereby predict, based on pedigree alone, which horses and stakes winners are likely to become racing's truly important horses.

Beyond educating the sport's breeders in the science of mating horses, and its auction buyers in the science of purchasing yearlings, Roman has extended a helping hand to handicappers, who are increasingly concerned about the science of picking winners. No handicapper in possession of the DI's for the 1982 Derby hopefuls should have invested a dollar in their prospects, as the pre-race favorites shaped up as statistical improbables. There are other important Dosage applications for handicappers, but first a basic explanation of the Dosage Index, one of the most inventive and scholarly contributions in the annals of the sport.

The Dosage Index is a statistical measure of speed and stamina in combination, calculated according to the performance aptitudes of the important sires (called chef-de-race sires) that appear in a horse's immediate four-generation family. As students of pedigree know, but many handicappers do not, the genetic aptitudes of racehorses are five: Brilliant, Intermediate, Classic, Solid, and Professional, the five arranged in order of increasing stamina, or, in order of decreasing speed.

By simple arithmetical calculations, explained below, the index describes a horse's ratio of speed to stamina. Roman's research with the tool persuades horsemen and handicappers that horses having too great a speed quotient (above 4.00) are not likely to become classic winners or important sires themselves. In a sport where classic traditions have lately yielded more and more authority to speed—indeed Roman has referred to a general inflation factor toward higher DI's in contemporary pedigrees—perhaps some find solace from a scientific method that assigns a kind of ultimate authority to horses possessing greater stamina.

Roman's practical approach to Dosage produces three statistics. First, a Dosage Profile (DP) is identified by assigning points to each of the five aptitudinal categories in a four-generation pedigree. Thus a DP looks like so: 7-5-9-1-2, where 7 means Brilliant points, 5 means Intermediate points, 9 means Classic points, etc., etc. The Dosage Index (DI) and another statistic called center of distribution (CD) are merely ratios among the points, and easily calculated.

To arrive at a Dosage Profile, handicappers must identify the chef-de-race sires in each of the first four generations. The influence of each of these sires is allotted a number or points, such that each of a preceding generation's chef-de-race sires can earn only half the points of the succeeding generation's. Thus, moving backward, we find a possible progression of 1-2-4-8 sires in the four generations, such that these sires contribute 16-8-4-2 points each. The chef-de-race sires have themselves been classified by aptitudinal groups, and points for each aptitudinal group represented by the fabulous sires are totaled.

A table of current chef-de-race sires by aptitudinal groups is presented at the end of this piece.A horse's point total in each aptitudinal group expresses its DP. Gato Del Sol's Dosage Profile is expressed as 6-3-5-2-2.

The Dosage Index is the ratio of the points in the speed wing to those in the stamina wing.

The speed wing is equal to the Brilliant points plus Intermediate points plus one-half the Classic points.

The stamina wing is equal to the other half of the Classic points plus the Solid points plus the Professional points.

When the speed points are divided by the stamina points, an elementary division calculation, the DI results.

What is the DI for Gato Del Sol? It is 1.77.

As the DI is directly proportional to the speed in a pedigree and inversely proportional to the stamina, a DI of 1.00 reflects a perfect balance of the two qualities. A DI of 2.00 indicates twice as much speed as stamina.

The CD of Roman's pedigree is the single point where the combined influences of all the chef-de-race sires concentrate most strongly. Its calculation requires nothing more than a sequence of addition, subtraction, and multiplication operations.

Multiply the Brilliant points by 2 and add the product to the Intermediate points.

From the sum subtract the Solid points.

Next multiply the Professional points by 2 and subtract that product from the preceding difference.

Divide the resulting number by the total number of points in the DP.

What is the CD for Gato Del Sol? It is 0.50.

Roman's research with his Dosage methodology has been continuous, pragmatic, and greatly important to the production of knowledge concerning relations between bloodlines and racetrack performances. He has concentrated his studies on stakes winners, and rightly so, as the classic purpose of mating Thoroughbreds, largely forgotten in the recent industrialization of the stud in numerous stateside factories throughout the land, has been the improvement of the breed. That improvement is most likely to occur when the highest grade of stakes winner is involved in the mating.

Consider Roman's most significant findings:

1. Champions and leading sires have significantly lower DI's and CD's than do the normal population of stakes winners.

2. A DI of 4.00 and a CD of 1.25 separate the classic winners and champions from the other stakes winners with astonishing reliability. In 62 years exactly three horses with DI's exceeding 4.00 have won the Kentucky Derby, only two the Belmont Stakes, and just one with a CD above 1.25 has won either classic. In contrast, of stakes winners as a class, approximately 40 percent have a DI exceeding 4.00, but these horses rarely win the sport's definitive events.

3. Studies of stakes-winning sprinters, middle-distance horses, and routers have revealed a direct correlation between the DI and distance potential. The sprinters have the highest DI's, the routers the lowest, and the middle-distance horses fall in between. The differences among the groups are statistically significant, eliminating chance as the cause of the results.

4. Although the DI's and the CD's for successive generations have been rising in general, the relative importance of stamina in top-class horses, compared to the entire population, has remained stable. Breeding practices may now churn out more speed burners than ever, but these still do not often advance to the top of the class.

Of applications to handicapping, handicappers can obviously eliminate horses in the classics if their DI's exceed 4.00, and without hesitation.

A narrow application to handicapping? Perhaps.

There are at least two wider applications. Of the stakes population at any major track, horses with DI's and CD's within the classic ranges can be considered at advantage when the distance lengthens to 1¼ miles or farther and the quality of the competition becomes the highest. Regular, older stakes campaigners will be fairly evaluated from the past-performance lines, but lightly raced, nicely bred four-year-olds and similar late-blooming five-year-olds might be moving toward the top at any time of the season. If the contest is now Grade 1 at a classic distance, demanding of horses the proper blend of speed and endurance, handicappers benefit if they consult the Dosage Indexes. Horses should qualify within the 4.00 and 1.25 limits.

Another application of Dosage is far more interesting, easily more advantageous. Each season the better three-year-olds sort themselves out in increasingly demanding stakes competition. The Roman approach helps handicappers predict which should go the farthest against the best. If handicappers prepare a file of DI's and CD's for stakes winners and outstanding allowance winners in the three-year-olds divisions, they have accumulated useful evidence as to which hopefuls might end as sprinters, middle-distance types, and routers, as well as which might be genuine graded-stakes stars and classic contenders. As between sprinters and middle-distance horses, Roman's research with Dosage has not yet established a DI value line separating the two groups. That's an empirical problem worth its solution.

Similarly, Dosage analyses of juvenile stakes show the winners have DI's that become lower as distances increase.

At the five-furlong dash the winners average 10.50 or greater but the typical DI's drop to 9.75 or so at 5½ furlongs. At six furlongs the average DI of two-year-old stakes winners has fallen two sharp points, to slightly below 7.50. The sprints of two-year-olds really do differ from the dashes.

In longer races—routes of 1⁄₁₆ miles, for example—two-year-old DI's clearly become lower throughout the second part of the year. During fall the typical route winner has a DI ranging from roughly 6.00 to 4.50. The winners of the dashes of spring are less likely to win the routes of fall. The two populations of two-year-olds differ significantly in their racing attributes and potential.

The handicapper's difficulty with Roman's practical approach to Dosage is precisely the practical problem of obtaining a four-generation pedigree. The expedient sources of information are either *Daily Racing Form*'s columns or local pedigree services that might provide the information—for a fee.

For handicappers who wish to calculate Dosage statistics of their own, the chef-de-race sire table below is the basic source. The table is revised or expanded periodically, and listed sires may be assigned concurrently to two aptitudinal groups, as the letters in parentheses denote.

There are presently only 156 sires worth all the attention.

Chefs-de-Race as of May 2003, Listed Alphabetically

Chefs-de-race are listed alphabetically with their aptitudinal designations in parentheses (B=Brilliant, I=Intermediate, C=Classic, S=Solid, P=Professional)

Abernant (B)	Discovery (S)	Mossborough (C)	Royal Charger (B)
Ack Ack (I/C)	Djebel (I)	Mr. Prospector (B/C)	Run the Gantlet (P)
Admiral Drake (P)	Donatello II (P)	My Babu (B)	Sadler's Wells (C/S)
Alcantara II (P)	Double Jay (B)	Nashua (I/C)	Sardanapale (P)
Alibhai (C)	Dr. Fager (I)	Nasrullah (B)	Sea-Bird (S)
Alizier (P)	Eight Thirty (I)	Native Dancer (I/C)	Seattle Slew (B/C)
Alycidon (P)	Ela-Mana-Mou (P)	Navarro (C)	Secretariat (I/C)
Alydar (C)	Equipoise (I/C)	Nearco (B/C)	Sharpen Up (B/C)
Apalachee (B)	Exclusive Native (C)	Never Bend (B/I)	Shirley Heights (C/P)
Asterus (S)	Fair Play (S/P)	Never Say Die (C)	Sicambre (C)
Aureole (C)	Fair Trial (B)	Nijinsky II (C/S)	Sideral (C)
Bachelor's Double (S)	Fairway (B)	Niniski (C/P)	Sir Cosmo (B)

Bahram (C)	Fappiano (I/C)	Noholme II (B/C)	Sir Gallahad III (C)
Baldski (B/I)	Forli (C)	Northern Dancer (B/C)	Sir Gaylord (I/C)
Ballymoss (S)	Foxbridge (P)	Nureyev (C)	Sir Ivor (I/C)
Bayardo (P)	Full Sail (I)	Oleander (S)	Solario (P)
Ben Brush (I)	Gainsborough (C)	Olympia (B)	Son-In-Law (P)
Best Turn (C)	Gallant Man (B/I)	Orby (B)	Speak John (B/I)
Big Game (I)	Graustark (C/S)	Ortello (P)	Spearmint (P)
Black Toney (B/I)	Grey Dawn II (B/I)	Panorama (B)	Spy Song (B)
Blandford (C)	Grey Sovereign (B)	Persian Gulf (C)	Stage Door Johnny (S/P)
Blenheim II (C/S)	Gundomar (C)	Peter Pan (B)	Star Kingdom (I/C)
Blue Larkspur (C)	Habitat (B)	Petition (I)	Star Shoot (I)
Blushing Groom (B/C)	Hail To Reason (C)	Phalaris (B)	Sunny Boy (P)
Bois Roussel (S)	Halo (B/C)	Pharis II (B)	Sunstar (S)
Bold Bidder (I/C)	Havresac II (I)	Pharos (I)	Sweep (I)
Bold Ruler (B/I)	Heliopolis (B)	Pia Star (S)	Swynford (C)
Brantome (C)	Herbager (C/S)	Pilate (C)	T.V. Lark (I)
British Empire (B)	High Top (C)	Polynesian (I)	Tantieme (S)
Broad Brush (I/C)	His Majesty (C)	Pompey (B)	Teddy (S)
Broomstick (I)	Hoist The Flag (B/I)	Precipitation (P)	The Tetrarch (I)
Bruleur (P)	Hurry On (P)	Pretense (C)	Ticino (C/S)
Buckpasser (C)	Hyperion (B/C)	Prince Bio (C)	Tom Fool (I/C)
Bull Dog (B)	Icecapade (B/C)	Prince Chevalier (C)	Tom Rolfe (C/P)
Bull Lea (C)	In Reality (B/C)	Prince John (C)	Tourbillon (C/P)
Busted (S)	Intentionally (B/I)	Princequillo (I/S)	Tracery (C)
Caro (I/C)	Key to the Mint (B/C)	Prince Rose (C)	Traghetto (I)
Chateau Bouscaut (P)	Khaled (I)	Promised Land (C)	Tudor Minstrel (B)
Chaucer (S)	King Salmon (I)	Rabelais (P)	Turn-to (B/I)
Cicero (B)	King's Bishop (B/I)	Raise A Native (B)	Ultimus (B)
Clarissimus (C)	La Farina (P)	Relko (S)	Vaguely Noble (C/P)
Colorado (I)	Le Fabuleux (P)	Reviewer (B/C)	Vandale (P)
Congreve (I)	Luthier (C)	Ribot (C/P)	Vatellor (P)
Count Fleet (C)	Lyphard (C)	Right Royal (S)	Vatout (S)
Court Martial (B)	Mahmoud (I/C)	Riverman (I/C)	Vieux Manoir (C)
Creme dela Creme (C/S)	Man O' War (S)	Roberto (C)	War Admiral (C)
Crepello (P)	Massine (P)	Rock Sand (C/S)	What A Pleasure (B)
Damascus (I/C)	Midstream (C)	Roman (B/I)	Wild Risk (P)
Danzig (I/C)	Mieuxce (P)	Rough'n Tumble (B/C)	Worden (S)
Dark Ronald (P)	Mill Reef (C/S)	Round Table (S)	

CHAPTER 29

THE INFORMATION-MANAGEMENT APPROACH TO HANDICAPPING

FOR THOSE HANDICAPPERS who play to win conspicuous money, the most significant developments of the modern pastime are:

a. an explosion of handicapping information that is meaningful and potentially decisive;

b. the accelerated and corresponding increase in exotic-wagering opportunities.

The two conditions invite part-time practitioners to achieve a lofty purpose previously beyond their scope—beating the horses for substantial money (thousands)—in the short run of the season. The information avalanche facilitates the discovery of overlays and of various scenarios for attacking the same race. Combination betting occasionally delivers huge overlays that win, the best shortcut to collecting robust mutuels at a few flashpoints of the year.

In concert with major trends, the new methodology for finding overlays and beating the races is an array of knowledge and skill I have termed information management. The phrase parallels unstoppable trends in the larger society. Following are six propositions that frame the new approach. All are integral. That is, they relate to one another in indispensable ways. If one is missing, the methodology suffers seriously. Near the end the procedures of information management are contrasted with the traditional handicapping practice.

The six central themes can be summarized succinctly:

1. Make decisions, not selections.

Applying everything handicappers know to every race they study normally results in two or more plausible outcome scenarios. Each scenario presents an alternative decision. Well-informed handicappers must decide which decision is best when winning chances are juxtaposed with public odds.

An analogy to risk-management behavior strategy is apt. This is a fascinating approach to handicapping, vastly dissimilar from a philosophy of making selections that figure to win. In the age of information, handicappers equipped to make decisions will conquer contemporaries equipped only to make selections. That anticipates the second imperative.

2. Rely on various and diverse types of information, not on systematic methods.

The proposition does not imply that systematic methods should be abandoned, just broadened, to encompass unfamiliar kinds of information that have a meaningful and consistent impact on race outcomes.

Considerable research shows that problem solving and decision making will be improved in relation to the amount of information that has been accessed. Is there a better real-time application than to Thoroughbred handicapping? Practitioners should not discount the point. The more information handicappers use, the more overlays they will find. The more successful therefore they will be.

3. Use personal computers and databases to manage the plethora of information and to identify the data relations of greatest value.

It's possible to implement an information-management approach by resorting to manual systems. But, why bother? Manual systems become laborious, inefficient, and time-consuming. They are prone to error. They are fantastically less productive than the electronic counterparts. Those averse to computers should make up their minds to bite the bullet and invest. Acquire the necessary training. Use the machines to store, process, and retrieve the data of interest.

Constructing databases makes more sense than developing computer models of the handicapping process, though both are compatible. Databases supply the flexible data management and problem-solving tools that are otherwise unimaginable.

Examine the following table.

Taken from *High-Tech Handicapping in the Information Age* (1986), it represents a hypothetical database of crucial performance characteristics for every racehorse on the grounds. By relating the data in the 20 columns to one another technically, the database quickly responds to numerous queries handicappers will submit. In this way databases enhance information productivity tremendously.

					Competitive Level	Class Rating	Back Class	Key Race	Ability Figures	Stakes Designations	Speed Figure	Pace Figure	Pace Rating	Race Shape	Wins When Fresh	Longest Layoff/Win	Form Cycle	Best Distance	Distance Range	Dosage Index	Turf I.V.	Mud Rating
	Name	Age	Sex																				
	MY COUNTESS	4	F		NWI	21	C32				93	85	228	AA	0	23	N	8.5	8–9	10.00	NA	B
	MAX'S LADY	4	F		NWI	23	NA				0	96	93	251	SA	0	9	N	8.5	8–8.5	7.36	1.80	A
RECORD	SOCIAL WHIRL	4	F		C45	20	C20	C50	26		0	93	92	256	SA	0	27	R	8.5	7–8.5	11.44	0.61	NA
	PETITE FLEUR	3	F		MONU	15	NA				0	93	88	250	SS	0	27	N	8.5	8–8.5	3.55	1.15	B
	SARATOGA ROXIE	5	M		C50	22	NWI				0	94	90	254	AA	1	64	F	8	8	15.15	0.44	B
	GOLDEN SCREEN	4	F		MON	30	NA				0	91	91	243	AS	0	NA	NA	8.5	8–8.5	4.66	0.75	P
	BUENA FE II	4	F		C100	9	NA				0	97	93	272	AF	0	42	N	6.5	6–8	NA	NA	A
	PRINCESS POLEAX	4	F		C12		M12				0	97	94	145	SS	0	16	N	8.5	8–8.5	6.79	2.22	A

Racehorse (table heading)

PRIMARY KEY   DOMAINS

A *relation* of handicapping data items called *Racehorse*.
A data base constructed of relations or tables is called a *relational data base*.
Racehorse has eight rows or data records. Each record consists of twenty *domains* or columns. Each domain represents a data item type. The table values are data items.
The relation has a *primary key*, the name of the horses. The primary key identifies a record uniquely.

4. Expert decisions most often result from intuitive reasoning skills, not from logical deductive reasoning.

Logical deductive thinking proceeds from the general to the particular, as from the general principles of handicapping to specific races in which those principles apply. Intuitive thinking proceeds from the specific to the general, as from specific facts, data items, and pieces of information to general conclusions about the weight of evidence. Unknown to handicappers and most others, the real experts in many unrelated fields have been found to make their key decisions intuitively. In fascinating university experiments the researchers found difficult at first to explain, human chess experts consistently beat computers programmed to play errorless chess. They accomplished the feat by calling into play extensive knowledge and experience that allowed them to maneuver in atypical, unpredictable patterns the computers did not comprehend.

Handicappers can learn to implement the same strategy. The fundamentals include knowledge, information sources, and experience. The more of each, the better. It's that elementary—know-how, information, experience. The most important factor: knowledge.

Intuitive reasoning, handicappers must understand, is not a guessing game and has nothing to do with whim, whisper, or getting in touch with feelings. It has instead a strong rational basis. The critical concept is the additive weighting of all the specifics relevant to a given situation or set of circumstances. Memory skills are employed to "chunk" several sources of knowledge, information, and experience together in ways that contribute to the widest possible constellation of problem-solving and decision-making skills.

Intuitive reasoning skills are learned. Moreover, they do not depend upon intelligence. As emphasized, they depend upon knowledge, information, and experience in combination. That holds out an intriguing possibility for all of us. We can all become experts.

5. Emphasize exotic wagering, not straight wagering to win.

The selections derived from systematic methods of handicapping have been referred to as prime bets. When backed to win, these are the horses by which proficient handicappers can profit season after season. Fair enough.

Unfortunately, at least three conditions conspire to thwart the win bettor's prosperity. First, a season's bounty from straight bets on prime selections amounts to modest profits. Computer simulations have revealed that with systematic win wagering it takes too long to win too little. For that reason recreational handicappers who seek substantial money in the short run—season—abandon systematic win wagering.

Second, while awaiting the two or three prime bets of an afternoon, systematic win bettors also dabble in the daily double, exactas, and other exotics, and they take flyers on longshots as well. The habits slice the profit margin noticeably.

Third, as the fields grow smaller and the odds on contenders go correspondingly lower, too many prime selections go postward as underlays. These must be forsaken, as any series of underlays guarantees loss. The profit margin grows thinner still, maybe disappears.

Exotic wagering presents the contemporary alternative. It offers the best-informed handicappers a chance to make important money in the course of a season, as straight wagering does not. Exotics serve three purposes at least:

1. They afford handicappers who become information managers the opportunities to use all the information they bother to collect.

2. They can be used to convert straight underlays to exotic overlays.
3. They facilitate the making of substantial profit at small risk, a fundamental principle of effective money management.

Techniques aside, the crucial consideration of exotic wagering is value, and not just fair value, as in the win pools, but generous value. Rewards must be relatively high. That is because the probability of any exotic wager actually winning will be relatively low. Handicappers will lose much of the time. Exotics that win must overcompensate for the losses and toss tidy profits besides.

6. Participate on Information Teams.

Few handicappers enjoy the time or possess the energy and know-how to store, process, and retrieve the multiple kinds of information that will be potentially decisive. The remedy can be information teams composed of generalists and specialists having various handicapping strengths. One might provide speed figures. A second trip and bias data. A third trainer statistics. A fourth body-language updates. The team contributes the vital information sources needed to enhance the day-to-day problem solving and decision making.

Final decisions remain individualized, of course. The bottom line for team performance is that the profits of the members should increase.

Those are the broad strokes of the methodology. The practical component is the computer and broader information system. If the computer is missing, the productivity and efficiency of the effort will be diminished.

The substantive component is the quality of the information. If high quality is missing, sticky problems will persist unsolved, and poor decisions will carry the cause. Effectiveness will be hampered.

The process of handicapping for information managers clearly differs from conventional practice. The two approaches can be contrasted as shown in the table at the top of the next page.

It should be evident that by conventional handicapping only method selections can be supported, even when various types of information are used in that context. Almost everything else is either missed or undervalued.

The information-management approach opens the race widely to its real possibilities. Horses and combinations of horses offering value at comparable probabilities can be considered equally. The new approach identifies more overlays and therefore works better.

Finally, a caution. Systematic method handicappers cannot transform themselves into information managers overnight. They should not expect

Systematic Method Handicapping	Information Management
1. Identify contenders and eliminate noncontenders, according to the principles of the method.	1. Consider the prerace information requirements: eligibility conditions, track conditions, biases, trainer and jockey stats.
2. Separate the contenders, in concert with the method.	2. Conduct an information search and analysis of the past performances.
3. Make a selection.	3. Solve problems, by resorting to the database and information system.
4. Inspect selection at paddock and during the post parade.	4. Develop alternative outcome scenarios that are probable.
5. Bet selection or pass the race.	5. Make decisions.

to change quickly. The transformation consumes a year at least, more likely two. It begins with planning and thinking, not with buying a computer. It continues by choosing the structure and content of the information system that will emerge. It gathers its lasting momentum by accumulating the expansive knowledge and skill in handicapping on which the system ultimately swings.

CHAPTER 30

THE CRUCIBLE OF EXPECTATION

IN RECENT SEASONS a pair of mathematical wizards has delivered four fascinating books to Thoroughbred handicappers. Emerging from the keenest of minds, the four share a most intriguing characteristic. The books tell practitioners practically nothing about the art of handicapping.

Instead they concentrate intensely on parimutuel betting and money management. On these matters the books reveal almost everything there is to know. Yet not many handicappers have benefited from the wisdom.

From the perspective of the nonmathematical mind, the problem with mathematicians is that they talk a foreign language. They might cry out excitedly, "The probability that John Henry will finish in the money is .87, and the Expectation to show of this type of bet is .34. The situation deserves the optimal Kelly bet-size!"

This means the John Henry shapes up today as a fantastic show overlay that deserves the player's maximum bet. On this type of wager, repeated hundreds of times, for each dollar invested the bettor can expect to collect $1.34, or 34 percent profit.

Andrew Beyer would put it differently. "I'm gonna kill this goddamn race!"

Unable to understand conversational math, handicappers shy away from the books and the authors. This is a dreadful mistake. It prevents them from correcting the awful betting and money-management habits most handicappers have picked up as baggage along the way.

The painful truth is that the fundamental parimutuel-wagering and money-management concepts are mathematical. No one learns how to bet intelligently or how to manage money expertly through the hard-boiled lessons of "experience."

If anyone cares to contradict this, let him read the texts of the leading handicapping authorities in the nation. Many recount the painstaking evolutions of the handicappers as bettors. After 10, 15, or 20 years of experimenting and floating, the leading authorities in the end arrive exhaustedly at the only betting and money-management principle that can be extracted from experience.

Handicappers, the experts conclude, must bet and manage money in ways best suited to the individual temperament and personality. It's rather sad, actually.

Experience at the races is not sufficiently rigorous to teach practitioners the correct principles of parimutuel betting and money management, but a few slow, thoughtful, difficult readings of the appropriate books turn wonderful tricks.

No one needs to master complex formulae and apply them steadfastly to the daily routine. That's not the idea. But grasping the fundamental ideas and strategies of intelligent betting and money management is exactly the idea. Handicappers will be amazed at the simplicity inherent in elementary mathematical truth. The lessons learned serve the highly practical purpose, besides, of answering all the pestering questions of loved ones and curious outsiders.

For example, "Well, if you're so good, why don't you just play the horses for a living and make yourself a fortune?"

The last time a curious outsider—a.k.a cynical outsider—put one to me, I replied, "Well, my Expectation to win is .26 when my handicapping methods are working in top form. I play approximately 90 days each year and get roughly three bets a day. That's 270 bets a season.

"If I bet $250 on each, I would earn a profit of $17,550. If I bet $50 on each, my profit would be $3,150. Not exactly a corporate salary. Does that answer your question?"

My retort was not only proper, it was mathematically precise. The crucial indispensable contribution of the mathematical models of handicapping is the concept of Expectation. It's a bottom line so loaded with impact that almost everything else the math authors do can be traced back to the handicapper's Expectation.

The concept refers to the rate of gain-loss on the dollar invested to be expected from a given handicapping proficiency across a representative sample of performance, approximately 250 plays. A synonym for positive Expectation (profit) is advantage. A negative Expectation, of course, refers to the dollar loss or the handicapper's disadvantage. As the mathematicians emphasize, no brand of systematic money management has ever been known to overcome a negative Expectation. That is, effective money management is dependent upon proficient handicapping.

No matter how averse to math they are, all regular handicappers should come to grips with the following formula:

$$E(x) = \text{Odds} \times P(W) - P(L)$$

This means that the dollar profit (E) of handicapper (x) is equal to the average odds on x's winners multiplied by the probability of winning (win percentage) minus the probability of losing (loss percentage). How complex is that?

A typical workout (200 races) of my class methods resulted in 35 percent winners (.65 loss probability) at average odds of 2.6 to 1. Expectation is therefore .26. This means that for each dollar I wager I can expect to get back $1.26.

This is what math authors mean to communicate when they state that the Expectation of a given bet or type of bet is .15. If handicappers bet $100 in a series of 50 $2 tickets, they will net roughly $15. The more frequently they make similar bets, the more inexorably the profit margin will approach exactly 15 percent of the amount invested.

Knowing a handicapping Expectation slays all the persistent dragons.

How much can I expect to win in a typical season, for instance, given my Expectation of .26?

The amount won or lost will be equal to the amount bet multiplied by the handicapper's Expectation.

If I play 90 days and bet three races a day, $250 flat, I shall invest $67,500. My profit will be $17,550. If I bet just $50 flat, the amount bet will be $13,500 and the profit will be $3,510.

Math also advises me that I can do better by varying the bet size. The optimal bet is the single-race Expectation (.26) divided by the dollar odds. If the odds are 5-2, the optimal bet is 10.4 percent of bankroll. If the odds are 13-1, the optimal bet is 2 percent of bankroll. This has the happy effect of maximizing the rate of growth of the bankroll, which flat betting does not do.

After playing the races for a decade, most of what I have learned about parimutuel wagering and money management I absorbed within six months from one of the aforementioned authors, Dick Mitchell. Something about the logic underpinning the optimal bet size has disturbed me and I posed the problem to Mitchell.

I talked to him in his own language, sounding eerily like the math expert I am not.

Consider a handicapper having a 10 percent Expectation, I said. If the odds on his best bet of the day are 5-2, he should bet 4 percent of bankroll.

But if the best-bet odds are 10-1, he should bet just 1 percent of bankroll.

Isn't that betting more on lower-priced selections and less on higher-priced selections, thereby minimizing value?

Mitchell's answer dealt with the actual handicapping probabilities, of course. He pointed out that the 10-1 shot reflects public odds and might be judged by the individual handicapper a serious overlay. The correction is using the true winning odds, as determined by the individual handicapper.

So if a handicapper judges the 10-1 public choice an actual 4-1 shot, he should bet 2.5 percent bankroll. The more rigorously handicappers estimate probable odds, the more likely they will make optimal bets. That amounts to common sense, as math ultimately does, and is a greatly persuasive argument for constructing an accurate handicapper's odds line. We not only spot overlays as a result, but we understand as well the proper bet sizes.

The presupposition of optimal-betting procedures is accurate odds lines. Where these are missing, flat betting substitutes well, sacrificing maximum rate of growth but reducing the risks of overbetting correspondingly.

Expectation is nothing less than the most critical variable in handicapping for profit. Systematic method play depends upon it absolutely. All else swings on Expectation.

If Expectation is unknown, method handicappers are spinning wheels.

If Expectation has been overestimated, method handicappers will bet too much and will therefore lose.

If Expectation has been underestimated, handicappers will bet too little and will therefore win less than they are capable of winning. Needless to say, underestimation is the lesser evil.

What is the Expectation of a 30 percent handicapper who gets 5-2 on winners? It's .05.

If that handicapper slips $100,000 through he windows on method selections for the season, how much will he win? He wins $5,000.

What is the optimal bet size on a 5-2 shot? It's 2 percent of bankroll. Handicappers keeping copious records of their play gain an advantage otherwise unmatched. A full season's research is enough. Those handicappers can determine their Expectation for playing the races and possibly for specific types of races—maiden races, claiming races, allowance races, stakes races, turf races, routes and sprints, races for three-year-olds, maiden-claiming races, races for fillies and mares, races for juveniles, races at classic distances.

The list is lengthy. Something is bound to be learned. If handicappers know their single-race Expectation on each of the specialties and construct a reasonably accurate odds line for each race, they can invest the optimal amounts each trip to the window and get full benefits from their hard-earned handicapping proficiency.

When those most fruitful of years finally arrive, the compliments can be sent to mathematics.

CHAPTER 31

IN THE AGE OF EXOTIC WAGERING: WHERE WE ARE NOW

SINCE THE ORIGINAL edition of this anthology (1987), the betting menus of racetracks have exploded with exotic wagers the executives would have considered destructive when the exacta on the ninth race first appeared at Hollywood Park in 1969. Instead of exactas on the third, fifth, seventh, and ninth, and two trifectas perhaps on other races—so the pools will not dilute one another, in the official view—bettors can now construct exacta and trifecta combinations at every race. They can roll the pick threes from the top of the cards to the bottom. If they cannot roll the doubles, as at Hollywood Park and Santa Anita, they can pursue the early double and the late double anywhere. Parlays are available.

And not a day passes anywhere that bettors cannot chase the four- and five-figure payoffs brandished routinely by the pick fours and superfectas, the newest exotica still limited to selected spots on the daily programs. The New York Racing Association, apparently still in thrall to the dilution factor, prohibits its bettors from playing the pick three on the same race that begins its pick four, an encroachment on freedom of choice that cost me a couple of hundred just the other day, but the decades-long complaints of the bettors that they should be allowed to bet any race they choose in any way they choose have largely carried the cause. The exotic-wagering game has been won.

Not to be neglected is the peculiar charm of the southern California pick six, inexorably a national pool, where the single-day 2002 carryovers on occasion spilled over the $200,000 mark. When the pools go international, how long will it be before the southern California pick-six carry-overs will exceed $500,000? Undoubtedly, exotic bettors have this and other new developments to whet the appetite even more.

Unlike the track executives who have resisted the onslaught at every turn, most handicappers and casual racegoers have come to understand that exotic wagering represents a healthy development that has altered the racetrack experience for its regular customers like none other since parimutuel wagering replaced bookmaking early in the 20th century.

Why?

What have we learned by now?

How should we proceed from here?

For recreational customers, practically all, the exactas, trifectas, pick threes, pick fours, superfectas, and the mighty pick six, extend the opportunities to win substantial profits in the short run, as straight wagering to win does not, and without losing their shirts. All they need to remember, well understood in a fogged, slippery corner of their consciousness at the track, is the first principle of exotic wagering: bet small, win big. If they will follow that prime principle, recreational handicappers can stay in the game until something wonderful happens.

To appreciate the contrast, computer simulations have revealed how difficult it will be for recreational handicappers to amass important profits in the short run of a season by betting to win, even when risking sizable amounts and implementing the most powerful systematic money-management methods. "Important profits" means a middle manager's salary.

Consider that the competent handicapper exhibiting 30 percent proficiency at average odds on winners of 2.75 to 1 and wagering 5 percent of a $1,000 bankroll across 700 bets can expect to win approximately $4,000. The same improving handicapper exhibiting 35 percent proficiency at average odds of 2.6 to 1 for the season can expect to win roughly five times as much, or $21,000.

The elite corps of serious recreational handicappers—well read, highly motivated toward profits, up to date on the information fronts, widely experienced, in attendance regularly, larger bettors—who exhibit the same 35 percent proficiency on key horses, average odds of 2.5 to 1, and betting $250 flat, can expect to take home approximately $42,000 for the hard work and long season. As Dick Mitchell has observed, "Not exactly Rolls-Royce wages."

Another melancholy observation is not only relevant but prevalent. For most recreational handicappers who care, the 35 percent proficiency and $250 bets on prime horses sail far wide of the mark. The more realistic benchmarks will be 30 percent proficiency and $20 bets. For this beleaguered group, the grind-it-out approach to winning becomes too long, too hard a grind. For this reason alone, systematic wagering to win has been almost completely abandoned.

This reality can be juxtaposed with three modern developments in the game to explain the bettors' unrestrained support of exotic-wagering opportunities: (1) the dramatically increased availability and accessibility of meaningful handicapping methods and information, (2) the oversupply of underlays to win provided by the small fields, and (3) the truly tremendous payoffs supplied routinely by the superfectas and pick fours, numerous trifectas and pick threes, and the southern California pick six.

The information explosion has persuaded thousands of tutored handicappers they can find more than one way to skin a race. Exotic wagering supports a reliance on multiple, diverse sources of information. The smaller fields have generated abundant underlays in the straight and in the exacta pools, the cruelest development of contemporary racing. Exotic wagering has provided the alternative. It presents racing's best customers with several advantages they need:

1. Exotic wagering permits the concurrent use of the several sources of handicapping information now available and widely distributed.
2. Many underlays in the win pools can be converted to overlays in the exotic pools.
3. The relatively large payoffs of combination betting supports the fundamental money-management principle that encourages bettors to maximize gain at minimal risk.
4. Exotic wagering allows recreational bettors to maximize profits in the short run of a day, week, two weeks, or a month, when skill, luck, and opportunity coincide for a time.
5. Exotic wagering gives the smallest bettors a chance to make substantial profits at the races, and allows the inspiring thoughts of the lifetime score, even as the possibility of the top horse allows the small owner to dream of a lifetime's success.

A COUNTERVAILING FORCE preventing the general progress resulting from the several advantages, however, becomes for most bettors an overarching disadvantage. Recreational handicappers in the main lack any degree of coherent knowledge and skill in exotic wagering. A glaring omission in handicapping instruction has been empirical evidence of the most effective strategies and techniques of exotic wagering. Most bettors therefore do what comes naturally, which can be disastrous.

In the past decade and a half the situation has improved. Important books by Barry Meadow, Dick Mitchell, William T. Ziemba, and Andrew Beyer have provided new directions and useful tips. Meadow and Ziemba have provided mathematically determined betting charts that allow handicappers to distinguish the underlay and overlay combinations in exacta wagering, and these have been terrifically helpful.

In *Betting at the Racetrack*, Ziemba (with Donald Hausch) has identified the win probabilities and cutoff values of the $2 and $5 exactas for all possible odds combinations. The values were derived from extensive studies of exacta wagering in New York and southern California, but they should generalize widely. The estimates depend upon the public's ability to estimate the winning probabilities of horses exceedingly well. Examine Table 1 (pages 160–161). It represents the cutoff values at 15 percent advantage for the $2 exacta in New York, where the odds on the top selection range from 6-5 to 8-1, and the odds on the bottom selections range from 7-2 to 10-1. The values on the top line represent the probabilities the combinations will actually occur.

Handicappers should notice the low probabilities associated even with low-odds combinations. A 6-5 shot atop a 7-2 shot has a 10.9 percent chance of occurring. The combination must pay $21 to make sense. A 2-1 shot atop a 5-1 shot will occur less than 5 percent (4.5 percent) of the time. The combination must pay $51. Handicappers must appreciate that a pair of 8-1 shots will occur only seven times in a thousand attempts (0.7 percent). On a $2 bet, that combination must return $310, and it frequently will not. Not only is catching exactas analogous to catching butterflies, but also handicappers must get generous value, not fair value.

Recognizing the poison that underlays in exactas can spread, Meadow insists each combination represent a 50 percent overlay. I concur. Table 2 (page 162) presents the exacta combinations at 50 percent advantage for $2 bets at customary takeouts at all tracks. Handicappers might clip the table and place it at a convenient position on the desk or table. Meadow cautions that when multiple combinations are pursued, the amounts of the losing tickets must be subtracted from the projected payoffs before overlays can be identified accurately.

In *Money Secrets at the Racetrack*, Meadow provides a one-paragraph tutorial on calculating exacta payoffs at 50 percent advantage, once handicappers have assigned win probabilities to their contenders. He describes a hypothetical exacta between Fetlock and Pastern, where a handicapper

Table 1

Cutoff Values at 15% Advantage to the Bettors for $2 Exactas in New York, Based Upon Public Win Odds

COLUMN: *Odds on the Horse You Think Will Win This Race*
ROW: *Odds on the Horse You Think Will Finish Second*

Quoted Odds	6-5	7-5	8-5	9-5	2-1	5-2	3-1	7-2	4-1	9-2	5-1	6-1	7-1	8-1
7-2	10.9	9.4	8.4	7.6	6.4	5.3	4.5	3.8	3.3	2.9	2.5	2.1	1.8	1.6
	21	24	27	30	36	43	52	60	69	79	92	109	127	144
4-1	9.7	8.4	7.5	6.7	5.7	4.8	4	3.4	2.9	2.6	2.2	1.9	1.6	1.4
	24	28	31	34	40	48	58	68	78	89	104	123	143	162
9-2	8.7	7.5	6.7	6.0	5.1	4.3	3.6	3	2.6	2.3	2	1.7	1.4	1.3
	27	31	34	38	45	54	65	76	87	99	116	137	159	181
5-1	7.6	6.5	5.8	5.3	4.5	3.7	3.1	2.7	2.3	2	1.7	1.5	1.3	1.1
	30	35	39	44	51	62	74	87	100	113	132	157	182	207
6-1	6.5	5.6	5.0	4.5	3.9	3.2	2.7	2.3	2	1.7	1.5	1.3	1.1	1
	35	41	46	51	60	72	86	101	116	132	154	183	212	241
7-1	5.7	4.9	4.4	4.0	3.4	2.8	2.3	2	1.7	1.5	1.3	1.1	1	0.8
	40	47	52	58	68	82	98	115	132	150	176	209	242	275
8-1	5.1	4.4	3.9	3.5	3.0	2.5	2.1	1.8	1.5	1.4	1.2	1	0.8	0.7
	45	53	59	65	77	92	111	130	149	169	198	235	272	310
9-1	4.5	3.9	3.5	3.1	2.7	2.2	1.9	1.6	1.4	1.2	1	0.9	0.8	0.7
	51	59	66	73	86	103	124	145	167	189	222	263	305	347
10-1	4.1	3.5	3.1	2.8	2.4	2.0	1.7	1.4	1.2	1.1	0.9	0.8	0.7	0.6
	56	65	73	81	95	115	137	161	185	210	246	291	338	385

	0.5	0.6	0.7	0.8	0.9	1	1.2	1.4	1.7	2.0	2.4	2.6	2.9	3.4
12-1	0.5 / 463	0.6 / 407	0.7 / 351	0.8 / 296	0.9 / 253	1 / 223	1.2 / 194	1.4 / 165	1.7 / 138	2.0 / 114	2.4 / 98	2.6 / 88	2.9 / 79	3.4 / 68
14-1	0.4 / 546	0.5 / 480	0.6 / 414	0.7 / 349	0.8 / 298	0.9 / 263	1 / 228	1.2 / 195	1.4 / 163	1.7 / 135	2.0 / 115	2.2 / 104	2.5 / 93	2.9 / 80
16-1	0.4 / 634	0.4 / 557	0.5 / 480	0.6 / 405	0.7 / 346	0.8 / 305	0.9 / 265	1 / 226	1.2 / 189	1.5 / 157	1.7 / 134	1.9 / 121	2.1 / 107	2.5 / 93
18-1	0.3 / 727	0.4 / 638	0.4 / 551	0.5 / 464	0.6 / 397	0.7 / 349	0.8 / 304	0.9 / 260	1.1 / 217	1.3 / 179	1.5 / 153	1.7 / 138	1.9 / 123	2.2 / 107
20-1	0.3 / 825	0.3 / 725	0.4 / 625	0.4 / 527	0.5 / 451	0.6 / 397	0.7 / 345	0.8 / 295	0.9 / 246	1.1 / 204	1.3 / 174	1.5 / 157	1.6 / 140	1.9 / 121
25-1	0.2 / 1181	0.2 / 1038	0.3 / 895	0.3 / 755	0.4 / 645	0.4 / 568	0.5 / 494	0.5 / 422	0.7 / 352	0.8 / 292	0.9 / 249	1.0 / 225	1.1 / 200	1.3 / 173
30-1	0.2 / 1511	0.2 / 1327	0.2 / 1145	0.2 / 965	0.3 / 825	0.3 / 726	0.4 / 631	0.4 / 539	0.5 / 450	0.6 / 373	0.7 / 319	0.8 / 287	0.9 / 256	1.0 / 222
35-1	0.1 / 2143	0.1 / 1883	0.1 / 1624	0.2 / 1370	0.2 / 1171	0.2 / 1031	0.3 / 896	0.3 / 765	0.4 / 639	0.4 / 529	0.5 / 452	0.6 / 408	0.6 / 363	0.7 / 314
40-1	0.1 / 2797	0.1 / 2457	0.1 / 2120	0.1 / 1788	0.2 / 1528	0.2 / 1345	0.2 / 1169	0.2 / 999	0.3 / 834	0.3 / 691	0.4 / 590	0.4 / 532	0.5 / 474	0.6 / 410
50-1	0.1 / 3743	0.1 / 3288	0.1 / 2836	0.1 / 2392	0.1 / 2044	0.1 / 1800	0.1 / 1564	0.2 / 1337	0.2 / 1115	0.2 / 924	0.3 / 789	0.3 / 712	0.4 / 634	0.4 / 549
80-1	0 / 8211	0 / 7214	0 / 6222	0 / 5248	0.1 / 4485	0.1 / 3949	0.1 / 3432	0.1 / 2933	0.1 / 2447	0.1 / 2028	0.1 / 1732	0.1 / 1561	0.2 / 1392	0.2 / 1205
100-1	0 / 32192	0 / 28280	0 / 24394	0 / 20574	0 / 17582	0 / 15481	0 / 13454	0 / 11497	0.0 / 9592	0.0 / 7950	0.0 / 6788	0.0 / 6121	0.0 / 5456	0.0 / 4724

$2 Exacta Overlay Prices

	1/5	2/5	1/2	3/5	4/5	1	6/5	7/5	3/2	8/5	9/5	2	5/2	3	7/2	4	9/2	5	6	7	8	9	10	11	12	15	20	25	30	50	100
1/9																							4	4	4	5	6	7	9	15	31
1/5																		4	4	5	5	6	7	7	9	12	15	18	31	61
2/5													4	5	5	6	7	8	9	10	11	13	15	16	20	26	32	38	62	122
1/2												5	5	6	7	8	8	10	11	12	14	16	17	18	23	31	38	46	77	152
3/5										5	5	6	7	8	8	9	10	12	14	16	17	19	22	24	28	37	46	55	91	181
4/5							5	5	6	6	7	8	9	10	11	13	14	16	18	21	23	26	28	31	38	50	63	75	123	242
1						6	7	7	7	8	8	10	11	13	14	16	17	20	23	26	29	32	35	38	47	62	77	92	152	302
6/5					7	7	8	8	9	10	10	12	14	16	17	19	21	25	28	32	35	39	43	46	57	75	93	111	183	363
7/5					8	8	9	10	10	11	11	12	14	16	18	20	23	25	29	33	37	41	46	50	54	67	88	109	130	214
3/2					8	8	9	10	11	11	12	13	15	17	20	22	24	26	31	35	40	44	49	53	58	71	94	116	139	229
8/5					8	9	10	11	11	12	13	14	16	18	21	23	26	28	33	38	43	47	52	57	62	76	100	124	148	244
9/5					8	9	10	11	13	13	15	16	18	21	24	26	29	32	37	43	48	53	59	64	70	86	113	140	167	275
2				9	10	11	13	14	14	15	16	17	20	23	26	29	32	35	41	47	53	59	65	71	77	95	125	155	185	305
5/2				11	11	13	14	16	17	18	19	20	22	26	29	33	37	41	44	52	59	67	74	82	89	97	119	157	194	232
3			12	13	14	16	17	19	21	22	23	25	26	31	35	40	44	49	53	62	71	80	89	98	107	116	143	188	233	278
7/2			14	15	16	18	20	23	25	26	27	29	31	36	41	47	52	57	62	73	83	94	104	115	125	136	167	220	272	324
4			16	17	18	21	23	26	28	29	31	33	35	41	47	53	59	65	71	83	95	107	119	131	143	155	191	251	311	
9/2			18	20	21	24	26	29	32	33	35	37	40	47	53	60	67	74	80	94	107	121	134	148	161	175	215	283		
5			20	22	23	26	28	32	35	37	38	41	44	47	59	67	74	82	89	104	119	134	149	164	179	194	239	314		
6		21	25	26	28	32	35	39	43	44	46	50	53	62	71	80	89	98	107	125	143	161	179	197	215	233	287			
7	25	29	31	33	37	41	46	50	52	54	58	62	73	83	94	104	115	125	146	167	188	209	230	251	272	335				
8	28	33	35	38	43	47	52	57	59	62	67	71	83	95	107	119	131	143	167	191	215	239	263	287	311					
9	32	37	40	43	48	53	59	64	67	70	75	80	94	107	121	134	148	161	188	215	242	269	296	323						
10	32	35	41	44	47	53	59	65	71	74	77	83	89	104	119	134	149	164	179	209	239	269	299	329						
11	35	39	46	49	52	59	65	72	79	82	85	92	98	115	131	148	164	181	197	230	263	296	319							
12	39	43	50	53	57	64	71	79	86	89	93	100	107	125	143	161	179	197	215	251	287	323								
15	49	53	62	67	71	80	89	98	107	111	116	125	134	157	179	202	224	247	268	314										
20	65	71	83	89	95	107	119	131	143	149	155	167	179	209	239	269	299	329												
25	82	89	104	111	119	134	149	164	179	187	194	209	224	262	299	337														
30	98	107	125	134	143	161	179	197	215	224	233	251	269	314																

has assigned Fetlock a 40 percent chance to win, and Pastern a 20 percent chance to win. To wit:

"Out of a 100% round-book line, you've assigned Fetlock 40%. The rest of the field has 60%, of which Pastern has 20%, or one-third of the remainder. Thus the chance of this combination finishing one-two is .40 $\times$ ($^{.20}/_{.60}$), or 13.3 chances in 100. Checking our friendly odds-percentage table (or calculating $\frac{1}{.133} - 1$), we find this equals about 6.5 to 1 (handicappers are urged to use the odds-percentage table at the end of this essay). For a $2 bet, anything below $15 for this combination is an underlay. Since we demand a 50% overlay for all exacta bets, we need $22 to play."

Handicappers without betting charts can rely upon calculators to make the computations, once win probabilities have been assigned. A few practice sessions will reveal how simple the process becomes. All that is left is checking the projected payoffs, and backing the combinations that will pay well enough.

A troubling paradox haunts the exotic-wagering habits of many racetrack regulars. The same handicappers who demand value when betting to win casually accept numerous underlay combinations in the exotic pools, presumably because the raw dollars appear acceptable. This devastates the bankroll long haul. As Ziemba has shown, keep in mind that the actual probabilities that exotic combinations will occur are low. The rewards must overcompensate for the risks.

Regarding strategies, below are a number of techniques for the exactas and other exotica that will be more likely to reward the bettors with overlays.

1. Far more often than not, favorites in exactas are overlays on the bottom but underlays on top. If favorites or low-priced contenders would be exploited in exacta wagering, they normally make better sense in the two-hole. No principle of exotic wagering deserves greater allegiance than this. Yet it is violated daily by multitudes of recreational bettors. As a practical imperative, recreational bettors must require themselves to know that favorites represent exacta overlays before supporting them on top.

Andy Anderson, of San Francisco, and the inventor of the excellent Exacta-Perfecta Gauge of fair cutoff values, has discovered a particularly charming application of this principle.

Odds-on favorites, even-money shots, and low-priced horses that are favored will return substantial profits over time when wheeled on the bottom in 11- and 12-horse fields. In Anderson's longitudinal study of the procedure (five years), these bottom wheels have thrown profits upward of 800 percent on investment.

At the Second National Conference on Thoroughbred Handicapping (Expo '84), at The Meadowlands, Anderson emphasized the tactic in a seminar and that same evening demonstrated its power. In an 11-horse lineup, Spend a Buck went off at even money in the Grade 1 Young America Stakes. Anderson and several conference participants back-wheeled the favorite. The winner was the longshot Script Ohio, at 37-1. Spend a Buck finished second. The $2 exacta paid $282, or 140-1.

In *Smart Money*, Las Vegas pro Gordon Jones supported Anderson on the charms of back-wheels of overbet favorites. Jones reported that back-wheels and partial back-wheels outperformed the backing of odds-on favorites to place by a significant sum.

2. Extreme favorites (odds-on) that figure to win can sometimes be supported on top of medium-priced horses and longshots, especially when the second and third public choices are overbet and can be eliminated.

Handicappers can anticipate profits from the partial wheels they construct from this guideline.

Author Steve Davidowitz years ago pointed out that when confronted with authentic outstanding horses that figure, the crowd instinctively overbets its second choice, which does not figure so well. It may do the same to its third choice, which also does not deserve it. Find the better-priced overlays in the field. Play all combinations having a handicapper's fair chance and paying generous value.

Where overlays abound in unpredictable circumstances, multiple keys transform unplayable races into beatable races.

3. Two medium-priced horses represent the most generous kinds of exacta overlays.

Many races become indecipherable in terms of a single selection at acceptable odds. Multiple keys to exacta bonanzas become the alternative. Compare the expected and projected payoffs. Play all combinations having a handicapper's fair chance and paying generous value.

Where overlays abound in unpredictable circumstances, multiple keys transform unplayable races into beatable races.

4. Two longshots are invariably overbet as exacta combinations.

Unless one horse represents the kind of fantastic overlay that has been miscalculated by the crowd, longshots of 13-1 or greater are best pursued in the win pools, where they pay boxcars as well. In Ziemba's tables a pair of 20-1 shots has a .1 percent chance of actually occurring and must pay $2,319 ($2 exacta) to equal a 15 percent edge for the bettor. And they never pay that!

5. Exacta wheels and baseballs are normally nonsense bets.

This is because too many of the combinations will be underlays. Not only do bets on underlays guarantee losses, they detract from the value of overlay combinations.

Following Meadow, Mitchell, and others, if three or more horses must be combined, check the cutoff values on the monitors, and cover the 50 percent overlays only. Following Beyer, if handicappers prefer, use the overlays evenly; the higher the value, the greater the coverage. When reducing costs, always eliminate the lower-odds horses first. San Francisco pro Paul Braseth believes a handicapper's top combination that will overpay should be hammered strongly, as great as 10 times any other preferred combination, an especially agreeable thought.

If quinellas are offered, and handicappers intend to combine a favorite or low-priced contender with a longshot, proceed in this way. Use the longshot on top of the low-priced favorite in one-way exactas only, then combine the favorite-longshot combination in quinellas. As a rule, the quinella should pay half the exacta. When the longshot wins, the exacta will pay significantly more than twice the quinella. When the underlay wins, the quinella will pay significantly greater than half the exacta.

At a seminar years ago during Oak Tree at Santa Anita, a lady liked a 40-1 shot and the even-money favorite. She bought a $20 quinella on the two. The 40-1 shot beat the 1-1 underlay by a nose. The $2 quinella paid $65. Our hero collected $650, and she was ecstatic. But if she had invested the same $20 in a slightly different way, the handicapper could have almost doubled her pleasure; $10 exacta with the 40-1 shot on top and a $10 quinella. The exacta with the 40-1 shot atop the 1-1 shot paid $185 for two, or a return on $10 of $925. The $2 quinella at $65 would have returned $325. The profit soars to $1,250 for the same $20 bet. Of course, if the 1-1 shot wins, the lady collects $325, not $625, a tradeoff handicappers must accept. In exotic wagering, it's crucial to play the upside. In the Oak Tree example, as the instructors insisted to the lady's chagrin, if the mistake is repeated 10 times a year, that's $6,000 lost, and nobody can afford that tradeoff at the races. That crestfallen woman will not make the same mistake again, and neither should regular handicappers.

6. In general, the trifecta offers the same fair-value propositions as the exacta.

That means that combinations of favorites, longshots, and overbet favorites keyed to win will represent poor bets.

Barry Meadow has warned the trifecta should be passed, unless handicappers can eliminate the favorite or the second choice. When both are covered, the trifectas underpay, even as the probabilities of winning remain excessively low.

Regarding favorites in trifectas, Beyer prefers to key legitimate favorites to win only. If favorites are false or vulnerable, ignore them. The reason: The public tends to bet favorites evenly to win, place, and show, making the trifectas relative underlays when favorites finish second and third.

San Diego pro Andy Cylke, on the other hand, has collected extensive trifecta data at several tracks that indicate the favorites to show can be extremely generous when longshots finish first and second. If longshots are combined in the top two holes, cover the favorites to show.

Dick Mitchell recommends the following trifecta ($1) strategy for casual bettors in competitive situations that promise to pay well:

3 horses to win	A-B-C
the same 3 horses to place add a 4th horse	A-B-C-D
the same 4 horses to show, add a 5th horse	A-B-C-D-E

The coverage is extensive, notably to win, and the cost ($1 tickets) is low; $27. Trifectas are best avoided in fields smaller than eight.

7. The superfecta is most attractive when handicappers can key on a nonfavorite to win, or bet against a favorite or low-priced second choice.

Experience with the superfecta has been so limited, almost nothing of value exists in the books and periodicals. Still, the empirical evidence can be inspiring, as when the superfecta at Santa Anita pays eight to 10 times the trifecta. Five-figure payoffs are rather routine, such that a superfecta or two in the calendar year might turn losses to profits. Still, the losses can be stiff and amount to thousands annually.

In the April 2001 edition of his excellent newsletter, *Meadow's Racing Monthly*, Barry Meadow explores the superfecta with his customary parimutuel aptitude and restraint. Meadow makes a number of important points:

- When handicappers key a horse to win, they should insist that at least one, and preferably two, other horses finish in the top four.
- Several horses must be eliminated from serious consideration.
- Longshots are best covered to finish third and fourth, as that's where they typically do finish.

The eliminations are crucial, as the cost of the tickets otherwise will add up uncomfortably and so will the losses. Meadow urges handicappers to hesitate before playing the superfecta, to pose to themselves these questions:

- Can you leave out either the favorite or the second choice; if not, no play.
- Are there longshots you can use, keying them to run third or fourth, because a longshot is much more likely to run third or fourth instead of first or second?
- Can you abandon several horses altogether?
- Is there a pace scenario that might put several horses with a particular running style in or out of the superfecta?
- Is there a discrepancy between the crowd's opinion and your own? If so, that's the best time to play.

As basic as the advice sounds, Meadow stresses that handicappers must pass the superfecta whenever the race should run to form. He cautions that many races are comprised of obvious combinations, as when a maiden-claiming race contains five horses that can run a little, and seven that cannot run at all. Wait for sweeter opportunities.

Meadow presents three simple strategies that often will make sense:

- Key one horse to win, expand the ticket in the deeper positions ($48):
  1 with 2-3-4 with 2-3-4-5-6 with 2-3-4-5-6

- Go short to win and place, then go deep in the third and fourth slots ($60):
  1 with 2-3 with 2-3-4-5-6-7-8 with 2-3-4-5-6-7-8
- Key two longshots in the fourth position ($72):
  1-2-3 with 1-2-3-4-5 with 1-2-3-4-5 with 6-7

Meadow cautions that handicappers should not seek the all-encompassing Superfecta Plan, a single strategy that does not exist. A number of single strategies such as the above three must be applied to specific situations. The basic principles are more important than specific strategies. Remember:

- Don't play unless there's an opportunity to score.
- Key, don't box.
- Look to eliminate at least one low-priced horse.
- Strive to include at least one high-priced horse.
- Avoid using the "all" button.
- Bet in one-dollar ($1) increments.

The final guidepost is critical. If the superfecta pays $527 for $1, or less than 600-1, handicappers won't be forced to sign a tax slip. At least at the self-service machines (SAMs), handicappers can hit the "repeat" button several times. At the window or on the phone, ask the clerk to punch the $1 button repeatedly.

8. If structured carefully, the pick three frequently will combine the best value with the strongest probability of winning.

A melancholy disadvantage of chasing exotic combinations is the low probability of winning. Losing runs can be prolonged and painful. In pick-three wagering, only winners must be selected. If handicappers cover the contention of each leg such that they have a 50 percent or greater chance of hitting each, the probability of hitting the pick three will be .50 × .50 × .50, or 12.5 percent. The fair-value odds will be 7-1. The pick three must pay 8-1 to break even. Handicappers should play when they estimate the pick three will pay 12-1 or greater, a 50 percent overlay. If handicappers invest $72, the payoff must be $864. Handicappers can examine each three-leg win combination, as Meadow urges, and abandon the combination that obviously will underpay.

Adventurous pick-three bettors can treat any sequence of three races as a series of parlays. In each of the three legs, a key horse is selected, and linked to the contention in the other two legs. Three tickets are purchased. Obviously, to cash, at least one of the three key horses must win. If two of the key horses win, and the contention in the other leg has been identified correctly, handicappers collect the pick three twice. That will happen regularly, if handicappers find a pair of key bets in any three-race sequence. On rare occasions, all three keys will win, and handicappers collect the payoff three times.

One of the key horses can be a favorite, but odds-on favorites are taboo.

In *The Winning Horseplayer,* Beyer promotes an approach to exotic wagering where the bets vary in accord with the strength of handicappers' opinions. The ceiling bet equals the largest bet the individual has risked during the past two seasons, such that bettors remain within their comfort zones. Typical bets are scaled downward from the ceiling bet. As Beyer notes, the approach allows recreational handicappers repeated opportunities for big scores in the short run. Two or three times a season they should expect to make a killing, when the key horses and all the circumstances of the races appear to be ideal—and, in fact, happen.

The recommended scaling is 5 to 10 percent of the ceiling on typical combinations. As opinions strengthen, bet size increases to 20 to 25 percent. A strong opinion might deserve a 50 percent outlay. Extra-strong opinions warrant as much as 75 to 80 percent of the ceiling amount. Specifics aside, handicappers must not forget the key consideration of all exotic bets is added value, and not merely fair value. The subjectivity of Beyer's approach means it should work best in confident, highly experienced hands. A certain level of betting artistry is desirable. Recreational handicappers that suffer a tendency to lose the big ones while winning the small ones should benefit instead from a more objective and disciplined style.

The pick six is the most exotic racetrack bet of all. It has a unique appeal that is almost primal and urgent to a number of the most talented handicappers and biggest bettors in the country. Its separate treatment therefore in this anthology is proper, and comes to handicappers from one of the most successful pick-six proponents anywhere. Nonetheless, even without a pick-six plum, handicappers capable of complementing consistent profits in the win pools with occasional exotic windfalls will have the best chance of ending the seasons far ahead. Even without a pick-six plum, that middle manager's salary is entirely feasible.

CHAPTER 32

EUREKA! FIXED PERCENTAGE-MINIMUM

A 100-RACE FIELD STUDY at Santa Anita Park and numerous computer simulations have revealed that the racetrack money-management method presented for the first time here can

(a)   Outperform flat betting by a significant margin
(b)   Control for the profit erosion characteristic of fixed-percentage wagering during losing runs
(c)   Increase in power as the number of bets increases

Labeled *fixed percentage-minimum* (FP-M) by the author, the method invests a fixed percentage of capital following a win bet, but just a minimum amount following a loss. It's an important variation of fixed-percentage wagering, whereby bettors bet a fixed percentage of capital each time. As will be seen immediately and convincingly, FP-M wagering not only minimizes the losses of accumulated profits during typical losing streaks at the racetrack but also makes it possible for handicappers to regain considerable losses quickly, or even pull ahead of previous profit margins, merely perhaps with a pair of winners.

Handicappers capable of a .35 win proficiency, at average odds of 2.6-1, attainable results, can be expect to earn a middle management's corporate salary over a season's play. But at .30 proficiency FP-M does not perform nearly as well and may bust once of every five times attempted.

The Problem: Fixed-percentage wagering to win has long been championed as an effective money-management method at the races, as bettors bet more when winning, less when losing, thereby maximizing gain and minimizing loss. At conventional win-proficiency levels, the method avoids bankruptcy wonderfully well. As others have shown, racegoers who take $100 to the track and bet 5 percent of it consistently will have $45 remaining after 20 consecutive losses.

But the method suffers a fatal flaw. I call it the erosion effect. In any continuous sample of play, as of a season, even the most competent handicappers can expect to suffer losses of 10 to 15 races in succession. When this happens, profit erosion with fixed-percentage investments becomes unacceptably steep. The greater the accumulated profits, the deadlier the erosion effect. Handicappers who have begun play with a $5,000 bankroll, for example, and have doubled it by betting 5 percent of capital consistently, but suddenly lose 10 straight races, will see a $5,000 gain dwindle to $985, a profit reduction greater than 80 percent. If few handicappers can be found betting fixed-percentage amounts, perhaps this is the explanation. Sooner or later, they experience the erosion effect.

A pleasantly inviting alternative is fixed percentage-minimum.

Rationale. The FP-M method derives from the proposition, confirmed by empirical study, that successful handicappers win and lose in clusters almost as frequently as they win and lose alternately.

Four patterns of winning and losing can be represented as follows:

1. Win Clusters WW WWW WWWW WW WW
2. Loss Clusters LL LLL LLL LLLL LLLLLL LLLLL
3. Alternating Win- WW LLL WWW LLLL WW LLLLL
 Loss Clusters
4. Alternating Wins WLWLWLWLWLWLWLWLWLWLWL
 and Losses

The first two patterns are sensitive to fixed-percentage wagering, as bettors bet more when winning, less when losing, and therefore maximize profits and minimize losses. In Pattern 3, Alternating Win-Loss Clusters, losses during dry runs are further minimized using FP-M, as only the first loss in a cluster equals a fixed-percentage amount, and subsequent losses equal the minimum bet multiplied by the loss N. Thus the greater number of losses in a cluster, the greater the loss reduction with FP-M. When a win cluster follows, the second bet is a fixed-percentage amount, and of a capital amount that now has not decreased as much as it would have with unmodified fixed-percentage wagering.

In Pattern 4, Alternating Wins and Losses, the cumulative loss is maximized using FP-M. Following a win, the higher fixed-percentage amount is bet, and loses. Following a loss, the minimum is bet, and wins. To the extent that this pattern is repeated, loss is maximized, gain minimized, and any cumulative profits eroded. The research question is whether FP-M investments protected during Pattern 3 overcompensate sufficiently for the FP-M losses maximized during Pattern 4 throughout representative betting experiences.

Two studies have supplied provocative evidence. In the Santa Anita field study, the writer won 37 of 100 plays, average win odds at 2.99-1. A starting bankroll of $500 was increased to $2,304, a $1,804 profit. The fixed-percentage bet following a win was 5 percent, and the minimum bet following a loss was $25 (an original 5 percent of $500). The dollar return on investment was .57, unusually high, yet a particularly positive characteristic of FP-M, which invests considerably less than fixed-percentage betting.

By comparison, a series of $25 flat bets across the 100-race sample grossed $1,690.75, a $1,190 profit. Return on the dollar invested was a high .47.

Interestingly, a fixed-percentage bet at 5 percent of capital would have returned approximately $2,300, exceeding FP-M by some $500, with the dollar return a healthy .36. In the Santa Anita workout of 100 races, however, the longest losing streak was seven (twice). Computer simulations of seasonal play replicated what sad experience has so often proved. With all but exceptionally conservative styles of handicapping, losing runs of 12 to 15 are absolutely normal during any season. They pop up at least once or twice, and FP-M has been designed to eliminate precisely the effects of longer losing runs.

In the example where a $5,000 stake has been doubled by fixed-percentage betting, but 80 percent of that profit eroded during a 10-loss sequence, the FP-M loss for the 10 races would total $2,750, leaving a $7,250 bankroll intact. When the next two horses win, FP-M rebounds more strongly than the fixed-percentage method does. As play continues and success accumulates, these differences intensify.

To appreciate this, examine a fixed 5 percent flow of bets in contrast to FP-M where the $5,000 original bankroll has swelled to $20,000 but that inevitable 10-race loss skein strikes, followed at last by two consecutive winners, each paying odds at 2.6-1.

	FIXED PERCENTAGE		FIXED PERCENTAGE-MINIMUM	
Play	Bank	Loss	Bank	Loss
1	$20,000	$1,000	$20,000	$1,000
2	19,000	950	19,000	250
3	18,050	900	18,750	250
4	17,150	858	18,500	250
5	16,292	815	18,250	250
6	15,477	744	18,000	250
7	14,703	735	17,750	250
8	13,968	700	17,500	250
9	13,268	663	17,250	250
10	12,605	630	17,000	250
Play	Bank	Gain	Bank	Gain
11	$11,970	$1,500	$16,750	$ 650
12	13,470	1,749	17,400	2,262
Totals	$15,219	($4,781)	$19,662	($338)

During the 10-race slide, fixed-percentage wagering cost $8,030, fully 53 percent of $15,000 in profits. Alternatively, FP-M cost $3,250 to a bank of $16,750, for an overall loss approximating .25. Following the two wins at plays 11 and 12, FP-M has drawn practically even with its profitable point of departure. The power of the method during win-loss clusters characterized by multiple losses can be readily appreciated.

Nonetheless, handicappers win and lose alternately as well as in clusters. As previously remarked, during these sequences the aggregate loss is intensified using FP-M. What of this? The records of many regular handicappers indicate they win and lose in clusters almost as frequently as they alternate wins and losses. The question remained. Does the number of win-loss clusters in a handicapper's season overcompensate significantly for the number of alternating wins and losses during the season?

The field study of 100 bets proved inconclusive on that point. But computer simulations of conventional handicapping proficiency have indicated that the best of handicappers can do better by switching to FP-M. Before examining the field study in more detail, let's turn our attention to the simulations.

COMPUTER SIMULATIONS

A computer was asked to determine whether FP-M wagering gains accumulated by attainable levels of handicapping proficiency during a season overcompensated for the losses intensified by that method when alternating wins and losses occur. The criterion of success was the ability of FP-M to exceed profits yielded by flat bets at three levels of proficiency, that is, 30 percent winners, 35 percent winners, and 40 percent winners, each at odds of 2.6-1, and without busting out.

A season was defined as 440 bets, approximately one-third of the races available at major tracks during a six-month calendar. The starting bankroll was $5,000, and a 5 percent bet of capital was used as the FP-M bet after a win, $250 as the minimum bet following a loss. Flat bets were at $250 also.

A flat bet of $250 on each of 440 plays at the three levels of attainable results and paying 2.6-1 on winners yields the following:

	Investment	Profit	Dollar Return
30%	$110,000	$8,800	.08
35%	110,000	28,600	.26
40%	110,000	48,400	.44

Numerous simulations indicated that the FP-M profit at the .30 proficiency level did not differ from the flat-bet profits and often fell considerably below $8,800. With FP-M at 30 percent winners, handicappers might go broke in three out of 10 replications. Losses of smaller amounts can be expected about 50 percent of the time.

Prospects brighten sharply at .35 handicapping proficiency. At that performance level FP-M profit exceeds flat-bet profit by some $10,000 after 440 bets. Not only that, the simulations also show the FP-M profits exceed flat-bet profits more substantially as the number of bets increases. After two thousand bets, for example, flat-bet profit at .35 proficiency (2.6-1 odds on winners) would reach $130,000, but FP-M profit would approach $202,000, a .55 advantage to FP-M wagering.

To digress, no computer bet exceeded $1,000. Whenever the bankroll totaled $20,000, profit-taking was simulated, and the computer reverted to a $5,000 bankroll and continued to play.

The computer simulations demonstrated that FP-M profit margins at .35 proficiency or better are not seriously eroded or tilted substantially backward by the alternating wins and losses that occur during long, representative periods of betting. Thus, while winning, the method controls for the erosion effect common to fixed-percentage betting. Handicappers capable of .35 proficiency at 2.6-1 averaged odds are encouraged to maximize profit with FP-M wagering. The method requires users to achieve a slightly higher win percentage than the general public does (.33), while avoiding those overbet favorites that lower the crowd's dollar odds ($1.60). These are attainable results, to be sure.

THE FIELD STUDY

During the core of the Santa Anita winter racing season 1982, the author from February 11 through April 18 (37 racing days), and starting with a $500 bankroll and betting a fixed 5 percent following a win, a $25 minimum following a loss, used the FP-M method to study 100 consecutive win bets.

At .37 handicapping proficiency, averaged win odds at 2.99-1, the method recorded $1,804 in profits, a .57 dollar return on an investment of $3,129, far surpassing flat-bet profit for the same sample of play and surpassing the fixed-percentage rate of return. Table 1 presents the dollar profits (rounded) and rate of return for the three methods during the field study of 100 races:

Table 1
Profits and Rate of Return for Three Methods
During the Field Study

	Flat Bets	Fixed Percentage	Fixed Percentage-Minimum
Amount Invested	$2,500	$ 7,686	$3,129
Gross	$3,690	$10,986	$4,933
Profit	$1,190	$ 2,300	$1,804
Dollar Return	.47	.36	.57

The 100-race sample can be considered representative of a major racing calendar and was unbiased by extreme odds on winning selections, unbiased by atypical winning or losing runs. Among 37 winning selections the odds range was 0.8 to 10.1. Only five winners returned odds higher than 5-1. The longest losing cluster was seven (twice), longest winning cluster was three (five times). Handicapping proficiency and average win odds can be accepted as representative of successful handicapping performance at the racetrack.

Regarding clusters, the field-study sample contained 10 win clusters and 13 loss clusters. Alternating win-loss sequences occurred 20 times.

Of the wagers on 37 winners, 15 were at fixed-percentage amounts (22 minimum bets of $25 apiece), and these overcompensated significantly for fixed-percentage bets on 20 of the 63 losers.

Handicappers should examine the two seven-race losing runs, as presented in Table 2 (next page). The first, of plays 23-29, resulted in an FP-M loss of $202, while fixed-percentage betting lost $332, a $130 difference. During the second, of plays 85-91, FP-M lost $260, but fixed-percentage betting lost $737, a difference between the two methods of $467. Thus as parimutuel betting continues, the loss difference between the two methods grows significantly greater, more so as the size of the bets increases and number of consecutive losses increases.

Where handicapping proficiency warrants, the Santa Anita field study indicates that FP-M not only beats flat betting but controls for the erosion of profits incurred by fixed-percentage betting during longer losing streaks, notably when bets are of higher amounts.

SUMMARY

The studies in combination support the following assertions:

1. FP-M wagering works best for seasonal investments among handicappers whose win percentages and dollar returns exceed those of the crowd.
2. FP-M controls for the profit erosion common to fixed-percentage wagering during longer losing streaks, particularly when substantial profits have accumulated and amounts to be wagered will be relatively high.
3. The power of FP-M increases as the number of bets increases. On that point, handicappers are advised to postpone profit-taking until the size of the bets arouses the kind of psychological discomfort that distorts ordinary judgment, or instead distorts the odds.
4. The power of FP-M increases as the differences between the size of the winning bets and losing bets in alternating win-loss clusters increase.
5. The method works best where frequent win-loss clusters characterize play, but this should occur normally among successful handicappers.

Table 2: Dollar Losses as Between FP-M and Fixed-Percentage Wagering During Similar Losing Streaks at Two Points in the Season at Santa Anita

Early Losses Bets 23-29		FP-M	Bank	Fixed Percentage	Bank
Feb. 20	6th	(52)	$1,011	(55)	$1,044
	7th	(25)	986	(52)	994
	8th	(25)	961	(50)	611
Feb. 21	7th	(25)	936	(47)	897
	8th	(25)	911	(45)	852
Feb. 24	4th	(25)	886	(43)	809
Feb. 25	5th	(25)	861	(40)	769

FP-M Loss $202

Fixed Percentage Loss $332

Later Losses Bets 85-91		FP-M	Bank	Fixed Percentage	Bank
Apr. 9	5th	(110)	$2,211	(139)	$2,636
	6th	(25)	2,086	(132)	2,504
	8th	(25)	2,061	(125)	2,379
Apr. 10	3rd	(25)	2,036	(119)	2,260
	9th	(25)	2,011	(113)	2,147
Apr. 14	1st	(25)	1,986	(107)	2,040
	3rd	(25)	1,961	(102)	1,938

FP-M Loss $260

Fixed Percentage Loss $737

LIMITATIONS

The constraints of FP-M betting are apparent from its positive aspects. Handicappers should consider the following:

1. FP-M wagering requires a relatively high proficiency in selecting winners at acceptable odds. At lower levels of proficiency the more frequent occurrences of alternating wins and losses counterbalances the basic design of the method.
2. A season's play or longer generates the kind of profits the method is designed to yield. Profit-taking on a monthly or bimonthly basis does not apply.

3. The method is most sensitive to longer losing runs. Where these do not occur, the power of the method will be counteracted. As in the Santa Anita field study, fixed-percentage wagering will yield higher profits where loss clusters remain relatively small.

CHAPTER 33

BARRY'S MONEY
SECRETS AND CHARTS

EVERY BET, EVERY DAY, Barry Meadow plays the races in harmony with his betting lines. In three decades of chasing the money at racetracks, I can think of no other player that resembles Barry on the point. The objective is to find value, and to make money. If the wager should overpay, Barry may play. If the wager should not overpay, Barry never plays. The trick is to estimate with a pronounced degree of precision what the payoff should be to render good value, the mark of expertise in handicapping. I imagine nobody does that as carefully, and as effectively, as Barry.

Years ago, to cite a classic case, the pick six at Del Mar featured a seductive carryover, and Barry took the Amtrak from his spot in Anaheim to the station at Del Mar. Minutes later he arrived unannounced at the box. It's unfailingly fun to spend a day at the races with Barry, because not only is he smart and clever, but also he's full of good humor. Knowing that Barry was chasing the carryover, I immediately pricked him by saying I had no interest in betting the pick six, but he countered by notifying me that that would not stop him. Unknown to Barry at the moment, something else would stop him. In the box that day too were a handful of nationally renowned handicappers, each of them eager for the pick-six races to begin.

On the train ride, Barry had isolated the horses he liked in each of the six legs. As is his custom, he had arrayed the numbers of the horses he liked in several six-race combinations, e.g., 2-5, 3-6-7, 8, 1-7-9, 3-5, 6-7 (72 combinations) such that his singles and A-horses (top choice in a spread race) would dominate each ticket. He had constructed as many as a dozen potentially playable tickets. Using his betting lines, Barry estimated the chances that each ticket would win. Using the morning lines, the size of the pool, and the win probabilities he had attached to each ticket, Barry next estimated the number of winning tickets and the pick-six payoffs he could expect. The pick-six races looked formful to a fault, and following the numerous calculations, Barry announced he had found no bets.

If memory serves, Barry's cost to play would have amounted to $1,200 or thereabouts, and he had estimated the pick-six payoff at no greater than $7,000 to $8,000, or less than 7-1; no value, no play. His colleagues in the box were not similarly deterred. One of Barry's colleagues had invested $2,500 and when he hit the pick six, he was thrilled, except in short time the payoff was posted at $8,000, and the thrill was gone.

Barry's commandment is to make a betting line. The betting line must be a 100 percent line, which equals the chances of all the horses in the race, and Barry is insistent that the handicapper's line correspond to 100 percent, even if that means agonizing on whether Contender C should be 4-1 or 9-2. Barry juggles his original line until he has reached between 99 and 100 percent. He suggests to inexperienced linemakers this may take as long as 15 minutes to begin, while causing tension headaches, but soon enough the process can be completed pain-free in a couple of minutes.

In making a betting line, Barry is merely asking handicappers to quantify their opinions. Instead of saying, "I like the 6 best," or "It's a closely matched race among the 4, 7, and 9," or "The 5 sticks out but he'll probably be overbet," or "As many as six horses can win here," assign each of the horses a fair-value betting line by asking rhetorically how often each would win if the race were repeated a hundred times. Once the percentage chances have been assigned to each horse, sum them. The percents should sum to 100. If they do not, juggle the line, adding and subtracting points for each horse, based upon the various handicapping factors that apply.

Once the 100-point line has been established, the next step is easy. The percentage chances are converted to fair-value odds, using the odds-percentage table opposite. If Contender A has 38 points, the fair-value odds will be 8-5. If Contender B has 28 points, the fair-value odds will be 5-2. If Contender C has 18 points, the fair-value odds will be 9-2, and so forth. Barry urges handicappers to memorize the percentages and the corresponding fair-value odds, a sensible and elementary task.

The next step is crucial, and it's Barry's signature point. Handicappers

Odds Percentage Table

1-10	90.91	4-1	20.00
1-5	83.33	9-2	18.19
2-5	71.42	5-1	16.67
1-2	66.67	6-1	14.29
3-5	62.50	7-1	12.50
4-5	55.56	8-1	11.11
1-1	50.00	9-1	10.00
6-5	45.45	10-1	9.09
7-5	41.67	11-1	8.33
3-2	40.00	12-1	7.69
8-5	38.46	15-1	6.25
9-5	35.71	20-1	4.76
2-1	33.33	25-1	3.85
5-2	28.57	30-1	3.23
3-1	25.00	50-1	1.96
7-2	22.22	99-1	1.00

should not bet at any time, unless they are getting a 50 percent bonus. Contender A, with 38 points and a fair-value line of 8-5, must be 5-2. Contender B, with 28 points at 5-2, must be 7-2. Contender C, with 18 points at 9-2, must be 7-1. Fair value is converted to good value. Barry's chart, "Win Overlays" (on the next page), presents the 50 percent bonus line for horses having a handicapper's fair-value line of 2-5 to 6-1. Memorize these adjusted lines now.

The 50 percent bonus is not pulled from midair, but is subjectively biased. In *Money Secrets at the Racetrack* (TR Publishing 1987, 1990), his signature book, Barry reports that after studying thousands of his personal bets, he has concluded the 50 percent bonus will guarantee profits of 8 to 10 percent. Any smaller bonus percentage may convert profit to loss. This happens because (a) handicappers have a tendency to overestimate their horses' winning chances, especially the low-priced contenders, (b) late betting often lowers the odds to the player's disadvantage, and (c) the race will be susceptible to a relatively large error factor, which is not considered in setting the betting lines.

Win Overlays

Your Line	Odds Required
2-5 or below	4-5
1-2 or 3-5	1-1
4-5	6-5
1-1	3-2
6-5	9-5
7-5 or 3-2	2-1
8-5 or 9-5	5-2
2-1	3-1
5-2	7-2
3-1	9-2
7-2	5-1
4-1	6-1
9-2 or 5-1	7-1
6-1	9-1
7-1 or above	exactas only

If handicappers have no access to the odds-percentage table, but have assigned the percentage chances on a 100 percent betting line, fair-value odds are estimated easily with a calculator by dividing the percentage chance of each horse into 100, and subtracting one. Contender A above has 38 percentage points, so 100 divided by 38 equals 2.63, minus one, equals 1.63, or 8-5.

As demanding that Barry can be that handicappers must make a betting line, or they're probably kidding themselves, he compromises to the extent that the line might be set for the authentic contenders only. Eliminate the horses having a nominal chance. Instead of a 100-point line, now use an 80-point line, allowing the noncontenders a 20 percent chance. In other words, the handicapper's contenders should be winning four of five bettable races, a proficiency standard that can be examined, and should be. Barry's records show his noncontenders win 15 percent of the races he bets. Handicappers without records can assume their noncontenders will win 20 percent of the races. The weakness of the 80 percent line, however, extends in undesirable ways to exacta wagering, a topic Barry covers exceedingly well, and which we address next.

Reiterating the importance of setting the betting line, Barry summarizes his betting procedure succinctly:

1. Analyze the chances of every horse in the race.
2. Determine the fair-value odds using the odds-percentage table.
3. Bet to win on any horse having odds 50 percent higher than the betting line.

The betting lines accomplish all the important money-management objectives:

1. They force handicappers to quantify their opinions, such that they can consider intelligently, not just one horse, but several horses, and how each relates to the others—make decisions, not selections.
2. They allow handicappers to test abilities that can be measured with personal records across the seasons, e.g., do your even-money shots win half the time, 2-1 shots a third of the time, 4-1 shots 20 percent of the time, 9-1 shots 10 percent of the time; how much money do you make on horses that go at 5-2 and below; has your handicapping been improving, or is it in decline?
3. Best of all, the line enables handicappers to spot the true overlays, the horses and combinations by which bettors can win, not only in the straight pools, but also in double pools, exacta pools, quinella pools, and the pick-three, pick-four, and pick-six pools.

Barry accomplishes something else, quite wonderful, in *Money Secrets at the Racetrack*. He presents an amazing array of charts that tell handicappers exactly how much they should bet in relation to the odds and what the cut-off points are for finding his 50 percent overlay combinations in doubles, exactas, quinellas, and the serial bets. I counted 32 charts, and eight of them displayed pick-six cards and scenarios that featured various combinations of singles, A horses, and B horses (backup horses), how many combinations must be covered for each scenario, how to fill out the several betting cards exactly, leg by leg and horse by horse, and is easily the best, most accurate material for pick-six shoppers on record.

In his chapter "How Much To Bet," a brief treatment of the Kelly Criterion, Barry explains the dangers of overly aggressive betting and reminds handicappers the optimal bet size is equal to the edge divided by the odds. If handicappers enjoy a 15 percent edge when wagering to win (33 percent winners at average odds of 5-2) and the odds on Contender A will be 3-1, the optimum bet is 5 percent of the bankroll. To bet more is to overplay your edge, and risk ruin, and to bet less is to win less than you're capable of winning. That is, the Kelly Criterion guarantees the maximum growth of a bankroll, as no other money-management method does. But as Barry explains, the problem with the Kelly Criterion in parimutuel settings (racetracks) is that the edge is always subjective, not objective. Handicappers believe they have a 20 percent edge in an exacta, but the handicapping has been less than perfect.

The correction is a fractional Kelly. Barry suggests a half-Kelly, such that a 15 percent edge to win on a 3-1 shot is no longer an optimal bet of 5 percent ($^{15}\!/_3$), but half of 5 percent, or 2.5 percent. Few handicappers have records that inform them of their betting edge to win, not to mention the edge in doubles, exactas, and the serial bets. An *a priori* edge when betting to win might be assumed at 15 percent, if handicappers are confident they can win 33 percent of their bets at average odds of 5-2, an attainable goal for competent handicappers. Divide the 15 percent by the odds to win on selections, and bet a 50 percent Kelly. A 2-1 shot would warrant 3.75 percent of the bankroll ($^{15}\!/_2 \times .50$). A 5-1 shot would warrant 1.5 percent of bankroll ($^{15}\!/_5 \times .50$). A 10-1 shot would warrant 0.75 percent of bankroll ($^{15}\!/_{10} \times .50$). This follows Kelly, as the percentage amount should decline as the odds grow greater.

Barry recommends a $2,000 bankroll for each of the several parimutuel pools—win, place-show, exactas, doubles, pick threes—and his charts reveal the optimal bet sizes for the $2,000 bankroll at the various odds levels. Examine the Win-Bet Chart on the next page. It shows the optimum bet size where the handicapper's line (on the left) varies from 1-5 to 6-1 and the tote odds (top) vary from 4-5 to 10-1. If handicappers believe a best bet should be 3-2, and the public offers 2-1, the optimal bet for a $2,000 bankroll is $26. To bet more is to risk converting profit to loss. To bet less is to win less than the handicapper is capable of winning. If an overlay is not listed on the chart, play the highest listed number, e.g., your 3-5 standout that is sent away at 8-5 deserves an $80 bet.

Barry's discussion of place and show wagering is concise and excellent, and will have tremendous appeal to contemporary handicappers finding an unprecedented abundance of underlays in the win pools. Underlays to win are often overlays to place and show, as the oversupply of win wagering is not reflected in the place and show pools, where the casual customers will be supporting their favorite longshots. As Barry tells, the crowd gen-

WIN BET CHART
(Capital = $2000)

	4/5	1	6/5	7/5	3/2	8/5	9/5	2	5/2	3	7/2	4	9/2	5	6	7	8	9	10
1/5	125																		
2/5	100																		
1/2		80	83	85															
3/5		60	66	71	80														
4/5			50	57	66	75													
1					40	50	55	60											
6/5						35	40												
7/5							30	32	33	34									
3/2							26	27	29	31	33								
8/5								24	26	28	30	31							
9/5								21	23	25	27	28	29						
2									20	22	25	26	28						
5/2										17	20	22	24						
3												13	16	16	17				
7/2													12	13	14	15			
4													10	11	12	13	14		
9/2														8	10	11	12		
5														5	7	8	10		
6																	6	8	

erally overbets longshots to place and underbets favorites and low-priced contenders to place. An overlay occurs when a horse's percentage of the place pool is significantly less than its percentage of the win pool. A favorite that has 50 percent of the win pool, but just 25 percent of the place pool, and 20 percent of the show pool, is probably an overlay to place and show.

But is it? How seriously must a horse be underbet to place and show to qualify as an overlay? Barry provides the chart that tells. Using the crowd's well-known efficiency when betting to win, Barry has estimated the maximum percentages of the place and show pools that expose the overlay opportunities. Examine the chart on page 195, Place-Show Maximum Percentages. The even-money favorite that has 25 percent of the place pool can be bet to place, as that percentage is less than the 26.95 maximum percentage the horse can have to place. Similarly, the 1-1 favorite that has just 20 percent of the show pool can be bet to show, as 20 percent is less than the 23.99 maximum percentage.

Ignoring the win pools, if handicappers have a calculator, they can calculate the place-show percentages and compare them to Barry's friendly charts. Overlays are identified quickly. Handicappers leave literally thousands of dollars untouched among their place and show overlays annually, as I discovered on my inaugural day at the races with Barry, at Santa Anita, in 1987. Overlays I covered to win in the first and second races were overlays to place and show as well, the first paying $6 to place and $5 to show, and the second paying $6.20 to place and $4 to show. Their percentages of the place and show pools fell significantly below Barry's cut-off percentages, but I did not realize that. Handicappers should notice that Barry's place-show percentages have been estimated for horses at 4-1 and below, and not for the midlevel and longer-priced horses that inevitably underpay to place and show.

Barry loves the exactas, and he wants handicappers to love them just as much. He salutes the prevalence of silly money, as people play birthdays, phone numbers, and numbers they like, such as 1-2, and 7-11. As Barry notes, millions of these dollars become available to good handicappers year after year. The logical reason Barry prefers exactas is he can determine whether the combinations are yielding value. On the monitors, now the computer screens, the payoffs for the various combinations are projected. Barry needs the monitors to answer two of the three questions he poses:

1. What is the chance the combination will finish one-two?
2. What is the payoff?
3. Is the payoff an overlay?

Barry notes that handicappers must make two calculations, each of them simple. First, what are the chances that a horse will win? Second, assuming the first horse has won, what is the chance the other horse will finish second?

He relays the hypothetical exacta of Fetlock and Pastern. A handicapper gives Fetlock a 40 percent chance to win, and Pastern 20 percent. To calculate the fair-value exacta payoff, proceed as follows.

Out of the 100 percent betting line, Fetlock has been assigned 40 percent. So the rest of the horses are assigned 60 percent, of which Pastern has 20 percent, or one-third of the remaining percentage chance. The chance of the combination finishing one-two is $.40 \times (^{.20}\!/_{.60})$. Your calculator shows that outcome will be equal to 13.3 chances in 100. Checking the odds-percentage table (or calculating $^{1}\!/_{.133} - 1$), handicappers discover the fair-value odds will be 6.5-1. For a $2 bet, anything less than $15 for the

Fetlock-Pastern combination will be an underlay. Since Barry demands a 50 percent overlay at all times, handicappers following Barry must receive $22 ($15 × 1.5, or $22.50), or they should not bet. By this procedure, exacta overlays are readily spotted. Handicappers should resolve to follow the procedure, notably in the context of small fields that dominate the nonclaiming races and deliver so many underlays among the exacta combinations.

Once again, Barry provides a betting chart for handicappers who prefer to avoid the calculations. Review the $2 Exacta Overlay Prices (next page), which include Barry's 50 percent bonus payment, where the betting lines are your own and the odds on the top horse are on the left and the odds on the second horse are along the top. What is the 50 percent overlay payoff for a 5-1 shot on top of a 5-2 favorite? It's $47. How about your 3-2 shot on top and your 2-1 shot on bottom? The 50 percent overlay pays $13.

In playing multiple exacta combinations, the 50 percent overlay payoff must be adjusted to account for the number of losing combinations. If a half dozen $2 combinations are backed, the overlay price of each is adjusted upward by $10, to account for five losing tickets. As Barry says, it's often a cheerless world. Barry supplies overlay charts for the $3 and $5 exactas too, as well as a chart that reveals the optimal bet size for a $2,000 bankroll when the $2 exactas will be returning $6 (or less) to $43 (and more).

Despite the prevalence of numbers, numerical relationships, and arithmetic sprinkled throughout its pages, *Money Secrets at the Racetrack* is written in a colloquial style that is user-friendly, even among people averse to math. Because Barry is a professional player who understands not only the complexities and nuances of parimutuel wagering, but also the practical situations and decisions the bettors confront routinely, the author emerges as less an instructor than a sidekick. He is especially comforting on the popular psychology of decision-making at the track, inevitably sticking to the guidance provided by his betting lines, and urging handicappers to do the same.

Here's Barry on the final decision-making about an exacta box, after he has set his lines, calculated the exacta payoffs that would yield his 50 percent bonus, and has checked the projected payoffs on the monitors. "Let's say I make Silly Skipper 2-1 and Billy Bret 5-1. I need $35 to play Silly Skipper-Billy Bret and $44 for Billy Bret-Silly Skipper. If the numbers are below these [projected payoffs], no play." The conversational tone places the bettor alongside Barry at the monitors. The pragmatic tone dominates the text. And beyond the math and numerical relation-

$2 Exacta Overlay Prices

	1/5	2/5	1/2	3/5	4/5	1	6/5	7/5	3/2	8/5	9/5	2	5/2	3	7/2	4	9/2	5	6	7	8	9	10	11	12	15	20	25	30	50	100
1/9																							4	4	4	5	6	7	9	15	31
1/5																			4	4	5	5	6	7	7	9	12	15	18	31	61
2/5														4	5	5	6	7	8	9	10	11	13	15	16	20	26	32	38	62	122
1/2													5	5	6	7	8	8	10	11	12	14	16	17	18	23	31	38	46	77	152
3/5											5	5	6	7	8	8	9	10	12	14	16	17	19	22	24	28	37	46	55	91	181
4/5								5	5	6	6	7	8	9	10	11	13	14	16	18	21	23	26	28	31	38	50	63	75	123	242
1							6	7	7	7	8	8	10	11	13	14	16	17	20	23	26	29	32	35	38	47	62	77	92	152	302
6/5						7	7	8	8	9	10	10	12	14	16	17	19	21	25	28	32	35	39	43	46	57	75	93	111	183	363
7/5					8	8	9	10	10	11	11	12	14	16	18	20	23	25	29	33	37	41	46	50	54	67	88	109	130	214	
3/2					8	8	9	10	11	11	12	13	15	17	20	22	24	26	31	35	40	44	49	53	58	71	94	116	139	229	
8/5					8	9	10	11	11	12	13	14	16	18	21	23	26	28	33	38	43	47	52	57	62	76	100	124	148	244	
9/5				8	9	10	11	13	13	13	15	16	18	21	24	26	29	32	37	43	48	53	59	64	70	86	113	140	167	275	
2				9	10	11	13	14	14	15	16	17	20	23	26	29	32	35	41	47	53	59	65	71	77	95	125	155	185	305	
5/2			11	11	13	14	16	17	18	19	20	22	26	29	33	37	41	44	52	59	67	74	82	89	97	119	157	194	232		
3		12	13	14	16	17	19	21	22	23	25	26	31	35	40	44	49	53	62	71	80	89	98	107	116	143	188	233	278		
7/2		14	15	16	18	20	23	25	26	27	29	31	36	41	47	52	57	62	73	83	94	104	115	125	136	167	220	272	324		
4		16	17	18	21	23	26	28	29	31	33	35	41	47	53	59	65	71	83	95	107	119	131	143	155	191	251	311			
9/2		18	20	21	24	26	29	32	33	35	37	40	47	53	60	67	74	80	94	107	121	134	148	161	175	215	283				
5		20	22	23	26	28	32	35	37	38	41	44	47	59	67	74	82	89	104	119	134	149	164	179	194	239	314				
6	21	25	26	28	32	35	39	43	44	46	50	53	62	71	80	89	98	107	125	143	161	179	197	215	233	287					
7	25	29	31	33	37	41	46	50	52	54	58	62	73	83	94	104	115	125	146	167	188	209	230	251	272	335					
8	28	33	35	38	43	47	52	57	59	62	67	71	83	95	107	119	131	143	167	191	215	239	263	287	311						
9	32	37	40	43	48	53	59	64	67	70	75	80	94	107	121	134	148	161	188	215	242	269	296	323							
10	35	41	44	47	53	59	65	71	74	77	83	89	104	119	134	149	164	179	209	239	269	299	329								
11	39	46	49	52	59	65	72	79	82	85	92	98	115	131	148	164	181	197	230	263	296	319									
12	43	50	53	57	64	71	79	86	89	93	100	107	125	143	161	179	197	215	251	287	323										
15	53	62	67	71	80	89	98	107	111	116	125	134	157	179	202	224	247	268	314												
20	71	83	89	95	107	119	131	143	149	155	167	179	209	239	269	299	329														
25	89	104	111	119	134	149	164	179	187	194	209	224	262	299	337																
30	107	125	134	143	161	179	197	215	224	233	251	269	314																		

ships, Barry encourages the adoption of exotic strategies that make sense and will save money.

He conveys muffled enthusiasm toward the trifecta, for example, noting in the book's first chart that among the various exotica, only the tri-fecta falls down on two critical questions: Can the true odds be deter-mined (questionable); are the crowd's odds posted (no). As Barry asks rhetorically, and rather unrealistically, is the 2-4-7 combination returning $68 or $680? In a later chapter on the three-horse bet, Barry admits the trifecta can be a seductive proposition—mainly because the crowd's silly money on so many irrational combinations impregnates the pools—but he quickly denounces the common reliance on boxes and wheels. Barry's prescription avoids the trifecta altogether, unless the favorite or the sec-ond choice can be eliminated, and his guiding principle is rooted in good handicapping: *Without a key horse or horses, don't play the trifecta.*

On the practical level, Barry shows in detail how trifecta bettors might structure the several tickets where, ". . . let's say you like #2 best, #4 next best, and you give #1, #5, and #8 small shots." Barry's tickets are con-structed to guarantee success if the handicapping has been correct; i.e., either #2 wins and #4 runs second, or #4 defeats #2. All other possibili-ties are covered; fascinating.

In another late chapter, "Multiple Win Exotics," Barry deals with his personal favorite, the pick six, and the text virtually leaps to a higher form of life. With the southern California pick-six carryover now as great as $200,000-plus after one weekend day, and going higher every year as the gigantic bet has become literally a national pool, the stakes have increased tremendously. When War Emblem lost the 2002 Belmont Stakes, the one-day carryover to Sunday in New York was $685,751. It's too tempt-ing for good handicappers not to care.

Barry sees no reason to play the pick six, a desperately low-percentage bet, unless handicappers will benefit from the positive-expectation situ-ations provided by the carryovers; i.e., the track will distribute more money to the winners than it collects, or free money. On days when the track has guaranteed a $1 million pool, by contrast, no positive expecta-tion exists. A couple of weeks before the 2002 Belmont Stakes carryover, Hollywood Park offered a $1 million guaranteed pick-six pool, the favorites dominated the series, and the payoffs to winners fell below $500, which is not the chance to win that savvy bettors prefer.

As he does with trifecta wagering, in tackling the pick six, Barry again places the emphasis where it belongs, on good handicapping. He empha-sizes the importance of key horses and the setting of accurate lines, and he scorns the pitiful practices of scrambling and stabbing. Saying the small bettors are essentially contributing to the pool, a form of charity, with a minuscule chance of winning, Barry recommends that small bet-tors instead form partnerships and teams, such that a $200 contribution to a $1,200 ticket creates a far greater opportunity to win than does a $200 individual play. The trick to partnerships and team play, however, is the designation of the team captain, who elicits opinions perhaps, but takes responsibility for the final decisions, a sticky circumstance at best.

THE SUBSTANCE OF Barry's discussion is provocative and should be of interest to good handicappers everywhere with the hope of hitting a huge pick six. As usual, Barry begins by estimating the fair-value odds of each horse in each leg. He presents the following example:

1st #5 (.45), #4 (.20), #7 (.15)	3 (.80)
2nd #1 (.50)	1 (.50)
3rd #6 (.30), #3 (.25), #1 (.15), #5 (.15)	4 (.85)
4th #2 (.60)	1 (.60)
5th #3 (.25), #4 (.25), #7 (.15), #9 (.12)	4 (.77)
6th #4 (.35), #1 (.20), #3 (.15)	3 (.70)

The ticket is $3 \times 1 \times 4 \times 1 \times 4 \times 3$, or 144 combinations, a cost of $288. When the probability of hitting each leg is multiplied one by another, Barry has an 11 percent chance of hitting six winners, a relatively good chance of getting the pick six. The fair-value payoff would be $2,618, but Barry's 50 percent bonus requirement means the payoff must be $3,927. Barry concedes he cannot be certain what the pick six will pay, but he can estimate the payoffs well enough by relating the size of the pool, the takeout (usually 25 percent), and his estimate of the percentage of the pool that will be bet on each of his winners, which he equates to his personal betting line on each horse.

Barry makes two calculations, the first with his longest-priced horses winning each leg, the second with his favorites winning each leg. He takes the midpoint of the two estimates as his best estimate. But since favorites win more often that longshots, Barry assumes the payoff will fall below his midpoint. He next estimates the number of winning tickets, based upon his calculations, and dependent upon the size of the pool, finally he estimates the size of the payoff. It's heady stuff, entirely rational, and handicappers in pursuit of the pick six are encouraged to pursue Barry's discussion in detail.

For the above ticket, Barry shows that at Obscure Downs, with a pick-six pool of $7,000 and a 25 percent take, with the track distributing only 50 percent of the pool to the winners, the distribution to the winners would be $2,625 and if Barry had the lone ticket, he would receive no value. Switching to Big-League Park, pool of $500,000, same take, and 75 percent distributed to the winners, interestingly enough, even with his longshots winning, Barry's calculations estimate 30 winning tickets and a payoff of $9,375. As Barry tells, it's crucial to realize that under no circumstances will the ticket be worth $100,000.

The practical contribution Barry makes to pick-six bettors, and it's a huge gift, is showing how to reduce the costs of the tickets significantly, without reducing the chances of winning significantly, and accomplishing the trick by depending upon good handicapping. Referring again to the sample ticket, notice in the first leg, #5 has a much greater probability of winning, and in the sixth leg, #4 has a significantly better chance of winning. Barry calls these the "A" horses in any spread. On a card with two singles, if handicappers demand that two of their "A" horses also win, two tickets can be constructed, as follows:

5	1	6,3,1,5	2	3,4,7,9	4,1,3
4,7	1	6,3,1,5	2	3,4,7,9	4

The two tickets instead of one cut the cost from $288 to $160, a 45 percent reduction, while the chances of winning have been reduced just 19 percent, the chance that both #5 in the first leg and #4 in the sixth leg will both lose.

In a remarkable series of charts, Barry reveals how to combine pick-six singles with A-horses in the other legs, and B-horses (backup horses) in the same legs. No matter how many A-horses handicappers will combine with singles, and allowing as many as a half dozen B-horses, Barry's charts show how many combinations must be covered, and how many tickets will be purchased, and how the tickets should be filled out. The chart on page 192 shows the combinations and tickets where handicappers use two singles, combined with three, two, one, or no A-horses, and various numbers of B-horses.

Suppose a handicapper combines two singles with two horses in another race, five in a fourth race, and six horses in the remaining two legs; that is, SS2566 on the chart. Using zero A-horses, the handicapper covers 360 combinations, a prohibitive cost of $720. Using three A-horses, the handicapper covers 16 tickets, an untenable chance to score. Using two A-horses, the handicapper covers 95 combinations, for a cost of $190, and fills out 11 tickets (2A in the left margin), a nifty compromise. Barry's combinations are cost-effective combinations, with excellent coverage at a reasonable cost, and without lowering the chances of winning to subterranean depths. However rocky, partners and teams can find no straighter path to the pick-six riches.

PICK 6

2 singles

4A (1 ticket)
1st... A
2nd...A
3rd... A
4th... A
5th... S
6th... S

3A (4 more = 5)
1st... A A A B
2nd...A A B A
3rd... A B A A
4th... B A A A
5th... S S S S
6th... S S S S

2A (6 more = 11)
1st... B A A B A B
2nd...A B A A B B
3rd... A A B B B A
4th... B B B A A A
5th... S S S S S S
6th... S S S S S S

1A (4 more = 15)
1st... B B B A
2nd...B B A B
3rd... B A B B
4th... A B B B
5th... S S S S
6th... S S S S

0A (1 more = 16)
1st... B
2nd...B
3rd... B
4th... B
5th... S
6th... S

	3A	2A	1A	0A		3A	2A	1A	0A
SS2222	5	11	15	16	SS3333	9	33	65	81
SS2223	6	15	22	24	SS3334	10	40	84	108
SS2224	7	19	29	32	SS3335	11	47	103	135
SS2225	8	23	36	40	SS3336	12	54	122	162
SS2226	9	27	43	48	SS3344	11	48	108	144
SS2233	7	20	32	36	SS3345	12	56	132	180
SS2234	8	25	42	48	SS3346	13	64	156	216
SS2235	9	30	52	60	SS3355	13	65	161	225
SS2236	10	35	62	72	SS3356	14	74	190	270
SS2244	9	31	55	64	SS3366	15	84	224	324
SS2245	10	37	68	80	SS3444	12	57	138	192
SS2246	11	43	81	96	SS3445	13	66	168	240
SS2255	11	44	84	100	SS3446	14	75	198	288
SS2256	12	51	100	120	SS3455	14	76	204	300
SS2266	13	59	119	144	SS3456	15	86	240	360
SS2333	8	26	46	54	SS3466	16	97	282	432
SS2334	9	32	60	72	SS3555	15	87	247	375
SS2335	10	38	74	90	SS3556	16	98	290	450
SS2336	11	44	88	108	SS3566	17	110	340	540
SS2344	10	39	78	96	SS3666	18	123	398	648
SS2345	11	46	96	120	SS4444	13	67	175	256
SS2346	12	53	114	144	SS4445	14	77	212	320
SS2355	12	54	118	150	SS4446	15	87	249	384
SS2356	13	62	140	180	SS4455	15	88	256	400
SS2366	14	71	166	216	SS4456	16	99	300	480
SS2444	11	47	101	128	SS4466	17	111	351	576
SS2445	12	55	124	160	SS4555	16	100	308	500
SS2446	13	63	147	192	SS4556	17	112	360	600
SS2455	13	64	152	200	SS4566	18	125	420	720
SS2456	14	73	180	240	SS4666	19	139	489	864
SS2466	15	83	213	288	SS5555	17	96	369	625
SS2555	14	74	186	250	SS5556	18	126	430	750
SS2556	15	84	220	300	SS5566	19	140	500	900
SS2566	16	95	260	360	SS5666	20	155	580	1080
SS2666	17	107	307	432	SS6666	21	171	671	1296

In its straight talk about money management and betting, *Money Secrets at the Racetrack* is aimed primarily at experienced handicappers, and in particular good handicappers. Barry Meadow is the voice of reason at the windows. Few handicappers, however practiced, however successful, would be unable to benefit from a studious immersion in this telltale book. Winners should win more money than ever. Capable handicappers who manage to lose money might be converted from losers to winners, which would be no small feat.

Meadow's Racing Monthly is a hard-nosed periodical on handicapping and parimutuel betting for experienced and regular players, available by subscription. It's highly recommended.

How to Cut the Cost and Fill Out Multiple Pick-Six Tickets

To use Barry's illustration and lingo, let's say you have a pick-six ticket, $4 \times 1 \times 4 \times 2 \times 1 \times 5$. Looking under the previous chart for two singles, the combination SS2445 costs $320 ($160 \times 2$). The two singles are #5 in the second leg and #3 in the fifth leg. As shown below, your top choices in the four races to be spread are #6 in the first leg, #4 in the third, #1 in the fourth, and #8 in the sixth.

Leg 1	6 3 4 5	
Leg 2	5	
Leg 3	4 1 2 7	
Leg 4	1 5	
Leg 5	3	
Leg 6	8 2 4 5 6	160 combinations, cost of $320

If two of your top choices in the races to be spread, referred to as "A" horses in the charts, were required to win, you would need to invest only $110 instead. In the chart for two singles, under 2A, for SS2445, notice you would be covering 55 combinations, instead of 160 combinations. On the left of the chart for 2 singles, see how to mark the tickets for 3A, and another ticket for 2A.

The 11 tickets are completed on page 196.

After marking the horses' numbers for each leg, Barry circles the A-horse for easy reference. Since the horses will not change from ticket to ticket, Barry first marks singles on each card, e.g., #5 in the second leg and #3 in the fifth leg. He next marks the A-horse on the first ticket, e.g., A A A A , proceeds to A A A B, and proceeds to complete the 11 tickets. Review the 11 tickets and track the S A B horses as marked.

For practice, select another pick-six combination from the chart for two singles and repeat the process of marking the tickets. It's easy with practice, but the procedure will require some time. A reliable time to fill out multiple pick-tix tickets is following the late scratches.

Race	Main	Backup
1	6	5
2	2-7-9	3
3	1-4	2-12
4	2-6	4-8-9-10-12
5	7	5
6	3-8	

Our main ticket, consisting of our prime contenders, the horses in the left-hand column, costs $48 ($1 \times 3 \times 2 \times 2 \times 1 \times 2 \times \$2$). Now we fashion a ticket that includes our longshot, #5; we substitute him for our top choice in the first race and use him on a ticket that includes the main contenders in the other races, as follows:

Race	Horse
1	5
2	2-7-9
3	1-4
4	2-6
5	7
6	3-8

This ticket costs $48, too. Now we move on and substitute our backup horse for the main horses in Race 2:

Race	Horse
1	6
2	<u>3</u>
3	1-4
4	2-6
5	7
6	3-8

This ticket costs a mere $16. We proceed to fill out five such backup tickets (we had no backup horses in the sixth race) in addition to the main ticket; the total cost comes to $328.

Place-Show Maximum Percentages

Your Odds	Place	Show
1-9	48.55	43.22
1-5	44.92	39.98
2-5	38.50	34.27
1-2	35.93	31.98
3-5	33.69	29.98
4-5	29.94	26.65
1-1	26.95	23.99
6-5	24.50	21.81
7-5	22.45	19.99
3-2	21.56	19.19
8-5	20.73	18.45
9-5	19.25	17.13
2-1	17.97	15.99
5-2	15.40	13.71
3-1	13.47	11.99
7-2	11.97	10.66
4-1	10.78	9.59
9-2 +	no play	no play

AAAASS

A·AABSS

AABASS

ABAASS

BAAASS

BAABSS

ABABSS

AABBSS

BABASS

ABBASS

BBAASS

CHAPTER 34

READY-MADE
BETTING LINES FOR
CONTENDERS ONLY

W HEN BOB BAFFERT'S War Emblem upset the 2002 Kentucky
Derby at 20-1, a number of hard-boiled handicappers, who had realized too late that they should have known better, slapped themselves in
the face, a belated wake-up call. Andrew Beyer wrote that he had never
felt so stupid, as War Emblem had carried the top Beyer Speed Figure
(112) into the Derby, and by several lengths. Yours truly had backed War
Emblem at 6-1 in the Illinois Derby (Grade 3), against the 1-2 pre-Derby
favorite Repent, and had watched him romp by a dozen lengths. I too
was looking the other way in the Derby.

When five weeks later the longshot Sarava upended War Emblem's Triple
Crown bid in the Belmont Stakes, and paid $142 to win, his trainer, Ken
McPeek, pondered out loud how the handicappers could have overlooked
his colt en masse. McPeek explained in detail how his colt had just won the
restricted Sir Barton Stakes by six open lengths on Preakness Day at Pimlico, earning an acceptable Beyer 99, and that Sarava was obviously a ram-
pantly improving three-year-old that had to be respected. How, McPeek
wondered, could everyone have ignored his talented colt so dismissively.

McPeek was not alone. In the next few days at least three colleagues
called to commiserate, asking whether I had backed Sarava in any way,
and conceding the colt might have been bet. My explanation for the oversight was terse and true. I had not bothered to make a betting line. It's the
same reason the handicappers missed War Emblem and it's the only

explanation that satisfies McPeek's curiosity. Nobody bets War Emblem in the Derby or Sarava in the Belmont, unless he has constructed a fair-value betting line on the classics, and has included War Emblem and Sarava as contenders. In that case, handicappers indeed might have bet on both colts to win.

In less dramatic circumstances, the same oversight occurs every day at every track, and horses that deserve respect as contenders win and pay more than they should, without the support of many of the best handicappers on the grounds. The sad explanation is always the same. The handicappers had failed to construct a betting line. They therefore had no way to know that the horse was about to get away as an absolutely good thing.

Nevada pro Steve Fierro once was a card-carrying member of the crowd that let too many good things get away, but no longer. Fierro transformed himself into a linemaker and value bettor, and because he now bets nothing but overlays on his lines, he has been a winner ever since. Displaying the evangelical passion of the convert, Fierro wants all serious handicappers that do not make betting lines to transform themselves as he did, and he has written a self-published, personal polemic on the topic, *The Four Quarters of Horse Investing* (2001), that qualifies as a business plan.

Fierro knows well the self-defeating habits that subvert the best efforts of good handicappers, and in his book he stresses the importance of business principles, if handicappers want to become consistent winners. Although Fierro's business plan has been developed in four-part harmony—contender selection, attaching value, performing while investing, and record keeping—the essence of the approach is the reliance on fair-value betting lines for the authentic contenders. Moreover, and this is the clever part, Fierro knows the majority of handicappers will not bother to make the betting lines, so he has completed the task for them. He calls his betting tools templates, and he insists handicappers will find them easy to use because they are not "percentage-based."

While reassuring handicappers they will not have to worry about establishing the percentages that various contenders will win, and converting those percentages to odds, Fierro reassures the same handicappers that he has done the dirty work for them. Fierro understands well that experienced handicappers will be adept at identifying contenders, the first quarter of his four-part business plan, at least much of the time, so he leaves that crucial task to the individual. Once the contenders have been isolated, the next step, attaching value, can be assigned exclusively to Fierro's templates, once handicappers have decided how strongly they prefer Contender A.

To see how the process works, examine Fierro's four-contender template (page 200), and assume Contender A has been established as a 5-2 shot. Contender B now will be assigned odds of 3-1, 7-2, 4-1, or 9-2, depending on how strongly Contender B compares with Contender A. If Contender B becomes a 7-2 shot, Contender C is automatically assigned odds of 5-1, and Contender D can only be 6-1. The task is done. Fierro is using an 80/20 percentage ratio between contenders and noncontenders, such that the contenders should win four of five bettable races, and the Contender line where A is 5-2, B is 7-2, C is 5-1, and D is 6-1, adds to 80 percent of the probabilities.

Fierro's Four-Contender Template consists of 28 betting lines, all of them ranging from 79 to 81 percent of the 100 percent betting line. Notice that when Contender A has been declared a legitimate 8-5 shot, Contender B-C-D must be 6-1 or greater to warrant a bet. When Contender A is considered a fair bet at 2-1, Contender B must be 4-1. The odds lines are derived from the empirical studies Fierro has engaged for years. His standard of success holds that the average payoff on Contender A, for example, must exceed the payoff for the highest betting line possible on Contender A, which is 4-1. The average Contender B winner must pay 9-2; Contender C must pay 6-1 on average, and so must Contender D horses that are winners.

Ignoring percentages, handicappers engage the process by deciding how strongly they prefer Contender A, and assigning the fair-value odds. With practice, the other three contenders will fall into place quickly on the odds line, according to Fierro. A process of linemaking that formerly has been tedious is now a fast track, with the odds lines ready-made. Fierro provides a Three-Contender Template (page 201) as well, and now Contender A is never greater than a 5-2 shot. Once more, in each of 27 betting lines, the contender line ranges from 79 to 81 percent of the 100 percent line.

When selecting contenders and attaching value, Fierro suggests handicappers complete a simple task he calls race typing, which means handicappers first decide what kind of race they will be attempting to decipher. He identifies three race types:

A. Formful
B. Positives and negatives for each contender
C. Unpredictable

In Race A, the relative strengths of the contenders are plain, and the odds on each will be easy to assign. In Race B, handicappers will be forced to analyze the advantages and disadvantages of each contender, and setting the odds line will be difficult. In Race C, contender selection

FOUR CONTENDER TEMPLATES

CONTENDER A ODDS	CONTENDER B ODDS	CONTENDER C ODDS	CONTENDER D ODDS	PCT%
8/5	6/1	6/1	6/1	80%
9/5	9/2	6/1	6/1	81%
9/5	5/1	5/1	6/1	81%
9/5	5/1	6/1	6/1	79%
2/1	4/1	6/1	6/1	81%
2/1	9/2	5/1	6/1	81%
2/1	5/1	5/1	5/1	81%
2/1	5/1	5/1	6/1	79%
5/2	3/1	6/1	6/1	81%
5/2	7/2	5/1	6/1	80%
5/2	4/1	5/1	5/1	80%
5/2	4/1	9/2	6/1	80%
5/2	9/2	9/2	5/1	80%
3/1	3/1	5/1	6/1	80%
3/1	7/2	4/1	6/1	81%
3/1	7/2	9/2	5/1	81%
3/1	7/2	9/2	6/1	79%
3/1	7/2	5/1	5/1	79%
3/1	4/1	4/1	5/1	81%
3/1	4/1	4/1	6/1	79%
3/1	4/1	9/2	5/1	79%
3/1	4/1	9/2	9/2	81%
3/1	9/2	9/2	9/2	79%
7/2	7/2	7/2	6/1	80%
7/2	7/2	4/1	5/1	80%
7/2	7/2	9/2	9/2	80%
7/2	4/1	4/1	9/2	80%
4/1	4/1	4/1	4/1	80%

THREE CONTENDER TEMPLATES

CONTENDER A	CONTENDER B	CONTENDER C	PCT%
1/1	5/1	6/1	80%
6/5	7/2	6/1	81%
6/5	4/1	5/1	81%
6/5	4/1	6/1	79%
6/5	9/2	9/2	81%
6/5	9/2	5/1	79%
7/5	3/1	6/1	80%
7/5	7/2	9/2	81%
7/5	7/2	5/1	79%
7/5	4/1	4/1	81%
7/5	4/1	9/2	79%
3/2	3/1	6/1	79%
3/2	7/2	9/2	80%
3/2	4/1	4/1	80%
8/5	5/2	6/1	80%
8/5	3/1	9/2	81%
8/5	3/1	5/1	79%
8/5	7/2	4/1	80%
9/5	5/2	9/2	81%
9/5	5/2	5/1	79%
9/5	3/1	4/1	80%
9/5	7/2	7/2	79%
2/1	2/1	6/1	80%
2/1	5/2	4/1	81%
2/1	5/2	9/2	79%
2/1	3/1	7/2	80%
5/2	5/2	3/1	81%

will be puzzling, but as Fierro tells, once the contenders have been isolated, the fair-value odds for each will be surprisingly clear.

To help further, Fierro supplies for free the Betting Line Templates handicappers should use (opposite page). Fierro provides his betting lines to the impressively successful *Today's Racing Digest,* of southern California, and his Betting Line Templates can be downloaded on the Web. Fierro practically demands that handicappers who want to succeed must fill out the templates before they arrive at the track or off-track parlor. Once developed, the templates become a fail-safe guide to the day's action. In a curious step the author insists has worked empirically, Fierro urges handicappers not to alter the templates, even to adjust for scratches, jockey changes, alterations in the probable pace, races taken off the turf, or other inconvenient factors that usually send handicappers scrambling to reevaluate their thinking and late betting.

In a provocative section of his text, Fierro provides handicappers with what he terms filters, which are empirically documented scenarios that can guide bettors as to whether races having more complicated betting lines are actually playable. Fierro's filters resulted from the study of more than 18,000 races across a four-year period. They are:

Top Contender 1-2-3-4
Pass, All Too Low
Three Overlays, Pass
Four Overlays, Pass
Two-Horse Play
Legitimate Favorite, Pass
Prohibitive Favorite, Pass

In the Top Contender 1-2-3-4 scenario, more than one of the contenders is an overlay. What to do? Fierro found he usually could not bet both overlays and expect a long-term profit. The situation demands attention, as it can be expected to occur in one of four races (26 percent). In a subsample of 2,242 races, Fierro found the best bet was the contender most likely to win, typically Contender A, or Contender B. The most likely contenders won more and paid more. Here are Fierro's results:

Highest-rated Contender   22%W $11.90 Ave.Mutuel   1.31 ROI
Lower-rated Contender   10%W $14.87 Ave.Mutuel   (.23)ROI

As Fierro's research tells, if Contender A is 7-2 and an overlay, and Contender D is 15-1 and an overlay, the wager belongs on Contender A.

STEVE FIERRO'S *THE FOUR QUARTERS OF HORSE INVESTING*
BETTING LINE TEMPLATES

TRACK: NAME: DATE: DIRT/TURF

P# 1st Race Type	Current Odds	Fair Odds
Analysis:		

P# 6th Race Type	Current Odds	Fair Odds
Analysis:		

P# 2nd Race Type	Current Odds	Fair Odds
Analysis:		

P# 7th Race Type	Current Odds	Fair Odds
Analysis:		

P# 3rd Race Type	Current Odds	Fair Odds
Analysis:		

P# 8th Race Type	Current Odds	Fair Odds
Analysis:		

P# 4th Race Type	Current Odds	Fair Odds
Analysis:		

P# 9th Race Type	Current Odds	Fair Odds
Analysis:		

P# 5th Race Type	Current Odds	Fair Odds
Analysis:		

P# 10th Race Type	Current Odds	Fair Odds
Analysis:		

Despite the lower odds, the most preferred contenders won more than three times as many races. To put it differently, the smaller the spread between a contender's fair-value odds and the overlay odds, the more likely that contender will win.

When Fierro's line identified three or four overlays, he could not secure a profit, no matter how he proceeded. When two overlays were found, the situation proved ripe for profits, but not easily. Fierro first set the overlay bar at 5-1 on both horses; no profit. He tested 6-1 on each overlay; no profit. The profits appeared only at 8-1, or higher, on each contender in a two-horse overlay scenario.

Fierro has copious advice too for handicappers who are hell-bent to bet against legitimate, and especially prohibitive, favorites. The overlays they believe they will be backing more often than not will be false overlays. "Whenever I set a line on a horse at 3-2 or less, and the public agreed and bet the horse below 3-2, the other listed contenders were false overlays. They reason they became false overlays is because of the heavy betting action on the overwhelming favorite. I lost an astonishing 44 cents on the dollar when betting into this type of contender/favorite."

Handicappers must avoid betting against the prohibitive favorites. "We have a prohibitive favorite in a race when: One of our betting-line contenders is sent to the post at 3-2 or less and no other entrant in the race is less than 5-1."

Although *The Four Quarters of Horse Investing* can be pedantic in parts and is a highly personalized presentation, its contents have been empirically documented across several seasons and they have been demonstrably effective for the author, who may be right in thinking its businessman's approach will transfer readily to most handicappers who want to win. The betting-line "templates" are readily transportable, to be sure, and they can correct the unfortunate habit widely dispersed among good handicappers to let too many overlays get away, and cry about the lost opportunities afterward.

A couple of weeks following the 2002 Kentucky Derby, I chatted with friend and partner Tom Brohamer. In the course of the conversation, Brohamer mentioned he had cashed a nice bet to win on War Emblem. I inquired as to how he had come to make the play.

"I didn't consider Came Home or Harlan's Holiday to be legitimate contenders," said Brohamer, "so I made a line on four horses. I had War Emblem at 12-1. When he came up greater than a 50 percent overlay, I made the play." Brohamer did not say as much, but the only way to "have" horses that pay as well as War Emblem and Sarava in the 2002 classics is to make a betting line.

CHAPTER 35

THE PICK SIX
IN A BOTTLE

IS THERE SUCH a species of the racetrack as a pick-six winner? The sightings have been rare, to be sure, but absolutely the species does exist. The markings of these rare birds can be considered equally rare. They include 10 or more seasons of passionate play, accompanied by triumphal results.

Although undoubtedly others will have acquaintances of their own, the three specimens I have known are Steven Crist, Barry Meadow, and my favorite, Gibson Carouthers. The first two should be familiar to denizens of the track, and devotees of the pick six, but Gibson is not. As introduction, Gibson is a Minneapolis pro, a terrific player, who sits on the board of fan-friendly Canterbury Park, not to mention the inventor of that track's three-year-old Claiming Crown, and whose pick-six methods differ in their entirety from the other two, and until lately, may have been unique to himself.

But the cat got out of the bag in *The HorsePlayer Magazine,* Volume 9, Issue 2, of March and April 2002, when Gibson penned the best pick-six article ever written, entitled, "20 Years of Playing the Pick Six . . . and Still Alive!," a heading that fits the passion and the personality perfectly. Formerly an advertising prodigy, responsible for Burger King's "Double Whopper" of a hamburger (the response to McDonald's Big Mac), and other successfully familiar advertisements, and currently an entrepreneur of creative and gimmicky gadgets and stuff (his latest is a key chain that supports the campaign for youngsters to stop smoking by including a tag for the picture of a loved one), Gibson has even produced a T-shirt that promotes the pick six. On the back it says, "Play the Pick 6 at Canterbury Park." On the front, and this is the fabulous part, the shirt asks, mysteriously, "Are You Alive?"

As is true of ideas that hit the center marks with uncanny accuracy and force, Gibson's magazine piece on the pick six is succinctly elegant in its simplicity. Handicappers who adhere to its principles will have no need to wrestle with the probabilities of hitting the six legs of the complicated bet vis-à-vis the projected payoffs, which are virtually guaranteed to be generous. They will not be required to fill out 21 betting cards featuring the convoluted admixtures of singles, A-horses, and backup horses. They will not need partners or teams of bettors. And they will never be required to risk a small fortune to compete on a leveled playing field with the heavily financed syndicates.

The single requirement for success is excellence in handicapping. This means the best of handicappers should have the best of chances to win the pick six, such that the recommended strategy approaches the ideal. After admitting to the commoner's mistakes during the tender years, Gibson's turn of fate occurred once he realized that the thinner his ticket, the sturdier his chances long-term. As he puts the seemingly elementary point, "You can't play not to lose. You must play to win. It's easy to get suckered into including a bunch of horses that could win. That results in fat tickets. I have found that most of the time I've hit the Pick 6, I would have won with a much leaner play. Conclusion: You win the Pick 6 when your top plays are right. Not when you back up your top plays with all sorts of defensive combinations."

GIBSON'S LEANER, ASSERTIVE strategy combines only two types of horses, singles and covers. He identifies two types of singles, "separators" and "standouts," and each is critical to recognize, the standouts significantly easier for most handicappers than the separators. The "separator" is the play that eliminates to a startling degree the competition. The odds to win will be high, but the horse figures on fundamental dope. It's a serious overlay, if you will, but not a longshot, and certainly not a stab. As Gibson advises, the bigger the odds, the more likely the competition will disappear, but the distinction between the legitimate contender Gibson has in mind and a longshot is crucial to comprehend. The conventional definition of the longshot as a horse having a low probability of winning at high odds does not apply. Gibson's separators have a good chance to win, period, and they should be expected to outrun their odds routinely. I can testify that Gibson's horses do. His separators are authentic contenders.

In the *HorsePlayer* article, Gibson does not instruct handicappers at all in the search for separators. That remains the individual handicapper's private domain. He refers obliquely to his personal unconventional methods, described as "tedious" and "time-consuming." When he suggests he has never mastered speed and pace figures, and has discovered no shortcuts, but relies instead only on "tons of angles" and "stacks of chart books," Gibson understates his armament to a fault. It's true that Gibson has an aptitude for long-priced overlays that will outrun their odds, but like all successful masters of patterns and angles, the aptitude has become a function of fundamentally sound handicapping.

Gibson's style of play and the resulting overlays are heavily dependent upon pattern recognition. The "tedious" and "time-consuming" aspect is a lengthy, laborious consultation with the results charts. That's where Gibson finds his separators, which cannot be said of numerous experienced handicappers, who generally do not consult the charts, except perhaps to uncover specific bits of information that might be helpful. So Gibson enjoys that built-in edge, an untapped source, even as speed handicappers of a generation ago enjoyed an edge because few of their colleagues had access to the figures.

Similarly, the important search for separators is readily conducted by handicappers having an especially strong aptitude that fewer players will share. The aptitude might emphasize hidden form, or early-pace analysis, or class on the grass, or trainer patterns, or combinations of speed and pace figures, or pedigree plays, or anything else that (a) handicappers have recognized as personal strengths and (b) has rewarded its backers with a regular schedule of underbet winners. Handicappers as a group have learned to repeat the bets that have rewarded them royally in the past, and the habit, a form of pattern recognition, is readily transferable to a reliance on the horses as separators in the pick six.

Standouts are horses that are not worth the effort to defeat. Whether even-money, odds-on, 6-5, 8-5, 2-1, or even 5-2, the horses qualify as authentic standouts, at least by the handicapper's best judgment. Here handicappers best accept Gibson's studied experience, as he admits to years of misguided attempts to upset these favorites in the pick six. The turning point arrived once Gibson realized the pick six could deliver a bonanza of profits, even when the tickets included a couple of standouts. "I fought standouts for far too long. It's a reflection of my hatred of chalk.

All it takes is a couple of big scores with a couple of even-money standouts, and you'll change your mind. I sure did."

If the pick-six ticket is characterized by a separator and a couple of standouts, all that is left is the three (or four) races where handicappers will be forced to spread. In these less predictable races, handicappers are urged to rely on Gibson's "covers," and his definition of the term should not be denied. "'Covers' refer to races where *you go as deep as necessary* to insure having the winners." Handicappers must entertain no shortcuts. Cover *all* the horses having a handicapper's chance to win. As Gibson declares, if handicappers lose, they are shocked. They say, "I could not have covered that horse." They never say, "Oh, damn, I almost used that horse." In using covers, Gibson insists handicappers can fabricate no excuses for missing. In reading the piece, I realized that on this obvious yet underestimated point, Gibson might as well have been scolding me.

Although cost is a crucial consideration in Gibson's approach, he goes so far regarding covers as to encourage handicappers to hit the "all" button in the less predictable races, but only ". . . if you honestly think any horse in the race can win." On a variation of the point that has the potential to punish its abusers severely, Gibson advises that it's never acceptable to eliminate just one horse. He cautions handicappers too on the inherent contradiction of using as covers just two horses. "That's an admission you don't know who's going to win, yet you're probably not going deep enough to cover."

No one should doubt that the elegance of the approach, and the key to winning, is the separator. In reflecting on his winning days, Gibson encourages handicappers to concentrate on the notion they can win the pick six for as much as six figures ". . . *by making only one good pick.*" Examine the typical ticket below. Gibson submitted it during the opening week of Del Mar, 2001, and hit for $16,598.20.

Race 3	2,3,4,6,9	Covers, 5-deep	#2 won, paid $4.60
Race 4	8	Separator	#8 won, paid $23.20
Race 5	2,3,5,8	Covers, 4-deep	#5 won, paid $20.60
Race 6	3,4,8	Covers, 3-deep	#3 won, paid $10.20
Race 7	3,6	Standout (2)	#3 won, paid $4.40
Race 8	11	Standout	#11 won, paid $6.40

120 bets, $240 ticket

The pick six for Gibson's ticket returned 69-1. The separator (10-1) and the 9-1 winner in a "cover" race keyed the killing, despite the two standouts and the underlay that won one of the three "cover" races. In the magazine, Gibson chastises himself for breaking his rule regarding "standouts," and the two-horse play in Race 7. "I played stupid here. Took bad shot at beating favorite. Never a good idea." The "bad shot" doubled Gibson's cost, without enhancing his value. Handicappers will notice if Gibson had trusted his standout in Race 7, the ticket would have cost half as much, or $120. The pick-six return on investment would have soared to 138-1.

Unrelated in the magazine piece, Gibson hit the pick six again that week for roughly the same amount on roughly the same ticket. As mentioned, he is especially adept at foraging through the charts for the separators that will elude most of us. In his summary remarks on betting the pick six by this approach, Gibson offers handicappers these curiously comforting comments.

"One good thing about this style of playing is that you rarely feel bad when you lose. If your separator loses, you went down with your main play. If a standout loses, he still wasn't worth trying to beat. If a cover loses, you would have never used that pig."

I like that. Gibson Carouthers's pick-six prescription sounds so good, so easily digestible, it might be promoted shamelessly as a remedy for all good handicappers and for all times, rather like a potion that might be bottled and sold as a cure for whatever the pick-six ill that ails you. Have a problem hitting the pick six? Come right here, and get the winning formulae. Imagine that, the pick six in a bottle!

CHAPTER 36

THE HANDICAPPER'S DAY AT THE RACES: THE WTC BREEDERS' CUP EVENT-DAY PARTY

ANYONE WHO WAS on-track on that inaugural Saturday in 1984, when the buzz in the Hollywood Park air was undeniable and unprecedented, knew that this would be the start of something big. Two decades later, John Gaines can rest assured and proud, because his vision of a day devoted to championship Thoroughbred racing is bigger and better than ever. The World Thoroughbred Championships Breeders' Cup event day, as it is now awkwardly called, has triumphed, in fact, as the sport's greatest idea ever, its grandest day annually. Breeders, owners, trainers, jockeys, track officials, and the fans, everyone who is anyone in this sport of clay-footed kings, bathes in the afternoon's glory. This was an idea whose time had come.

Not to be forsaken are the handicappers and bettors, who now gather on this singular afternoon from around the world to play the game they love. The WTC Breeders' Cup event-day party can be accepted too as the handicapper's greatest day at the races. The pools are huge, the payoffs astonishing, the handicapping challenging, and the game on this day, as on no other, proceeds with the promise that the best of handicappers can anticipate the greatest rewards. May the best and the brightest win. In 2001, for example, the two best horses in the world, Tiznow and Sakhee, finished one-two in a thrilling Breeders' Cup Classic, and the superfecta paid $24,496. With the sport and the game joining together like this, the party approaches the ideal.

With a year's income up for grabs several times in one afternoon, and six-figure bonanzas entirely feasible from the results on nothing more than good handicapping, handicappers are urged to play and to prepare. Of handicapping, players benefit if they follow the rocky road to the championship card carefully, not failing to purchase the advance edition of the *Daily Racing Form* past performances, and getting as fully acquainted with the horses as time allows. Of the betting, handicappers are urged to up the ante, for most players significantly, putting aside $100 to $200 a month during the calendar year. With so much profit at stake, handicappers best adhere—and strictly—to the trusty maxims that short money and scared money never wins. Aggressive betting is the only way to go. Out-of-pocket betting gets handicappers nowhere.

Table 1 presents the odds on the first three finishers in the eight races on the 2001 program at Belmont Park, and the $2 payoffs for the several pools. The odds and payoffs should be considered typical. Examine the table for a few minutes now.

Table 1: WTC Breeders' Cup Races 2001, Odds and Payoffs, Various Pools

	Odds 1-3	Win	Exacta	Trifecta	Super	Pick Three	Pick Four
		$2	$2	$2	$2	$2	$2
Distaff	12, 9-2, 32	$26.60	$133	$2,551	$X	$X	$X
Juv Fillies	11, 53,7-2	25.80	768	3,823	X	X	X
Mile	5, 8, 33	12.20	105	2,445	X	1,671	X
Sprint	9, 17, 11	21.20	290	2,162	27,799	2,396	X
F & M Turf	6, 13, 36	14.00	229	5,166	44,331	1,641	X
Juvenile	7, 42, 9	16.40	530	3,665	*56,927	1,609	X
Turf	7-5, 7, 8	4.80	33	211	**3,965	291	X
Classic	6, 9-2, 13	15.80	140	1,341	24,496	359	1,627

Pick Six ($2)	Pool $4,811,450	*4th Horse = 103-1
Races 5-10	Pick Six $262,442	**5th Horse = 51-1
	Pick Five $ 1,475	

Handle $98.6 Million

What's not to like? Of the $98.6 million handle, roughly $80 million was returned to the winners. Plenty of money for everyone, and the pot should only grow bigger.

Examination of the successful horses' odds reveal that only when over-bet favorites prevail, as with Fantastic Light in the Turf, do the exotic payoffs look normal, although a $4,000 killing in the superfecta from a 7-5 underlay may be begging the question. When medium-priced contenders win, as from 5-1 to 12-1 in 2001, the payoffs soar. Of the horses that ended in the money in 2001, only five had been sent off at 20-1 or greater. Still, when double-digit longshots partake in the payoffs, the profits go ballistic. Without a corresponding escalation in costs, the trifectas can exceed exactas by factors of 6-1 to 10-1, possibly by 20-1. Superfectas normally exceed trifectas by 10-1 to 20-1, an astonishing ratio.

On this day too, the pick threes, typically the handicapper's best friend, because only the winners must be found and the probabilities of hitting can be unusually strong among the exotic wagers, play a supporting role in relation to the trifectas and superfectas, the marquee stars of this show, where the longshots spike the payoffs by finishing second, third, and fourth. Needless to note, the longshots on this special day often possess seductively positive dope. Many of them might be expected to earn a share if the races proceed in ways that fatten their chances, and when they do, the horses must be covered.

The truly important point about the fabulous payoffs, however, is that effective handicapping is not as difficult as the odds would suggest. Nothing comes easily, to be sure, but on this day competent handicappers hold the edge. So how might handicappers proceed to get their share of the profits?

A point of departure honors the crucial distinction between picking winners and constructing the exotic combinations. If these are the best horses in the world, the winners, with important exceptions, more often than not will be the multiple Grade 1/Grade 2 stickouts. The principle applies reliably to the Distaff, Mile, Sprint, Filly and Mare Turf, Turf, and Classic. In 2001, the guideline missed the Distaff (Unbridled Elaine), but caught the Mile (Val Royal, $12.20), Sprint (Squirtle Squirt, $21.20), Filly and Mare Turf (Banks Hill, $14), Turf (Fantastic Light, $4.80), and Classic (Tiznow, $15.80).

The juveniles can be evaluated reliably using speed figures, with the fillies expected to show a Beyer Speed Figure of 94, and the colts a Beyer of 100, provided the early pace of the qualifying race was not slow. If the juveniles are improving, as many will be, handicappers can accept Beyer figures within two lengths of the guideline numbers, or 90 for fillies and 96 for colts. If the qualifying figures were recorded in Grade 1/Grade 2 stakes going long, award extra credit. If imports are entered, a la Johannesburg, accept one Group 1 title, provided the Timeform rating is 115 or greater. If the Timeform rating for the qualifying race is below 115, require two or more Group 1/Group 2 victories.

Of horses that match the standards, when betting to win, and keying exotic combinations, discount the underlays and consider the overlays.

As a rule, favorites will be underlays, and second, third, and fourth choices might be overlays. Make your fair-value betting lines, and stick strictly to them. In betting exactas, medium-priced overlays can be combined, and each of them used atop the underlays. Unless the overbet favorites are champions, near-champions, or division leaders that stand out, *and* the second and third betting choices can be tossed, do not key the favorites on top in exactas. If the favorite figures strongly, and the second and third choices can be dismissed, use the favorite on top to *all* the overlays that might outrun their odds, varying the amounts on each combination from highest to lowest in accord with the value offered.

The trick, of course, is constructing trifecta and superfecta combinations that make sense and should pay extravagantly well. It's crucial to assume the races will be *contentious*. The contention runs deep, not only to win, but also to finish second, third, and fourth. That means several horses can be considered for each hole.

Begin by dividing the field into thirds. The top third consists of the multiple Grade 1/Grade 2 contenders, and figure qualifiers, most likely to win, as described above. The middle third consists of horses rated a cut or two below the top echelon, as handicappers prefer. The bottom third consists of all the other horses. No horses are eliminated from consideration at this early juncture. Starting with the main contenders, make a betting line by asking if the race were run 100 times, how many times might each horse be expected to win. Write the percentage amount for each horse on a sheet. The percentages must sum to 100 percent. If they do not, juggle the line, adding and subtracting points for the various horses, until a 100-point line has been constructed. Convert the percentages to fair-value betting odds. Use the odds-percentage table at the end of this essay, or divide the percentage amount for each horse into 100, and subtract 1.

If a main contender might be expected to win 20 percent of the time, the fair-value odds are 100/20, or 5 minus 1, equals 4-1. If an outsider should win 4 percent of the time, the fair-value odds are 100/4, or 25, minus 1, equals 24-1.

Once the fair-value odds for each third of the field have been determined, the trifecta and superfectas can be contructed by linking the overlays in each third to the overlays in the other two-thirds. Several tickets will be purchased. Key the overlays in the top third of the field to win and place. Use the overlays/longshots in the middle third to place and show. Use the overlays/longshots in the bottom third to finish third and fourth. As Barry Meadow notes, longshots generally will finish third and fourth, not first or second, and that's the cost-effective way to cover them on the championship card. In trifectas and superfectas, favorites might be covered to finish third and fourth, notably when double-digit contenders have been covered to win and place.

A simple alternative can apply when any of the championship events appears more predictable. In the 2001 Classic, for example, four horses accounted for more than two-thirds of the probabilities: Galileo (3-1), Sakhee (9-2), Tiznow (6-1), and Aptitude (2-1).

Aptitude was the obvious underlay; out. Galileo was a mild underlay perhaps, while Sakhee and Tiznow represented mild overlays. Now the two overlays are boxed to win and place, and *all* the other horses having a handicapper's chance to finish well are boxed to finish second and third in trifectas, and to finish third and fourth in superfectas.

Serial bets can be constructed smartly by linking the overlays in the top thirds of the fields in each leg. Profits again run high. If handicappers allot themselves a 50 percent chance of hitting each leg of the pick three, for example, the probability of hitting the three races will be .5 × .5 × .5, or 12.5 percent. The fair-value odds will be 7-1 (100/12.5 = 8, minus 1, or 7-1), a handicapper's decent chance to collect. Payoffs must exceed costs by 8-1 to break even. In the 2001 Breeders' Cup, the approach collected the pick three in the three-race sequences ending with the Banks Hill in the Filly and Mare Turf ($1,641), Johannesburg in the Juvenile ($1,609), Fantastic Light in the Turf ($291), and Tiznow in the Classic ($359). The 120 combinations cost $240, and the payoffs totaled $3,900 (16-1), a handsome profit.

No matter what procedures are followed, handicappers will experience a busy afternoon. Preparation makes the difference, but handicappers best stay on alert for odds shifts, biases, and the overlay opportunities that will be legion. It's party time, but handicappers best let the partygoers eat, drink, and quarrel about the horses that figure to be best. Handicappers can deal with the championship races on the proper terms, as the contentious puzzles they are. And when the day is done, may the best handicappers enjoy their best results of the year.

Odds Percentage Table

1-10	90.91	4-1	20.00
1-5	83.33	9-2	18.19
2-5	71.42	5-1	16.67
1-2	66.67	6-1	14.29
3-5	62.50	7-1	12.50
4-5	55.56	8-1	11.11
1-1	50.00	9-1	10.00
6-5	45.45	10-1	9.09
7-5	41.67	11-1	8.33
3-2	40.00	12-1	7.69
8-5	38.46	15-1	6.25
9-5	35.71	20-1	4.76
2-1	33.33	25-1	3.85
5-2	28.57	30-1	3.23
3-1	25.00	50-1	1.96
7-2	22.22	99-1	1.00

CHAPTER 37

HOW TO HANDICAP
THE KENTUCKY DERBY

"We look for the athlete, never mind the bloodlines."
D. WAYNE LUKAS,
Los Angeles Times, 1984

"Where are the Dosage boys?"
BOB BAFFERT,
Churchill Downs press box, 1998,
after Real Quiet, DI of 5.86, had won.

IN THE 15 YEARS since D. Wayne Lukas had asserted his narrow point of view about bloodlines and the Kentucky Derby, only one colt with a high Dosage Index had won, and the colorful trainer had changed his mind. During the interim, it's fair to say, horsemen and handicappers alike had learned more than they ever had expected to know about the subtleties and intricacies of the Kentucky Derby, which remains, and ever will, the most complicated horse race of them all.

Then, in 1998, Real Quite, a Dosage improbable, won, and the new unofficial Derby spokesman, Bob Baffert, bellowed triumphantly to the media, "Where are the Dosage boys?" The next year, 1999, another Dosage improbable, Charismatic, won for Lukas, and the matter of bloodlines and the Derby appeared to have come full circle. The ground has shifted under the Kentucky Derby, to be sure, but as the French like to say, the more things change, the more they remain the same. It's true still that pedigree plus performance gets the roses, and it's just as true as always that colts having a severe imbalance of speed and stamina in their recent bloodlines, high Dosage, if you will, are highly unlikely to win the Kentucky Derby.

Perhaps it's simply characteristic of this widely misapprehended sport that the most popular race on the Thoroughbred calendar had also been the most misunderstood. Until the mid-1980's, year after year, in the fanfare surrounding the big race, the essential analysis had been missing. For example, the 1986 pre-Derby consensus choice, Snow Chief, would have been fortunate to finish in the money, and if he had won, would have become the first colt of his kind to have done so in modern racing history. The winner, Ferdinand, came romping home at 17-1, when he should have been no worse than a co-favorite.

Since 1929, no less, no horse having a ratio of speed to stamina (Dosage) in its immediate four-generation pedigree exceeding a guideline figure (4.00) had ever won the Kentucky Derby. Such colts possess an unacceptably high Dosage Index, a pedigree construct that refers to the blend of speed and stamina in the bloodlines. A perfect blend of speed and stamina is reflected by a Dosage Index (DI) of 1.00. A Dosage Index of 2.00 means twice as much speed as stamina. A DI of 0.50 means half as much speed as stamina.

Snow Chief had a DI of 5.00. Snow Chief was a statistical improbable in the 1986 Derby. The colt did not figure to win, and the experts should have told us so. Since Strike the Gold interrupted the flow in 1990, three colts having "high Dosage" have won, including Real Quiet (1998), and Charismatic (1999).

To bring matters into perspective, the problem of analyzing the Kentucky Derby is unique in Thoroughbred handicapping. How to predict the probable outcome of a race in which still-developing three-year-olds will compete over a distance of ground (1¼ miles) none has traveled, on a racetrack few have experienced. The main problem is the distance. A mile and one-quarter and farther represent classic distances in American horse racing. Unfortunately, a Thoroughbred's performances at middle distances (one mile, 1¹⁄₁₆ miles, 1⅛ miles) are not strongly related to its performances at classic distances.

Thus, the crucial consideration: can leading Derby candidates that have impressed at 1⅛ miles do well at 1¼ miles?

By conventional handicapping methods, evaluating the past performances in terms of demonstrated speed, class, form, pace preferences, and distance preferences, not to mention the interrelations among the several factors, it's difficult to say. What is well known is that numerous three-year-olds that have won smashingly at middle distances, including many Derby favorites, cannot duplicate the feats at 1¼ miles and beyond. Experts that have persisted in projecting Derby winners strictly from the past performances have regularly fallen flat on their predictions. So have the millions of recreational bettors that have followed their advice. Since Spectacular Bid, in 1979, exactly one favorite has prevailed.

A few memorable situations have been the most provocative. In 1984, the brilliant filly Althea smashed the track record at Oaklawn Park, in Hot Springs, Arkansas, for 1⅛ miles, taking the prestigious Arkansas Derby by 10 lengths. Trainer Lukas assured a Kentucky Derby dinner audience during Derby Week that the Dosage Index would be unmasked at last. Althea possessed fabulous speed, but lousy Dosage. Favored at 5-2, on Derby Day she finished 19th of 20.

The 1985 unanimous pre-Derby favorite, Chief's Crown, became the most intriguing case of all. An authentically top colt, Chief's Crown had followed his brilliant races as the nation's champion two-year-old with magnificent pre-Derby performances in Florida and Kentucky. No one expected, therefore, that Chief's Crown, DI of 5.00, would be unable to handle the stretch run of a 1¼-mile race. Victory was virtually preordained by the experts and horsemen at every station. In a southern California poll of horsemen and assorted insiders by *Daily Racing Form,* 96 percent selected Chief's Crown to win. Only one horseman—one!—selected Spend a Buck. Above all, it would be the 1985 running that changed perspectives, altered the conventional wisdom.

Just two horses qualified on Dosage to upset Chief's Crown: Spend a Buck and Stephan's Odyssey. They finished one-two. Chief's Crown labored throughout the Churchill Downs stretch and barely held third. The favorite ran his race but was not good enough. The defeat was inexplicable by conventional handicapping, and for the first time the insiders conceded they might have something new to learn about the relationship between performance and pedigree.

Again for the 1986 running, just two horses qualified to upset the can't-miss favorite. Following a horrendous trip the first mile, Ferdinand (DI 1.50) won. Snow Chief collapsed in ordinary style after chasing a fast pace. He failed to beat half the field.

In 1993, Sea Hero, a Dosage probable devoid of early speed, had failed to win at middle distances during winter and spring; indeed, had failed to threaten. He won the Kentucky Derby going away and paid $27.80. He next lost at another middle distance, before winning the 1¼-mile Travers Stakes at Saratoga going away.

In 1995, the Dosage probables in the bulky field included Thunder Gulch, Tejano Run, Timber Country, and two other colts. It happened again. Thunder Gulch won, and paid $51. The exacta to Tejano Run paid $480. The trifecta to Timber Country paid more than two thousand dollars. This was the last hurrah.

By 2002, every one of the 18 colts in the Derby gate possessed a Dosage Index below 4.00. Horsemen such as Lukas and Baffert will not hesitate to run a colt having high Dosage in the Derby, perhaps, but when they do, the odds will be heavily against their success.

IN 1981, DR. STEVEN A. ROMAN, a scientist who directs the basic research in chemical processes at Shell Oil, in Houston, Texas, and author of more than 60 patents in chemistry, published a longitudinal study of North American stakes winners that demonstrated irrefutably that when the highest-grade horses compete at classic distances, the determinant factor is usually the relationship between pedigree and performance.

Roman showed that horses having too much speed in relation to stamina were not likely to become racing's truly important stakes winners and leading sires. Of stakes winners as a group, approximately 40 percent have Dosage indices exceeding the guideline figure of 4.00, but these horses rarely win the sport's most definitive events.

More specifically, and controversially, Roman revealed that no horse having a genetic ratio of speed to stamina greater than a statistical index value of 4.00 had ever won the Kentucky Derby.

Roman also explained how to calculate and interpret the Dosage Index, a remarkably inventive tool that is merely a mathematical expression of a racehorse's inherent speed and endurance characteristics. The explanation and arithmetic is simple.

As students of pedigree know, but many handicappers do not, the genetic aptitudes of racehorses are five: Brilliant, Intermediate, Classic, Solid, and Professional, the five arranged in descending order of speed, or, if you wish, ascending order of stamina. To arrive at a horse's Dosage Index, Roman divided the five aptitudes into a speed wing and a stamina wing and allotted points to each by identifying the distinguished or "prepotent" sires found in a horse's most recent four generations.

These sires transmit outstanding racing qualities to their progeny consistently, in relation to sires that are not prepotent. Most great racehorses do not distinguish themselves at stud. They cannot pass along their abilities. In fact, in the sport's history, only some 150 sires have become prepotent.

The Dosage Index is merely the pedigree points in the speed wing divided by the points in the stamina wing. The higher index, the more unbalanced toward speed a horse's competitive quality.

Ever since Roman identified the value line separating truly important horses and classic winners from the others as 4.0, his followers delighted in evaluating Kentucky Derby candidates in terms of their Dosage figures and critics waited eagerly for the method to fall flat on its face.

In fact, Roman's two-step method for handicapping the Kentucky Derby has performed with astonishing reliability and has outperformed the public selectors by a wide margin. Roman advises handicappers to favor all Derby starters acceptable on Dosage and weighted within 10 points of the leader on the Experimental Handicap, the industry's scale of weights for new three-year-olds, based solely on two-year-old performance. Thus, Roman's method relates pedigree to performance.

Since Secretariat (DI 3.00) in 1973 through 1986, that mechanical two-step approach not only picked every Derby winner, itself remarkable, but a flat $2 wager on all 39 starters that qualified, a $78 outlay, returned winnings of $181.10, or profits of $103.10. The net on the invested dollar was an amazing 132 percent.

In some years the method's accuracy had been nothing short of sensational. Only Secretariat and Angle Light qualified when the great red horse set the standing Derby time record of 1:59⅖.

The next season, 1974, only the outsider Cannonade qualified; he won. In 1975, only Foolish Pleasure qualified; he won.

In 1982, the year after Roman had gone public with his Dosage research and statistical index, all the pre-Derby favorites had DI's well above the guideline figure. The qualifiers were three longshots: Cassaleria, Gato Del Sol, and Laser Light. So, what happened? Gato Del Sol won, paid $44.40. Laser Light finished second, paid $17 to place.

Twice, astonishingly, when only three starters qualified, the three finished one-two-three: Affirmed-Alydar-Believe It (1978); Spectacular Bid-General Assembly-Golden Act (1979).

IN 1983, THREE STARTERS qualified again, including winner Sunny's Halo. In 1984, three qualified again, including winner Swale. The two qualifiers of 1985 finished one-two.

Can anyone who understands the precarious fate of racing predictions, even under the best of circumstances, not be provoked by results of that kind?

A particularly intriguing part of doping the Derby with Dosage each season involved the starters of leading trainer D. Wayne Lukas. A goal-directed individual, Lukas had singled out the Kentucky Derby as his number-one priority. The trainer ached to win the race, badly. His plans and energies are focused in one direction for months.

The personification of the contemporary horseman, outstandingly successful with younger horses, especially in stakes, Lukas from 1981 to 1986 had started nine horses in the race, including a pair of favored entries. Many had DI's above the guideline figure. None finished in the money, notably Althea (1984), the 1983 favorite; Marfa (fifth); and the 1985 Preakness winner, Tank's Prospect (eighth).

In 1986, second favorite Badger Land, with a perfect DI of 1.00, finished fifth following an awful trip.

Ironically, the splendid three-year-old Codex, whom Lukas inadvertently failed to nominate in 1980, had a splendid Dosage Index of 1.50, and rightfully would have been favored.

Two weeks later in the Preakness Stakes at Pimlico, Codex trounced the popular Derby winner Genuine Risk by 4¾ lengths.

Codex remains the most interesting of the Lukas prospects, as the trainer did not buy the colt at public auction. Tartan Farm bred Codex and sent the horse to Lukas to train. Lukas much prefers to purchase his clients' horses at prestigious yearling auctions, a skill he has developed as well or better than any other horseman in history. At the sales Lukas emphasizes conformation, the physical appearance and gait of yearlings, but not pedigree.

The trainer has been quoted widely on the matter.

"I go for their looks, not their pedigree," Lukas told the *Los Angeles Times* in 1984. "I don't believe in getting your horses from your own farm and your family of studs and broodmares. It's like the NFL draft. You want to be able to draft from all schools, not be restricted to a certain few.

"And we look for the athlete, never mind the bloodlines."

Roman, an admirer of Lukas's expertise on conformation and conditioning, in 1986 suggested that the southern California trainer would do better in classics and erect the cornerstones of the empire he sought once he better appreciated the relations among conformation, bloodlines, and racetrack performances. Lukas finally began to pay more attention to pedigree and Dosage Indexes.

"I recognize it [the Dosage Index] as one factor among several," he says. "Obviously the reliability of the numbers cannot be ignored."

Ignoring Dosage, racing journalists analyze the Derby solely on past performances, but even here the experts could do much more than they have to clear the air. Presently some 30 stakes get promoted as preliminaries to Louisville, but one preliminary does not equal another.

Improving three-year-olds that win New York's Gotham Stakes (Grade 2) or Santa Anita's San Felipe Handicap (Grade 1) do not become important Derby contenders until they later win a more definitive prep. And the winner of Oaklawn Park's Rebel Handicap has not automatically propelled itself into the Derby picture—unless it wins the Arkansas Derby (Grade 2) as well.

In order to restore order on its farms and in international sales rings, the breeding industry in 1973 began the annual grading of stakes in terms of their competitive quality. Stakes races are now rated variously as Grade 1, Grade 2, Grade 3, listed, open, and restricted. When handicapping the Kentucky Derby (Grade 1), all the players need remember is that Grade 1/Grade 2 events are far superior to Grade 3 stakes and absolutely so to any lower-grade stakes.

A tenable variation of the Roman method for handicapping the Derby is to accept only horses that are admissible on Dosage and have won or have finished close (within two lengths) in any of nine definitive Grade 1/Grade 2 preliminaries. Four are for two-year-olds: the Champagne Stakes, the Breeders' Cup Juvenile, the Hollywood Futurity, and the Remsen Stakes. Five are for three-year-olds: the Florida Derby, the Santa Anita Derby, the Wood Memorial, the Blue Grass Stakes, and the Arkansas Derby. Three-year-olds also should have recorded a Beyer Speed Figure of 105 or greater, provided the performance followed an early pace that was normal to fast.

If pedigree remains as critical as ever, something else, rather basic, has changed. For a century, no less, Derby winners had exhibited "high class" as two-year-olds. Early maturity was considered by alert handicappers a prerequisite to success on the first Saturday of May in Louisville, and rightly so. On this, times have changed. Although dual qualifiers maintained an impact value of 2.00 throughout the 1990's—twice as many winners as probabilities would expect—and a wager on each was profitable, their predictive value has declined.

Since 1998, a majority of Derby heroes have lacked "high class" at two, including the past four winners. A trend toward notoriously lightly raced colts as Derby contenders has rendered the effective handicapping of the classic more chaotic than ever. In *Bet with the Best* (2001), *Daily Racing Form* national handicapper Mike Watchmaker reminds handicappers that although early maturity as reflected by high class at two may be less definitive than before, every Derby winner since Apollo in 1882 has had at least one start as a two-year-old. As Watchmaker notes, apparently the training and seasoning, physical and mental, that two-year-olds undergo in preparing to race are critical factors that shape them as legitimate Derby candidates. Sunday Silence in 1989 and Fusaichi Pegasus in 2000 started only once as juveniles, and without winning, and the two stand out as the most talented Derby colts of the past 15 years.

Watchmaker examined the Derby winners since 1990 closely and from many angles, and he reported the two-year-old profiles of the putative winners for the new millennium. Charismatic apart, the two-year-old profile favors either the traditional unmistakably talented colt, a la a dual qualifier, or a late-developing colt of fall whose starts have been carefully selected by an astute trainer. In addition, every Derby winner except Monarchos had recorded a two-year-old Beyer Speed Figure in the 90's, which merits respect, even if it's a sub-par substitute for high class.

Charismatic apart, the three-year-old profile is more finely focused, and includes (a) three to four starts, (b) three two-turn preps, (c) at least two triple-digit Beyer Speed Figures among the three-year-old races, (d) an in-the-money finish in a Grade1/Grade 2 prelim, (e) the most recent performance in the Santa Anita Derby, Wood Memorial, Blue Grass Stakes, or Arkansas Derby, and (f) an off-the-pace running style.

Watchmaker admits to an exception or two on each specific, and as if on the devil's cue, in 2002 War Emblem exited the Illinois Derby (Grade 2) at Sportsman's Park, a bullring, with one triple-digit Beyer, and at 20-1 scampered wire to wire. Regardless, Watchmaker's profiles should prove helpful to handicappers in doping the Derby.

Pedigree plus performance still gets the roses, all right, but the specific guidelines have been less conclusive than ever.

CHAPTER 38

BEYER ON SPEED (20 YEARS LATER)

TWO DECADES AFTER he had popularized speed handicapping to a degree even he could not have imagined, after he had altered the general practice, after his beloved figures had achieved a prominence in the past performances of first *The Racing Times* and then *Daily Racing Form*, bestowing on their founder and explorer a deserved niche in the history of the sport and game, Andrew Beyer returned in 1993 with ruminations as to how figure handicapping had changed, and how his experiences with figures indeed had changed him. An engaging attribute of Andy has always been the capacity to change his mind. As much or more than a professional treatment of the handicapping art, *Beyer on Speed* (Houghton Mifflin, 1993) unfolds as a personal journey.

Early in the exposition, speed figures still represent the most powerful tools in handicapping, but they are no longer the way, the truth, and the light. Not only has everyone been using them, reducing the odds on figure horses to miserly levels, but also Beyer has come to recognize, with fervor, the more complicated relationships among the figures and other important facets of handicapping. The most nourishing parts of his latest book are the chapters that document in personal detail Beyer's adjustments to the "realities" of speed patterns, pace analysis, and especially turf racing. As usual, he has lots to say about each topic that will be instructive and helpful.

Of the contemporary value of speed figures, Beyer relates a truly melancholy tale of his experience at Gulfstream Park, 1990, with the miserable maiden graduate Memorable Skater. Beyer found himself playing at the top of his form, his figures perfectly refined, his trip observations keen, detecting track biases more astutely than ever, and handling his money and emotions with skill and maturity, but getting nowhere. Memorable Skater had finished out of the money nine times against maiden competition, and now he was running against winners. Traditional handicappers, Beyer asserts, would have tossed the horse unblinkingly.

"But his speed figures were competitive with those of his rivals, and in his last start, he had been forced to race wide on a track with a strong rail-favoring bias." Beyer prepared to make a killing. "I thought Memorable Skater embodied all of the handicapping skills I had spent a lifetime learning." The race proceeded exactly as Beyer had expected. Memorable Skater hugged the rail and won by six. He paid $6.20.

Beyer returned from the wintry blues of Florida to Washington, D.C., feeling low and lost. Within months, however, he had discovered the antidote, and he relates with his customary enthusiasm how speed figures would key his killing of Laurel's double triple, not once, but twice, the first for $134,161 (one of 10 tickets out of a $1.3 million pool) and the second some five months later for $195,000. Beyer learned that figure standouts that once were 7-1 but now were 5-2 could be the triggers to exactas, trifectas, superfectas, pick threes, and pick sixes that would pay boxcars, and his worldview had been righted anew. Speed figures have been the keys to the exotic vaults ever since.

Beyer's innate skepticism of the value of figure patterns could be tested, once his speed figures began to appear in *Daily Racing Form* in April 1992, and he commanded access to the company's computer and programmers. The last running line had always represented for Beyer the best estimate of a horse's current form and ability. The question he had asked traditionally was whether the closely matched contenders could repeat or exceed the most recent race. Now he wanted to know whether other patterns of improvement and decline that had found support in the general practice could be validated empirically.

First, Beyer asked what margin constitutes a significant advantage. The answer was three points, but the horses produced a dollar loss of 7.5 percent. Imagining the loss might be erased by double-figure horses (each of two speed figures higher than any other figure in the field), Beyer discovered he could get 40 percent winners, but a dollar loss of 2 percent. Double-fig horses in sprints did better, tossing profits of 7.5 percent, but the sample size was small and the advantage inconclusive. Beyer reasoned it would be a waste of time to await double-figure standouts.

Aroused by the possibility of predicting the future by patterns of numbers, Beyer turned next to figure patterns, including prominent patterns promoted by others, namely the bounce patterns of Len Ragozin's The Sheets. He wanted to know what happened to horses that had run three consecutive improving figures. In a 4,518 horse sample, no less than 71 percent declined in the next race, and 51 percent of those declined by six points (three lengths) or more. Beyer was stunned. He christened the results as "the three-and-out pattern." The exceptions are younger, lightly raced, improving colts and fillies. But older horses are highly susceptible to the three-and-out phenomenon, and can be tossed.

Of the notorious bounce pattern, Beyer reiterated his skepticism whenever horses show a sudden towering speed figure, sticking out like a giraffe's neck. Those figures should always be discounted. A regression to normal heights can be expected. Of the layoff bounce, Beyer studied a profile of the pattern he had found in my *Figure Handicapping*. I wrote that a bounce is most likely to occur when a horse has experienced an overexertion following a layoff of five months or longer, winning or finishing within a length, if returned to competition within six weeks. Beyer examined 331 horses who fit the profile, and compared their speed figures in the comeback races with the figures they recorded in the subsequent race. The findings:

87 (26 percent) ran an improved figure in the subsequent start
22 (7 percent) ran exactly the same figure
222 (67 percent) ran a worse figure
158 (48 percent) ran a figure that was worse by 10 points or more

Beyer was convinced. He concluded a stressful race at any time—not just following a lengthy layoff—may take a heavy toll on horses and affect their next performances. In an amusing series of anecdotes in this context, Beyer accepted the bounce data as logical explanations of some his most humiliating public selections, as when in 1986 he told readers of *The Washington Post* to mortgage their homes and hock the family jewels so that they might make a lifetime score on Badger Land in the Preakness, following the colt's horrendous trip in the Kentucky Derby. "But a bedraggled Badger Land, suffering from the effects of that stressful race in Louisville, barely picked up his feet in Baltimore, and, indeed, he was never the same again. Nor, I suppose were some readers of the *Post*."

■　■　■

BEYER'S COMPUTER SEARCHES supported a variety of the conventional bounce patterns, the notion that most horses will regress following an unusually outstanding performance, and he accepts the assertion of Thoro-Graph's Jerry Brown that if horses do not bounce following a single towering performance, they almost certainly will following two towering performances. Beyer stops well short of others, however, on the expanding role of speed figures in handicapping. Beyer has always argued that speed figures can denote a horse's relative class, rather than the converse, that class barriers can prevent horses from recording their customary figures, but he resists the expanding tendencies in numerous quarters to rely upon the figures to explain form cycles and to predict the future.

"It is unrealistic to try to judge horses' form cycles and foretell the future by looking only at horses' figures—at a fraction of the evidence that indicates whether they ran well or poorly in their recent races. Any attempt to understand horses' past performances and form cycles must take into account the way their previous races were run."

And so Beyer launches his telltale chapter, "How Was the Figure Earned?" The critical considerations are three: pace, track biases, and trips. The interpretation of horses' figures should be guided by the advantages and disadvantages assigned to those key factors. Of the three, pace gets the most comprehensive coverage, and surprisingly so, as Beyer formerly disregarded the effects of pace on final time. He has changed his mind.

When horses get a clear lead on a moderate to slow pace, as Beyer explains, they will almost always deliver their best speed figures. But when early-pace pressure is applied, matters become complicated. Even top horses can fail to deliver their customary numbers, and ordinary horses can be severely disadvantaged. Beyer has determined that closers in slow-pace races will deliver weaker figures, and front-runners in fast-pace races will deliver weaker figures, results that can only be attributed to the effects of the early fractions. He relays several illustrations of the effects of early pace on final time, and alerts handicappers in particular to the front-runner engaged in a three- or four-horse pace duel in rapid time that puts away the other speed horses, and wins or finishes close. The results chart will show the other front-runners buried in the rear half of the field, saluting the performance of the front-runner that held well.

Even though he has become a convert to the impact of early pace on final time, Beyer remains bothered by the mathematics of pace handicapping, especially as it applies to the stalkers who sit closely behind the early fractions. His adjustment is simple, practical, and logical. Handicappers can construct track-specific charts of fractional times and pace figures that correspond to the same track's final times and speed figures.

Beyer presents the hypothetical chart below, which uses his standard figure-chart for six furlongs.

Four Furlongs		Six Furlongs	
:44	133	1:08	135
:44$\frac{1}{5}$	128	1:08$\frac{1}{5}$	132
:44$\frac{2}{5}$	122	1:08$\frac{2}{5}$	129
:44$\frac{3}{5}$	116	1:08$\frac{3}{5}$	126
:44$\frac{4}{5}$	111	1:08$\frac{4}{5}$	123
:45	106	1:09	120
:45$\frac{1}{5}$	100	1:09$\frac{1}{5}$	118
:45$\frac{2}{5}$	95	1:09$\frac{2}{5}$	115
:45$\frac{3}{5}$	89	1:09$\frac{3}{5}$	112
:45$\frac{4}{5}$	84	1:09$\frac{4}{5}$	109
:46	78	1:10	106
:46$\frac{1}{5}$	73	1:10$\frac{1}{5}$	103
:46$\frac{2}{5}$	67	1:10$\frac{2}{5}$	100
:46$\frac{3}{5}$	62	1:10$\frac{3}{5}$	98
:46$\frac{4}{5}$	56	1:10$\frac{4}{5}$	95
:47	51	1:11	92
:47$\frac{1}{5}$	45	1:11$\frac{1}{5}$	89
:47$\frac{2}{5}$	40	1:11$\frac{2}{5}$	86
:47$\frac{3}{5}$	34	1:11$\frac{3}{5}$	83
:47$\frac{4}{5}$	29	1:11$\frac{4}{5}$	81
:48	23	1:12	78
		1:12$\frac{1}{5}$	75
		1:12$\frac{2}{5}$	72
		1:12$\frac{3}{5}$	70
		1:12$\frac{4}{5}$	67
		1:13	64
		1:13$\frac{1}{5}$	61
		1:13$\frac{2}{5}$	59
		1:13$\frac{3}{5}$	56
		1:13$\frac{4}{5}$	53
		1:14	51

As Beyer shows, the numbers indicate that at a typical track, a six-furlong race run in 1:10 (a rating of 106) would normally be run with a half-mile time of 45 flat (also a rating of 106). Unfortunately, as Beyer tells, the relationship of fractional times to final times can vary greatly from track to track. He recommends the following procedure:

"Get a set of results for a track and compile a few decent-size samples of six-furlong races that were run in specific final times—say, exactly 1:10, exactly 1:11, exactly 1:12. Calculate the average half-mile time in each of these samples. Then compare the half-mile rating on the above chart with the six-furlong rating, as follows:

Final Time	Rating	Average Fractional Time	Rating	Difference
1:10	106	45⅕	100	Slow by 6
1:11	92	45⅗	89	Slow by 3
1:12	78	46⅕	73	Slow by 7

"The average half-mile fraction in this case is slightly more than five points slower than the norm. Add five points to the above chart for four-furlong times and the chart will now be tailored to this particular track." Beyer continues to alert handicappers that do not want to compile the averages that they might instead purchase *Par Times* from Cynthia Publishing Co., at 11390 Ventura Blvd., #5, Studio City, Ca. The pars show the average winning times and the associated fractional times for the various class levels at virtually every track in North America.

Beyer has abandoned the search for a pace figure that represents the abilities of front-runners, pressers, stalkers, and closers equally well, but he has emerged in this book as a rather strict devotee of pace analysis. It's as if Beyer is now saying, if trips and biases can misrepresent a horse's speed figures, so too can pace, maybe more so.

A second and excellent source of national *par times* is David Schwartz, who owns *Horse Street* publications, in Reno, Nevada. Schwartz can be reached on-line at DaveSchwartz@HorseStreet.com.

The other transformation of Beyer that rings true in his latest book is his new approach to turf racing. It happened primarily during Del Mar, 1992, where Beyer's association with San Diego pro Andy Cylke introduced him to the "Sustained Pace" ratings of the Sartin Methodology. Sustained pace is a velocity rating (feet per second), and is calculated as the *average* of a horse's velocity for the first six furlongs and his velocity for the final fraction (six-furlong call to the wire). Cylke advised Beyer the sustained-pace leaders had been dominating in turf routes. That summer, says Beyer, the ratings seemed to be ". . . infallible."

Beyer was so impressed, he began to alter his handicapping methods in grass routes. Once again, he devised a clever alternative that makes sense. Instead of using Sustained Pace, Beyer simply calculated a race's final fraction (final time minus six-furlong time), and modified it by a horse's lengths gained (or lost). If the raw times of a mile were 1:13⅕ and 1:37, the final quarter-mile was 23⅘. If Horse A lost three lengths during the final fraction, going from two lengths behind after six furlongs to five lengths behind at the wire, his final quarter-mile was 24⅖.

A complication for Beyer was that final fractions appeared in three distinct sizes: a quarter-mile, five-sixteenths of a mile (in 1¹⁄₁₆-mile races), and three-eighths of a mile (in 1⅛-mile races). Cleverly, Beyer converted the final fractions for 1¹⁄₁₆ and 1⅛ miles to their quarter-mile equivalents (see chart, below).

5/16 fraction in 1 1/16-mile races	Quarter-mile equivalent	3/8 fraction in 1 1/8-mile races	Quarter-mile equivalent
:29	:23 1/5	:35	:23 2/5
:29 1/5	:23 2/5	:35 1/5	:23 2/5
:29 2/5	:23 3/5	:35 2/5	:23 3/5
:29 3/5	:23 3/5	:35 3/5	:23 4/5
:29 4/5	:23 4/5	:35 4/5	:23 4/5
:30	:24	:36	:24
:30 1/5	:24 1/5	:36 1/5	:24 1/5
:30 2/5	:24 2/5	:36 2/5	:24 1/5
:30 3/5	:24 2/5	:36 3/5	:24 2/5
:30 4/5	:24 3/5	:36 4/5	:24 3/5
:31	:24 4/5	:37	:24 3/5
:31 1/5	:25	:37 1/5	:24 4/5
:31 2/5	:25 1/5	:37 2/5	:25
:31 3/5	:25 1/5	:37 3/5	:25
:31 4/5	:25 2/5	:37 4/5	:25 1/5
:32	:25 3/5	:38	:25 1/5
:32 1/5	:25 4/5	:38 1/5	:25 2/5
:32 2/5	:26	:38 2/5	:25 3/5
:32 3/5	:26	:38 3/5	:25 4/5
:32 4/5	:26 1/5	:38 4/5	:25 4/5
:33	:26 2/5	:39	:26

The new fractional-time charts moved Beyer up on the turf immediately. After brief but convincing experimentation with the fractional equivalents, Beyer soon confronted the Del Mar turf race that would assure him of a winning meeting, his first at tricky Del Mar. It was the Grade 2 Del Mar Oaks and the three contenders, who had started once apiece on the Del Mar grass, looked like this on Beyer Speed Figures and his new and novel fractional-time equivalents.

	Final Fraction	Equivalents	Beyer Speed
Golden Treat	24⅘	24⅘	92-88-99
Suivi	30	24	89-88-75
Morriston Belle	24⅘	24⅘	89-88-88

Although Suivi had slightly inferior speed figures, and the Beyer of *Picking Winners* in 1975 would have dismissed her chances out of hand and rushed to the side of Golden Treat instead, Beyer in 1992 backed Suivi with his customary force. "When she closed like a wild horse . . . and paid $10.60, I had broken my Del Mar hex."

Beyer elaborates on his "turf-racing education" in great detail, concluding the nature of turf racing is "antithetical" to dirt races. He notes, for example, that front-runners that go 1:12 on the main track to a final time of 1:36 and a solid Beyer Speed Figure would not impress many handicappers that honor the dynamics of pace vis-a-vis final time. But the same performance on the turf might deserve raves. The horse has finished in 24 flat on a surface where the ability to finish fast becomes an imperative. In the end, Beyer approaches turf races with an analysis that juxtaposes his speed figures with a high regard for late speed, and he is satisfied with the results.

In the final lengthy section of *Beyer on Speed*, the author is in his element absolutely, as he applies with verve and comprehension the contemporary role of speed figures; namely, using the standout figure horses as the linchpins in exotic betting. Nowhere is Beyer's application more timely and helpful than in betting the pick six. With the one-day carryovers in California on occasion surpassing $200,000 and the carryovers on "event" days reaching enormous ceilings—when War Emblem lost the 2002 Belmont Stakes to Sarava at $142, the one-day carryover in New York topped $685,000—handicappers have greater incentive than ever to confront the exotic wager.

Beyer shows how a pick-six ticket covering 84 combinations ($168), and characterized by two standout figure horses as singles, might be expanded to include other possibilities and reconstructed in a way that reduces the ultimate cost. On the ticket below, #3 in Race 1 and #7 in Race 5 are singles. Giving a special nod to Steven Crist as mentor, Beyer reconstructs the bet, such that the main ticket is chopped down significantly, five additional backup horses are added, and five additional tickets are purchased. The coverage is greatly expanded, as follows:

Original ticket:	
Race	Horses
1	3
2	2-7-9
3	1-4
4	2-4-6-8-9-10-12
5	7
6	1-2

The 84 combinations would cost $168. Beyer divides the contenders into two categories, the main contenders and the backup horses. He adds backup horses and buys several tickets, as follows.

From Beyer on Speed

Race	Main	Backup
1	3	7
2	2-7-9	3
3	1-4	2-12
4	2-6	4-8-9-10-12
5	7	5
6	1-2	

Beyer's main ticket, which consists of his prime contenders, the horses in the left-hand column, costs $48 (1 × 3 × 2 × 2 × 1 × 2 × $2). He then fashions a ticket that includes his longshot, No. 7. Beyer substitutes him for his top choice in the first race and uses him on a ticket that includes the main contenders in the other races.

Race	Horse
1	7
2	2-7-9
3	1-4
4	2-6
5	7
6	1-2

This ticket costs $48, too. Beyer moves on and substitutes his backup horse for the main horse in Race 2.

Race	Horse
1	3
2	3
3	1-4
4	2-6
5	7
6	1-2

This ticket costs $16. Beyer proceeds to fill out five such backup tickets in addition to the main ticket; the total cost comes to $328.

Partners and small teams of pick-six hunters can proceed in this way, and give themselves a decent chance to compete with the high rollers and syndicates whose gigantic tickets dominate on carryover days. To carry matters to an extreme that may appeal to some pick-six diehards, if handicappers proceed to buy even more tickets, such that they will win if any four of their main contenders win, they can combine the backup horses in Races 1 and 2 with the main horses in the other four races, then the backup horses in Races 1 and 3 with the main horses in the other four, and so forth, until every two-race combination of backup horses has been covered. Handicappers will find themselves filling out 24 pick-six tickets and the cost will rise. But so will the chances of hitting a life-altering pick-six payoff.

In revising and expanding this anthology, I found myself revisiting the several texts that have been published since 1987, the year of the original. I enjoyed none as much as *Beyer on Speed*, not so much because its contents are more compelling, and not just because Beyer more than other handicapping authors injects his personality into his writing, although I like that, but because the thoughts, experiences, and illustrations on every page so indelibly spring from the mind of a highly educated, greatly experienced, and obviously successful player. It's a treat to spend some time with Andy Beyer on our subject and to learn from his amazingly diverse and carefully examined experiences.

It's the same reason his columns for *The Washington Post* are the best on the game and sport by a wide margin. Beyer always seems to hit the nail on the head, whether it's evaluating the performances of horses, or dealing with the personalities and issues of the day. Happily, Steven Crist has included Beyer's *Post* columns in the *Daily Racing Form*. Beyer may swear he has dropped out of the book-writing business, but handicappers can find him routinely in the papers, and on the Internet.

CHAPTER 39

BROHAMER ON PACE

THE GENERAL PRACTICE of Thoroughbred handicapping took a giant leap forward in 1991 with the publication of *Modern Pace Handicapping* (William Morrow), by Tom Brohamer, of Los Angeles, the most important book and author on our great game in the past 15 years. With its innovative, unerring focus on the relationships among running styles, fractional times, and final times, the interrelated components of pace analysis, the book filled a fundamental gap in the literature. The contributions to the general practice the book would alter for all time included new, greatly improved pace ratings and new analytical tools—energy distribution, velocity ratings, track profiles, decision models, turn-time, pace figures, sustained pace, ESP—which by now have become part and parcel of the vernacular. The book has taken its rightful place as a standard in the field.

Once the authentic contenders have been identified as a function of form analysis, class evaluation, speed figures, and the rest, handicappers can be assured the final separation will be completed best by a reliance on Brohamer's power tools.

In a 2000 revised and updated edition published by DRF Press, Brohamer added a lengthy treatment of the Quirin-style speed and pace figures, to be used in combination to separate the legitimate contenders. That chapter puts pace analysis in the more conventional, familiar context of par times, track variants, speed figures, and race shapes, and its numerous practical illustrations will be nothing short of illuminating for most handicappers as to when front-runners, pressers, and closers should be at advantage or disadvantage.

In a further extension of the original work, in his chapter on pace in *Bet with the Best* (DRF Press, 2001), Brohamer expanded his treatment of running styles, revealing a new wrinkle that enhances the power of the ESP scenarios ("Early," "Pressers," "Sustained"), and he reiterated his fundamental principle that pace analysis beats pace ratings. All in all, this author and practitioner represents an exciting and progressive body of work.

A figure analyst from his early days during the late 1960's in southern California, Brohamer in the 1980's became a leading disciple of and major contributor to the Sartin Methodology, and up front in *Modern Pace Handicapping* he introduces handicappers to the advantages of velocity ratings in estimating horses' real speed. Whereas time is one-dimensional, and a rather crude estimate of horses' true speed, velocity is two-dimensional, equal to distance divided by time, and is measured as feet per second. Instead of noting a horse ran the first quarter-mile of a six-furlong sprint in 22⅗ seconds, handicappers might say he ran 58.92 feet per second (fps).

In a painstaking, laborious opening chapter, Brohamer guides handicappers through numerous feet-per-second calculations for the various fractional times and pace segments, and as the early fog drifts away the more precise estimates of horses' speed using velocity ratings becomes sky-blue clear. To appreciate Brohamer's pace concepts, handicappers need only a working knowledge of velocity ratings. Consider the A-B-C-D pace scenario below, where four horses with comparable final times will be going a mile and one-sixteenth at a hypothetical track where Brohamer's "track profile" (position and beaten lengths of the winners at the first and second calls) shows a track strongly biased toward early speed, such that none of the recent winners has been beaten by more than 1¾ lengths after six furlongs. If the value of one length for six furlongs at the mile and one-sixteenth is .15 fps, which horses can be quickly eliminated?

	Second Call/Early Pace
Horse A	54.92
Horse B	55.61
Horse C	54.60
Horse D	55.51

Horse B has the strongest early-pace velocity (55.61 fps). Since the track profile reveals the winners must be within 1¾ lengths after six furlongs and the value of one length at the six-furlong call is .15 fps, the potential winner must be no more than .26 fps (1.75 × .15) behind Horse B at the second call. Given this pace scenario, a second-call velocity rating below 55.35 would be unacceptable, and as Brohamer tells, rather abruptly, anyone willing to bet A or C ". . . had better stick to final times."

In similar manner, velocity ratings for the various pace segments are related to track profiles and decision models are elaborated, such that contenders are ranked on the various pace intervals—early pace, average pace, sustained pace, and others—and only the horses having a positive fit with the "Brohamer model" are backed. In the A-B-C-D scenario where the track profile heavily favors early speed, the decision model might offer handicappers the following rankings:

	EP (Early)	AP (Average)	SP (Sustained)
Horse A	3	2	3
Horse B	1	3	4
Horse C	4	4	1
Horse D	2	1	2

Since the decision model favors early pace, either Horse B or Horse D might be backed. The model might indicate handicappers can bet the top two horses on early pace. If that were the scenario, Horse D might shape up as an attractive overlay possibility, as he clearly outperforms the faster B (to the second call) on average pace and late pace.

The good news is that the relationships more precisely represented by velocity ratings can be comprehended just as well using the more familiar fractional times and final times. When fractional times and final times are understood in relation to running styles and track profiles, handicappers can arrive at the same decision models and prepare to support the contenders that fit the track model especially well. In identifying contenders, Brohamer in his seminars encourages handicappers to use Beyer Speed Figures and class-distance pars (Beyer pars), as well as the conventional guidelines on class evaluation (eligibility conditions) and form analysis. In separating the contenders, handicappers are encouraged to combine an extensive pace analysis with the Quirin speed and pace figures.

Pace analysis begins, and often ends, with the critical considerations of the probable early pace. Brohamer describes three archetype running styles: front-runners, or Early types (E), which only do their best when able to set or attend (within a length) the pace; Pressers (P), or stalkers, which normally run a length to three lengths behind the front flight; and closers, or Sustained types (S), which rally from behind the pace and with some exceptions will compete at the mercy of what happens up front. Thus, the shorthand of "ESP."

Handicappers designate horses' running styles by examining their winning races and close finishes, within half a length. Judgment calls will be required routinely, and numerous horses will show versatile styles, such as the ability to win as front-runners as well as pressers, a highly desirable E/P designation. Others horses will be designated P/S, which means they can win as pressers and as closers. Handicappers analyze the early pace by evaluating the "Early" scenario, the "Presser" scenario, and the "Sustained" scenario. The versatile horses must be included in each scenario to which their running styles belong.

Brohamer makes unambiguous assertions about the three running styles that handicappers can trust:

"Early-pace runners with pace figures that indicate that they cannot gain the lead should be considered non-contenders."

"Pressers able to establish their preferred positions are the most reliable horses at any racetrack."

"Closers that remain in the rear of the field and depend on a single late run in the final fraction of the race are the least dependable runners at any track at any time."

The complications inherent in clarifying the specific chances of front-runners and pressers in today's race were simplified greatly when a Las Vegas handicapper and researcher, Jim Cramer, suggested to Brohamer he designate the running styles more specifically, according to how fast the horses *typically ran at the first call*. Thus, using their customary fractional times at the first call, horses were designated as E1, E2, E3, and P2, P3, P4, and S3, S4, S5. If pressers will be fastest to the first call, they are labeled P1. The fastest front-runner in that race would be E2. Occasional closers might be an S3, and so forth, until the running times at the first call have been rated. Before the scrutiny that involves pace figures (second call) and their relationships with speed figures (final time), Brohamer alerts handicappers to the importance of understanding the probable early pace, which involves the start to the second call. A strong pace figure may be superfluous, if front-runners and pressers cannot establish their preferred positions.

Brohamer warns pace analysts that E3 front-runners, for example, win few races, far fewer than their rightful share, even when their pace figures are faster than par or best in the field. That's nice to know. Similarly, P4 horses will be less likely to win than will P2 and P3 horses. Among closers, the likeliest winners will be the S3 and S4 horses. It pays to spend the time and effort needed to designate the running styles accurately.

"The close-up position of a presser (P2, P3) in the earliest stages," cautions Brohamer, "seriously damages all but the E1's chances. It will become clear early on that certain types tend to produce more than their fair share of winners. E1's, P1's, P2's, and S3-4's will tend to outperform their counterparts unable to gain position." In other words, pace analysis supersedes pace ratings, a greatly reassuring thought to pace analysts without numerical ratings.

Once the running styles have been designated and rated, Brohamer advises handicappers to turn their attention to the importance of the second fraction. In sprints especially, the second fraction separates the men from the boys among the front-runners and pressers, and routinely will distinguish the pretenders from the contenders when horses are moving up in class. It's here too where sustained-pace horses will be required to establish striking position, or forever be forgotten. Brohamer insists the second fraction will be critical to comprehend when maidens graduate to the nonwinners allowances and whenever horses four and up jump multiple levels in claiming class. The critical indicators will be pace figures and turn-time.

Turn-time refers to the difference between the second-call and first-call fractional times, modified by lengths gained (or lost). If horses go the first quarter of a six-furlong sprint in 22 flat and arrive at the second call (four furlongs) in 45 flat, the turn-time of the race has been 23 seconds. The presser that has gained two lengths during the second fraction has completed a turn-time of 22⅘ seconds. The term "turn-time" refers to the ground during the second fraction that occurs on the far turn, which is maximal at six furlongs and minimal at seven furlongs. Although turn-time will be a more decisive indicator among front-runners and pressers, closers usually must gain ground on the front flight during the second fraction, as indicated by a strong turn-time. If closers fail to gain striking position at the second call, as indicated by a healthy turn-time, Brohamer refers mockingly to the horses as SS types. SS types are rarely backed to win, although they do complete many exactas and trifectas.

Although it's a simple concept and catchy phrase attractive to bettors, Brohamer posts a couple of warning signs about turn-time that handicappers must heed. First, turn-time is best evaluated in relation to turn-time pars. If nonwinners-once allowance horses deliver a turn-time of 23⅘, is that a positive or negative? It depends on the NW1X par at the specific track. A 23⅘ turn-time is par for the level at Delaware Park, two lengths faster than par at Sportsman's Park, and three lengths slower than par at Hollywood Park. Along with the $10,000 claiming pars at the regular sprint distances, Table 1 (on the next two pages) presents the 2001 turn-time pars (in parentheses) at the NW1X levels for 29 selected tracks. Handicappers can estimate the turn-time pars for the higher and lower class levels. For more advanced allowance races and ungraded stakes, subtract one length (one-fifth). For graded stakes, the Grade 1/Grade2 stakes especially, subtract two lengths (two-fifths). For low-level claiming races and maiden-claiming races, add two lengths (two-fifths). For mid-level claiming races, use the NW1XMC par. For higher-priced claiming races, subtract one length (one-fifth).

Among front-runners and pressers having closely matched speed and pace figures, a faster-than-par turn-time can be decisive. My initial acquaintance with "the importance of the second fraction" would prove memorable. A maiden graduate with an extremely strong speed figure had been entered in a NW1XMC allowance sprint at Santa Anita. Despite a soft pace figure and below-par turn-time, the horse went favored at even money. Another contender with a lower speed figure but stronger pace figure and faster-than-par turn-time was allowed to go at 13-1. When the even-money shot collapsed after four furlongs and the 13-1 shot drew off to victory, the lesson could not have been more practical.

Brohamer's second red flag about turn-time is that it is not an independent factor. The significance of turn-time will be dependent upon not only the turn-time par, but also a horse's speed and pace figures. If horses do not shape up as contenders on basic abilities, their turn-times do not redeem them. An exception will be relatively unpredictable, below-par races where none of the horses possesses qualifying speed figures, but a couple may possess qualifying pace figures. Among those pace standouts, a faster turn-time can carry the cause. It's nice to grab the lead into the stretch, with slow horses behind.

Among contenders that survive the early-pace analysis, the essence of Brohamer's pace analysis shifts to the fantastic interplay between pace figures and speed figures. In the revised edition of *Modern Pace Handicapping*, Brohamer delivers an exhaustive treatment of the Quirin-style speed and pace figures, which he has judged a worthy substitute for the velocity ratings of the Sartin Methodology. The Quirin speed and pace methodology is based upon the $10,000 claiming pars for the various racetracks, which are set equal to a figure of 100. At Churchill Downs, as seen in Table 1, the six-furlong pace-speed pars for $10,000 claiming horses are 45.6 (pace pars in tenths) and 1:11⅗, so the corresponding pace-speed figures are 100-100.

For every length, or fifth of a second, that horses have run faster than

$10K Claiming Pars/ Selected Tracks
Quirin $10k = 100   Beyer $10k = 83

Sprints (TT Par/NW1X)	6f	6.5f	7f
Aqueduct (23.0)	46.0 111.0	46.0 117.0	46.2 124.0
Aqueduct I (23.0)	46.6 111.3		
Belmont Park (23.0)	46.2 111.0	46.2 117.2	46.2 124.2
Saratoga (23.1)	46.0 111.2	46.2 117.3	46.0 124.1
Gulfstream (23.0)	46.0 111.3	46.0 118.1	46.0 124.4
Calder (23.2)	46.0 112.1	46.0 118.4	46.4 125.2
Churchill (23.8)	45.6 111.3	46.0 117.4	46.0 124.1
Keeneland (23.3)	45.8 110.2	45.4 117.0	45.4 123.3
Turfway Park (23.3)	45.8 111.4	46.4 118.4	
Arlington (23.1)	46.0 111.2	45.4 117.4	45.8 124.2
Hawthorne (23.2)	45.8 111.0	46.0 118.1	
Sportsmans (23.4)	46.8 112.0		
Fair Grounds (23.3)	46.0 111.2		
Oaklawn (23.3)	46.0 111.2		
Lone Star (23.0)	45.2 1103	45.2 117.0	43.8 123.3
Louisiana D. (23.1)	45.8 111.0	45.6 117.2	45.8 123.4
Monmouth (23.0)	45.2 110.4		
Meadowlands (23.0)	45.4 110.3		
Laurel (23.1)	46.2 111.0	46.4 117.4	46.6 124.3
Pimlico (23.1)	46.8 112.1		
Delaware (23.2)	45.8 111.2		
Golden Gate (22.3)	44.8 109.4		
Bay Meadows (22.3)	45.4 110.3		
Emerald D. (22.4)	44.8 109.4	45.0 116.3	
Turf Paradise (22.3)	44.8 109.4	44.8 116.1	
Woodbine (23.0)	45.8 111.4	45.6 118.1	45.6 124.3
Santa Anita (22.4)	45.2 110.3	45.2 117.0	45.6 123.3
Hollywood P.(22.4)	45.3 110.3	45.2 117.0	45.8 123.2
Del Mar (22.4)	45.2 110.3	45.2 117.1	45.4 123.3

Table 1.

Routes	1M		8.5f		9f	
Aqueduct	111.4	137.1			113.2	151.3
Aqueduct I	113.0	138.1	112.8	145.0	113.0	151.4
Belmont Park	111.6	137.2	111.8	144.2	112.2	151.1
Saratoga					112.8	151.2
Gulfstream Park			113.2	146.1	113.2	153.0
Calder	114.2	140.4	114.0	147.3	114.4	154.1
Churchill Downs	111.6	137.1	113.0	145.1	113.4	152.2
Keeneland			112.0	144.4	112.4	151.2
Turfway Park	112.6	139.2	112.8	146.0	113.4	153.2
Arlington Park	112.2	138.1			113.2	152.0
Hawthorne			112.8	145.3	113.0	152.1
Sportsmans Park	114.6	140.3	114.2	146.3	114.6	153.4
Fair Grounds	113.2	141.3	113.4	146.0	113.8	153.0
Oaklawn Park	112.8	139.1	113.4	146.0	112.8	152.3
Lone Star Park	113.2	138.3	113.4	145.0	113.8	152.0
Louisiana Downs			112.8	145.0	113.2	151.4
Monmouth Park	112.4	138.4	112.4	145.2	112.8	152.1
The Meadowlands	111.6	137.4	111.8	144.2	112.2	151.1
Laurel			113.4	145.2	113.4	152.1
Pimlico			113.0	145.4	113.2	152.4
Delaware Park	112.8	139.2	112.8	146.0	112.6	152.1
Golden Gate Fields	111.0	137.1	111.2	143.4	111.4	150.3
Bay Meadows	111.4	137.1	111.0	144.0	112.0	150.4
Emerald Downs	111.0	136.4	111.4	143.3	111.6	150.2
Turf Paradise	111.2	137.0	111.6	143.4	111.8	150.4
Woodbine			112.6	146.0	112.8	152.2
Santa Anita Park	111.5	137.3	111.7	144.1	111.8	151.0
Hollywood Park			111.8	144.2	111.8	151.1
Del Mar	111.3	137.3	111.5	144.1	111.7	151.0

Note: Pace pars are presented in tenths, final-time pars in fifths.

Table 1 (continued).

the $10k claiming pars, the Quirin figures will be a point higher, and for every length horses have run slower than the $10k claiming pars, the Quirin figures will be a point lower. The comparable abilities of $10k claiming horses at most tracks, and the incremental nature of par times between class levels at all tracks (claiming-class pars are usually faster by one length at each successively higher class level), means the track-to-track comparisons will be similar and meaningful. In addition, the relationship between horses' speed at the pace call and the finish line in the Quirin methodology is a convenient two-to-one, such that two points equals one length at the pace call and one point equals one length at the finish line. The relationships mimic reality quite well.

Brohamer explores the relations among speed and pace figures for numerous common handicapping situations, all of them nicely illustrated with examples from the racetrack. He shows too how combinations of speed and pace figures can be related to the various race shapes, and to the common running styles. If front-runners go slow early and fast late, the fancy speed figures can be entirely misleading, but the weaker pace figures will provide the clues for handicappers to stay away. If closers finish impressively to win where the race shape has been fast early, but slow late, the strong finish can be entirely misleading, such that when the pace will be normal to fast, the same closers will finish up the course. The speed and pace figures reveal the patterns all too well. It's a fascinating discourse on the complexities and intricacies of the speed and pace interplay.

As Quirin demonstrated, and Brohamer exploits, the basic relationship between the speed and pace figures is symmetrical. When the pace figure improves, the speed figure declines. When the pace figure declines, the speed figure improves. The symmetry holds for the great majority of Thoroughbreds, even for many top horses, although at the higher class levels the distinctions can be subtle. When young horses move ahead in class, for example, it's crucial to know whether their pace figures at the lower levels support the rise. If they do not, the horses can be expected to disappoint. Most will. Favorites and low-priced contenders can be abandoned confidently.

Handicappers who become familiar with the method will enjoy evaluating the three-year-olds and lightly raced four-year-olds as they attempt to establish their reputations at the top echelons of the sport. Many of the most heavily publicized colts and fillies will be susceptible to the pratfalls common to horses rising in class with a pace weakness, including each year's leading candidates for the Kentucky Derby. In the age of full-card simulcasting, Brohamer keeps a file of speed and pace figures for the leading three- and four-year-old prospects in the various stakes divisions.

Among the older claiming horses, where horses' running styles and their speed and pace capacities have been well established and can be readily evaluated, Brohamer's methods have been continually accurate and successful. His book includes chapters on making the Quirin-style figures, constructing the $10k claiming pars from small samples in the past performances, estimating track variants from *Daily Racing Form*'s old-style speed ratings and variants, and numerous practical applications. Brohamer's chapter on daily track variants and their application to actual times is the best treatment of that esoteric topic on record.

Whether pace analysts prefer velocity ratings or the more familiar fractional times, final times, and corresponding speed and pace figures, *Modern Pace Handicapping* is a text for the times; indeed, a text for all time. And handicappers that have not yet included an analysis of pace in their approach to beating the races dare not miss this fine book.

CHAPTER 40

QUINN'S
FIGURE HANDICAPPING
ON THE TURF

AFTER ARGUING THAT speed handicapping and pace ratings can amount to little more than faulty methods when evaluating horses going long on the grass, in *Figure Handicapping* (Quinn, William Morrow, 1992), the author presented his alternative methodology for figure handicapping on the turf. The method featured late speed and relative class, and the book included first renditions of turf-figure charts for 28 selected racetracks.

Before reviewing the method and its procedures, it's crucial to appreciate how turf races are distinct from races on the main track. First, the courses are distinct. Horses exit on straightaways or out of chutes. The rails are up, and the rails are down. The grass is long, or the grass has been cut short. Grass runners can be distinct too, with conformation characterized by shorter, more angular pasterns and dishlike feet. The effective grass stride is straight, gliding over the ground in a forward paddling motion, with less up and down curling movement of the front legs. Bloodlines count heavily, horses bred for the grass outperforming the others on the surface by a wide margin.

The pace is different. It's typically slower by as many as five lengths during the first quarter-mile, by six to 10 lengths during the first six furlongs. Jockeys prefer to take hold early, saving energy on the more tiring turf. The finish is then fast and furious, the margin of victory customarily narrow. Tiring horses rarely survive on the grass, as they regularly do on dirt. A 1990 study of turf routes for 50 days at Santa Anita documented the early-energy expenditures of winners to be significantly lower than the comparable energy expenditures of winners in dirt sprints and dirt routes.

Dirt sprints	52.72%	Early-energy expenditure
Dirt routes	51.72%	Early-energy expenditure
Turf routes	50.60%	Early-energy expenditure

In 50 days of racing, only one turf winner had expended as much as 51 percent of its energy at the pace call. On average, the turf winners' early-energy expenditures amount to a savings of energy equal to 11-12 lengths. On eight of the 50 days, the early-energy output of turf winners was less than 50 percent, a phenomenon I have not experienced on the dirt.

If the courses, horses, and races are different, so should be the methods that handicappers rely upon to disentangle turf contests. While the final times and fractional times of dirt races become relatively predictable for specific classes of horses, the pace and final times of turf routes can be relatively unstable, far more various, depending upon running styles, course configurations, and jockey tactics. Fractional times fluctuate wildly, impacting final times in ways that can make conventional speed figures misleading.

The prevailing circumstance on the turf is a relatively slow pace, followed by a furious all-out finish. Figure handicapping on the turf should conform to the common circumstance.

As a point of departure, Quinn's figure handicapping on the turf invokes the grass pars of classified allowance horses as the key indicators of the late-speed standard at a specific racetrack. Classified allowance races are used as the basis of comparison because Bill Quirin has demonstrated that track class is best determined by references to a track's maidens and classified allowance horses. Most tracks limit the grass routes to better horses. Classified allowance races represent the higher echelons of a track's horse population, including as they normally do an admixture of high-priced claiming horses, inveterate classified horses, and varieties of stakes horses.

Consider the grass pars and late-speed pars of classified horses at two dissimilar tracks at opposite ends of the country.

Hollywood Park			
	1M	1¹⁄₁₆M	1⅛M
Clf Alw Pars	1:10.1 – 1:35.2	1:10.2 – 1:41.2	1:11 – 1:48.1
Late-Speed Pars	25.1	31.0	37.1
Laurel			
	1M	1¹⁄₁₆M	1⅛M
Clf Alw Pars	1:11.4 – 1:36.3	1:11.4 – 1:43.0	1:11.4 – 1:49.3
Late-Speed Pars	24.4	31.4	37.4

At a mile and one-sixteenth on the grass, the late-speed par at Hollywood Park is 31.0, and the late-speed par at Laurel is 31.4, four lengths slower. If each of these pars is assigned a figure of 100, equating classified allowance runners on the grass at Hollywood Park and Laurel, a basis of intertrack comparisons is set. The late-speed pars for a track are calculated as the difference between the final times and fractional times of classified allowance winners for the various distances.

Since a horse's turf figure would be determined based upon its closing fraction from the six-furlong call to the wire, the critical consideration was how to value one length during that race segment. The concept of proportional time promoted so effectively by Andrew Beyer in his figure methods, such that faster is better, and the value of one length should depend upon the distance, is perfectly compatible with rating late speed on the turf, except that now the farther the finish, the higher the rating.

To implement the strategy, numerous weightings and rating procedures were tested. The breakthrough occurred when the basic unit of analysis was set as a quarter-mile of 25 seconds, which corresponds well with the classified allowance late-speed pars at a mile at most tracks. At Hollywood Park and Laurel, 25 seconds is within one length of the actual late-speed pars of classified horses, which are 25.1 at Hollywood Park and 24.4 at Laurel. The value of a fifth of a second, or one length, at a quarter-mile of 25 seconds (⅕₂₅) is .008. Instead of multiplying by 1,000 to reflect the value of one-fifth in an entire race, I multiplied by 100, to reflect the value of one-fifth during a portion of the race.

A weighting of 0.8 (.008 × 100) proved to be remarkably suitable for evaluating grass runners at the mile, especially when doubled arbitrarily to account for the faster finishes during the short race segments. Thus, the weighting of one-fifth of a second at a quarter-mile was set equal to 1.6. The next step followed logically, although not immediately. Three-eighths of a mile is half again as far as a quarter-mile. Thus, for races at nine furlongs, the value of one-fifth at three-eighths of a mile might be half again as great as 1.6, or 2.4.

The value of one-fifth at five-sixteenths, the late-speed interval at $1\frac{1}{16}$ miles, merely splits the difference between 1.6 and 2.4. It became 2.0 Using these values for one-fifth of second at the standard distances, a turf-figure chart can be constructed for any racetrack. Review the turf-figure chart for Hollywood Park.

Instantly, or so it seemed, these figures generated improved results. The comparisons and evaluations they facilitated proved to be accurate

Hollywood Park

	1 M		1 1/16 M		1 1/8 M		
Classified Alw Pars	110[1]	135[2]	110[2]	141[2]	111	148[1]	
Par Zone/Late Speed Pars	110[1] - 111[1]	25[1]	110[2] - 111[2]	31	111 - 112	37[1]	
Unusually Slow Pace	111[2] and Slower		111[3] and Slower		112[1] and Slower		Adj's 6 - 6
Faster Than Par Pace	110 and Faster		110[1] and Faster		110[4] and Faster		

1/4 M		5/16 M		3/8 M	
3	121	29	120	35	126
4	119	1	118	1	124
23	118	2	116	2	122
1	116	3	114	3	119
2	114	4	112	4	117
3	113	30	110	36	114
4	111	1	108	1	112
24	110	2	106	2	110
1	108	3	104	3	107
2	106	4	102	4	105
3	105	31	100	37	102
4	103			1	100
25	102	1	98		
1	100	2	96	2	98
		3	94	3	95
2	98	4	92	4	93
3	97	32	90	38	90
4	95	1	88	1	88
26	94	2	86	2	86
1	92	3	84	3	83
2	90	4	82	4	81
3	89	33	80	39	78
4	87	1	78	1	76
27	86	2	76	2	74
1	84	3	74	3	71
2	82	4	72	4	69
3	81	34	70		
4	79				
28	78				

Unusually Slow Pace (race): Add 100 (Par) to Late Speed Figure and divide by 2.

Faster Than Par Pace (race): For each 1/5-second frontrunners and pace pressers have exceeded par at the pace call, add 2 points to their late-speed figures. Does not apply to off-pace horses and closers.

and reliable. They picked winners routinely. After several promising trials, I knew I had something valuable after handicapping the Grade 2 Bay Meadows Handicap at nine furlongs on the grass during fall of 1989. I had just completed what I had hoped would be the final adjustments to the basic rating procedures and I considered the Bay Meadows stakes a test case.

At $250,000 guaranteed, the field featured an amazing array of talented horses from Bay Meadows, Gulfstream Park, Arlington Park, Hollywood Park, Laurel, and Santa Anita. By conventional handicapping, the race was puzzling. Using the new figure charts from the various tracks to evaluate the horses, the method indicated Ten Keys (from Laurel), figure of 125, should beat Colway Rally (from Gulfstream Park), figure of 118, by three lengths. Ten Keys won by three lengths and paid $18.20. Colway Rally finished second, and the $2 exacta paid $77.80. Eureka! In moments like these, far apart, Thoroughbred handicapping qualifies as the greatest game of all.

Before enumerating the few adjustments to the basic method that can make a difference, here is a step-wise summary of the procedure:

1. Calculate the classified allowance pars on grass at the track's regularly run distances.
2. Calculate the classified allowance pace pars (six-furlong call) at the same distances.
3. Calculate the late-speed pars for classified horses at each of the regularly run distances. A horse's late speed will be equal to the difference between the final pars and pace pars, modified by lengths gained (or lost).
4. Assign a turf figure of 100 to the late-speed pars of the classified allowance horses. A figure greater than 100 means a horse has finished faster than the typical classified allowance winner. A figure below 100 means a horse has finished slower than the typical classified allowance winner. Stakes horses would be expected to earn turf figures above 100, and lower-level claiming horses would be expected to earn turf figures below 100.
5. Use the standard weightings below to value one length faster and slower than the 100 figure of classified allowance winners.
   a. At a quarter-mile, one length, or one-fifth, is equal to 1.6
   b. At five-sixteenths of a mile, one length, or one-fifth, is equal to 2.0
   c. At three-eighths of a mile, one length, or one-fifth, is equal to 2.4

6. Use the classified late-speed pars and the values of one length at the standard distances to construct a turf-figure chart for any race-track.

7. In calculating the late speed of horses, make the standard calculations, and apply the adjustments below, as needed.

8. Assign turf figures to horses for the good performances of the past six turf races.

The adjustments will be few and trusty. No adjustments for sex and age, as the differences between the final time and pace pars for age and sex are not sufficiently large to affect the late-speed pars. For the same reason, happily, the method is not sensitive to *normal fluctuations* in running times resulting from the application of the daily track variant. Unless the turf variant will be unusually large, ignore it.

Apply these adjustments:

1. If the turf variant is five lengths or greater, apply the variant to the final time and half the variant to the pace-call time, before calculating a horse's late speed.

2. If the pace has been unusually slow, defined as six lengths or more slower than the six-furlong par for the distance, after calculating a horse's late speed, and assigning its turf figure, add 100 to the turf figure, and divide by two. The adjustment recognizes that an unusually slow pace allows turf horses to retain too much energy for the final fraction, and scales the turf figure back toward the 100 figure, i.e., a regression to the average, or mean.

3. If the pace has been unusually fast, add two points to the turf figure of any front-runner and pace-presser that has been within one length of the six-furlong pace. The method favors late speed, and the adjustment rewards horses that have set and pressed a faster-than-par pace.

4. On surfaces labeled soft or yielding, handicappers must make a judgment call. If the surface has distorted the running times seriously, calculate a horse's late speed, based upon the actual times in the past performances, and subtract one length. That is, a 26⅘ final quarter on a yielding course might be converted to 25⅘ arbitrarily, and the turf figure assigned based on the adjusted time.

Experience with the method has indicated it's usually best to evaluate horses by using races at distances within half a furlong. Races as far apart as a mile and a mile and one-eighth, for example, can be compared reliably only when the pace pars for the two distances are similar. Refer to the pace pars for Hollywood Park and Laurel again. At a mile, the Hollywood Park pace par is 1:10⅘, while at 1⅛ miles the pace par is four lengths slower at 1:11.0. The horses will finish faster at the longer distance. At Laurel, the pace par is the same for the three regularly carded distances; no problem. "Know your racetrack," an ancient axiom, applies here too.

The ratable races include the past six, as these six races can be considered a cycle of recent consistency. Use the top two figures.

When evaluating inexperienced and younger horses on the turf, rely primarily on pedigree and running style. Prefer the off-pace and closing styles, and discount the front-runners and pace-pressers, notably as favorites and low-odds contenders.

In races at 1¼ miles and longer, especially the stakes, use the quarter-mile turf figures, but rate horses using races at the exact distances. If handicappers compare the late-speed figures of horses at the mile with horses at the mile and a quarter, the figures will be unreliable.

The turf-figure charts of *Figure Handicapping* (1992) will be outdated. New charts are needed. The chart at the conclusion of this piece presents the 2001 late-speed pars for the classified horses at the standard distances for 25 major tracks, along with the unusually slow six-furlong times that will require the recommended rating adjustment. Set the late-speed pars on the chart equal to 100 and use the standard weightings to construct turf-figure charts for any track of interest. The task can be completed in one long night of sweat equity, accompanied by a bottle.

Finally, handicappers are urged to remember that late speed, in combination with relative class, is often the determining factor in grass routes. If two or more horses, four years old and up, are closely matched on the turf figures, it's usually preferable to favor the horse that has finished fastest against the best competition. If three-year-olds and younger four-year-olds have recorded impressive turf figures, and will be moving ahead in class by the next logical step, that's acceptable. If the younger, still-developing horses have earned a classy figure in one, two, or three turf attempts, those youngsters often will be better than acceptable. They like the grass, and may be prepared to record an even stronger turf figure against better horses today.

Late-Speed Turf Pars, Classified Alw, Selected Tracks
With Unusually Slow Six-Furlong Pace Pars

Track	1M		8.5F		9F		10F		11F/1 3/16M	
Santa Anita	24.0	112.3			35.4	113.3	23.3	113.3		
Hollywood	23.3	112.1	29.4	112.2	35.1	113.1	23.2	113.1	41.1	113.4
Del Mar	24.4	112.1	30.3	113.0	36.4	113.2			37.3	113.4
Aqueduct	24.1	113.3	30.4	113.3	36.4	114.1			37.0	114.1
Belmont	24.1	111.3	29.1	112.2					36.4	112.4
Belmont I					35.4	113.3	24.1	113.3	36.3	114.0
Saratoga			29.3	112.3	35.4	112.4			42.0	113.3
Saratoga I	23.3	112.2	29.4	113.4	36.0	113.2			36.2	113.4
Gulfstream	23.2	111.2	29.0	112.4	35.4	114.0			36.0	114.1
Calder	24.1	112.3	29.2	112.3	36.1	113.2			36.4	114.0
Churchill	24.1	113.4	30.2	114.1	37.0	114.3			37.4	115.0
Keeneland	24.0	113.3	30.1	113.3	37.0	113.3			42.1	115.0
Ellis Park	24.1	113.1	30.2	112.3	36.1	113.2				
Arlington	24.0	113.2	30.2	113.3	37.0	113.3	23.2	113.3	42.4	114.2
Hawthorne	24.0	112.1	29.1	112.3	37.1	113.0				
Fairgrounds	24.4	116.0	31.3	115.4	37.4	116.4				
Louisiana D	24.3	113.0	31.0	113.3			24.1	113.3		
Lone Star	24.4	114.1	31.1	114.1	37.3	114.3			37.1	114.2
Pimlico	24.1	112.2	31.0	112.3	36.2	113.4			36.3	113.4
Laurel	23.4	113.4	30.2	113.4	36.3	114.0	24.0	114.4	43.1	114.1
Monmouth	24.2	112.0	30.2	112.2	36.3	112.3			35.4	112.3
Meadowlan	24.3	112.1	31.0	112.3					37.1	112.3
Delaware	24.4	112.1	30.3	113.0	36.4	113.2			37.3	113.4
GoldenGate	24.4	113.2	31.2	113.2	37.3	113.4			37.3	113.4
BayMeado	24.3	112.4	31.2	112.3	36.0	114.2			38.2	115.3
Turf Parad	24.4	114.0	32.0	113.2	37.2	114.3			38.2	115.1
Woodbine	24.4	112.0	31.0	112.3	37.1	113.1	25.2	113.1	37.1	113.1

CHAPTER 41

DAVIDOWITZ REDUX

I N A REMARKABLE revision of a handicapping standard, author Steve
Davidowitz in the new *Betting Thoroughbreds* (Dutton, 1995) not only
escorts handicappers through familiar terrain in a contemporary setting,
but also extends a contribution none of us had a right to expect. Davidowitz presents a method of converting the Beyer Speed Figures to a corresponding scale of pace figures that handicappers might utilize to
complete numerical pace analyses.

The revised *Betting Thoroughbreds* is so thoroughly, comprehensively
good, the book takes its rightful place as a standard having equal elements
of appeal to everyone from novices to experts. The paperback original
(1979) covered 212 pages. The 1995 revision runs 347 pages. From start
to finish, the content reverberates against the actual playing experience
of the author so specifically that handicappers realize they are in the company of a widely practiced practitioner. Davidowitz's writings persistently
have reflected an eclectic point of view, as befits a professional who has
applied his craft from one end of the country to the other. This book com-
pletes the odyssey. Even the appendices are extensive and savvy.

The author Davidowitz is associated with track bias, key races, and
trainer patterns, but he is expert as well on class evaluation, speed handicapping, and exotic-wagering strategies. The original edition of *Betting
Thoroughbreds* argued passionately that track bias should be considered
the most influential handicapping factor of all. Davidowitz had coined

the term, in fact, and he was the first to reveal the elements of a bias, such that handicappers were alerted to inside biases, speed biases, outside biases, and closer biases, and combinations of the forms, such as inside-speed biases and outside-closer biases. Davidowitz even named names, and in the revision he again describes the biases handicappers might generally anticipate at specific tracks.

In the latest edition, the new emphasis is on pace (four chapters), which was the hot topic of the 1990's, and in a clever twist handicappers will like, Davidowitz relates his unwavering concern with track bias to the concept of pace. In a chapter titled "Pace and the Single-Race Bias," the author argues that unusually fast and unusually slow fractions can "bias" race outcomes as severely as do surface biases. The unusual configurations of pace favor horses having certain running styles, and are juxtaposed by Davidowitz to Bill Quirin's "race shapes." When the winners (and losers) return to the races, handicappers can discount (or upgrade) the prior performances as a function of track biases.

In the latest edition's most provocative chapters, Davidowitz proposes a method for associating the Beyer Speed Figures with complementary pace figures. Focusing on the well-documented, widely accepted role of the second fraction in pace analyses, Davidowitz contends that pace pars should represent the "normal fractions" associated with each final time.

If handicappers know the final-time pars at a track, they can identify the array of fractional times that have been associated with those par times, and select the midpoint. The midpoint of a representative range of fractional times for each final time constitutes the pace par. Hypothetically, the midpoint of the fractional times for a final time of 1:08.80 might be 44.80. For a final time of 1:12.20, the fractional midpoint might be 46.50; proportionately slower.

From these origins, Davidowitz constructs a chart of speed-pace figures for the customary final times at Aqueduct. As a starting point for converting Beyer Speed Figures to pace figures, Davidowitz arbitrarily selects the final time associated with a Beyer Speed Figure of 100. At Aqueduct, that final time is 1:10.40. The corresponding pace par (midpoint) is 45.50. That fractional time also is set equal to 100. For each .20 difference in final times (one length), Davidowitz adjusts the pace figure by one point. A final time of 1:10.20 corresponds to a pace figure of 101. A final time of 1:10.60 corresponds to a pace figure of 99.

As a length on the Beyer scale will equal 2½ points for sprints (approximately), and two points for routes (approximately), by the Davidowitz approach the corresponding pace figure will equal roughly half as much. Complications arise as the Beyer Speed Figures grow proportionally from the 100-figure starting line for sprints and routes, respectively, as shown on the chart for Aqueduct's six-furlong pars. When the Beyer Speed Figure has settled at 120 for the nation's top horses, the corresponding pace figure is 108, a difference of 12 points, or five to six lengths. At a Beyer 103, which is par for typical stakes horses at major tracks, the corresponding pace figure is 101, a difference of one length. The proportionality suffers, but the approach offers Beyer-figure followers—practically everybody—a method of pace analysis that might be studied empirically.

AQUEDUCT SIX-FURLONG PACE PARS

¼ MI.		½ MI.		6 FURLS.		BEYER FIG.		CONVERTED PACE-SPEED #
21.80	=	44.40	=	1:08.20	=	131	=	112
22.00	=	44.50	=	1:08.40	=	129	=	111
22.10	=	44.80	=	1:09.00	=	120	=	108
22.10	=	45.00	=	1:09.40	=	115	=	106
22.20	=	45.20	=	1:09.80	=	109	=	104
22.20	=	45.30	=	1:10.00	=	106	=	103
22.20	=	45.40	=	1:10.20	=	103	=	101
22.30	=	45.50	=	1:10.40	=	100	=	100
22.30	=	45.60	=	1:10.60	=	98	=	99
22.30	=	45.70	=	1:10.80	=	95	=	98
22.40	=	45.80	=	1:11.00	=	92	=	97
22.40	=	46.00	=	1:11.40	=	86	=	95
22.50	=	46.20	=	1:11.70	=	82	=	93
22.50	=	46.40	=	1:12.00	=	79	=	92
22.50	=	46.50	=	1:12.20	=	76	=	91
22.60	=	46.60	=	1:12.40	=	73	=	90
22.70	=	46.90	=	1:13.00	=	64	=	87
22.70	=	47.00	=	1:13.20	=	62	=	86
22.90	=	47.40	=	1:14.00	=	51	=	82
23.10	=	47.90	=	1:15.00	=	37	=	77
23.40	=	48.40	=	1:16.00	=	25	=	72

Following Davidowitz, local figure analysts can identify their track's final time for a Beyer figure of 100, calculate the midpoint of the associated fractional times, which will be set equal to 100, and develop a speed-pace chart. If results improve, the method makes sense.

Throughout the book, Davidowitz is concerned, as only an experienced, successful handicapper would be, with the subtleties, nuances, and variations of his several handicapping themes. The overlays are in the details, Davidowitz might say. Whether they have absorbed the original editions or not, handicappers are recommended to engage the 1995 release from beginning to end. It's a powerful text that gathers a cumulative force as the chapters unfold. The book's a definite winner, and the same prosperity awaits its faithful disciples.

Chapter 42

PATTERN RECOGNITION AND LITFIN'S EXPERT ILLUSTRATIONS

AMONG PRACTICED HANDICAPPERS, the game's sturdy veterans, study of the past performances can be viewed as a process of pattern recognition. Which performance patterns have been known to be positive predictors? Successful pattern recognition becomes crucial in the handicapper's search for overlays that might win, not to mention the spotting of underlays that figure to lose.

The best material on pattern recognition comes to us from Dave Litfin, *Daily Racing Form*'s New York handicapper. *Dave Litfin's Expert Handicapping* (Little, Brown, 1995) is exactly that. Weaving its contents from speed figures, to trainer patterns, to pace and track biases, to four negative patterns to be steadfastly avoided, and to an amazing array of angles that constitute positive patterns, Litfin's patterns are notable, not only for relating the fundamental to the incidental, but also for delivering the kinds of medium-priced overlays (not longshots) that make sense, and can be replicated time and time again. Litfin's patterns qualify too as the most meticulously, perfectly illustrated of any in print. An author's first book is usually handled with special care, and this one certainly has been.

Since professional speed figures made their debut first in *The Racing Times* in 1991, and soon after in *Daily Racing Form,* figure analysts inexorably have reveled in using figure patterns to interpret horses' cycles. The relations between horses' figure patterns and their current form is intriguing, and for most handicappers it breaks new ground. Litfin begins here, and before delving into the patterns of greatest interest, he espouses an incredibly important and greatly unappreciated point. Litfin assures handicappers the same patterns can be inferred, regardless of the speed-figure methods engaged; i.e., whether handicappers are analyzing The Sheets or the Beyer Speed Figures. Despite the amusing protestations of some that their figures are distinct, Litfin's illustrations on the point are convincing.

Although Litfin deals with the bounce, bounce-back patterns that have become common currency among contemporary handicappers, his signature pattern has not. He refers to the pattern, quite appropriately, as "explosive horses." To borrow Litfin's profile, three-year-olds that have recently run a figure equal to or slightly superior to their best two-year-old figures are strong candidates to improve again in the near future, especially if the "slight forward move" occurred soon after a return from a layoff. Best of all, the near-future improvement will often be "explosive," of multiple lengths, and will surprise the majority of bettors. The price will be right.

In describing how the pattern crawled into his consciousness, Litfin returned to Saratoga in 1992. A three-and-up maiden event for New York-breds contained a third-starting three-year-old named Lochrima, who had returned on July 8 at Belmont Park from a November 22 layoff with a Beyer Speed Figure of 46, which had equaled his best at two. In his second start, Lochrima regressed badly, although it's hard to imagine a regression following a Beyer 46. Regardless, The Sheets' Bob Beinish in a seminar issued what Litfin described as an unshakable opinion that Lochrima was poised to deliver a lifetime best performance by several lengths. This disturbed Litfin, as every New York-bred in the maiden lineup had recorded a higher Beyer Speed Figure than had Lochrima. As matters proceeded, Lochrima did not win, but he finished third by a length at 20-1 to a 6-5 favorite and a 3-1 second choice, following a horrible trip. Lochrima improved on The Sheets from 24 to 16¾ (lower is better), and his Beyer Speed Figure improved from 46 to 58, good enough to win most maiden races limited to New York-breds.

Litfin describes the improvement pattern of Russian Bride, a filly that had been racing regularly and in her second start at three suddenly equaled her best race at two, a 16 on Thoro-Graph. In her next start, the barn moved from a NW1XMC allowance romp to the Grade 2 Comely Stakes, and as Litfin tells, they knew what they were doing. Review the past performances and the filly's Thoro-Graph sheet on the next page.

At 10-1, Russian Bride exploded to a seven-length improvement, good enough to finish second to the 3-1 second choice in the Comely, while

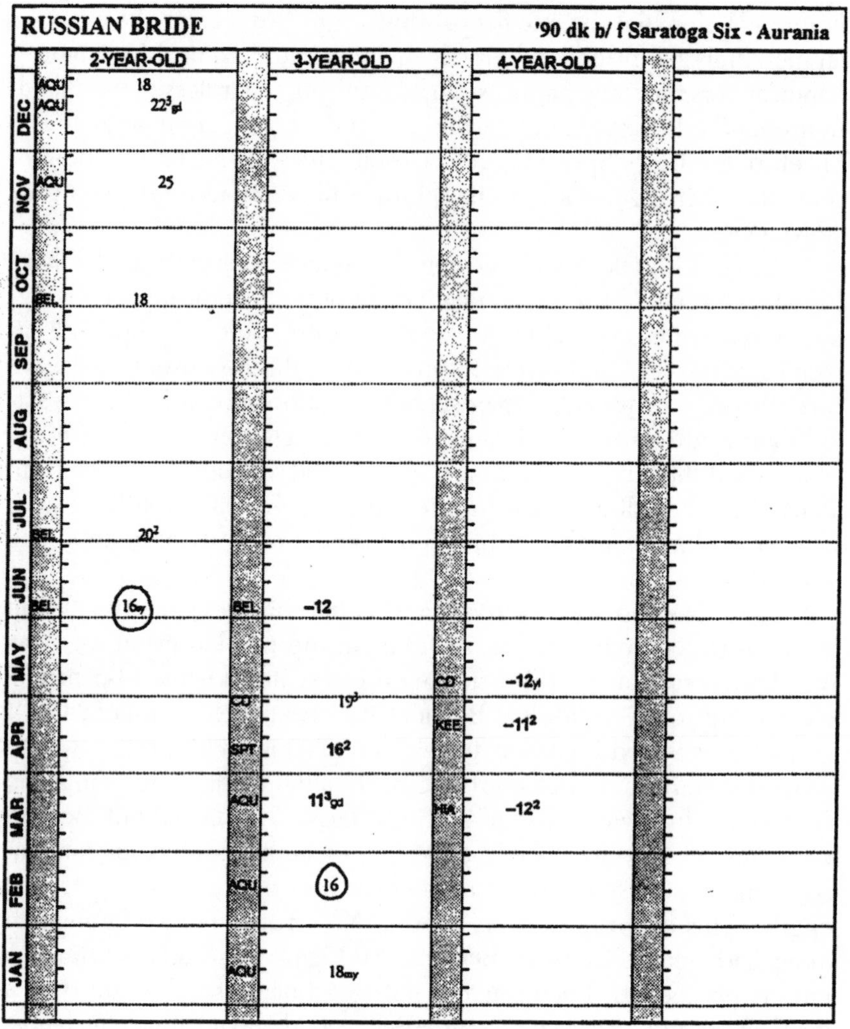

RUSSIAN BRIDE
'90 dk b/ f Saratoga Six - Aurania
2-YEAR-OLD
3-YEAR-OLD
4-YEAR-OLD
DEC
NOV
OCT
SEP
AUG
JUL
JUN
MAY
APR
MAR
FEB
JAN
AQU 18
AQU 22³gd
AQU 25
BEL 18
BEL 20²
BEL 16my
BEL -12
CD 19³
SPT 16²
AQU 11³gd
AQU 16
AQU 18my
CD -12yl
KEE -11²
HIA -12²

Russian Bride Dk. b. or br. f. 3(Feb), by Saratoga Six—Aurania, by Judger

MIGLIORE R (97 16 12 13 .16) Br.—Eaton Lee (Ky)

Own.—Kentucky Blue Stable Tr.—Jolley Leroy (7 1 0 1 .14)

116

Lifetime					
11 3 2 1 $89,736	1993	5 2 1 1			$70,936
	1992	6 1 1 0			$18,800
	Wet	2 2 0 0			$27,600

29Apr93- 8CD	fst	7f	:22^4	:46^2	1:24^1	ⒻLa Troienne	70	3	10	9^4	10$^{5\frac{3}{4}}$	6$^{6\frac{3}{4}}$	6$^{8\frac{1}{2}}$	Santos J A	b	113	5.40e	80–08 TrvrsCty116^{hd}AdddAsst113$^{1\frac{1}{2}}$Blld113	Sluggish brushed	10
10Apr93- 8Spt	fst	1 1/16	:47^3	1:12^3	1:45	ⒻN J Clb Oak	73	3	3	3$^{2\frac{1}{2}}$	3$^{2\frac{1}{2}}$	3^4	3$^{8\frac{1}{2}}$	Bourque C C	b	115	4.30	82–11 TruAffr120$^{3\frac{3}{4}}$Boots'nJck122$^{4\frac{3}{4}}$RssnBrd115	Bore out turn	7
21Mar93- 8Aqu	gd	1 1/16	⊡:48^3	1:13^2	1:44	ⒻComely	88	4	4	4$^{2\frac{1}{2}}$	2$^{\frac{1}{2}}$	2$^{\frac{1}{2}}$	2^2	Migliore R	b	113	10.50	83–25 PrivtLight112^{2}RussinBrid113$^{1\frac{1}{2}}$TruAffir118	Good effort	6
21Mar93-Grade II																				
17Feb93- 7Aqu	fst	6f	⊡:23	:46^3	1:11^2	ⒻAlw 27000	70	1	8	5^2	2^{hd}	1^1	1$^{6\frac{3}{4}}$	Bravo J	b	116	6.80	86–09 RussinBrd116$^{6\frac{3}{4}}$HghBrgr116^{1}ThThTth116	Drifted, drvng	8
14Jan93- 6Aqu	my	6f	⊡:23	:46^4	1:13^1	ⒻClm 50000	70	2	6	2^1	2^2	2^{hd}	1$^{2\frac{1}{4}}$	Migliore R	b	116	2.90	77–19 RussinBrid116$^{2\frac{1}{4}}$PromisdRlc118$^{1\frac{1}{2}}$TrckCtyGrl111	Driving	8
14Jan93-Claimed from Kentucky Blue Stables, Jolley Leroy Trainer																				
26Dec92- 2Aqu	fst	6f	⊡:23^1	:47^2	1:13^2	ⒻClm 35000	62	11	1	3^1	3^2	2$^{3\frac{1}{2}}$	2$^{1\frac{1}{2}}$	Migliore R	b	116	5.00	74–20 PnmJne102$^{1\frac{1}{2}}$RussinBrid116^{4}TnksforLunch116	2nd best	11
18Dec92- 7Aqu	gd	6f	⊡:23^1	:47	1:12	ⒻAlw 27000	46	6	1	2$^{\frac{1}{2}}$	3$^{3\frac{1}{2}}$	6$^{9\frac{1}{2}}$	6$^{15\frac{1}{2}}$	Davis R G	b	116	6.10	67–18 NiceCrne116$^{5\frac{1}{2}}$Woodmn'sGirl109$^{3\frac{1}{2}}$Incinrt116	Weakened	6
19Nov92- 7Aqu	fst	7f	:23	:46^3	1:24^2	ⒻAlw 27000	47	7	1	5^2	4^3	9^{12}	9$^{19\frac{1}{4}}$	Migliore R		116	3.10e	64–16 TouchOfLove117$^{1\frac{1}{2}}$InHrGlory118^{5}Mgroux116	Wide,tired	9
3Oct92- 8Bel	fst	6f	:22^2	:45^2	1:10^4	ⒻPrsnl Ensign	74	8	7	7^7	8^8	8^{11}	5^9	Krone J A		116	10.70	77–17 MssdthStorm116$^{4\frac{1}{2}}$FmlyEntrprz118$^{\frac{3}{4}}$TyWn118	No factor	8
3Jly92- 8Bel	fst	5½f	:22	:45^1	1:04^2	ⒻAstoria	58	7	8	5$^{3\frac{1}{2}}$	5^4	5$^{6\frac{1}{2}}$	5^8	Cruguet J		112	4.70	85–11 DstnctHbt112$^{2\frac{1}{2}}$D'Accrdrss119^{3}TryInThSk116	Four wide	8
3Jly92-Grade III																				

LATEST WORKOUTS May 29 Bel 4f fst :51^2 B May 22 Bel 6f fst 1:13^4 H May 13 Bel Ⓣ 5f fm 1:03 B (d) Apr 20 Kee 4f fst :49^2 B

236 DAVE LITFIN'S EXPERT HANDICAPPING

SAR p71 WILLIAMSTOWN 90 race 8

10 RACES 92 5 RACES 93

12+ Ywt AWTP12

17" AWCD28

17" Y AWCD 8

.17" t AWKE16

22- w AWTD 3

21- YwT] AWSrPMV

17" AWSrPMV

19- Y AWSrPMV

21 Yw MSEL14

26" Y[MSCD21

'4" vw AWBEPMV

14 v AWKE18

11 Yt AWKE 6

edging clear of the 3-5 favorite. The Thoro-Graph number plunged from 16 to 11¾ and the Beyer figure soared from 70 to 88. These horses represent a fabulous source of overlays that do improve, and by several lengths.

An important and common variation of the pattern finds the new three-year-old that has just matched or slightly improved its two-year-old top disappointing with a declining performance, notably if wheeled back to action in a couple of weeks. Examine the telltale pattern on The Sheets of Williamstown (page 259), another third-starting three-year-old that had exceeded his two-year-old top of 12¼ with an 11 first back at three, and then regressed to a 14. But the colt had returned from the 11 in 12 days, much too soon, and bounced. The third start was the Grade 2 Withers, and Williamstown was sent away at 10-1.

Williamstown won the Withers by a head, and paid $23.60. On the sheets, the colt exploded to a 4. In relating the incident, Litfin juxtaposed the "explosion" pattern with a perceptive pace analysis that favored Williamstown's running style and would compromise the chances of the 2-1 favorite, a strength of Litfin's book from cover to cover; good, in-depth handicapping, not just pattern recognition. Handicappers need to remember the three-year-old explosion pattern can happen immediately following a new "slightly improved" top, or if the new three-year-old has regressed in the next start following a quick return to action, the explosion can occur in the second start following the new top.

Next, Litfin tackles the "forging" pattern, another figure pattern that can be a precursor to peaking form, but undoubtedly the most difficult to recognize. Simply stated, forging horses are held to be "looping" back to their best performances.

Russian Bride's Thoro-Graph sheet indicated an explosive pattern when she was entered in the Grade 2 Comely Stakes for three-year-old fillies at Aqueduct on March 21, 1993. She was unable to get back to her debut figure of 16 until her eighth start, when she recorded another 16 in winning a preliminary allowance on February 17. Significantly, there had been several gaps between her races at age two. Handicappers can use the pattern to evaluate older, more heavily campaigned horses whose form cycles should reveal the patterns of speed figures that count. The patterns will be several and dissimilar. Litfin cautions the patterns can be perplexing to the untrained eye. He emphasizes handicappers will be looking for a more extended period of time between best efforts and he recommends the presence of evidence other than speed figures that horses should be moving in a positive direction.

In relating how he came to back the filly Groovy Feeling at 12-1 to win Aqueduct's Grade 2 Ladies Handicap of 1993, Litfin not only related the figure pattern he recognized in persuasive detail, but also explained how Groovy Feeling should benefit by moving from turf to dirt, from a pair of exceptionally strong recent workouts, from a favorable change in posts, and from her new trainer, Peter Ferriola, perennially among the New York leaders. Although the figure pattern may be the telltale clue, forging patterns will work best for expert handicappers who can not only recognize the pattern, but also can evaluate its full-blown handicapping context. A figure handicapper I rub elbows with at Santa Anita occasionally has explained to me that he collected on a double-digit winner I could not fathom because it was rounding back to its top figure, leaving me in the dark even as I revisited the past performances. He must have been referring to forging patterns that escaped me, and largely still do.

The first 106 pages of *Dave Litfin's Expert Handicapping* deal with the relations between speed figures and form cycles, beautifully and persuasively illustrated, and the material is highly recommended to everyone.

Litfin is equally assured in dealing with trainers and conditioning patterns. He reminds handicappers that trainers are notorious creatures of habit, and insists their favorite patterns should be readily recognizable. My favorite, which should be highly prized among those who follow New York racing, is the Florida-to-New York "wake up" pattern. A specialty of New York's Nick Zito for years, the Florida-to-New York wake-up pattern features horses that have looked dull during the winter at Gulfstream Park, but can be expected to improve dramatically on their return to New York during spring.

Litfin illustrates the wake-up pattern repeatedly, but emphasizes the variations on the theme will be numerous; that is, the repetition of a trainer pattern that wins. His adjustment to the infinite variety is clever and simple. As he does anew in his chapter on keeping records in DRF Press's *Bet with the Best*, Litfin urges handicappers to compile manually a file of past performances for a trainer's winners. For any trainer of interest, clip the past performances of the horses that have won and arrange them chronologically in a notebook. Litfin recommends that handicappers record for each winner the distance, the eligibility conditions, the win mutuel, equipment changes, and personal comments. Litfin swears the positive patterns will be leaping off the pages in short time. Litfin affords no fewer than 82 pages of his book to recognizing successful trainer patterns.

In introducing his negative patterns, Litfin asserts there are but two reasons to play a race: a legitimate contender is underbet, or a vulnerable favorite is overbet. In each situation, the handicapper enjoys an edge. He believes the second situation, the overbet favorite—a condition he perceives as chronic in New York, especially—is vastly underrated as a source of value. This is true particularly in constructing exactas and trifectas, because the vulnerable favorites can be eliminated from two or more wagering positions, thereby facilitating the possibility of the score.

According to Litfin, several situations, rather common, will be ruinous to vulnerable favorites, and he implores handicappers to recognize each of the following patterns:

1. disadvantaged by the probable pace, the worst condition of all
2. unsuited to the footing
3. graded-stakes winners prepping in allowance races
4. chronic money-burners
5. basement-level inconsistent claimers
6. suspicious class drops
7. favorites that open well above their morning line

As always, the patterns have been illustrated smartly, and in a context of expert, full-dress handicapping.

Litfin concludes his discourse on pattern recognition with a panoply of "angles" handicappers must learn to perceive for the added value they usually offer. In selecting his examples, Litfin has been careful to invoke winners that pay generous, but not outrageous odds, enhancing the credibility of the pattern play. Below is a sampling of Litfin's patterns that pay and the odds on the winners he chose to illustrate his points.

- First time for a tag (9-2)
- First try against restricted claimers (7-1)
- First try against older (9-2)
- Out of jail, up in class (12-1)
- Reclaimed (6-1)
- Turf-to-dirt (6-1)
- Won pace duel, lost the race (21-1, 16-1)
- Weight and trainer intent (7-1)

Once again, the illustrations make the case, and Litfin indulges himself and treats his audience to a broader context of expert handicapping.

Dave Litfin's Expert Handicapping is a handbook on pattern recognition that begs to be devoured. It serves its purpose better, as I have discovered, on the second reading, and the greater the expertise that handicappers bring to the exchange, the more likely they will appreciate the lessons to be learned.

CHAPTER 43

OUT OF CHAOS,
A DEGREE OF ORDER:
REAL SPEED

WITH A BACKGROUND in psychology, I occasionally will be pressed to comment on the psychology of the racetrack; more specifically, whether certain personality types should be expected to do better or worse. My response has been short and sharp. Winners may come in numerous sizes and shapes, but the personalities that can expect nothing but heartaches at the races are the control freaks.

Money management apart, handicappers and bettors exercise no control over events at the track. The troubled trips, inept horsemen, jockey mistakes, form reversals, stewards' decisions, betting patterns, all the annoying upsets of one kind or another, none of it falls under the player's jurisdiction. People having a desperate need to control their environment probably do not belong at the racetrack. A fascinating variation of the controlling personality is the scientific mind. The scientist feels the need for control, in the scientific manner, by observing, measuring, testing, and solving all problems at a terrifically high degree of objectivity and confidence.

So it has come to pass in the arid lands of Socorro, New Mexico, near the ovals of Albuquerque and Ruidoso Downs, that the archaeologist Charles Carroll has allotted a good majority of his free time to the scientific pursuit of beating the races. As demonstrated in his unheralded but provocative *Handicapping Speed* (Lyons & Burford, 1991), he has partially succeeded, rather almost succeeded, at least in relation to his own scientifically elevated standards. As the title of his book denotes, Carroll has fastened on the speed factor because it alone lends itself to scientific inquiry, and as the subtitle, ". . . The Thoroughbred and Quarter Horse Sprinters," denotes, he is concerned with sprints only, and for scientific reasons. Only linear relationships are solvable, and the speed of the race-horse, a function of distance divided by time, is linear, testable, and solvable, under optimal conditions up to seven furlongs.

When Charles Carroll views a horse race, he perceives chaos. Not the pedestrian kind of chaos, a jumble of disorder, but the scientific kind, an absence of *testable, solvable* order. To put it in scientific terms, the horse race is not a system that might be divided into its fundamental parts, such that each of those parts might be understood, and the system put back together again, such that the newly constituted system might be completely understood and predictable. Suggesting that horse-race handicapping began to shift from art to science in the 1960's and 1970's, Carroll draws analogies between handicappers and scientists in "other" fields. Physicists reduced, from atoms to quarks; biologists reduced, from cells to electrochemistry; handicappers reduced, from hot tips to track variants and par times.

Carroll assigns the important role of chaos in understanding dynamic systems to the MIT meteorologist Edward Lorenz, who was working with a mathematical model of weather systems when one day he introduced a tiny element of noise. Lorenz merely rounded one of the numbers in his equations from seven digits to three. He went to lunch. An hour later the same model that should have been predicting the same numerical changes in the weather was fluctuating wildly and randomly; i.e., chaos. Naturally, Lorenz wrote a paper. He described what would evolve in chaos theory as the "butterfly" effect. Weather patterns were affected and changed by factors as remote and seemingly trivial as the beat of a butterfly's wings. Lorenz concluded that the weather could be predicted only in terms of general patterns.

It turns out the scientists soon recognized that in *dynamical* systems—weather patterns, heating systems, horse races—no less than millions of "butterflies" are flapping their wings. The conclusion was difficult for the scientists to accept; that is, random aberrations—butterfly wings flapping, horses stumbling at the gate—are not noise in the system; rather, *order* is the system within the chaos. Scientists in many fields, handicappers included, accepted two new fundamentals: You can't know all the parameters, and the ones you do know are not connected in any linear fashion. This is crucial, as most nonlinear equations cannot be solved. You cannot, for example, connect a horse stumbling at the gate to future performance, as trip handicappers are prone to do.

As Carroll tells, the order within the chaos that is a horse race is the horses' true speed. That's in part because the second law of thermodynamics holds that all systems run out of gas, which means that horses running across a distance of ground will eventually get tired. Moreover—and this is the scientific part—the relationship between the expanding distance and a horse's running time is linear; it can be plotted with amazing accuracy. Carroll shows the linear relationship between the expanding distance and time in a horse race up to 10 furlongs is as great as .9994, which means handicappers can be 99.94 percent certain that a horse that runs six furlongs in such-and-such time will run seven furlongs in such-and-such time. With exceptions for exceptionally small segments, the shorter the distance, the more precise the relationship, and the less likely any noise will interfere, in accord with the second law. Scientists prefer a confident level of precision. Carroll will concentrate on the sprints.

In a provocative illustration of the linear relationship between distance and time, Carroll notes the absence of a world record for 7½ furlongs on the dirt, although he cites an American record of 1:26⅘. "With a correlation coefficient of .9994, you can plug 7.5 into the equation for the line in Figure 7.9 [shown below] and be 99.94 percent certain that the world record for the distance should be 86.6 seconds, or 1:26⅗."

If Carroll perceives horse races as chaos in which subsystems of order might be found, handicappers can imagine his reaction to the indices of

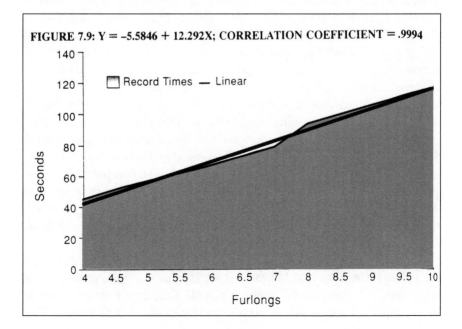

FIGURE 7.9: $Y = -5.5846 + 12.292X$; CORRELATION COEFFICIENT $= .9994$

speed handicapping that have persisted as our most effective tools—class-distance pars, track variants, one-fifth equals one length. "The problems with many of the baselines, particularly homemade ones that attempt to follow the lead of the various writers, are mainly caused by class-par time charts that incorporate false averages and flyers. And the concomitant overuse of daily track variants derived from the same pars. They are compounded by the widespread acceptance of the old axioms that one losing length is equal to 10 feet and one-fifth of a second." Beyer Speed Figures are dismissed, or perhaps merely discounted for what he considers their gross inaccuracies, and so are all other methods of speed handicapping where millions of butterflies can be imagined flapping their wings.

In Carroll's search for more scientific methods, a fundamental problem was the establishment of the baseline, or standard of comparison, by which horses' real speed might be calculated. First, Carroll is careful to define real speed, not as time, but as distance divided by time, or feet per second. No argument there. Carroll settled on a baseline of *top speed.* By top speed, he meant the fastest rate of speed any Thoroughbred could be expected to run across a given distance. The laws of physics, in combination with the second law of thermodynamics (horses running out of gas at some point), postulate the existence of a theoretical ceiling upon a horse's speed at any distance, such that no horse would be capable of running faster than the ceiling speed. Carroll's trade-off with the theoretical top speed is the world record for each of the regularly run distances. If a horse's *real speed* is compared to the prevailing *top speed*, the ratio should provide handicappers with the most advanced methodology of speed handicapping.

Carroll's methodology approaches its finest estimate of horses' speed quotients by reliance on another measure of real speed, *time per length.* "Another measure of speed is time per length. In order to calculate it, you first need to decide how long a length is. There has been some debate over the years about whether eight or nine feet should be used." This cannot be reassuring to the thousands of unscientific feet-per-second devotees who have invoked 10 feet (because convenience counts) as the length of the average Thoroughbred. In his personal computations, Carroll experimented with seven and nine feet. He got impossibly fast and slow speeds, ". . . which makes it clear that eight feet is the best average." He continues, "Maybe there is a quintessential average, like 7.839 or 8.021—but it is not 7.5 or 8.5; they've been tested."

With eight feet as the average length of the horse, Carroll next divided the various distances into lengths. At a mile, for example, consisting of 5,280 feet, a horse runs for 660 lengths. To calculate time per length, handicappers simply divide a horse's time by its number of lengths. For a mile completed in 1:36 flat (96 seconds), the time per length would be $^{96}\!/_{660}$, or 0.145 seconds per length. To arrive at his baseline, or standard of comparison, for calculating any horse's real speed, Carroll simply used the world records at the various distances. For each world record, he calculated the number of lengths a Thoroughbred must run and the time per length. Carroll's Thoroughbred baselines can be examined below.

At six furlongs, the world record of 1:07⅕ (estimated), or 67.2 seconds,

---

Thoroughbred Base Points

Distance	Time	Lengths	Time-Per-Length
4 furlongs	44.2	330	.134
4.5 furlongs	50.4	371.25	.1357
5 furlongs	55.2	412.5	.1338
5.5 furlongs	61.4	453.75	.1353
†6 furlongs	67.2	495	.1358
6.5 furlongs	73.6	536.25	.1372
7 furlongs	79.4	577.5	.1375
8 furlongs	92.2	660	.1397
††8.182 furlongs	95.0	675	.1407
††8.318 furlongs	96.7	686.25	.1409
*8.5 furlongs	98.4	701.25	.1403
*9 furlongs	105.0	742.5	.1414
*9.5 furlongs	112.4	783.75	.1434
*10 furlongs	117.8	825	.1428

†See text
††1m 40yds and 1m 70yds extrapolated times
*American Dirt Course Record

With this baseline, you can get away with murder. Even though handicapping can be considerably improved with the addition of track constants and (in some cases) race variants, a weekend handicapper can get by at most tracks with conservative betting and this ultimate-horse baseline alone.

---

would require 495 lengths, and the superstar's time per length is .1358. In the same way, any horse's real speed can be calculated as time per length. The final step divides the superstar's time per length by any horse's time per length. The calculation shows how fast a horse has run in relation to the world-record speed, and becomes the most accurate way to distinguish a field of horses on real speed.

Suppose a handicapper's best bet of the day was beaten by 4½ lengths in a seven-furlong race where the winner was timed in 1:23⅗, or 83.4 seconds. Using a calculator (computer software is available), the winner's time of 83.4 seconds first is divided by the number of lengths in a seven-furlong race (577.5). The winner's time per length is 0.1444. The loser beaten by 4½ lengths has a time per length slower than the winner by 4.5 × 0.1444, which equals 0.65 seconds slower. Add 0.65 to 83.4 seconds and you have a "close approximation" of the loser's time, which is 84.05 seconds.

Now the loser's time is converted to time per length easily, as 84.05 divided by 577.5., or 0.1444 seconds per length. To get the best bet of the day's speed rating, divide the seven-furlong baseline speed (0.1375 time per length) by the horse's real speed (0.1455 time per length).

$$0.1375 / 0.1455 = 0.945$$
$$0.945 \times 1,000 = 945$$

To remove the decimal points, as shown, multiply by 1,000. The best bet of the day has a speed rating of 945. Handicappers might say the horse has run 94.5 percent as fast as the world-record holder for the distance. An astonishing revelation of Carroll's methodology that may shock experienced handicappers—it did me—is that the range of speed ratings for all horses, even for hopeless maiden claimers, seldom drops below 90 percent of the superhorse. Carroll comments, "A figure in the 800's is extremely poor. A horse can be 90 percent as fast as Secretariat or Dr. Fager, and never win a race."

In later chapters of *Handicapping Speed*, Carroll applies his methods to actual races. Examine the speed ratings for a field of $4,000 claimers at Longacres who have not won a race since April 3. It's August 25, 1990.

Western Nifty	6f	952
Green Echo	6f	951
Green Echo	6.5f	946
Seatonic	6.5f	944
Big Time Louie	6.5f	942
Nijinsky's Promise	6.5f	938
My Picture Time	6f	933
Kalahari Kid	6f	932

Emphasizing that much work is still to be done once handicappers possess the speed ratings, and that a majority of speed handicappers would have preferred Western Nifty in the Longacres sprint, Carroll opted instead for Green Echo, mainly because he had recorded higher, more consistent figures in several races at different distances. Carroll concluded the three horses most likely to finish in the money after extensive handicapping—Western Nifty, Green Echo, and Seatonic—also had been rated 1-2-3 on the numbers. Without a strong enough opinion to bet substantial amounts to win, Carroll instead keyed Green Echo top and bottom with the other two high-rated horses in exacta and trifecta boxes. Although he did not say as much, on reviewing the results chart, I concluded that Carroll must have enjoyed a banner day at Longacres.

ELEVENTH RACE **6 FURLONGS. (1.07⅘) CLAIMING. Purse $4,200. 4-year-olds and upward which have not won a race since April 3. Weight, 122 lbs. Non-winners in 1990 allowed 3 lbs. Claiming price $4,000.**

Longacres

AUGUST 25, 1990

Value of race $4,200; value to winner $2,310; second $800; third $610; fourth $375; fifth $105. Mutuel pool $50,377. Exacta pool $37,698. Trifecta pool $83,715.

Last Raced	Horse	M/Eqt.	A.Wt	PP	St	¼	½	Str	Fin	Jockey	Cl'g Pr	Odds $1
17Aug90 10Lga 7	Green Echo	LBb	4 119	9	3	3 ½	1 hd	1 3	1 ½	Delgadillo C	4000	7.30
3Aug90 1Lga 7	Western Nifty	LBb	4 119	6	5	5 hd	3 1	3 ½	2 1½	Boulanger G	4000	10.80
18Aug90 11Lga 3	Seatonic	B	8 119	10	6	6 2½	4 1	5 2½	3 1½	Cedeno E A	4000	2.30
15Aug90 11Lga 8	My Picture Time	LB	4 119	7	1	1 2	2 1½	2 1	4 ½	Barnese V J	4000	5.50
8Aug90 3Lga 3	Nijinsky's Promise	LBb	4 119	1	11	11	9 1½	6 3	5 1½	Corral J R	4000	9.60
8Aug90 10Lga 3	Big Time Louie	LB	4 119	5	8	8 3	6 hd	7 3	6 ½	Maelfeyt B J	4000	13.00
15Jun90 2Lga 7	Kalahari Kid	LBb	4 117	2	7	4 1	7 3	4 2½	7 2½	Belvoir V5	4000	9.70
9Aug90 5Lga 9	Memory Lapse	LBb	4 122	3	9	9 1	8 ½	9 3	8 2	Drexler H	4000	25.10
28Jly90 10HaP 3	Lord Emmaus	LB	8 122	11	2	2 1	5 ½	8 hd	9 ¾	D'Amico D L	4000	8.00
11Aug90 11Lga 8	Sir Edward	B	4 119	4	10	10 ½	10 2	10 3	10 5	Southwick W E	4000	12.90
4Aug90 3Lga 7	Smoother Sailing	LB	4 119	8	4	7 hd	11	11	11	Jauregui L H	4000	17.20

OFF AT 5:59. Start good. Won driving. Time, :21⅘, :45⅕, :57⅖, 1:10⅗ Track fast.

$2 Mutuel Prices:			
9–GREEN ECHO	16.60	12.00	5.40
6–WESTERN NIFTY		10.40	7.40
10–SEATONIC			2.80

$2 EXACTA 9–6 PAID $229.40. $1 TRIFECTA 9–6–10 PAID $407.60.

B. g, by Greenough—Forest Echo, by Tompion. Trainer Mullens H R. Bred by Roffe S (Wash).

GREEN ECHO, within striking distance early, drove through along the inside on the turn to take command, gradually drew clear and just lasted in the final sixteenth. WESTERN NIFTY, never far back, rallied slightly wide into the stretch and closed strongly. SEATONIC lacked early foot, came wide for the drive and finished willingly. MY PICTURE TIME sprinted clear early, could not match strides with GREEN ECHO nearing the stretch, gave way gradually. BIG TIME LOUIE raced wide. LORD EMMAUS stopped after showing brief speed.

Owners— 1, Gentry J; 2, Western S Stables; 3, Holland L & P-Lang T; 4, Jensen Luella M; 5, Macadams R & Sea Horse Six Stable; 6, Gray-Harwood-Hudson; 7, Jones O M or Jean C; 8, Dbts Stable; 9, Smith Jenny L; 10, Jones & Hagan Jr; 11, Collicott G L & Mercer Betty.

Trainers— 1, Mullens H R; 2, Smith Larry; 3, Holland Peter; 4, Kenney Dan; 5, Chambers Mike; 6, Drebin Keith; 7, Fisher Steve; 8, Samuels Bruce; 9, Smith Derry B; 10, Jones Michael David; 11, Collicott Gary L.

Because precision matters when working with numbers, Carroll concludes too that his methodology will uncover more overlays than the conventional methods of speed handicapping, or any other style of handicapping. Although he liked Seatonic as a factor in the Longacres race, for example, Carroll castigates the crowd for making the eight-year-old its 2-1 favorite, based upon two respectable showings in his two most recent races. "This is a traditional handicapping approach that sometimes works," says Carroll, dismissively, and no one can dispute the assertion.

Although Carroll refines his methodology further by providing "constants" and "variants" to enhance the ratings, he insists the relatively simple procedures associated with the baseline standards above will place speed handicappers well in front of the crowd. He does recommend precise decimal equivalents when valuing beaten lengths of a neck (.20), a head (.15), and a nose (.06).

Out of chaos comes a certain degree of order, based upon the power of scientific inquiry, and scientific procedure. In his chapter "Chaos— Why There Are Horse Races," in which the author draws delightful analogies between racetrack handicappers and the scientists of renowned disciplines, Carroll offers bettors a scientific explanation at last for all the irrational, seemingly inexplicable upsets of the racetrack, as when a clearly superior horse loses to clearly inferior foes, or when suddenly a dismal horse runs faster than it ever has in its life, or ever will again. In trying to comprehend it all, think fondly of weather patterns, Edward Lorenz of MIT, the butterfly effect, and the chaos inherent in dynamic systems.

As to the order Carroll has extracted from the chaos that is the horse race, I have not experimented with his time-per-length speed ratings, and by not doing so I may have missed the most powerful approach to handicapping yet invented. An endorsement in support of Carroll's scientific endeavor has been posted by a speed handicapper of national repute, and someone who should know. Andrew Beyer himself. And among the people that should not miss this book are the engineers, physicists, biologists, meteorologists, archeologists, chemists, and even the social scientists who are also handicappers.

CHAPTER 44

UPDATES ON THE CLASS, SPEED, AND PACE FACTORS

This essay appeared in an abridged, differently edited version in the May-June 2001 issue of The HorsePlayer Magazine *as "Quinn on Class."*

IN MIDSTRETCH OF the 2001 Breeders' Cup Classic, devotees of the class factor might have tripled their wagers on Giant's Causeway. The imaginary escalation should be considered rational, even advantageous. With Europe's ranking handicap star at 7-1, and only the California-bred supplemental nominee Tiznow to be headed, nearing the sixteenth pole Giant's Causeway looked absolutely like the overlay of the season.

When Tiznow (9-1) dug in, fought furiously, and prevailed by a neck, not only were most observers surprised, but the unexpected outcome also brought sharply into focus the difficulties contemporary handicappers can experience when evaluating class. Tiznow had won a single Grade 1 event. Giant's Causeway had won six. Tiznow had romped on the front end by six in the Super Derby (Grade 1) at Louisiana Downs in a six-horse field of sophomores. The Beyer Speed Figure (114) had exceeded par for three-year-olds of fall, but runners-up Commendable and Mass Market had impressed no one except their connections. Giant's Causeway had defeated the cream of Europe's older elite. His Timeform rating had crested at a sensational 130, although it should be noted that Timeform ratings do not correspond numerically to Beyer figures.

In his latest race during Oak Tree at Santa Anita, Tiznow had been extended fully at nine furlongs and following an ordinary uncontested pace (47 seconds and 1:10⅘) to withstand the sustained challenge of the three-year-old Captain Steve in the Goodwood Handicap (Grade 2), which was open to older runners, but empty of talented ones. Facing a $360,000 late-nomination fee and feeling indecisive, Tiznow's owner and trainer had waited several days and had depended upon jockey Chris McCarron's verdict before making the commitment to run.

A three-year-old Cal-bred having zero support as Horse of the Year before the Breeders' Cup Classic would soon be the runaway winner of the honor, further illuminating the problems handicappers can encounter nowadays when evaluating class.

In fact, although he had never defeated an important horse, by standards that can be accepted as reliable in the modern sport, Tiznow's upset in the Classic was supported by the record. He had entered the race a multiple Grade1/Grade 2 winner, with above-par and still-improving speed figures. In Grade 1 stakes of today, horses four and up should have won *two* or more Grade 1/Grade 2 events; three-year-olds may have won merely one.

Backers of Giant's Causeway may have felt unfortunate to have lost, but they were beaten by an authentic Grade 1 contender.

The Class Factor Today An ex-claiming horse won the 1999 Kentucky Derby. That year's Breeders' Cup Classic and 2000's Belmont Stakes were won by imposters. It's true too that too many graded stakes are being snatched by unimpressive horses in unimpressive time and manner.

At Del Mar in 2000, no less than one of every four races (28 percent) was a maiden-claiming procession. No wonder many handicappers have concluded the class factor is less important than ever, and a few have argued ridiculously that class does not exist.

A better explanation concedes that when approximately 40 percent of the past 20 select U.S. yearling crops have been purchased by foreign interests, the majority of the youngsters exported to faraway lands, an inevitable consequence will be too many stakes races chasing too few stakes horses, reducing field size and lowering quality. From year to year now, the older handicap divisions and the three-year-olds may be strong, but they may be unusually weak.

The class factor applies regardless. No doubt it's disingenuous to identify the "best" horses in slow fields, and handicappers need not try. Where relative abilities will be unclear, or depressingly weak, it's legitimate to pass, or to skin the races by applying other factors.

Although the class factor will be decisive most often in stakes races and in turf routes, class considerations are never unimportant, and class standouts at bettable prices might be spotted on a regular schedule in races of every kind. As an agreeable irony of the modern game, even as standard race conditions have been altered to accommodate horsemen, certain class drops and class rises have emerged as more meaningful than ever.

These relatively recent developments have resulted in new applications when evaluating class:

1. the publication of the Beyer Speed Figures
2. the use of optional-claiming conditions to fill allowance fields
3. an oversupply of three-year-old claiming races
4. an innovative starter race for maiden-claiming grads
5. a renewed emphasis on pace figures, or pace analysis, as indicators of which three-year-olds might move ahead in class effectively

In sum, even as cheaper races and smaller fields have weakened traditional applications of the class factor, new and fascinating applications have rushed to the class handicapper's rescue. As ever, the class factor cannot be viewed independently. In place of the customary class-form interplay, today's most progressive handicappers will emphasize the interdependence between the class factor and speed and pace.

The Class-Speed Interplay Long before his speed figures made their debut in *The Racing Times* and then *Daily Racing Form,* Andrew Beyer observed that the most reliable indicator of whether a claiming horse might survive a multiple rise in claiming price was its speed figure. No matter the step-up, if the speed figure supports the maneuver, make the play.

It was good advice. Not only did Beyer's observations prove correct, but also the horses paid sizzling odds, the betting public unwilling to back the steep escalation in claiming class.

In 1986, professional speed figures still years removed from the daily paper, on Gold Cup morning at a Hollywood Park seminar, Tom Brohamer advised a group of visiting Canadians that a claimer jumping from $10,000 to $32,000 represented the best bet of the day. A few of the visitors snickered.

When the class climber won by daylight and returned $38 or thereabouts, the snickers turned to cheers. No one in that group will doubt again the power of speed figures in predicting rises in claiming class.

By publishing Beyer Speed Figures as part of the past performances, the *Daily Racing Form* has facilitated comparisons between class and speed that were untenable for the recreational market—and most regulars—only a decade ago. As Bill Quirin demonstrated, class and speed are perfectly correlated (better horses run faster), and no one should trifle with the implications of that.

By comparing Beyer pars, and benchmark figures, to the horses' figures presented by the *Daily Racing Form,* handicappers can compare what horses have actually done to what they should be expected to do at today's class level.

In most claiming races, speed and pace will be primary and dominant. If the matter at hand is a $40,000 claiming sprint for four-year-olds and up in southern California, for example, the Beyer par is 98 (males). Horses that have not recorded a Beyer Speed Figure within two lengths of 98 (93) at least twice in the last six or seven races will be unlikely to win, regardless of recent wins and competitive finishes at various class levels. Favorites and low-priced contenders lacking the adequate speed figures can be abandoned.

If the $40,000 sprint has been limited to March three-year-olds, the Beyer par may shift by as many as five lengths to 85, and the same class evaluations apply. By becoming familiar with the Beyer pars at the local tracks and at common shipping tracks, class lovers earn enormous dividends.

In the modern claiming game, where cheaper brands now predominate, speed figures more often will alert class analysts that horses attempting multiple-level leaps should not land safely. That information can be precious.

Early in 2001, a mare claimed by leading southern California trainer Bill Spawr out of a $20,000 claiming race, which she had won, promptly won again for $25,000. Spawr raised the mare two additional levels to $40,000. Inspired by the trainer-jockey tandem of Spawr and Laffit Pincay Jr., as well as the confident class ride, the bettors backed the mare to even money.

Spawr's claim's speed figures at the $20,000 and $25,000 levels were 80 and 81. Par for $40,000 females was 90. Handicappers might have accepted figures as low as 85. The Spawr-Pincay even-money favorite got trounced.

When claiming horses enter the nonwinners allowance series, and vice versa, the class-speed dynamic can reveal the contenders well suited to the class levels. Examine the comparisons below for seven major tracks having winter dates:

	Nonwinners Allowance Levels and the Comparable Claiming Classes		
	NW1X	NW2X	NW3X
Fair Grounds	20,000	35,000	50,000
Hawthorne	14,000	18,000	30,000
Gulfstream Park	32,000	40,000	62,500
Aqueduct Inner	35,000	50,000	75,000
Delaware Park	17,500	25,000	40,000
Laurel	14,500	30,000	50,000
Santa Anita	40,000	62,500	100,000

A Fair Grounds shipper exiting a $20,000 claiming race there and entered under NW1X allowance conditions at Hawthorne might carry a definite edge. New York shippers should do well under advanced allowance and claiming conditions in Florida. Delaware shippers can match Maryland horses at lower and middle levels, but not yet at the higher classes.

Santa Anita claiming horses might ship successfully anywhere they roam, although the southern California circuit remains isolated and the claiming horses stay there.

None of this applies to claiming races restricted to three-year-olds; more on those low-level races below.

To solidify further the class-speed comparisons simulcast handicappers increasingly must make effectively, the *Daily Racing Form* presents daily a short list of benchmark Beyers that should translate reasonably well across various tracks and class levels.

115+   Best horses in the country
109   Grade 1/Grade 2 stakes pars (writer's add-on)
105   Leading three-year-olds en route to the Triple Crown (add-on)
100   Good allowance and low-grade stakes
90   Typical $25,000 claiming race
80   Typical $10,000 claiming race
57   Bottom-level $2,500 claimers at smaller tracks

The benchmarks can be adjusted readily to narrow circumstances at local tracks. As one length on the Beyer scale approximates 2.5 points in sprints, 2 points in routes, a $35,000 claiming race at Calder might be expected to be run two lengths faster than a $25,000 race. The benchmark Beyer would be 95 (four-and-up males).

In the contemporary context it's crucial to appreciate that numerous races at the various class levels will be won by horses that have run slower than par. Accept as suited to the class horses that have run within two to three lengths of par (5 to 7 points), provided four-and-up horses have delivered the desired performance more than once. A single Beyer standing out in the record like a giraffe's neck is invariably suspect, and often false.

The class-speed interplay gained in importance significantly for southern California handicappers studying allowance races beginning January 1, 1998, when a new horse-racing board regulation stipulated that Cal-breds that had won a NW1X allowance race limited to state-breds could compete at the same level in open company.

Dozens of Cal-breds began to take advantage of the situation. Their chances under open NW1X allowances hinged absolutely on the speed figures they had recorded while beating the state-breds. Where the speed figures had been soft, the Cal-breds could be tossed. Where the speed figures had been strong, the Cal-breds might be expected to win again at a class level they had already surpassed. Many did, and as overlays.

Optional-Claiming Races To enlarge the small fields, a twist on the conditions of eligibility for the nonwinners allowance series has been introduced on an expanding scale; the optional-claiming race. As a result, the mix of allowance horses and claiming horses in these mid-level encounters has become more complicated than ever.

Under optional-claiming conditions, horsemen can enter under allowance conditions or for a designated claiming price. Thus high-priced claiming horses that previously have won under today's allowance conditions will be facing younger, still-developing three and fours that have not yet won one, two, or perhaps three allowance races.

The class handicapper's first line of defense in any optional-claiming race is to favor the authentic allowance types. These will be the younger, lightly raced threes and fours that are moving impressively through their basic conditions and might soon be stakes material. If their speed figures have been low, probably the younger colts and fillies will be false, but if their figures fit the class, prefer them.

Only when the allowance timber is missing should handicappers prefer the older, heavily raced claiming horses, although precisely that situation can be expected to arise regularly. When it does, the ripest overlays will be hard-knocking platers that recently have been winning or performing well at a claiming class superior to today's allowance level.

During Oak Tree at Santa Anita in October of 2000, trainer Bobby Frankel recognized his chance to steal a juicy allowance purse at no risk when he entered an older grass router that had been competitive at the $80,000 claiming level under nonwinners-twice allowance conditions. The optional-claiming price designated for the NW2X level recently had been raised from $62,000 to $80,000. Frankel's high-priced claimer outran a number of inveterate NW2X allowance losers easily and paid $9, when he might have been 8-5.

In any nonwinners allowance race contested under optional-claiming conditions, look hungrily for consistent claiming horses that need only defeat an array of inveterate allowance failures at today's level.

Claiming Races Limited to Three-Year-Olds No situation poses thornier problems for class handicappers than the claiming races limited to three-year-olds. Still, at times these lackluster contests can present golden opportunities for backing overlays, notably during the first six months of the year.

Three-year-old claiming horses tend to be cheaper than they look and confoundingly inconsistent. Good races are not repeated. Form reversals are legion. Most importantly, the three-year-old claiming horses as a group are far inferior to their nonclaiming counterparts. Moreover, from January to June especially, to protect owners' investments, three-year-olds entered to be claimed tend to be entered at claiming prices much too high.

When they lose ugly, the claiming threes will be dropped, probably repeatedly, until competitive class levels can be found.

Handicappers best avoid the pitfalls inherent in three-year-old claiming races by limiting their bets to win to allowance dropdowns. The single requirement is the switch out of an allowance race, provided the youngster has demonstrated some ability in the classier division: early speed, a mid-race move, an even effort, a finish within six lengths, and best of all, a willingness to track or stalk a rapid pace to the pre-stretch call before fading.

If handicappers can restrict themselves to allowance dropdowns in three-year-old claiming company during winter and spring, and to a lesser degree during summer and fall, the number of bets will plunge, but the profits will rise. Odds on the allowance droppers frequently enough will be fair to generous.

It is crucial to stress a counterpoint regarding three-year-old claiming horses. No matter the margin of victory, no matter the speed figure, no matter the connections, when winners of three-year-old claiming races attempt to re-enter the nonclaiming divisions, reject them. A faster pace, the greater mid-race acceleration, and the more competitive finish, featuring better horses at every stage, are likely to defeat even the most impressive of them.

The cheaper front-runners often will finish out of the money. The occasional magnificent exception, a la Charismatic, will not compensate for the losses.

In late October of 2000, the three-year-old gelding Three Amigos made his debut on the turf at a flat mile at 7-1 and blasted a field of $62,500 claiming three-year-olds by 5½ lengths. The speed and pace figures looked super. Three Amigos had completed the final quarter-mile in 24⅕ seconds.

Trainer Paul Aguirre was duly impressed. Having won twice going away with the three-year-old following his $25,000 claim of September 8, Aguirre next entered Three Amigos under NW1X allowances on the Hollywood Park grass.

The bettors surveyed the past performances and sent Three Amigos off against the allowance field as their mild favorite at 3-1.

The allowance horses slaughtered Three Amigos. He pressed a rapid pace for six furlongs, and faded quickly. Three Amigos finished seventh of nine, beaten 13½ lengths.

The class rise from three-year-old claiming to three-year-old nonclaiming may be the steepest, least successful in horse racing.

Starter Races for Maiden-Claiming Grads These innovative but pitiful races amount to a refuge for bad horses. In southern California, the conditions of eligibility invite horses that have won a maiden-claiming event with a $40,000 tag or lower, and have never won two races.

Because the horses cannot be claimed, class handicappers might imagine horsemen would drop horses that have been running well at comparable open claiming levels, but they do not. The fields instead are brimming with maiden-claiming winners only, many of which also have failed repeatedly under the same starter conditions.

Class evaluation does not apply. Speed handicapping will be unreliable. Combinations of speed and pace figures might be expected to sort these horses fairly well, but inevitably the entire fields will be unforgivably slow.

Instead of doubling the starting price, as class analysts are encouraged to do under traditional starter conditions for claiming-race winners, now handicappers should reduce the starting price by half. Horses that have impressed near those levels can be preferred.

Even so, the results so far have proved to be poor. Not only do the $20,000 horses refuse to enter, but also the winners of the starter races for $40,000 maiden-claiming grads have yielded average speed figures closer to $10,000 claiming horses.

These starter races persist as unpredictable. If dropdowns from open $20,000 claiming (or higher) are spotted, or the occasional allowance dropdown becomes available, make the play. Otherwise, class handicappers best proceed to the next race.

Class, Pace, and the Nonclaiming Three-Year-Olds.

Probably the most overlooked, underrated element of class evaluation regards the pace capacities of talented three-year-olds. Nothing so impedes a nonclaiming three-year-old rising in class as a swifter pace sustained to the six-furlong call of routes.

Until the nonclaiming threes have proved they can cope with a faster-than-par pace while moving ahead in class, they must be suspect, notably in Grade 1 and Grade 2 company. The predicament can be especially beneficial to handicappers in possession of pace figures.

Talented three-year-olds that have recorded strong speed figures and impressive victories in classy company will be severely overbet, setting the table for an upset, whenever the fancied horses' pace figures remain dubious (more than two lengths slower than par). It happens every spring.

In this context it's instructive to review the past performances of Tiznow, who as a three-year-old seized the early lead in the Breeders' Cup Classic and prevailed at 9-1, following a stretch-long determined effort against a legitimate champion.

Examine the Quirin-style speed and pace figures assigned to Tiznow by figure handicapper Tom Brohamer in the colt's three races in southern California before the Classic.

	Par	Pace	Speed	
Swaps (Gr.1)	111	111	109	2nd by 2½
Pacific Classic (Gr.1)	113	114	114	2nd by 2
Goodwood Handicap (Gr.2)	113	109	115	1st by 1½

The performances in the Swaps Stakes and Goodwood Handicap qualify as classic illustrations of three-year-olds unlikely to win the Classic. As the pace figure (2 points = 1 length) goes up, the speed figure goes down, and vice versa. The profile indicates the three-year-old cannot set or attend a rapid pace, and still finish well.

The Pacific Classic at Del Mar alters the situation in a positive way. In that 10-furlong Grade 1 test, Tiznow exceeded par at the pace call *and* at the finish, only to succumb by two to the front-running Skimming. When Tiznow was afforded a sluggish early pace (47⅗ and 1:12) in the Breeders' Cup Classic, he retained sufficient energy to withstand Giant's Causeway.

In contrast, review the past performances and corresponding speed and pace figures recorded by the talented colt War Chant during January, March, and April of 2000, as he prepared for the May 6 Kentucky Derby.

	Par	Pace	Speed	
Alw, NW1X	105	104	110	1st by 5
San Rafael (Gr.2)	108	117	107	1st by ½
SA Derby (Gr.1)	111	109	111	2nd by 1

Favored at 2-1, War Chant could be expected to disappoint in the Santa Anita Derby. And he might finish up the course. Class analysts experienced with combinations of speed and pace figures would have wagered against War Chant aggressively. Instead, although he lost, War Chant delivered a par performance following a slightly soft pace.

Based upon his Santa Anita Derby performance, War Chant's case for winning the Kentucky Derby would be considered marginal, although not hopeless. By comparison, when Silver Charm defeated a powerful crop of three-year-olds in the 1997 Kentucky Derby, he had exited a loss by a head to Free House in the Santa Anita Derby with a Quirin combination of 122-112, a tremendous performance for an April sophomore. Silver Charm would have pickled War Chant.

War Chant resurfaced during October, of course, to sparkle on the turf, where he won from behind, untroubled by the early pace. It's true too that talented three-year-olds that cannot dispense above-par combinations of speed and pace figures while moving up in class during spring frequently can do exactly that in top company during late summer and fall. Seasoning and physical maturity do matter.

The class-pace dynamics among developing three-year-olds persists as perhaps the most intriguing aspect of class evaluation in the modern game. The best of handicappers are well advised to pay attention to the developing colts and fillies from January to November.

CHAPTER 45

THE XTRAS

A NEW VOICE FOR the new millennium belongs to Cary Fotias, and he comes in loud and clear. His contribution is both contemporary, one might even say postmodern, and significant. He uses velocity-based pace numbers and energy-distribution concepts to identify horses coming to peak condition. The horses can be expected to deliver their best efforts next time, and many do.

A number and variety of figure analysts have depended upon numerical patterns to infer improving form, even peaking form, but none has succeeded with a high degree of reliability, until now. The main problem has been an overreliance on final figures, and final figures can be influenced by several factors—pace, class, trips, distance, bias, track condition—that do not reflect variations in the form cycle. In particular, early pace bears directly on final time. As the increasing numbers of users of Quirin-style speed and pace figures will testify, when the pace figure improves, the final figure declines, and vice versa, at least for the large majority of horses.

So it's hardly shocking that early pace in relation to final time might be a predictor of peaking form, as Fotias has discovered, but the critical relationships extend beyond the typical speed and pace interplay, notably to prior pace figures and to horses' overall patterns of development. Notable too, Fotias's use of speed and pace figures in combination is not devoted to pace analysis, or race shapes, as in the Quirin approach, but to considerations of horses' current condition. Fotias wants to know when horses should be in condition to run their best races.

In his superb paperback *Blinkers Off,* Fotias tells of his considerable playing background, with emphasis on the two latter-day influences that have shaped his current thinking, Len Ragozin's The Sheets and the Sartin Methodology. Allowing that The Sheets trace overall development but suffer the weaknesses inherent in the reliance on final-time figures, while the Sartin Methodology focuses narrowly on a representative pace line that ignores overall development and may be insensitive to the form cycle, Fotias has combined and expanded the methodologies of the two approaches in the quest to predict when horses can be expected to deliver a top performance.

The author refers to the telltale information as The Xtras. The Xtras are numbers, or figures, that give context and meaning to final-time figures, and are intended to help handicappers relate performance to the form cycle. The Xtras include a pace number, a "turnback" number, and in dirt sprints only, a two-furlong number. At all distances, the pace number occurs at four furlongs, which in figure handicapping is the conventional pace call of sprints, but a radical departure from the conventional pace call of routes, which occurs at six furlongs. All the numbers are velocity-based, crafted by hand, and adjusted for wind, weight, track configurations, and Fotias's proprietary track variants. Users work with conventional numerals, e.g., $^{69}\!/_{4}+$, not with feet per second.

As with The Sheets and the Thoro-Graph figures, The Xtras are presented on a graph, but instead of providing a horse's complete record, Fotias gives the information for the past three seasons. The graphs will look reassuringly familiar to most figure handicappers, including the various symbols for half-points, quarter-points, sprints and routes, grass races, and off tracks. Final-time numbers are centered and the four-furlong pace numbers appear in parentheses to the right of the final numbers and within their personal lines. The value of a point varies with distance, such that one point equals one length at four furlongs (the constant pace call), 1½ lengths at six furlongs (so two points equals three lengths, a huge difference), two lengths at a mile (now two points equals four lengths), and 2½ lengths at a mile and one-quarter (two points equals five lengths). With skimpy practice, The Xtras are easy to read. A legend for The Xtras and the graph for the good New York sprinter-miler Affirmed Success can be found on pages 284–285.

In a chapter on general handicapping principles that proceeds the method's most significant discovery, Fotias enumerates and discusses briefly 12 "key variables" that can affect how horses distribute their

LEGEND

THE XTRAS are the definitive handicapping tool for evaluating thoroughbred performance and form cycles.

THE XTRAS will allow you to interpret "the race within the race" and focus on condition angles overlooked by the public and other figure players. At a glance, you will be able to isolate horses with "hidden" moves.

On each XTRA page, the last three years of a horse's performance are presented. The **final numbers** are graphed in the larger area of each yearly column, and the extra numbers are to the right. The number in parentheses ( ) is always the 4 furlong or **pace number**. If a dirt race was longer than 6f, the smaller number to the left of the pace number is the 6f **turnback number**. In dirt sprints only, the **two furlong number** is to the right of the pace number.

All our numbers are hand crafted and velocity based. They are adjusted for wind, weight, track configurations, and our proprietary track variants. The graphed final numbers are reported in 1/4 point increments, while the extra numbers are rounded to whole numbers. The higher the number, the better the performance. Weight is already factored into previous races. If contenders are not carrying equal weights **today**, credit horses carrying lower weight by .20 "final number" points per lb.

SYMBOLS

+ 1/4 point
" 1/2 point
- minus 1/4 point

\> wet fast
^ good
/ sloppy
\ muddy
< slow
+ heavy
: frozen
= turf
^= good turf
.= yielding turf
:= soft turf
+= heavy turf
*= hard turf

w won race
( ) no pace number calculated
-- no final number calculated
xx did not finish/eased

TRACK CODES AND OTHER INFO

two letter track codes on left
(see EQUIFORM.COM for list)

M in final number column
denotes missing race(s)

last race at top of right column

age at top of yearly columns

weight at right of horse's name

DISTANCE CODES

light italic	< 6f	70
light	6f - 7-1/2 f	70
bold	8f - 9-1/2 f	**70**
bold italic	10f or longer	*70*

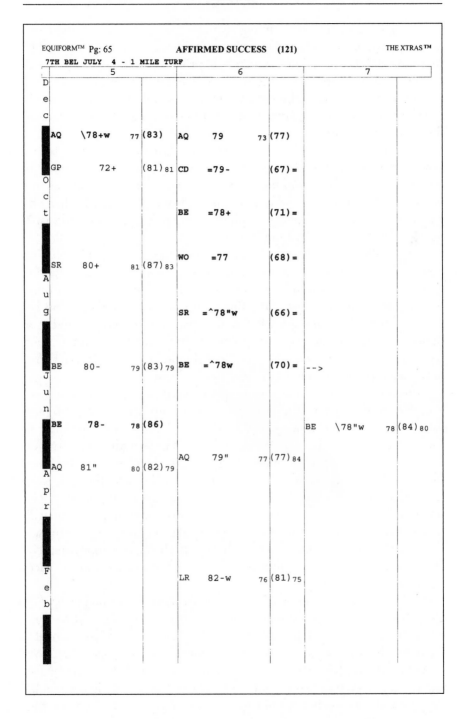

7TH BEL JULY 4 - 1 MILE TURF

	5			6			7	
D								
e								
c								
	AQ	\78+w	77 (83)	AQ	79	73 (77)		
	GP	72+	(81) 81	CD	=79-	(67) =		
O								
c								
t				BE	=78+	(71) =		
	SR	80+	81 (87) 83	WO	=77	(68) =		
A								
u								
g				SR	=^78"w	(66) =		
	BE	80-	79 (83) 79	BE	=^78w	(70) =	-->	
J								
u								
n								
	BE	78-	78 (86)				BE	\78"w 78 (84) 80
	AQ	81"	80 (82) 79	AQ	79"	77 (77) 84		
A								
p								
r								
F				LR	82-w	76 (81) 75		
e								
b								

energy. The 12 factors are running style, the pace demands of the race, distance, surface, track bias, the jockey, the trainer, weight, post position, final-time ability, racing luck, and in bold print for emphasis, the current condition of the horse. The discussion of general principles is solid and insightful, and Fotias cautions that The Xtras should be used in combination with *Daily Racing Form* past performances, a guidepost too many figure addicts ignore.

In summarizing the role of the 12 variables affecting energy distribution, Fotias asserts his allegiance to the primary importance of current condition: ". . . all of them taken together are not as important as the horse's current form or condition. If a horse is not physically in shape to run a competitive race, all the sophisticated analysis in the world isn't going to land him in the winner's circle."

Fotias follows with his method's most salutary finding. The clue to peaking condition is "a new pace top." The context is crucial, however, and in its most elementary form includes a final-figure decline. Fotias does not indicate how severe the final-figure decline should be, but he cautions that a "double top," where a new pace top is accompanied by a final-figure improvement of two points or more, represents a different pattern, which can knock horses out and should not be confused with a new pace top accompanied by a final-figure decline.

Conventional pace analysis using speed and pace figures in combination also indicates that when the pace figure improves the final figure usually declines, but Fotias's pattern is distinct. Now the improvement at the pace call is represented by the horse's best pace figure in a series of performances. Because the most energy will be distributed to the four-furlong call and this is the most stressful part of the race, the new pace top and a final-figure decline not only will presage a top performance, but also the situation will remain hidden to most handicappers, who will notice mainly the decline in final-time performance. Fotias reports horses showing the pattern will rebound with a top performance approximately 70 percent of the time. Handicappers are urged not to confuse pace analysis with form analysis.

To illustrate, Fotias presents the seventh race at Aqueduct on January 26, 2001, an inner-dirt route where two horses were coming off new pace tops, but with highly anticipated results that fooled the New York bettors badly. Examine The Xtras for John Paul Too and Pure Harmony (pages 287–288).

As Fotias tells, John Paul Too was coming off a double top, a new pace top accompanied by a two-point final-figure gain. Although figure handicappers and pace analysts would applaud the obvious improvement, the extra expenditures of energy early and late could be expected to weaken

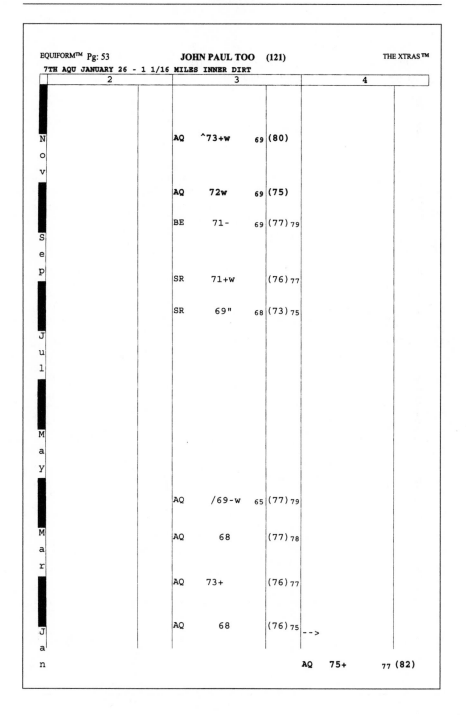

JOHN PAUL TOO (121)

7TH AQU JANUARY 26 - 1 1/16 MILES INNER DIRT

2	3	4
	AQ ^73+w 69 (80)	
	AQ 72w 69 (75)	
	BE 71- 69 (77) 79	
	SR 71+w (76) 77	
	SR 69" 68 (73) 75	
	AQ /69-w 65 (77) 79	
	AQ 68 (77) 78	
	AQ 73+ (76) 77	
	AQ 68 (76) 75 -->	
		AQ 75+ 77 (82)

(Left margin: N o v ... S e p ... J u l ... M a y ... M a r ... J a n)

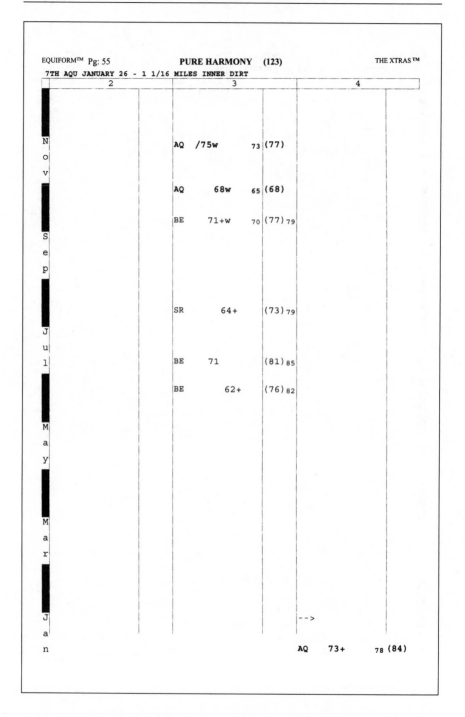

EQUIFORM™ Pg: 55   **PURE HARMONY** **(123)**   THE XTRAS™

7TH AQU JANUARY 26 - 1 1/16 MILES INNER DIRT

	2	3	4

Nov

AQ   /75w   73 (77)

AQ   68w   65 (68)

BE   71+w 70 (77) 79

Sep

SR   64+   (73) 79

Jul

BE   71   (81) 85

BE   62+   (76) 82

May

Mar

Jan

-->

AQ   73+   78 (84)

John Paul Too's current condition. Fotias insists these horses typically will need recovery time.

Pure Harmony, alternatively, already had recorded a final-figure 75 in November and had followed with a 73+ while running his new pace top (84). Although Pure Harmony might be expected by figure analysts to "bounce" off the much-improved 75, and apparently did, in doing so he exhibited continued good form by staying above his previous final-figure tops of 71 and 71+, while the new pace top of 84 indicated Pure Harmony actually had reached the best form of his career. The hidden form would pay excellent dividends. John Paul Too went favored at 2-1. Pure Harmony romped to a front-end score at 13-1.

Fotias describes two variations of the new-pace-top pattern where The Xtras can supply adherents with numerous opportunities. One is the cyclical pace top, the other the delayed pace top. Whereas the new pace top typically will be descriptive of younger, lightly raced horses that are still developing and capable of reaching new heights, the cyclical pace top applies to older, established runners, the bread-and-butter claiming horses absolutely, whose figure patterns and form cycles have largely stabilized. Now the horses have cycled back to a pace-figure top that previously has prefaced a stronger winning performance. The horses are achieving peak condition again.

In the delayed pace top, horses record a new pace top but do not demonstrate peak performance until the second race afterward, due to one of four intervening factors. The four are an intervening turf race, an equipment change, a legitimate excuse, and a race against a track bias. Fotias provides provocative illustrations of each, and an especially agreeable characteristic of the patterns should be higher odds on peaking horses.

As must be true of the important advances in handicapping theory and practice, The Xtras not only extends our understanding of the game as a whole, i.e., how energy- distribution patterns can reflect improving form, but also broaden, strengthen, and alter our comprehension of the interrelationships among the several handicapping factors, in this book among form, pace, and final time. Pace as a fundamental of handicapping has been studied extensively and in-depth as much or more than any other factor throughout the 1990's, ostensibly as a remedy to counteract the widespread public use of speed figures and the depressing odds that have resulted from the general practice. The resulting guidelines have been many and useful, entirely capable of tossing profits, but pace analysts will be introduced in *Blinkers Off* to empirical evidence that will challenge them to alter certain established routines.

The most intriguing alterations apply to lightly raced horses and to turf races. Regarding lightly raced horses, the maidens and maiden-claiming horses making their first and second starts, especially, Fotias's research debunks one of the most common interpretations of pace and speed figures used in combination. Using the customary fractional and final times, Fotias presents Horse A and Horse B, as follows:

Horse A	22.0	45.1	1:10.3
Horse B	22.5	45.8	1:10.3

As the author notes, using conventional pace analysis and the match-ups of the Sartin Methodology, for instance, Horse A possesses the superior pace ability and should bury Horse B. Fotias concedes that the common interpretation is usually valid when dealing with older, experienced horses, but he begs to differ if the menu is lightly raced younger horses, especially maidens, and most notably the second starters that handicappers generally will expect to improve. Now Horse B deserves the nod. The reason is persuasive. In these situations, handicappers should be concerned with evaluating condition, and not pace match-ups.

In the terminology of The Xtras, Fotias refers to "plunge lines" and "compression lines," such that Horse A represents a plunge line, where the pace figure is significantly greater than the final figure. Horse B represents a compression line, where the pace figure and final figure are well balanced. If A and B are second starters, pace analysts invariably would favor Horse A, but they would typically be wrong. Horse A has expended too much energy too soon, and has an extraordinarily good chance to suffer a loss of conditioning. Horse A is likely to regress. Horse B, on the other hand, has distributed his energy efficiently. Horse B should benefit from improved conditioning, and is capable of exploding with a forward move in his second start.

In similar circumstances, Fotias depicts Horse A and Horse B as maiden winners at seven furlongs who in a few weeks will meet under nonwinners-once allowance conditions at six furlongs. Review the speed and pace figures, as they might appear on The Xtras graphs:

	Final	6f	4f	2f
Horse A	71	71	(80)	84
Horse B	71	70	(71)	74

Traditional pace analysts again would favor Horse A. Fotias disagrees sharply. "When evaluating one-number horses, this is simply not the case.

Second-time out compression horses, with a competitive final number, will usually defeat other one-number horses with a better pace figure." How about that!

Fotias introduces his treatment of grass races by reinforcing the conventional wisdom that turf racing is different and late speed usually predominates over early speed. That is, the distinguishing characteristic of winning grass horses is the ability to unleash the bulk of their energy late. While the signal of peaking condition on the dirt is the new pace top, on the grass it's the turf pace low. Just as the new pace top identifies horses that are running stronger in the most stressful stages of the race, the turf pace low serves the same purpose on the grass.

As on the main track, the context of the turf pace low is crucial. A grass horse that reveals the requisite pace figure must also retain a final figure within two points of his previous figure. And the turf pace low does not necessarily mean the horse's lowest pace figure lifetime. Fotias refers to an important subset of the phenomenon as the "turf decline line." The turf decline line is simply a decline in successive turf pace figures of six points or greater. The pattern denotes the ability to finish faster. As Fotias states, "If they are going slower early, but running roughly the same final number, they are finishing better. This is a powerful conditioning angle on the weeds."

In an example involving the mare Stetson Lady at Santa Anita on March 29, 2001, Fotias shows how the mare finished her five-year-old campaign with three final numbers near 70, improving to a 73– top in December. After beginning her 2001 season with a combination $^{71}\!/_{70}$ (pace figure appears first), Stetson Lady next dispensed a $^{64}\!/_{71}$–, a turf decline line of seven points. In her third start Stetson Lady defeated a field that was deeply contentious on final figures, and paid $26.20.

The turf-pace-low pattern has been especially curious to me, because it seemingly conflicts with an aspect of evaluating grass racing I have pursued rather confidently, and rather effectively, for years. When evaluating horses' final fractions (from the six-furlong call to the wire), unusually strong final fractions become suspect whenever the pace figure has been unusually slow, precisely because the horses have retained too disproportionate a share of their energy. When forced to chase an honest pace, even a six-furlong pace that has been slower than par, but by six to seven lengths only, perhaps by as much as two seconds (10 to 12 lengths), the same horses often cannot duplicate the powerful closing fractions. They no longer retain the deeper reserves of energy and their closing fractions will be weaker.

Fotias controls for the distortions by requiring that the final-time figures remain robust. Instead of fastening on the final fraction, The Xtras emphasize the ability to finish strongly against the sluggish pace. If the final figures have remained relatively stable (within two points), now it's the "turf spread" (subtract the pace figure from the final figure) that counts. The greater the turf spread, the stronger the finishing ability, a reflection of improving condition.

In an amusing account of the complications inherent in making conventional speed figures on the grass, Fotias reports how illogical projection techniques were employed (inadvertently and regrettably) to assign greatly dissimilar Beyer Speed Figures to a NW1X allowance winner and a Grade 1 stakes winner that had run final times within one length of each other at marathon turf distances on the same Belmont card.

The allowance winner Formal Consent was given a Beyer 91 while the Grade 1 stakes winner and champion Fantastic Light was given a Beyer 106. Class distinctions aside, Fotias concluded that the speed figures made no sense, given the raw data, and were dependent solely on projection techniques that were highly subjective. Examining the relations among the fractional times and final times of the two grass marathons, Fotias invoked The Xtras to demonstrate that Fantastic Light indeed was the better horse, but not because his final figure was significantly higher; it was not. Formal Consent at $^{51}\!/_{4}$ had a turf spread (final figure minus the pace figure) of 23, while the classy Fantastic Light at $^{43}\!/_{6}$ had a turf spread of 33. As Fotias points out, "Fantastic Light had demonstrated a sizeable edge in finishing ability, and that is usually decisive in grass races."

Throughout an adult lifetime, Cary Fotias has exhibited a passion for mathematical games, including poker, bridge, blackjack, and currency trading. He played poker full-time for a few years and traded currencies for eight years, and for the past 10 years he has turned to professional handicapping. His academic credentials include an undergraduate degree from the University of Michigan and an MBA from Indiana University, and happily his grasp of math and statistics has found a platform for innovation and practical application in Thoroughbred racing and handicapping. The results should prove beneficial to handicappers everywhere.

The formulas that produce The Xtras are proprietary. The information is not available for public consumption and handicappers cannot learn how to construct The Xtras by inhaling *Blinkers Off*. The information is distributed instead by Equiform, a dotcom company that has published *Blinkers Off* and for which Fotias has been founder and president. A new and important author and book that can enhance handicapping proficiency is always cause for celebration. This one is cause for jubilation.

CHAPTER 46

IDEAS THAT
NO LONGER APPLY

THE MONUMENTAL PROBABILITY studies conducted by researchers Fred Davis and William Quirin have alerted handicappers at all major tracks as to the traditional practices in need of revision or abolition. That laundry list appears immediately below. Where local studies contradict the national samples, local results can apply, provided (a) the research questions are identical; (b) local samples are sufficiently large and representative, such that random samples contain at least 200 races and non-random samples contain at least 500 races; (c) the local statistical methods obtained probability values by dividing the percentage of winners having a past-performance characteristic by the percentage of starters having the characteristic; and (d) the local samples are not subjectively biased, that is, only represent the selections or winning selections of a particular public selector or small group of selectors.

Handicappers whose methods of selection, or methods of separating contenders, or rating methods, or methods of making figures are influenced by the past-performance characteristics reflected in the scientific findings reported here can improve their effectiveness either by eliminating the factor or by doing the opposite, whichever the data suggests.

Horses with a blowout on the day preceding a race enjoy no statistical advantage. All studies demonstrate that a recent race is more influential than a recent workout.

Inconsistency is no basis for eliminating horses and contenders.

Although consistent horses win more than a fair share of their races, inconsistent horses win enough, and horses that have won only one of their previous 10 starts win almost their fair share of the races they enter. This is particularly true in claiming races.

The stretch gain is overrated as an impending sign of victory. Horses able to pass one or two others inside the stretch call or gain one to two lengths at that point usually retain the sharp form, but are at no significant advantage.

Points for less weight, points off for higher weight, turns reality upside down. Higher-weighted horses race at such a statistical advantage, the researchers argue, that racegoers who have no time for handicapping might as well support the top weight in each field. In stakes and handicaps it is risky to bet against the heavyweights.

Favorites on the turf win at approximately the same rate as their counterparts on dirt, but their rate of loss on a series of wagers is half again as great.

Apprentice jockeys perform almost as well as journeymen, even at the route. Horsemen who have long held that the horse makes the rider have been statistically sustained.

Excepting inside posts on grass or in certain route races, post position has incidental effect on race outcomes.

Leading claiming trainers win more than their share of the races, but are overbet. Handicappers should require that their horses deserve the odds the crowd allows.

Speed duels do not ruin the chances of the horses that engage in them, particularly in sprints. Early speed is so important that horses are not fairly eliminated because they figure to contest another horse early.

The inside horse in a speed duel has no real advantage.

Almost every North American racetrack, under normal racing conditions, favors horses with good early speed. Quirin has referred to early speed as the universal track bias.

On drying tracks, early-speed horses do not tire enough to lose their customary advantage to come-from-behind types. Early speed does best on sloppy tracks, but statistics suggest that tiring tracks tire the other horses as much as they do the speed burners.

At mile tracks the number 1 post position is at no disadvantage in sprints. The 1 post in fact is the most powerful. It is less potent in one-turn routes (mile or longer), but still at slight advantage.

Routers dropping back to sprints do not win nearly their fair share, but sprinters stretching out do. The likeliest sign of success is a recent sprint finish in the money or within two lengths of the winner.

Impressive maiden-special winners do move into nonwinners allowance competition successfully, winning half again their rightful share of the allowance starts.

In sprints, freshened horses fare better in the second start after a layoff, but only if the first start reveals a good and not overexerting performance. The third start can be a peak performance provided the second start is clearly better than the first.

Freshened routers do best if they return to competition in a pair of sprints before stretching out. Only one sprint warm-up has deteriorating effects.

All-out stretch drives from the quarter pole or eighth pole do not sap horses' energy reserves. These competitors win better than expected next out. The data hold for sprints and routes.

Better than the stretch gainers are horses that bid at the second or third calls, but flattened in the drive, losing, yet finishing in the front half of the field.

Horses that flash surprise early speed, which they usually lack, are not good bets next time. Typically, these simply revert to their familiar style, which does not include early speed.

Weight shifts are of little importance, in either sprints or routes.

When entered in races limited to their sex, females can repeat previous victories as often as males, can carry high weight as effectively, and can withstand all-out stretch drives just as well.

Recent action is unimportant in two-year-old racing.

Early speed does not stand up on turf as on dirt. The single exception is the lone front-runner, capable of securing the clear lead. These win, paying a profit of 20 percent on the dollar.

Short layoffs of 30 to 60 days do not disqualify horses as contenders on form, provided they show a four-furlong workout within the past seven days; the time of the workout is unimportant. The horses win their fair share.

Long layoffs of 61 days to a year, even longer, do not disqualify horses as contenders on form, provided they show a five-furlong workout or longer within the past 14 days; the time of the workout is unimportant and the five-furlong workout might have occurred more than 14 days ago if it has been part of a regular pattern. The horses win their fair share.

Claiming horses can rise in class by more than 20 percent, even 50 percent, provided the speed figure they recorded in the lower-level performance equals par for today's class level.

The general purse inflation, and the premium purse values provided to state-bred races in many states, means that purse comparisons track to track in the nonclaiming races and the stakes will be less reliable than ever.

CHAPTER 47

ONLINE INFORMATION RESOURCES

WHETHER HANDICAPPERS WANT entries, results, odds, selections, or information of any kind, Thoroughbred racing's online information resources will provide the supply lines at a couple of clicks.

Here are the major suppliers, and the important features of each.

Daily Racing Form (www.drf.com) The primary source for entries and results at all U.S. racetracks, *Daily Racing Form* provides its online subscribers with the past performances for the upcoming action at all tracks two days in advance. A unique feature appreciated by hundreds of trip handicappers is Stable Mail, whereby handicappers can identify horses to watch on their personal lists and *DRF* will forward a convenient notice via E-mail whenever and wherever the horses will be running again.

Another unique feature is a free download of the software Formulator 3.0, which allows users to customize the past performances in various ways. For instance, handicappers can manipulate the data, such that the fractional times at each point of call are presented, which greatly facilitates pace analysis and the calculations of final fractions on the turf. The latest version of Formulator (3.0) allows handicappers to view the lifetime past performances of horses, instead of the 12 to 20 lines that normally appear. The complete records can supply a valuable edge when evaluating the current form and class of older runners in relation to their faraway past. The complete records are helpful too with pattern recognition that may not be visible in the limited array of standard past performances.

Other features include a Newcomer's Corner; a private Clocker's Report, provided to *DRF* from the respected Handicapper's Report, of Los Angeles, for the races of the southern California circuit, where the "national" pick six resides; and on a subscription basis, access to the excellent *DRF Simulcast Weekly*, which contains the results charts for all races for the previous week, along with Beyer Speed Pars, the Beyer Speed Figures for all recent winners, and articles delivered by leading handicappers.

Needless to say, *Daily Racing Form*'s editorial coverage offers the most complete and up-to-date news stories and features on the Web. Business reporter Matt Hegarty is an outstanding reporter, and he provides continuous and in-depth coverage of the important business stories of the sport and industry.

Bloodstock Research Information Services (www.brisnet.com) BRIS, the company's well-known acronym, provides its subscribers with an excellent version of the past performances, developed by a stable of talented professional handicappers. Important features include the speed and pace pars, and pace figures, for every point of call. The report also provides uncommonly timely trainer stats and pedigree information suitable to each specific race. BRIS also features a free daily newsletter, the *Handicapper's Edge*.

Axcis Information Network, Inc., a subsidiary of Equibase, Inc. (www.trackmaster.com) TrackMaster offers subscribers a version of the past performances, called TrackMaster Plus, characterized by the usual array of handicapping information and by the company's proprietary "power" ratings. TrackMaster offers the same past-performance products and services exclusively for followers of harness racing.

The TrackMaster site offers a comprehensive national selection service for all operating tracks on a fee-for-service basis. The selection service has been available for years, remains cost effective, and is managed expertly, as it has been from the start, by the excellent handicapper Ellis Starr.

The National Thoroughbred Racing Association (www.ntra.com) The NTRA site is also the Web site for the World Thoroughbred Championships, run by Breeders' Cup Ltd., and an attractive feature is the Road to the World Thoroughbred Championships, which presents the rankings of the horses by points earned in graded stakes for all eight divisions. The rankings are updated weekly. Everything handicappers and others want to know about the races and their preliminary events can be found here.

The NTRA also presents a well-designed interactive horse-racing game, BetTheNet, an especially entertaining and instructive way for new-comers, beginners, and even experienced racegoers to learn the basics, and more, for playing the races. Participants can earn points and prizes for completing various stages of the game, and the pop-up facts about handicapping and wagering intelligently should appeal to regular race-goers and handicappers alike.

TurfPedia, Inc. (www.turfpedia.com) Turfpedia.com is the author's site, and the intention long-term is to become the brand name on the Web for player development, or fan education. Turfpedia is the Thorough-bred-racing segment of a fantastically larger Pedia Network, Inc.—auto-pedia, winepedia, huskerpedia, et.al.—an Irvine, California-based network information "superbrand" that ultimately is intended to consist of more than 2,000 "pedias." Although the network remains in its infancy, turfpedia.com currently contains more than 300 pages of information and instruction on the art of Thoroughbred handicapping and the skill of parimutuel wagering. The information has been targeted variously at newcomers, beginners, and intermediate regulars, as well as to profes-sional players, and all the leading ideas and methods are treated.

Turfpedia.com also presents regular columns by authors Tom Bro-hamer, Mark Cramer, Steve Roman, and me, as well as selected links to other horse-racing sites and "pedia" sites. Mark Cramer's coverage of European races has been particularly well received by U.S. handicappers. (For excellent links to many European handicapping sites, go to www.racenews.co.uk.)

Needless to say, individual racetracks invite their customers and horse-racing enthusiasts to visit their sites and many of them can be considered outstanding. Daily entries and results are posted. A special nod goes to Del Mar (www.dmtc.com), which was the first kid on the Internet block, has been managed superbly for years by Mary Shepardson, and features a unique pedigree database, developed by the brilliant Berkeley dropout Miles Michaelson. The pedigree information can be accessed directly at www.dmtc.com/dmtc98/pedigree.

The new kids on the Internet block are the providers of account-wagering services. The major players are Television Games Network

(www.tvg.com), Magna Entertainment Corporation (www.expressbet.
com), and YouBet, Inc., (www.youbet.com). Wagers can be placed con-
veniently via the Web and by telephone, from the home, office, or anywhere else in the world.

CHAPTER 48

AINSLIE'S
COMPLETE GUIDE TO
THOROUGHBRED
RACING

THE LITERATURE OF handicapping passed the high-water mark in 1968 when Simon and Schuster of New York published *Ainslie's Complete Guide to Thoroughbred Racing,* by Tom Ainslie, also of New York. The substance and exposition of this work proved so influential in their effects that the publication's impact far exceeded giving racegoers the most complete codification of handicapping theory and method yet elaborated. There would be enormous external rippling effects, the most important of which was that the intellectual character of racing and handicapping had been persuasively and gracefully communicated to interested publics as not before, and these publics would come to accept the ideas as they never had.

Playing the races became legitimized, intellectually, and not just to horseplayers who suddenly became handicappers, but also to book publishers, the marketplace, and even the racing establishment. With sales in excess of 100,000 and still selling strong in the 1980's, the *Complete Guide* had established itself as the undisputed leader and classic in the dubious field of handicapping instruction. The content and integrity of the book marked it at once as the fundamental source for newcomers as well as an advanced and fully integrated kind of handicapping for professionals. To be sure, all who read the book emerged from the experience with a deeper respect for the sport of racing and the joys of handicapping—hardly an inconsequential legacy.

Of effects that go beyond the practice of handicapping, handicappers might consider these:

1. Tens of thousands of reasonably bright racegoers came to understand their sport in its participative aspects, thereby enhancing their personal pleasure and satisfaction when playing the game, even while thousands more took up the pursuit of a game that had been fully exposed as a stimulating and rewarding pastime.

2. The market for handicapping literature of substance opened widely and expanded fantastically. Thus came to die the ancient but much-revered myth that horseplayers can't read. The message had been sounded loudly, clearly. Racing is formful, skillful players can beat the game, and here's practically everything you need to know. It was all absolutely so.

3. In consequence of the two effects just discussed, publishers of books discovered a surprisingly large market for handicapping instruction. The several important books that have since come to life trace directly or indirectly to the commercial success of the *Complete Guide*. Publishers now appreciate that the handicapping market can be strong, with annual sales remaining brisk for those works perceived by the market to be standards.

4. The comprehensive and integrated body of knowledge about the nature of racing and handicapping contained in the *Complete Guide* became the hypotheses and propositions stimulating the first truly scientific investigations of handicapping ever conducted. The probability studies of Fred Davis and Bill Quirin, conducted on a national scale, were completed and published, affording handicapping a scientific basis at last. There followed numerous local, smaller-scale studies, and countless personal studies conducted most seriously by individuals in quest of handicapping's profits. In the subsequent findings of these studies, for the most part the *Complete Guide* was sustained. Portions that science indicated were in need of revision received precisely such revisions in 1979 and 1986, when Ainslie refined parts of the content.

5. At least seven of the prominent handicapping authors of the 1970's and 1980's trace in lineage to the *Complete Guide*, or to its author, in writer Ainslie's various capacities as publisher, editor, and co-author of handicapping works of merit. To wit, Fred Davis, Steve Davidowitz, William Quirin, Henry Kuck, Bonnie Ledbetter, James Quirin, and William L. Scott. Authors that might never have been published otherwise, or if they had been, would otherwise have

found a much more restricted market for themselves, owe the *Complete Guide* a nod for their own special place in the specialized field.

6. The attitudes, values, and personal qualities attached by the book to successful handicappers, to handicapping, and to racetrack participation, of the deliberate, informed, and goal-directed kind, were of an ambience widely and happily reinforced by anyone professionally concerned with the substance, integrity, and professional conduct of the sport. This was a book indeed that men of such stature as Santa Anita Director Emeritus of Racing Jimmy Kilroe could applaud and promote it as representing the best of the sport. No unimportant matters, these.

7. Author Ainslie established himself as a leading authority on handicapping. The skill of handicapping and its instruction enjoyed a contemporary figurehead, such that others might establish themselves as figures in the field as well. And others did. In this important role Ainslie continuously conducted himself as a model that served the field and all that are a part of it.

Of handicapping as an art and a game, the book's contributions were several, including classic chapters on the class and form factors, but on these matters times have changed. Class comparisons dependent on purse values are passé and Ainslie's archly conservative elimination guidelines on current form—e.g., no horse is acceptable on form without a race and a workout in the past 21 days—have experienced a form reversal of their own. Modern handicappers best remain flexible, even liberal, with their standards of recent action and acceptable form. Layoff horses of today, short and long, do win their rightful share of the races, even with a minimal regimen of training between races.

In addition, Ainslie, at least in the *Complete Guide*'s original version, adopted a jaundiced view of speed handicapping accentuating the shortcomings of par times, track variants, and the adjusted final times and speed figures the numerical calculations were intended to produce. He flatly asserted that pace analysis was generally superior to speed handicapping and he insisted the adjusted final times and speed figures would be meaningless where horses were unsuited to the distance, or should be uncomfortable with the pace, or would be susceptible to a decline in form. Ainslie wanted handicappers to relate the speed figures to the other fundamental factors of handicapping, hardly a marginal idea.

As events have shown, the shortcomings of the methodology notwithstanding, professional speed figures have proved to be more rigorous and reliable than Ainslie had imagined, not only from distance to unrelated distance, but from track to unfamiliar track. In his 1986 revision of the *Complete Guide,* Ainslie acknowledged as much, and he saluted the role of speed handicapping in evaluating the real abilities of horses.

The specific selection and elimination guidelines aside, the lasting contribution of the *Complete Guide* is the theory and method of "comprehensive handicapping," as Ainslie christened his approach. Comprehensive handicapping holds that all of the factors of handicapping will play a part in the outcomes of races, their relative importance and the disadvantages of each, varying from situation to situation. The whole should exceed the sum of its parts, such that class evaluation, speed handicapping, pace analysis, form analysis, trip handicapping, trainers and jockeys, post position, pedigree, and the rest obtain the greatest meaning when each has been related to the others. Handicappers are urged to apply everything they know to every race they play. Ainslie concedes that excellent speed handicappers, as well as other method players, may do as well as anybody, but he argues the most successful of handicappers will have absorbed the most knowledge and skill, and will have applied all of it most effectively from situation to situation.

Surely this was a bellwether book.

CHAPTER 49

SECRETARIAT

L ET HORSEMEN, OWNERS, racing officials, and racing fans quarrel about the history of events if they must, but handicappers have united on the argument as to which horse is the greatest of them all. It is Secretariat, the phenomenal son of the great Bold Ruler. The red colt raced only at two and three, in that second season altering for all time the conduct of the sport and its business by contributing within the six months from May 5 to October 28, 1973,

(a)   The first Triple Crown sweep in 25 years and in such consummate style that new—and still standing—stakes and racetrack time records were established for the Kentucky Derby and the Belmont Stakes;

(b)   The ground-shattering breeding-syndication price of $6 million for services at stud;

(c)   The most devastating series of top-level stakes triumphs ever witnessed at American racetracks; and

(d)   The single greatest racing performance yet delivered in the history of Thoroughbred racing.

To the testament of others it is greatly appropriate to conclude a first comprehensive review of the handicapping literature by adding to the praise of the horse, as Secretariat has left to handicappers the very real-time model of Thoroughbred class and speed. When Secretariat's name appears in the literature of handicapping, it is invariably invoked as a simile or metaphor that illuminates the author's point about class. At those moments the horse and his races return vividly to the mind.

Of course the single greatest performance of them all was Secretariat's glorious dance in the Belmont Stakes of 1973, and handicapping authors Andrew Beyer and Steve Davidowitz have borrowed from the virtuoso act to illustrate special considerations in handicapping. Beyer asserts that speed handicappers enjoyed the earliest insight as to the horse's special dimensions. For Secretariat at two, Beyer had recorded a speed figure of 129, by far the highest figure ever accorded a two-year-old, and almost the highest figure ever accorded any horse. On the Monday following the 1973 Belmont Stakes, Beyer sat down to record his figures for that day's races in New York. He wrote:

Secretariat earned a figure of 148 that day—so much higher than any race I had ever seen that the horse had seemed to step into a different dimension. . . .

Romantics could appreciate Secretariat for his strength, his grace, his exciting style of running. But for me the most awesome moment of his career came two days after the Belmont Stakes, when I sat down with my paper, my pencil, and the Belmont charts, calculated my track variant and wrote down the number 148 for the eighth race that day. For a true addict, speed figures are the most beautiful part of the game.

Steve Davidowitz experienced a different kind of peak on that exciting Saturday in New York. He recalls the remarkable Sham's valiant efforts to beat the great horse in the Kentucky Derby and the Preakness:

In the Derby Secretariat went very wide on both turns and with power in reserve outdrove Sham from the top of the stretch to the wire. . . .

In the Preakness, while under no special urging, Secretariat made a spectacular move around the clubhouse turn—from last to first—passing Sham in the backstretch. For the final half of the race Pincay slashed his whip into Sham with wild fury. Turcotte, aboard Secretariat, never moved a muscle. But Sham never gained an inch. At the wire he was a tired horse.

As the Belmont Stakes approached, Davidowitz focused on the exacta. Secretariat was coming to the race of his life, while Sham was a tired and already beaten horse. Given an overbet second choice in small fields, where one horse figures a legitimate standout, Davidowitz tells how to benefit from exacta overlays. Merely eliminate the overbet second choice. Wheel the prime selection to the nondescript others. When Sham disappeared in the Belmont, Secretariat ran off into history, and Steve Davidowitz not only reveled in the moment, but also cashed a $2 exacta worth $35.

Here for the reading pleasure of handicappers are reprints of the results charts for six remarkable stakes races, four of them Grade 1's, in which Secretariat astonished the racing world (see pages 305–309). During the series this incredible racehorse erased four racetrack time records, from 1⅛ miles to 1½ miles, on dirt and turf. Against older horses in the inaugural running of the Marlboro Cup at Belmont Park in New York, Secretariat set the world record for 1⅛ miles. Given just two attempts on grass, Secretariat demonstrated that he was also the greatest turf runner of all time. As the charts and the races they signify are recalled, handicappers should remember, too, that in 1973 both the three-year-old and older handicap divisions luxuriated in a surplus of some of the finest racing talent of the decade. In none of the races was Secretariat fully extended.

Kentucky Derby

NINTH RACE CD May 5, 1973 — 1¼ MILES. (2:00). Ninety-ninth running KENTUCKY DERBY. SCALE WEIGHTS. $125,000 added. 3-year-olds. By subscription of $100 each in cash, which covers nomination for both the Kentucky Derby and Derby Trial. All nomination fees to Derby winner, $2,500 to pass the entry box, Thursday, May 3, $1,500 additional to start, $125,000 added, of which $25,000 to second, $12,500 to third, $6,250 to fourth, $100,000 guaranteed to winner (to be divided equally in event of a dead-heat). Weight, 126 lbs. The owner of the winner to receive a gold trophy. Closed Thursday, Feb. 15, 1973 with 218 nominations.
Value of race, $198,800. Value to winner $155,050; second, $25,000; third, $12,500; fourth, $6,250.
Mutuel Pool, $3,284,962.

Last Raced	Horse	EqtAWt	PP	¼	½	¾	1	Str	Fin	Jockeys	Owners	Odds to $1
4-21-73^{7} Aqu^{3}	Secretariat	b3 126	10	11^{h}	$6^{\frac{1}{2}}$	5^{1}	$2^{1\frac{1}{2}}$	$1^{\frac{1}{2}}$	$1^{2\frac{1}{2}}$	RTurcotte	Meadow Stable	a-1.50
4-21-73^{7} Aqu^{2}	Sham	b3 126	4	5^{1}	3^{2}	2^{1}	$1^{\frac{1}{2}}$	2^{6}	2^{8}	LPincayJr	S Sommer	2.50
4-26-73^{6} Kee^{2}	Our Native	b3 126	7	$6^{\frac{1}{2}}$	$8^{1\frac{1}{2}}$	8^{1}	5^{h}	3^{h}	$3^{\frac{1}{2}}$	DBrumfield	Pr'ch'd-Thom's-R'q't	10.60
4-26-73^{6} Kee^{5}	Forego	3 126	9	$9^{1\frac{1}{2}}$	$9^{\frac{1}{2}}$	$6^{\frac{1}{2}}$	6^{2}	$4^{\frac{1}{2}}$	$4^{2\frac{1}{2}}$	PAnderson	Lazy F Ranch	28.60
4-28-73^{7} CD^{2}	Restless Jet	3 126	1	$7^{1\frac{1}{2}}$	7^{h}	$10^{1\frac{1}{2}}$	$7^{1\frac{1}{2}}$	$6^{1\frac{1}{2}}$	$5^{2\frac{1}{4}}$	MHole	Elkwood Farm	28.50
4-28-73^{7} CD^{1}	Shecky Greene	b3 126	11	$1^{1\frac{1}{2}}$	1^{3}	$1^{1\frac{1}{2}}$	3^{3}	5^{1}	$6^{1\frac{1}{2}}$	LAdams	J Kellman	b-5.70
4-26-73^{6} Kee^{6}	Navajo	b3 126	5	$10^{1\frac{1}{2}}$	10^{1}	11^{4}	$8^{1\frac{1}{2}}$	8^{2}	7no	WSoirez	J Stevenson-R Stump	52.30
4-26-73^{6} Kee^{7}	Royal and Regal	3 126	8	3^{1}	4^{3}	4^{3}	4^{1}	$7^{1\frac{1}{2}}$	$8^{3\frac{1}{2}}$	WBlum	Aisco Stable	28.30
4-26-73^{6} Kee^{1}	My Gallant	b3 126	12	8^{h}	$11^{1\frac{1}{2}}$	12^{3}	11^{2}	$10^{\frac{1}{2}}$	9^{h}	BBaeza	A I Appleton	b-5.70
4-21-73^{7} Aqu^{1}	Angle Light	3 126	2	4^{h}	$5^{1\frac{1}{2}}$	7^{1}	$10^{1\frac{1}{2}}$	$9^{1\frac{1}{2}}$	$10^{1\frac{3}{4}}$	JLeBlanc	E Whittaker	a-1.50
5- 1-73^{8} CD^{5}	Gold Bag	b3 126	13	2^{h}	2^{h}	$3^{\frac{1}{2}}$	9^{1}	11^{1}	11no	EFires	R Secr'st-M G'td'nk	68.30
4-28-73^{7} CD^{6}	Twice a Prince	b3 126	6	13	13	13	13	12^{2}	$12^{1\frac{1}{2}}$	ASantiago	Elmendorf	62.50
4-26-73^{6} Kee^{3}	Warbucks	3 126	3	12^{1}	12^{3}	9^{h}	$12^{1\frac{1}{2}}$	13	13	WHartack	E E Elzemeyer	7.20

a-Coupled, Secretariat and Angle Light; b-Shecky Greene and My Gallant.

Time, :23$\frac{2}{5}$, :47$\frac{2}{5}$, 1:11$\frac{4}{5}$, 1:36$\frac{1}{5}$, 1:59$\frac{2}{5}$ (new track record). Track fast.

$2 Mutuel Prices:			
1A-SECRETARIAT (a-Entry)	5.00	3.20	3.00
5-SHAM		3.20	3.00
8-OUR NATIVE			4.20

Ch. c, by Bold Ruler—Somethingroyal, by Princequillo. Trainer, L. Laurin. Bred by Meadow Stud, Inc. (Va.).

IN GATE—5:37. OFF AT 5:37 EASTERN DAYLIGHT TIME. Start good. Won handily.

SECRETARIAT relaxed nicely and dropped back last leaving the gate as the field broke in good order, moved between horses to begin improving position entering the first turn, but passed rivals from the outside thereafter. Turcotte roused him smartly with the whip in his right hand leaving the far turn and SECRETARIAT strongly raced to the leaders, lost a little momentum racing into the stretch where Turcotte used the whip again, but then switched it to his left hand and merely flashed it as the winner willingly drew away in record breaking time. SHAM, snugly reserved within striking distance after brushing with NAVAJO at the start, raced around rivals to the front without any need of rousing and drew clear between calls entering the stretch, was under a strong hand ride after being displaced in the last furlong and continued resolutely to dominate the remainder of the field. OUR NATIVE, reserved in the first run through the stretch, dropped back slightly on the turn, came wide in the drive and finished well for his placing. FOREGO, taken to the inside early, veered slightly from a rival and hit the rail entering the far turn, swung wide entering the stretch and vied with OUR NATIVE in the drive. RESTLESS JET saved ground in an even effort. SHECKY GREENE easily set the pace under light rating for nearly seven furlongs and faltered. NAVAJO was outrun. ROYAL AND REGAL raced well for a mile and had nothing left in the drive. MY GALLANT, outrun at all stages, was crowded on the stretch turn. ANGLE LIGHT gave way steadily in a dull effort and was forced to check when crowded by GOLD BAG on the stretch turn. GOLD BAG had good speed and stopped. TWICE A PRINCE reared and was hung in the gate briefly before the start and then showed nothing in the running. WARBUCKS was dull.

Preakness Stakes

EIGHTH RACE
Pim
May 19, 1973

$1\frac{3}{16}$ MILES. (1:54). Ninety-eighth running PREAKNESS STAKES. SCALE WEIGHTS. $150,000 added. 3-year-olds. By subscription of $100 each, this fee to accompany the nomination. $1,000 to pass the entry box, starters to pay $1,000 additional. All eligibility, entrance and starting fees to the winner, with $150,000 added, of which $30,000 to second, $15,000 to third and $7,500 to fourth. Weight, 126 lbs. A replica of the Woodlawn Vase will be presented to the winning owner to remain his or her personal property. Closed Thursday, Feb. 15, 1973 with 194 nominations.

Value of race $182,400. Value to winner $129,900; second, $30,000; third, $15,000; fourth, $7,500.
Mutuel Pool, $922,989.

Last Raced	Horse	EqtAWt	PP	St	¼	½	¾	Str	Fin	Jockeys	Owners	Odds to $1
5- 5-73^{9} CD^{1}	Secretariat	b3 126	3	6	$4\frac{1}{2}$	$1\frac{1}{2}$	$1^{2\frac{1}{2}}$	$1^{2\frac{1}{2}}$	$1^{2\frac{1}{2}}$	RTurcotte	Meadow Stable	.30
5- 5-73^{9} CD^{2}	Sham	b3 126	1	4	$3^{3\frac{1}{2}}$	4^{3}	$2^{1\frac{1}{2}}$	2^{5}	2^{8}	LPincayJr	S Sommer	3.10
5- 5-73^{9} CD^{3}	Our Native	b3 126	4	5	5^{h}	5^{8}	4^{3}	3^{3}	3^{1}	DBrumfield	Mrs M J Pritchard	11.90
5-12-73^{6} Pim^{1}	Ecole Etage	b3 126	6	1	$1^{1\frac{1}{2}}$	2^{2}	$3\frac{1}{2}$	4^{10}	4^{10}	GCusimano	Bon Etage Farm	11.30
5- 5-73^{7} Pen^{1}	Deadly Dream	b3 126	2	3	6	6	6	6	5^{3}	ASBlack	Wide Track Farms	35.50
5-12-73^{6} Pim^{5}	Torsion	3 126	5	2	$2\frac{1}{2}$	3^{h}	5^{14}	5^{3}	6	BMFeliciano	Buckland Farm	39.00

Time, :24⅖, :48⅕, 1:11⅖, 1:35⅗, 1:54⅖. Track fast.
(Daily Racing Form Time 1:53⅖ New Track Record).

$2 Mutuel Prices:			
3-SECRETARIAT	2.60	2.20	2.10
1-SHAM		2.20	2.20
4-OUR NATIVE			2.20

Ch. c, by Bold Ruler—Somethingroyal, by Princequillo. Trainer, L. Laurin. Bred by Meadow Stud Inc. (Va.).
IN GATE—5:40. OFF AT 5:40 EASTERN DAYLIGHT TIME. Start good. Won handily.

SECRETARIAT broke well and was eased back and relaxed nicely as the field passed the stands the first time. He was guided outside two rivals entering the clubhouse turn and responding when Turcotte moved his hands on the reins, made a spectacular run to take command entering the backstretch. SECRETARIAT was not threatened thereafter and was confidently hand ridden to the finish. SHAM broke to the right and brushed with DEADLY DREAM leaving the gate, then drifted in and hit the rail entering the clubhouse turn. Pincay swung SHAM out entering the backstretch and roused him in pursuit of the winner but he could not threaten that rival in a game effort. OUR NATIVE, reserved between rivals early, rallied to gain the show. ECOLE ETAGE, hustled to the lead, gradually weakened after losing the advantage. DEADLY DREAM stumbled then was brushed by SHAM just after the break and was outrun thereafter. TORSION, stoutly rated early, could not menace when called upon.

(The :25, :48⅘, 1:12, 1:36⅕ and 1:55 as posted by the electric timer during the running was invalidated after a 48-hour interval by a stewards' ruling, and the above time reported by official timer E. T. McLean Jr. was accepted as official.

Scratched—The Lark Twist.

Belmont Stakes

EIGHTH RACE
Bel
June 9, 1973

$1\frac{1}{2}$ MILES. (2:26$\frac{3}{5}$). One Hundred-fifth running BELMONT. SCALE WEIGHTS. $125,000 added. 3-year-olds. By subscription of $100 each to accompany the nomination; $250 to pass the entry box; $1,000 to start. A supplementary nomination may be made of $2,500 at the closing time of entries plus an additional $10,000 to start, with $125,000 added, of which 60% to the winner, 22% to second, 12% to third and 6% to fourth. Colts and geldings. Weight, 126 lbs.; fillies, 121 lbs. The winning owner will be presented with the August Belmont Memorial Cup to be retained for one year, as well as a trophy for permanent possession and trophies will be presented to the winning trainer and jockey. Closed Thursday, Feb. 15, 1973, with 187 nominations.

Value of race $150,200. Value to winner, $90,120; second, $33,044; third, $18,024; fourth, $9,012.
Mutuel Pool, $519,689. Off-track betting, $688,460.

Last Raced	Horse	EqtAWt	PP	¼	½	1	1¼	Str	Fin	Jockeys	Owners	Odds to $1
5-19-73^{8} Pim^{1}	Secretariat	b3 126	1	1^{h}	1^{h}	1^{7}	1^{20}	1^{28}	1^{31}	RTurcotte	Meadow Stable	.10
6- 2-73^{6} Bel^{4}	Twice a Prince	3 126	4	4^{5}	4^{10}	3^{h}	2^{h}	3^{12}	$2\frac{1}{2}$	BBaeza	Elmendorf	17.30
5-31-73^{6} Bel^{1}	My Gallant	b3 126	3	3^{3}	3^{h}	4^{7}	3^{2}	2^{h}	3^{13}	ACorderoJr	A I Appleton	12.40
5-28-73^{8} GS^{2}	Pvt. Smiles	b3 126	2	5	5	5	5	5	$4\frac{3}{4}$	DGargan	C V Whitney	14.30
5-19-73^{8} Pim^{2}	Sham	b3 126	5	2^{5}	2^{10}	2^{7}	4^{8}	$4^{1\frac{1}{2}}$	5	LPincayJr	S Sommer	5.10

Time, :23$\frac{3}{5}$, :46$\frac{1}{5}$, 1:09$\frac{4}{5}$, 1:34$\frac{1}{5}$, 1:59, 2:24 **(new track record) (against wind in backstretch). Track fast.**

$2 Mutuel Prices:

2-SECRETARIAT	2.20	2.40	...
5-TWICE A PRINCE		4.60	...

(NO SHOW MUTUELS SOLD)

Ch. c, by Bold Ruler—Somethingroyal, by Princequillo. Trainer, L. Laurin. Bred by Meadow Stud, Inc. (Va.).
IN GATE—5:38. OFF AT 5:38 EASTERN DAYLIGHT TIME. Start good. Won ridden out.

SECRETARIAT sent up along the inside to vie for the early lead with SHAM to the backstretch, disposed of that one after going three-quarters, drew off at will rounding the far turn and was under a hand ride from Turcotte to establish a record in a tremendous perfomance. TWICE A PRINCE, unable to stay with the leaders early, moved through along the rail approaching the stretch and outfinished MY GALLANT for the place. The latter, void of early foot, moved with TWICE A PRINCE rounding the far turn and fought it out gamely with that one through the drive. PVT. SMILES showed nothing. SHAM alternated for the lead with SECRETARIAT to the backstretch, wasn't able to match stride with that rival after going three-quarters and stopped badly. **Scratched—Knightly Dawn.**

Marlboro Cup Handicap

SEVENTH RACE
Bel
Sept'ber 15, 1973

$1\frac{1}{8}$ MILES (chute). 1:46$\frac{1}{5}$). First running MARLBORO CUP HANDICAP. By invitation. Purse $250,000. Purse to be divided 60% to the winner, 22% to second, 12% to third and 6% to fourth. Trophies to be presented to the winning owner, trainer and jockey.

Value of race, $250,000. Value to winner $150,000; second, $55,000; third, $30,000; fourth, $15,000.
Mutuel Pool, $595,169. Off-track betting, $325,311.

Last Raced	Horse	EqtAWt	PP	St	¼	½	¾	Str	Fin	Jockeys	Owners	Odds to $1
8- 4-73^{7} Sar^{2}	Secretariat	b3 124	7	6	5^{4}	5^{4}	3^{2}	1^{2}	$1^{3\frac{1}{2}}$	RTurcotte	Meadow Stable	b-.40
8-21-73^{7} Sar^{1}	Riva Ridge	b4 127	6	2	2^{1}	2^{1}	$1\frac{1}{2}$	2^{6}	2^{2}	EMaple	Meadow Stable	b-.40
7-23-73^{8} Hol^{1}	Cougar II.	7 126	2	7	7	7	7	3^{1}	$3^{6\frac{1}{2}}$	WShoemaker	Mary F Jones	a-4.00
9- 8-73^{7} Bel^{7}	Onion	4 116	3	4	$1\frac{1}{2}$	1^{h}	2^{h}	$4\frac{1}{2}$	$4^{2\frac{1}{2}}$	JVelasquez	Hobeau Farm	14.30
8-25-73^{8} Mth^{2}	Annihilate 'Em	3 116	4	3	$4^{1\frac{1}{2}}$	3^{h}	4^{h}	5^{2}	$5\frac{1}{2}$	ACorderoJr	Patricia Blass	21.70
8-18-73^{7} Dmr^{1}	Kennedy Road	5 121	5	1	3^{1}	4^{h}	5^{5}	$6^{1\frac{1}{2}}$	6^{2}	DPierce	Mrs A W Stollery	a-4.00
7-21-73^{7} Aqu^{1}	Key to the Mint	b4 126	1	5	6^{6}	6^{4}	6^{1}	7	7	BBaeza	Rokeby Stable	3.50

b-Coupled, Secretariat and Riva Ridge; a-Cougar II. and Kennedy Road.

Time, :22$\frac{3}{5}$, :45$\frac{3}{5}$, 1:09$\frac{1}{5}$, 1:33, 1:45$\frac{2}{5}$ **(new American and world record) (against wind in backstretch). Track fast.**

$2 Mutuel Prices:

2B-SECRETARIAT (b-Entry)	2.80	2.80	2.40
2-RIVA RIDGE (b-Entry)	2.80	2.80	2.40
1-COUGAR II. (a-Entry)			3.00

Ch. c, by Bold Ruler—Somethingroyal, by Princequillo. Trainer, L. Laurin. Bred by Meadow Stud, Inc. (Va.).
IN GATE—4:50. OFF AT 4:50 EASTERN DAYLIGHT TIME. Start good. Won ridden out.

SECRETARIAT, unhurried away from the gate, moved around horses to reach contention after going the half, drifted out a bit leaving the turn, headed RIVA RIDGE with three sixteenths remaining and drew away under brisk handling. RIVA RIDGE prominent from the outset, took over when ready racing into the turn, remained well out in the track while making the pace into the stretch but wasn't able to stay with SECRETARIAT while holding COUGAR II. safe. COUGAR II., off slowly, settled suddenly approaching the stretch, altered course when blocked attempting to split horses nearing midstretch and finished with good energy. ONION showed good early foot while racing well out from the rail but had nothing left for the drive. ANNIHILATE EM made a run along the inside approaching the end of the backstretch and was finished soon after going three quarters. KENNEDY ROAD, steadied along while between horses on the backstretch, gave way approaching the stretch. KEY TO THE MINT showed nothing.

Man o' War Stakes

SEVENTH RACE
Bel
October 8, 1973

1½ MILES (turf). (2:25⅗). Fifteenth running MAN O' WAR. Weight For Age. $100,000 added. 3-year-olds and upward. By subscription of $200 each, which shall accompany the nomination; $500 to pass the entry box; $500 to start, with $100,000 added. The added money and all fees to be divided 60% to the winner, 22% to second, 12% to third and 6% to fourth. Weight for age. 3-year-olds, 121 lbs.; older, 126 lbs. The N.Y.R.A. to add The Man o' War Bowl to be won three times, not necessarily consecutively, by the same owner before becoming his or her property. The owner of the winner will also receive a trophy for permanent possession and trophies to the winning trainer and jockey. Closed Monday, Sept. 24, 1973 with 23 nominations.
Value of race $113,600. Value to winner $68,160; second, $24,992; third, $13,632; fourth, $6,816.
Mutuel Pool, $428,256. Off-track betting, $188,300.

Last Raced	Horse	EqtA	Wt	PP	¼	½	1	1¼	Str	Fin	Jockeys	Owners	Odds to $1
9-29-73^{7} Bel^{2}	Secretariat	b3	121	3	$1^{1\frac{1}{2}}$	1^{3}	1^{3}	$1^{1\frac{1}{2}}$	1^{3}	1^{5}	RTurcotte	Meadow Stable	.50
9-27-73^{8} Atl^{1}	Tentam	b4	126	1	$3^{1\frac{1}{2}}$	3^{3}	2^{2}	2^{8}	2^{10}	$2^{7\frac{1}{2}}$	JVelasquez	Windfields Farm	3.60
9-22-73^{7} Bel^{2}	Big Spruce	b4	126	7	7	7	7	7	5^{2}	$3^{\frac{1}{2}}$	ASantiago	Elmendorf	6.90
9-22-73^{7} Bel^{3}	Triangular	6	126	4	5^{h}	6^{5}	6^{2}	$4^{\frac{1}{2}}$	$3^{\frac{1}{2}}$	$4^{2\frac{1}{2}}$	RCSmith	Hobeau Farm	25.40
9-22-73^{7} Bel^{1}	London Company	3	121	6	6^{4}	5^{1}	5^{1}	$3^{\frac{1}{2}}$	4^{2}	5^{7}	LPincayJr	Chance Hill Farm	8.40
8- 4-73^{7} Sar^{5}	West Coast Scout	b5	126	5	4^{2}	4^{2}	$4^{1\frac{1}{2}}$	6^{3}	6^{3}	6^{6}	ACorderoJr	Oxford Stable	25.90
9-21-73^{7} Bel^{1}	Anono	b3	121	2	2^{1}	$2^{1\frac{1}{2}}$	$3^{1\frac{1}{2}}$	5^{h}	7	7	MVenezia	A D Schefler	38.60

Time, :23⅘, :47, 1:11⅗, 1:36, 2:00, 2:24⅘ (new course record) (against wind in backstretch). Track firm.

$2 Mutuel Prices:			
1A-SECRETARIAT	3.00	2.40	2.20
2-TENTAM		3.00	2.60
7-BIG SPRUCE			3.20

Ch. c, by Bold Ruler—Somethingroyal, by Princequillo. Trainer, L. Laurin. Bred by Meadow Stud, Inc. (Va.).
IN GATE—4:48. OFF AT 4:48 EASTERN DAYLIGHT TIME. Start good. Won ridden out.

SECRETARIAT, away in good order, moved to the fore from between horses nearing the finish line the first time, saved ground after opening a clear lead around the first turn, responded readily to shake off a bid from TENTAM after going three-quarters, turned back another bid from that rival approaching the stretch and drew away under a hand ride. TENTAM, never far back while saving ground, eased out to go after SECRETARIAT entering the backstretch, wasn't able to stay with that one after going three-quarters, made another run midway of the far turn but was no match for the winner while besting the others. BIG SPRUCE, outrun to the stretch, passed tired horses. TRIANGULAR was always outrun, as was LONDON COMPANY. WEST COAST SCOUT was finished at the far turn. ANONO showed good early foot but had nothing left after going a mile. **Scratched—Dendron, Star Envoy, Apollo Nine, Riva Ridge.**

Canadian International Stakes

EIGHTH RACE
WO
October 28, 1973

1⅝ MILES (Marshall course). (2:41). Thirty-sixth running CANADIAN INTER-NATIONAL CHAMPIONSHIP STAKES. $125,000 Added. 3-year-olds and upward. Weight for age (European scale). 3-year-olds, 117 lbs.; older, 126 lbs. Fillies and mares allowed 3 lbs. (No Canadian-bred allowance.) By subscription of $150 each which shall accompany the nomination and an additional $750 when making entry. The added money and all fees to be divided 65% to the winner, 20% to second, 10% to third and 5% to fourth. Closed Saturday, September 15, 1973, with 58 nominations.

Value of race $142,700. Value to winner $92,755; second, $28,540; third, $14,270; fourth, $7,135.
Mutuel Pool, $181,485.

Last Raced	Horse	EqtAWt	PP	¼	½	1	1⅜	Str	Fin	Jockeys	Owners	Odds to $1
10- 8-73⁷ Bel¹	Secretariat	b3 117	12	24½	28	26	15	1¹²	16½	EMaple	Meadow Stable	.20
10- 8-73⁷ Bel³	Big Spruce	b4 126	4	12	11h	106	5h	41	21½	ASantiago	Elmendorf	13.45
10-13-73⁸ Spt³	Golden Don	b3 117	6	11¹	9h	8²	85	52½	3¾	MManganello	Don'lds'n-Goldchamp	28.90
10-20-73⁷ WO³	Presidial	4 126	9	3¹½	3h	41½	3½	3h	44	SHawley	Winfields Farm	23.15
10-20-73⁷ WO¹	Fabe Count	5 126	8	4¹	5½	65	6h	6h	5¾	LDuffy	Parkview Stable	24.40
10- 8-73⁷ Bel⁴	Triangular	6 126	1	8¹	84	5¹	72	83	6nk	RCSmith	Hobeau Farm	32.55
10-20-73⁷ WO⁴	Top of the Day	3 117	2	10¹²	11½	9h	95	7¹½	RPlatts	Gardiner Farm	85.10
10-20-73⁷ WO²	Twice Lucky	b6 126	7	7½	42	32½	43	71	8½	HDittfach	C Smythe	45.40
10-21-73⁶ WO¹	Kennedy Road	5 126	5	1¹½	11½	1½	27	2h	95	AGomez	Mrs A W Stollery	9.25
10-21-73⁷ WO²	Tico's Donna	5 123	10	5¹	6h	7½	105	103	103½	WMcMahon	F Stronach	57.65
10-20-73⁷ WO⁵	Roundhouse	b5 126	3	9¹	10h	12	114	118	11¹¹	RGrubb	M J Resnick-Walsh	121.70
10-20-73⁷ WO⁶	Fun Co K	b4 126	11	6h	73	9h	12	12	12	JVasquez	Mrs M D Keim	90.70

Time, :24, :47⅖, 1:11⅗, 1:37⅗, 2:41⅘. Track firm.

$2 Mutuel Prices:

12-SECRETARIAT	2.40	2.50	2.10
4-BIG SPRUCE		4.40	2.90
6-GOLDEN DON			4.50

Ch. c, by Bold Ruler—Somethingroyal, by Princequillo. Trainer, L. Laurin. Bred by Meadow Stable, Inc. (Va.).

IN GATE—4:52. OFF AT 4:52 EASTERN STANDARD TIME. Start good. Won ridden out.

SECRETARIAT stalked the early pace while under restraint, came outside of KENNEDY ROAD in the backstretch, dueled with that one to the far turn, took command thereafter to open up a long lead a furlong out and was under mild intermittent pressure to prevail. BIG SPRUCE, well back early, closed willingly. GOLDEN DON came outside into the home lane and outfinished the balance. PRESIDIAL saved ground early while stalking the leaders but never threatened. FABE COUNT could not keep up. TRIANGULAR was never a serious threat. TWICE LUCKY, a mild contender at the mile, faded thereafter. KENNEDY ROAD set the early pace under restraint, dueled with SECRETARIAT in the backstretch but could not stay into the far turn.

Exacta (12-4) Paid $7.60; Exacta Pool, $129,545.

ANNOTATED
BIBLIOGRAPHY

THE BOOKS ON this list warrant the horseplayer's serious attention. They represent the best in the field and encompass the tenable theories and methods of Thoroughbred handicapping and parimutuel wagering.

Ainslie, Tom. *Ainslie's Complete Guide to Thoroughbred Handicapping*. New York, Simon &Schuster, 1968, 1986. The classical concepts, principles, and practices of Thoroughbred handicapping; in-depth discussion of each of the fundamental factors of handicapping; the procedures of comprehensive handicapping; basic facts of breeding and conformation; evaluation of 77 systems and methods; a glossary of handicapping terms.

Beyer, Andrew. *Picking Winners*. Boston, Houghton Mifflin, 1975. The definitive treatment of modern speed handicapping; par times; daily track variants; speed charts based upon the concept of proportional times; projected times; a trilogy of chapters on making speed figures: rationale and method; procedures and illustrations; interpretation and use.

_____. *The Winning Horseplayer*. Boston, Houghton Mifflin, 1983. A comprehensive discussion of trip handicapping; methods and notation of trip handicapping; speed and trip handicapping in combination; money-management guidelines.

_____. *Beyer on Speed*. Boston, Houghton Mifflin, 1993. The value of speed handicapping; figure patterns; factors that affect speed figures; the mathematics of pace; turf racing on two continents; exotic betting strategies.

Beyer, Andrew et.al., *Bet with the Best*. New York, DRF Press, 2001. Nine essays by professional practitioners on the leading ideas and methods of Thoroughbred handicapping and parimutuel wagering. In addition to Beyer's, the chapters are by Tom Brohamer, Steven Crist, Steve Davidowitz, Dave Litfin, James Quinn, Alan Shuback, Lauren Stich, and Mike Watchmaker.

Brohamer, Tom. *Modern Pace Handicapping*. New York, William Morrow, 1991,and DRF Press, 2000. Velocity ratings and calculations; concepts and procedures of the Sartin Methodology; running styles; turn time; energy distribution; track profiles; decision models; Quirin-style speed and pace figures; par-time charts; practical applications.

Carroll, Charles. *Handicapping Speed*. New York, Lyons & Burford, 1991. Handicapping the sprints; the mechanics of time; chaos theory applied to horse racing; the elements of speed; baseline standards for evaluating real speed; computing speed; time per length as a measure of real speed.

Cramer, Mark. *Fast Tracks to Thoroughbred Profits*. Secaucus, New Jersey, Lyle Stuart, 1984. The concept of wager value; the dialectics of handicapping information; opposite logics in handicapping; handicapping factors and information having high wager value.

_____. *Kinky Handicapping*. Annapolis, Maryland, TBS Publishing, 1993. Contrarian thinking in handicapping; unconventional and nontraditional patterns and angles.

Davidowitz, Steve. *Betting Thoroughbreds*. New York, Dutton, 1977, 1983, 1995. Fundamental handicapping principles and practices; track biases; the key-race method; the trainer window; basic, clear discussions of speed and pace handicapping; exotic betting strategies.

Davis, Frederick. *Thoroughbred Racing: Percentages and Probabilities*. New York: Millwood Publications, 1974. Introduction to the concept and computation of impact values (I.V.'s); the win percentages and probabilities of numerous handicapping factors.

Fabricand, Burton. *Horse Sense*. New York, David McKay, 1965. Mathematical methods and racetrack betting; the expected and actual win probabilities of odds ranges; the principle of maximum confusion; a systematic method of wagering on favorites.

Fierro, Steve. *The Four Quarters of Horse Investing*. San Diego, Today's Racing Digest LLC, 2001. Playing the horses as a business venture;

betting lines for contenders; templates of fair-value betting lines for contenders; empirical studies of effectiveness.

Fotias, Cary. *Blinkers Off: New Frontiers of Form Cycle Analysis.* Pace, velocity, and Thoroughbred condition; The Xtras (figure charts); the new pace top; distance switches; plunge lines; compression lines; turf pace lows; track biases.

Gaines, Milt. *The Tote Board Is Alive and Well.* Las Vegas, Nevada, GBC Press, 1981. Trend analysis of the totalizator board; charting procedures; betting trends that yield seasonal profits; illustrations.

Ledbetter, Bonnie. *The Body Language of Horses.* New York, William Morrow, 1980. Descriptions of equine body language; six profiles of racehorse body language at the track; handicapping guidelines.

Litfin, Dave. *Dave Litfin's Expert Handicapping.* Boston, Little Brown, 1995. Speed figures and condition; figure patterns; trainers and workouts; pace and track bias; negative patterns; angles; excellent illustrations.

Meadow, Barry. *Money Secrets at the Racetrack.* Anaheim, Ca., TR Publishing, 1988, 1990. The mathematics of parimutuel betting; constructing fair-value betting lines; overlays; how much to bet; win betting; place and show betting; exactas and trifectas; multiple win exotics; pick-six betting strategies and bet cards; excellent wagering charts; calculating the betting edge.

Mitchell, Dick. *A Winning Thoroughbred Strategy.* Los Feliz, Ca., Cynthia Publishing Company, 1985. The concept of mathematical expectation applied to Thoroughbred handicapping; a computerized model of handicapping and betting; odds lines based upon probabilities; money-management techniques; win, place, show, and exacta wagering; formulae; an innovative method for assigning probabilities to handicapping ratings.

Quinn, James. *The Handicapper's Condition Book.* New York, William Morrow, 1986, and DRF Press, 2000. In-depth analyses of the conditions of eligibility in major racing; the class factor; class demands of eligibility conditions; selection and elimination guidelines for 20 variations of racing conditions.

_____. *Figure Handicapping.* New York, William Morrow, 1992. Rationale for making figures; explanations and applications; figure patterns; figure handicapping on the turf; original turf-figure charts for 28 racetracks.

Quirin, William. *Winning at the Races: Computer Discoveries in Thoroughbred Handicapping.* New York, William Morrow, 1979. The scientific bases of effective handicapping; percentages and probabilities associated with numerous handicapping factors; impact values; the importance of early speed; leading turf-sire lines; computer-generated multiple regression models of handicapping.

_____. *Thoroughbred Racing: State of the Art*. New York, William Morrow, 1984. Key probabilities of handicapping; using speed and pace figures in combination; nine configurations of pace (race shapes); pedigrees and turf racing; computer simulations of five money-management methods.

Roman, Steven A. *An Analysis of Dosage*. The Thoroughbred Record, April, 1984. Evolution of pedigree evaluation; the concept of dosage; the Dosage Index and calculations; Dosage studies of open stakes winners; applications to handicapping and findings; how to handicap the Kentucky Derby.

Scott, William L. *How Will Your Horse Run Today?* Baltimore, Maryland, Amicus Press, 1984. Investigations of the form factor; form defects and form advantages; procedures of form analysis; applications and methods.

Ziemba, William T. and Hausch, Donald B. *Beat the Racetrack*. New York, Harcourt Brace Jovanovich, 1984. Inefficiency of market principles for identifying place and show overlays; a mathematical method of place and show betting; the Z-system; Kelly wagering techniques applied to place and show pools; formulas; charts; illustrations; fair-value cutoff values for $2 and $5 exactas in New York and southern California; foreword by Edward O. Thorp.